palgrave advances in
modern military history

Palgrave Advances

Titles include:

Richard Whatmore and Brian Young (*editors*)
INTELLECTUAL HISTORY

Saki R. Dockrill and Geraint A. Hughes (*editors*)
COLD WAR HISTORY

H.G. Cocks and Matt Houlbrook (*editors*)
THE MODERN HISTORY OF SEXUALITY

Patrick Finney (*editor*)
INTERNATIONAL HISTORY

Jonathan Harris (*editor*)
BYZANTINE HISTORY

Marnie Hughes-Warrington (*editor*)
WORLD HISTORIES

Helen J. Nicholson (*editor*)
THE CRUSADES

Alec Ryrie (*editor*)
EUROPEAN REFORMATIONS

Jonathan Woolfson (*editor*)
RENAISSANCE HISTORIOGRAPHY

Matthew Hughes and William J. Philpott (*editors*)
MODERN MILITARY HISTORY

Forthcoming:

Jonathan Barry and Owen Davies (*editors*)
WITCHCRAFT HISTORIOGRAPHY

Katherine O'Donnell, Leann Lane
and Mary McAuliffe (*editors*)
IRISH HISTORY

palgrave advances in modern military history

edited by
matthew hughes
brunel university

and

william j. philpott
king's college london

contents

notes on contributors

Joanna Bourke is Professor of History at Birkbeck College, University of London. She has published seven books, on Irish history, gender and 'the body', the history of psychological thought and modern warfare. Her books have been translated into Chinese, Italian, Portuguese, Spanish, Catalan and Turkish. *An Intimate History of Killing: Face-to-Face Killing in Twentieth Century Warfare* (1998) won the Fraenkel Prize in Contemporary History for 1998 and the Wolfson History Prize for 2000. Her book entitled *Fear: A Cultural History* was published by Virago in 2005. She is currently writing a history of rapists in the nineteenth and twentieth centuries, to be published in late 2006.

John Buckley is Reader in Military History at the University of Wolverhampton. Dr Buckley has written widely on many aspects of military studies, particularly the inter-war years, the Second World War and air power. He is the author of *The RAF and Trade Defence: Constant Endeavour* (1995), *Air Power in the Age of Total War* (1999) and *British Armour in the Normandy Campaign 1944* (2004).

John P. Cann is Professor of National Security Studies at the US Marine Corps Command and Staff College, Quantico, Virginia. Dr Cann earned his doctorate at King's College London in 1996, and is the author of *Counterinsurgency in Africa: The Portuguese Way of War, 1961–1974* (1996). A retired naval captain and flight officer, he was awarded the Silver Medal of Dom Afonso Henriques for his studies on conflict in Lusophone Africa.

Warren Chin is Senior Lecturer in the Defence Studies Department at the Joint Services Command and Staff College and Academic Director of the British army's command and staff course. Dr Chin also teaches at the Royal College of Defence Studies and was a Lecturer in War Studies at the

Royal Military Academy, Sandhurst. He specializes in British defence policy, weapons acquisition and the study of land warfare.

Nikolas Gardner teaches military history and theory at the University of Salford in Greater Manchester. Dr Gardner is the author of *Trial by Fire: Command and the British Expeditionary Force in 1914* (2003), as well as articles in *War & Society*, *War in History* and *The Journal of Military History*.

Laurent Henninger is *chargé de mission* at the *Centre d'études d'histoire de la défense* (based at Chateau de Vincennes, Paris), where he works on the philosophy and impact of 'military revolutions' over the *longue durée*, and runs a seminar on 'new battle history'.

Matthew Hughes is Senior Lecturer in History at Brunel University. His recent publications include *Allenby in Palestine: The Middle East Correspondence of Field Marshal Viscount Allenby, June 1917–October 1919* (2004) and (with Gaynor Johnson) *Fanaticism and Conflict in the Modern Age* (2005). Dr Hughes is a Fellow of the Royal Historical Society and Honorary Editor of the *Journal of the Society for Army Historical Research*.

Alan James is Lecturer in the Department of War Studies at King's College London, and a member of the 'Laughton Naval History Unit'. Dr James is the author of *The Navy and Government in Early Modern France, 1572–1661* (2004) and *The Origins of French Absolutism* (2006), along with a number of articles on naval, military, and confessional conflict in the sixteenth and seventeenth centuries.

Andrew Lambert is Laughton Professor of Naval History in the Department of War Studies at King's College London. A Fellow of the Royal Historical Society, his books include *The Crimean War: British Grand Strategy against Russia 1853–1856* (1990), *The Last Sailing Battlefleet: Maintaining Naval Mastery 1815–1850* (1991) and *The Foundations of Naval History: John Knox Laughton, the Royal Navy and the Historical Profession* (1998). His latest book, *Nelson: Britannia's God of War* was published in October 2004. He wrote and presented the three-part series 'War at Sea' for BBC2, broadcast in February 2004.

Michael S. Neiberg is Professor of History and Co-Director of the Center for the Study of War and Society at the University of Southern Mississippi. His recent publications include *Fighting the Great War: A Global History* (2005) and *Warfare and Society in Europe: 1898 to the Present* (2004).

William J. Philpott is Senior Lecturer in War Studies in the Department of War Studies, King's College London. Dr Philpott is the author of *Anglo-*

French Relations and Strategy on the Western Front, 1914–1918 (1996) and co-author (with Matthew Hughes) of *The Palgrave Concise Atlas of the First World War* (2005) and academic editor of the Palgrave monograph series *Studies in Military and Strategic History*.

Peter Stanley is Principal Historian at the Australian War Memorial, Canberra, where he has worked since 1980. Dr Stanley has published 18 books including *The Remote Garrison: The British Army in Australia 1788–1870* (1986), *White Mutiny: British Military Culture in India, 1825–1875* (1998) and *For Fear of Pain: British Surgery 1790–1850* (2003).

Bruce Vandervort is Professor of Modern European and African History at the Virginia Military Institute in Lexington, Virginia, USA. He is the author of *Wars of Imperial Conquest in Africa, 1830–1914* (1998) and serves as editor of *The Journal of Military History*.

introduction

matthew hughes and william j. philpott

For too long military history has sat uncomfortably on the margins of mainstream academic study. Its subject matter – all too readily dismissed as the antiquarian study of regimental details and tactical minutiae – has been seen as both technically abstruse and morally suspect, with its supposedly central focus on weapons and the killing that they facilitate. As recently as 1989, the introduction to one influential edition noted condescendingly of one of its contributors: 'The first essay... is by a military historian. However, [his] concerns are not those of the traditional military historian; battles, campaigns and generalship are replaced here by a broad introduction to current debates among historians about the nature of "total war" and its effects on social change.'[1] The implication of this prejudice is that the study of war is more academically legitimate if it deals with the people at war, rather than the conduct of war. This long-established intellectual snobbery contrasts with the enduring popularity of military history – whether it is accounts of battles and wars, or the lives of great commanders – that pervades the popular media.

Military historians have therefore fought a long battle for recognition of their sub-discipline, and of the centrality of war in all its myriad dimensions to human existence and endeavour. Definitions of the genre are problematic.[2] Arguably, 'true' military history should focus predominantly on the working of armies and the conduct of wars in the narrow sense of strategy, manoeuvres and battles – what some would call 'warfare' or 'warfighting'. However, broadly defined, military history can encompass all that goes on in wartime (and during low-level conflicts or insurgencies), whether it be the doings of soldiers or the actions of civilians, and indeed might also encompass the preparations that precede wars, and the peacemaking and demobilization which follow. In short, there is very little in modern human history which has not been determined or touched by war – and in the last 3,421 years only 268 of them

1

have been free of war.[3] Taking this wide-ranging definition, the study of armies and of war has as much claim to recognition as the historical study of governments and international relations, workers and trade unions, gender and class, or industry and finance. It is this holistic approach that the editors and authors of this volume have adopted, looking at war both in its strictly military dimensions and in its broader socio-cultural context.

Despite the potential range of the sub-discipline, the study of war and armed forces was until fairly recently marginalized by the historical profession and was typically taught in military academies and staff colleges. This was partly the fault of military historians who traditionally preferred to focus narrowly on events on the battlefield. The writers and teachers of the subject were usually professional practitioners, and its students fighting soldiers. As Edward Coffman noted in surveying the development of military history in the United States, this professional focus, with its militaristic connotations, hindered its progress into the peaceful groves of academe: 'Professors who were likely to be antimilitary anyway tended to be suspicious of soldiers who looked for practical answers to direct professional questions in the study of history.'[4] Moreover, many of the influential writers of military history in the late-nineteenth and early- to mid-twentieth centuries – such as Basil Liddell Hart, G. F. R. Henderson, J. F. C. Fuller and S. L. A. Marshall – were serving or former soldiers. Academics in this period failed to fill the huge gap that was emerging between the military histories written by professionals and those written by non-academic civilians.[5] Paradoxically, the non-military, non-academic authors frequently made the most prescient points about war and its wider context. Thus, the Polish banker, Ivan (or Jan) S. Bloch, in his *The War of the Future in its Technical, Economic and Political Aspects* (1898–1900)[6] argued that any future war would be long and inconclusive, largely because of the tactical stalemate produced by modern weaponry; the British pacifist, Norman Angell, observed in *The Great Illusion* (1910) that any European war would be disastrous financially, socially and politically for any country involved.

At the turn of the twentieth century, in Germany, despite its well-established tradition of historical scholarship, Hans Delbrück, arguably the founder of the modern academic study of military history, was himself marginalized in his professional career and restricted in his influence by the all pervading sway exercised by the Great General Staff over military scholarship.[7] In Great Britain, a few lonely academic posts held the line for the study of military affairs at university level: the Chichele Professorship of the History of War at Oxford University, founded in 1909, and the chair of naval history held by Sir John Laughton at King's College London in the early decades of the twentieth century, being two notable establishments in an otherwise barren academic landscape.[8] In the United States, before the Second World War, military history made little impact beyond the armed forces themselves, although the establishment of the American Military History Foundation in

1933 by a group of army officers sowed the first seed for a post-1945 expansion of the subject.[9]

It took the conjunction of a century dominated by conflict – two world wars and a lengthy Cold War confrontation, myriad civil wars and wars of decolonization – and the expansion of higher education following the Second World War, for the study of military history to make the cross-over from the professional to the scholarly milieu. In part, this was because the personal experience of military service in the world wars gave scholars a practical insight into the nature of war and the workings of the military as an organization. One has only to read the works of, say, Marcus Cunliffe – a British wartime officer and then academic – to see how post-war scholars could effectively blend an understanding of military history into wider studies (in Cunliffe's case, of the United States).[10] Importantly, official sponsorship of the subject, through the many 'official histories' of the twentieth century's conflicts commissioned by governments and armed forces, increased vastly the number of practising military historians, and at the same time inspired the first debates on the nature and value of military history.[11] In the United States, university history departments began offering courses in military history from the late 1940s and early 1950s – boosted by the need in the USA for ROTC university officer cadets to have some military history education – although the percentage (7.5) was small.[12]

In the USA and elsewhere, this post-war shift was not a smooth transition, took time, and is far from complete. Thus, until the 1960s at least, 'it might be noted how many history courses, and how many history books, used peace treaties as their opening paragraphs and wars as their full stops'.[13] The experience of the 1960s exacerbated the hostility in US universities towards military history, a subject that was seen by the mobilized academic Left to be too close to US militarism and the war in Vietnam (and also to counterinsurgency campaigns supported by America in which there were human rights abuses). The big growth in history sub-fields such as social, ethnic and labour history in the hiring boom in the USA in the 1960s and 1970s largely passed by military history, still viewed by many academics as stale and elitist. While some 26 USA universities currently offer graduate programmes in military history,[14] it is noteworthy that in the US younger historians in different fields of history have replaced retiring military history academics, or in some cases the latter have not been replaced at all.

Struggling to escape its antiquarian, establishment connotations, military history adopted disparate forms and labels such as war and society, history of warfare, war studies and peace studies. These labels demonstrated the subject's broader appeal but they also meant something: whether the programme concentrated more on war in its wider context or war-fighting on the battlefield; whether the department was taking a sociological or historical approach to the subject; whether the focus was on understanding wars or ending them; even whether a department had a supposed Left or Right bias. Overall, the result has been very positive. 'Military history' is now a broad church: it includes cutting-edge 'military' analyses of tactics, operations and strategy alongside so-called 'new' military history that approaches war through the prisms of discourse analysis, culture, gender, race and memory. While there is antipathy between the 'traditional' and 'new' approaches that hampers full convergence, the generic term 'war and society' has been coined to indicate this shift of focus away from armies and combat to include societies and conflict.[15] By broadening its base and improving its methodologies, military history was at last able to take its legitimate place alongside the other humanities and social science disciplines in departments of history, politics, international relations and sociology. Indeed, a mark of progress was the decision by the annual conference of the American Historical Association to make conflict the theme of its 2004 conference.

While the numbers of dedicated military history departments are small, particular, high-profile units have done much to broaden the appeal of the subject. In Britain, for instance, the first tentative steps to legitimize the study of military history were taken as long ago as the 1960s with the establishment of the first university department dedicated to the study of military affairs in their many dimensions: the Department of War Studies at King's College London. This department's significance and influence, nationally and internationally, over the following 40 years cannot be underestimated: one of this book's editors teaches there, the other gained his doctorate from the department, and a number of the contributors have connections with the department. The impact of market forces on higher education should increase undergraduate military history provision as some less elite establishments look to draw in students by offering niche degrees.

The spread of military history has been accompanied by a publishing boom in the field. A number of monograph series devoted to the subject exist: Palgrave/Macmillan's 'Studies in Military and Strategic History'; Frank Cass's 'Military History and Policy' series; the Greenwood/Praeger series, 'Contributions in Military Studies'; Kansas University Press's 'Modern War Studies' series; Indiana University's 'Twentieth Century Battles' series; University of Oklahoma's 'Campaigns and Commanders' series; and the Texas A&M University Press 'Military History' series. There are also useful textbook series such as Fontana's 1980s 'War and Society' volumes and Routledge's ongoing 'Warfare and History' series. To this must be added the many studies of war, armed forces and wartime themes produced by the wider academic and commercial press. The growing number of specialist journals provides forums for airing new research and debating key issues. To the US-based *The Journal of Military History* which has been published continuously since 1937[16] (also the British-based *Journal of the Society for Army Historical Research,* founded in 1921), must be added more recent journals such as *The Journal of Strategic Studies* (GB, 1978), *War and Society* (Australia, 1983), *Military History Quarterly* (USA, 1988) and *War in History* (GB, 1994), as well as the in-house journals and bulletins published by the armed forces themselves. In Germany, there is *Militärgeschichtliche Zeitschrift* ('military history journal', formerly called *Militärgeschichtliche Mitteilungen*, 'military history notices'), and in France *Revue historique des armées* (previously *Revue historique de l'armée*), *Revue internationale d'histoire militaire, Guerres mondiales et conflits contemporains* (formerly *Revue d'histoire de la deuxième guerre mondiale*) and a new journal entitled *La France en guerre 39–45*. Germany also has two Federal Universities of the Armed Forces, one in Hamburg and one in Munich.

While few would now question the legitimacy of military history, broadly defined, as an appropriate field for scholarly enquiry, there remains a certain lingering insecurity within the military history profession, perhaps a consequence of the genre's long struggle for recognition. Thus, in 1997, John Lynn could write: 'military history has always been regarded as politically and morally questionable, but now military history also suffers because it represents the opposite of the dominant, and increasingly intolerant, trends in historical studies'.[17] He identified three new menaces to military history: the inexorable rise of political correctness (as 'dead white male' history par excellence, military history was an obvious target for criticism); the all-pervading influence of theory in history departments; and, finally, the trivialization of historical themes. The response Lynn proffered was 'if you can't beat them join them', and the exploration of the gender, race and cultural dimensions of armed forces and war has certainly been a rising trend over the last decade.[18]

Moreover, since the end of the Cold War and the terrorist attacks of 9/11 (and, more recently, those in Spain and Britain), there has been a boom in military and security studies that has benefited military historians, especially those whose expertise has a policy-relevant dimension. Far from war becoming a thing of the past, other forms of conflict – 'war on terror', counterinsurgency, 'operations short of war' – have emerged, or remerged, in an unstable and conflict-riven world, and the study of war more generally has rapidly expanded with them. Undergraduate and postgraduate courses in war studies, military history and conflict, and related fields have sprung up in recent years, attesting to the centrality of war as a subject for legitimate enquiry, and the enduring interest in the subject at the highest level. Military historians are no longer mere investigators of long-dead wars, but strategic analysts, policy advisers and theorists. Consequently, the discipline is thriving and central to contemporary world affairs. It would seem that military history is now, if not entirely unassailable, secure amongst the increasingly diverse sub-specialisms that characterize the historical profession in the early twenty-first century.

As the study of war has flourished, so it has developed its own historiography.[19] Only recently, however, have scholars turned their attention to analysing the nature of military history itself, and the practices of the sub-discipline.[20] This guide does not purport to break new ground either in the evaluation of the nature of the discipline, or the development of new lines of thought in the field. Rather it presents itself as a 'state of the art' introduction to key areas and themes of military history. Its authors endeavour to outline important issues and approaches, to summarize significant debates – past and ongoing – and to identify trends and issues which deserve further study. As well as three chapters which examine warfare at the sharp end, in its three dimensions – land, sea and air – two chapters look at particular aspects of warfare more generally: non-European warfare, and counterinsurgency warfare, the latter currently in vogue in a period of post-imperial and low-intensity conflicts. A separate chapter examines empire and war through the prism of Britain's former 'white' dominions (notably Australia). Four of the main themes in the historiography of war are addressed in separate chapters: the 'war and society' genre which emerged as a strong sub-field in the 1960s and 1970s; the interaction of warfare with science and technology, which is closely linked with wider debates on the role of technology in historical development; the ongoing debate about the nature of Revolutions in Military Affairs, their interrelationship and differences; and the rise of the so-called 'new military history' from the 1980s onwards, to a position where it has become one of the dominant paradigms in the sub-discipline. Two chapters look at two key phenomena in military history in different ages: firstly the interaction between warfare and the rise of the state in the early modern period; secondly, the phenomenon of total war from the late eighteenth to the late twentieth century. Rounding off the survey, the final chapter looks at the development of military thought in the modern world. Each chapter is intended as a concise and accessible introduction to its subject, supported by notes and a brief bibliography outlining further reading. Inevitably, the compartmentalization of topics is never entirely possible, and readers will find a certain degree of overlap between the coverage of the individual chapters. However, they will find in this guide a thorough introductory survey of the main themes of military history; they will understand how the discipline has developed over the years; and they will be able to identify areas for further study or their own original research.

notes

1. C. Emsley, A. Marwick and W. Simpson (eds), *War Peace and Social Change in Twentieth Century Europe* (Milton Keynes, 1989), p. 3.
2. For the opinions of a number of leading practitioners on the nature of military history, see the chapter 'What is Military History?' in J. Gardiner (ed.), *What is History Today?* (Basingstoke, 1998).
3. Will and Ariel Durant cited in Donald Kagan, *On the Origins of War* (London, 1997), p. 4.
4. E. M. Coffman, 'The Course of Military History in the United States since World War II', *Journal of Military History* 61/4 (1997): 761–75, 762.

5. See Michael Howard, 'Disciplinary Views of War' in John Whiteclay Chambers II (ed.), *The Oxford Companion to American Military History* (Oxford and New York, 1999), p. 224.
6. The last volume appeared in English as *Is War Impossible?*
7. See A. Bucholz, *Hans Delbrück and the German Military Establishment* (Iowa City, 1984).
8. A. D. Lambert, *The Foundations of Naval History: Sir John Laughton, the Historical Profession and the Royal Navy* (London, 1998).
9. Coffman, 'Course of Military History', 761–3.
10. Notably, Marcus Cunliffe, *Soldiers and Civilians: The Martial Spirit in America, 1775–1865* (London, 1968). See also Brian Holden Reid, 'Cunliffe, Marcus Faulkner (1922–1990)' in H. C. G. Matthew and Brian Harrison (eds), *Oxford Dictionary of National Biography* (Oxford, 2004).
11. Coffman, 'Course of Military History', 73–5. See also M. Blumenson, 'Can Official History be Honest History?', *Military Affairs* 26/4 (1962): 153–61; M. Howard, *The Causes of Wars* (London, 1983), p. 210. Controversies continue over specific official histories. See for example D. French, 'Sir James Edmonds and the Official History: France and Belgium' in B. J. Bond (ed.), *The First World War and British Military History* (Oxford, 1991) and A. Green, *Writing the Great War: Sir James Edmonds and the Official Histories, 1914–1948* (London, 2003).
12. Coffman, 'Course of Military History', 765.
13. Emsley et al. (eds), *War Peace and Social Change*, p. 4.
14. See the Society for Military History graduate programme website at <http://www.smh-hq.org/gradguide/geolist.html>.
15. See Peter Karsten, 'The "New" American Military History: A Map of the Territory, Explored and Unexplored', *American Quarterly* 36/3 (1984): 389–418, 389.
16. First called *The Journal of the American Military History Foundation*, it became *The Journal of the American Military Institute* in 1939; in 1941, the title was changed to *Military Affairs*; in 1989, it became *The Journal of Military History*.
17. J. M. Lynn, 'The Embattled Future of Academic Military History', *Journal of Military History* 61/4 (1997): 777–89, 782.
18. Ibid.
19. See for example Bond (ed.), *The First World War.*
20. See for example J. Black, *Rethinking Military History* (London, 2004) and the special issue entitled 'The History of War as Part of General History', *Journal of Military History* 57/5 (1993): 145–63.

1
military revolutions and military history

laurent henninger

For some 50 years, military historians have been debating the issue of whether there was or was not a 'military revolution' in western and central Europe in the early modern period, and what was the nature of this supposed revolution. It all began in 1955 when Michael Roberts, in an inaugural lecture at Queen's University Belfast, first presented the idea of a military revolution, referring to the way Dutch military leaders dealt with new weaponry and tactics during their fight against the Spaniards at the end of the sixteenth century. Consciously or not, Roberts was thus transposing the economical concept of 'industrial revolution' to the field of military history. In 1976, Geoffrey Parker published an article on the same topic, criticizing Roberts' assertions and, instead of Roberts' emphasis on infantry drill and use of individual firearms, he focused on the transformations resulting from new *trace italienne* fortifications. In 1988, Parker developed this argument further when he published his seminal book on the topic, *The Military Revolution: Military Innovations and the Rise of the West, 1500–1800*. Soon after, Jeremy Black in turn critiqued Parker in his volume *A Military Revolution? Military Change and European Society, 1550–1800* (1991). The debate continued throughout the 1990s without ever being truly resolved or brought to any definitive – or even semi-definitive – conclusion, although an important step toward an agreed synthesis was made in 1995 when Clifford Rogers published his edited volume *The Military Revolution Debate: Readings on the Military Transformation of Early Modern Europe*. This collection included Michael Roberts' original 1955 article, Parker's 1976 article, an article by Jeremy Black that was a digest of his book, and several other chapters written by other prominent writers on this subject (notably John Guilmartin, John Lynn, David Parrott and Clifford Rogers himself). The debate revolved around three main issues: was there a revolution in military affairs in the early modern period? Assuming that the answer to this was affirmative, this raised two other questions: what constituted the military revolution and when did it happen?

Most of the protagonists in this debate seem at least to agree on one point: in the early modern period, Europe experienced a series of radical changes in the techniques and technologies of war. The origins of this can be traced back to the late Middle Ages and the slow renaissance of infantry formations – from the thirteenth century onward – in various parts of western and central Europe.[1] Having previously been overshadowed by heavy cavalry, infantry became more important on the field of battle. This was part of a wider historical change: namely, the social and political struggles that erupted across Europe at this time as the Continent moved from the Middle Ages into the early modern period. Put simply, the classical feudal system, socially and militarily based on mounted nobility, was losing its pre-eminence. Urban bourgeoisies and rural peasantries were challenging the feudal system and, in the process, looked for ways to gain military power. As a result, commoners' militias developed fighting methods as well as weaponry that could counter the formidable frontal shock power of the mounted knights. At first strictly defensive, these innovations were based on mass tactics that emphasized discipline, collective action[2] and new 'mental software'[3] that were radically different from the chivalric ethos of the mounted knight, which was primarily based on qualitative principles such as individual prowess and courage. The new tactics utilized weapons that, although sometimes very different at first sight, had in common the battlefield purpose of denying mounted knights the possibility of engaging in their preferred combat method of close-quarter fighting. The aim was to put knights at a distance from their enemy. Amongst these military innovators can be listed: Flemish militiamen armed with primitive lances and protected behind edged poles, English long-bowmen, Italian cross-bowmen, Swiss pikemen and Bohemian Hussites with their arquebuses.[4] As these infantry formations became increasingly powerful and successfully challenged the dominance of mounted knights on European battlefields, they laid the foundations of a forthcoming military revolution that was military, social and political in nature. On the way, the tactical posture of the new infantry units often shifted from defence to offence, most obviously in the case of the Swiss, who, in the second half of the fifteenth century, regularly beat the powerful armies of the dukes of Burgundy and, on several occasions, badly mauled those of the French kings. In the fifteenth century, the gradual quantitative and qualitative power of infantry over cavalry coincided with a technological innovation: the man-portable individual firearm, namely the arquebus. At first, these primitive weapons possessed just about every possible flaw: they were expensive, took a long time to reload, could not operate in wet weather, were unreliable and not safe for their bearer to fire, and their performance – in terms of power, range and rate of fire – was lower, or at best equal, to that of mechanical missile weapons such as long-bows or crossbows which, at this time, had reached their optimum capacity. The question then arises: why did the arquebus eventually replace mechanical missile weapons? It seems that the answer lies in a very simple fact: while long-bows required five years' hard daily training for an archer to become militarily efficient, the arquebus could be used effectively after only a few weeks' practice. Provided enough money was available, it became possible to field infantrymen in quantities never encountered before. This phenomenon contributed to the continuous trend of growth in the size of armies, as well as to the systematic tactical bias of seeking decision on the battlefield through mass and a purely quantitative conception of power – in this case, firepower – as opposed to manoeuvre. Furthermore, this trend would also have consequences for the very nature of battlefield courage. Human nervous and cognitive systems could no longer cope with the speed of fire-weapons projectiles. This was partially true when one considers the already existing arrows and crossbow bolts, but humans would henceforth be overwhelmed by a radical quantitative leap. As Hegel would have said, after reaching a certain critical mass, a quantitative jump was leading the way to a qualitative one. Heroic courage, visible since the dawn of time, would rapidly become archaic and give way to stoical courage, more passive and fatalistic than that of the mounted knight, and more suited for modern combat.[5] While this would not become fully apparent until the invention of automatic weapons and quick-firing artillery in the second half of the nineteenth century, this development began with the advent of primitive gunpowder weapons at the start of the early modern period. Since the question of courage – and its corollary, fear – is at the very root of military tactics, this fact alone could be considered a major turning point in the history of warfare, if not the main one.

The rise of the power of infantry accentuated the socio-political problem embedded in this Military Revolution: the uncertain consequences of the arming of social groups not originally intended to participate in the ruling system. Some European states would deal with this problem through the generalization of parliamentarian political systems (mainly England and the Low Countries), others with the building or reinforcement of the centralized monarchical and bureaucratic state (mainly France and Spain). Recognizing that change was inevitable, from the end of the fifteenth century, the wealthy and mighty attempted to control the rise of infantry as the dominant force on the battlefield. The process had begun as revolutionary, and emanated from social groups fighting for themselves, but it would be appropriated by others, and would finally develop as a state-controlled and sponsored process. Ordinary people could no longer afford fire-weapons, nor could they manage the complex organization and training of new combined-arms infantry in which firearms were deployed alongside edged weapons such as pikes and halberds, the tactical system that was to become increasingly standard on the battlefield during the sixteenth century. Following the ideas of Michel

Foucault, one could also notice that firearms proved formidable tools of social control, not only of the people facing them, but also of the soldiers manning them:

> If there is a politics-war series that passes through strategy, there is an army-politics series that passes through tactics. It is strategy that makes it possible to understand warfare as a way of conducting politics between States; it is tactics that makes it possible to understand the army as a principle for maintaining the absence of warfare in civil society. The classical age saw the birth of the great political and military strategy by which nations confronted each other's economic and demographic resources; but also saw the birth of meticulous military and political tactics by which the control of bodies and individual forces was exercised within States.[6]

Alongside the renaissance of the infantry, one of the main features of the early modern military revolution was the development and spread of artillery. In Western civilization, if the infantry has always emanated from the lower and middle social classes (and the cavalry from the aristocracy), the states created and developed artillery. Simultaneously, during this period, states were trying – and often succeeding – in reducing alternative forms of socio-political powers, mainly the feudal aristocracy and the urban councils. Artillery became one of the main tools of this process of control. Its enormous cost could only be sustained by centralized power that later improved its capacity still further by developing increasingly efficient fiscal bureaucracies. In addition, cannons were of primary importance for bringing down the thin, high walls of feudal castles. The medieval aristocracy could not resist such a politico-military challenge, particularly in a situation where its socio-economic power was already badly mauled by a growing bourgeoisie. Tactically, artillery was at first used as a siege weapon, and its battlefield deployment proved to be problematic. These difficulties began to be overcome in the second half of the fifteenth century when engineers (notably in France) developed several technological improvements: new metallurgic processes enabled the forging of more resilient and cheaper tubes; new gunpowder increased range and striking power; and, last but not least, the tubes were mounted on wheeled gun-carriages and metallic pivots were forged on their sides, enabling easier movement and aiming of the gun. With the capabilities of field guns thus greatly enhanced, tacticians began to manoeuvre artillery on the battlefield. Along with individual fire-weapons, the battlefield use of artillery accelerated the increase in firepower that would transform forever the face of battle.

The other great feature of the military revolution, and the one that fuelled most of the debates among historians during the 1990s, was the radical transformation of the Western fortification system. Unable to resist artillery bombardment, high and (relatively) thin medieval-era fortress walls gave way to a new type of fortification called 'artillery fortresses' (or *trace italienne*, since the early designers were Italian engineers). These new fortifications were 'characterised by thick sunken walls and a snowflake-shaped plan that enabled the defenders to sweep every foot of the walls with enfilading cannon fire'. As Clifford Rogers writes, 'money, time, and methodical siegework, rather than battlefield victories, became the foundation of military success'.[7] Once Italian engineers had laid the theoretical and practical basis of the new system in the sixteenth century, other countries followed suit, principally France and the Low Countries, led, in the seventeenth century, by two prominent figures: Sébastien Le Prestre de Vauban and Menno van Coehoorn. Italian architects initially led the way in this type of engineering in the fifteenth and sixteenth centuries, aided by the political fact that dozens of Italian city-states were constantly at war with each other in this period. After the demise of Italian engineers, excellence in the art of fortress-building (and storming) went to the French and the Dutch. Geostrategical necessities compelled this change, in particular the will to defend, benchmark and sanctify the limits of the 'Square Field' (le pré carré) of the French absolutist monarchy, and the Dutch defensive war against Spanish imperialism. Even more than artillery, only states could afford the cost of these fortifications. In turn, the new fortification systems became one of the main direct and indirect tools working towards an increase in the power and centralization of modern states.

In this period, there was also a transformation in cavalry. The chivalry associated with the mounted knights of the Middle Ages evolved into 'heavy cavalry', a functional role without the social, economical, political, ideological or even aesthetical background of knightly warfare. Cavalry only retained the very specialized tactical roles of shock and breakthrough manoeuvres on the battlefield. Alongside heavy cavalry, the need arose for light cavalry for reconnaissance and screening purposes as well as for waging 'little war' (the term then in use for guerrilla and raiding operations). Since such a tactical tradition did not exist in Western civilization, light cavalry formations had to be imported from the 'Orients': southern Spain, eastern and south-eastern Europe. Initially, mercenaries from these regions fulfilled the part of light cavalry; eventually, locally recruited light cavalry units became an integral and customary part of Western armies. While light cavalry recruitment became purely Western, such units long retained 'oriental' features in their armaments and accoutrements, not to mention their tactical traditions of 'swarming', 'deep raid' and 'harassment' which Western commanders and theoreticians had difficulties conceptualizing and practising, and which were unusual in the 'Western way of war'.[8]

Changes in the size of armies as well as in their armament led to transformations in the theory and art of war. With the increasing complexity of battlefields and theatres of operations, the need arose for professional hierarchies and cadres able to manage the combined-arms combat of large forces equipped with 'high-tech' weaponry. Such an intellectual process would prove difficult to manage since empiricism had more or less been the rule in the West for centuries, and since the only theoretical apparatus available was that of Ancient (Greek and Roman) authors who proved of limited value when it came to theorizing the use and effect of fire-weapons, but who were nonetheless increasingly relied upon throughout the early modern period to provide theoretical guidance.[9] In the long run, some theoreticians would emerge who criticized the emphasis put on Ancient military writers and tried to develop new theories of war,[10] but the bias toward purely quantitative answers – such as mass[11] and destruction – and the mythical 'decisive battle' on a single point would endure until the 1920s and 1930s, when Soviet military theoreticians finally created new concepts more appropriate to modern warfare, most notably the concept of 'operational art' (that would find itself re-appropriated by the US military establishment in the 1980s). This constituted the first true theoretical attempt of the historical 'unblocking' of an aporia – a logical dead-end – that would hamper Western military thought and praxis for so many centuries.[12]

There was also a revolution in war at sea after *c*.1500. At first, nautical knowledge and technologies underwent major changes during the fifteenth century. The 'revolution of Atlantic shipbuilding', as some maritime historians name it, saw the 'round ship' with Nordic rigging impose its hegemony on sea warfare. It was only in the Mediterranean that the long, thin and oared galley with Latin rigging would continue to survive until the eighteenth century. These 'Northern' ships were more resilient, had much better sea-holding qualities as well as longer range, and had a bigger and more fragmented surface of sail which made them more mobile and manoeuvrable, therefore permitting them to sail close-hauled (in other words, to sail into the wind). Such qualities would prove essential for ocean crossings, augmented by improvements in knowledge of astronomy and cartography. From now on, navigation was freed from the restriction of staying in sight of the shore and from coastal 'leaps' from mooring to mooring. From a purely military perspective, these ships could now carry artillery in their lower decks (the 'broadside') since the guns had been lightened and the structures of the hulls strengthened to sustain more recoil and absorb more incoming gunfire. Naval artillery would from now on possess formidable firepower, and such weapon-systems would remain the most powerful armament available until the middle of the twentieth century, when a single plane carrying a nuclear bomb would supersede the firepower of a battleship. One gets a good idea of the weight of naval firepower when one considers that, during the important land battle of Rocroi in 1643, the two opposing French and Spanish/Imperialists armies fielded a total of 47 field guns. This was, at that time, the number of guns carried by a single ship-of-the-line. The English made one of the main improvements for naval artillery in the sixteenth century when they mounted guns on new four-wheel carriages (with small wheels) radically different from their terrestrial counterparts (two large wheels). This made for a more stable platform and more rapid reloading. These technological improvements increased the integration of the guns with the ship's hull, transforming it into a true weapon-system per se, in the modern sense of the term, and a truly maritime one; warships would now be highly mobile artillery platforms as opposed to infantry carriers designed for ship-to-ship boarding fights. Since the dawn of naval warfare, this latter type of fight had actually been more a land-battle transplanted to the surface of the sea than a true sea-battle.

Combined with the improvement of navigation and the extended range of the ships, these changes proved decisive not only for European expansion overseas but also for the creation of specifically naval tactics and, more especially, naval strategy. That constituted a radical shift in the whole history of strategy and not only in the history of Western strategy. The elaboration of a naval strategy involved a brand new *Weltanschauung* and, for the first time, strategy could become not only world-wide, but also global – that is, more than ever closely and directly related to other domains such as finance, commerce, law, politics, diplomacy, science, astronomy, technology and industry. In addition, naval power implied a resolute understanding of the fact that, on the oceans even more than on land, the strategic principles of permanence and endurance were of primary importance. This highlighted the vital importance of logistics and had an operational consequence too: victory in one naval battle could not win wars and even less the mastery of the sea; the decisiveness of a battle was even more impossible to obtain on sea than on land. Such a process would necessitate an intellectual 'quantum leap' or 'qualitative leap' (as continental philosophers would say) then only made by the English in the sixteenth century. Elizabethan England saw the emergence of a philosophical thought of might and power, which led to a very concrete result: the mathematical projection of reality which meant the geometrization of space[13] and therefore the projection of might.[14] Even though Mercator, the inventor of modern cartographical projection, was not English but Flemish,[15] he was strongly influenced by his personal friend, the English magician and astrologist John Dee.[16] The issue of space and power had already begun to be explored by philosophers such as Carl Schmidt in Germany, and Philippe Forget and Gilles Polycarpe in France, all of whom opened up intellectual avenues that would warrant further research.[17]

Navies thus became very 'high-tech' arms and one of the main drivers of scientific and technological progress. Moreover, they necessitated the creation of, for the time, gigantic industrial and logistical systems intended to build and then support navies. Thus, for historians, the naval shipyards such as the Venice arsenal were the matrix of modern industrial complexes, and therefore of the nineteenth-century industrial revolution. Marcus Rediker goes even further, arguing that the maritime society was the crucible for the rise of capitalism and of an international working class; for him, the workers' oppression and day-to-day conditions in nineteenth-century factories and mines are rooted in early modern era ships.[18] Also, the same logistical need for numerous naval bases reinforced in turn the intellectual and commercial need for a primitive sort of 'network-centric' strategic thought – already highlighted by the geometrization of space – long before the US army coined the term at the start of the twenty-first century. Until late in the eighteenth century, British imperialism avoided control of vast areas of landmass – as opposed to the French and, especially, the Spanish – in favour of control of sea networks, whether strictly maritime ones (sea-lanes) or islands, ports and towns. In support of this strategy, Britain only needed a few (relatively) tiny colonies. For instance, the will of North American colonists to expand to the west was strongly opposed in London and the rebels were thus compelled to seek their formal and political independence in order to do so. Since the beginning of Western expansion, England/Britain had understood that modern imperialism was network-oriented, and not land-oriented. Indeed, one can go further and argue that imperialisms such as in Spain were more archaic in that they were more 'agrarian' (i.e., with a tropism towards gaining mere acres and square-miles as the roots of power). Since the sixteenth century, England had sought for intensive trade with the Spanish (and Portuguese) territories of the Americas, but had to sneak its way in, through force, piracy or smuggling, sometimes on a very large scale. In 1713, after the Peace of Utrecht that ended the War of Spanish Succession with a British victory over Spain and France, London chose to reinforce its strategic network rather than gain vast territories. Leaving the mundane inner management of the Spanish American colonies to Madrid, London preferred to secure the de facto quasi-monopoly of trade with these colonies. By this means, the power and glory of Spanish might was put to a definite end.

As the above descriptive analysis of the early modern 'military revolution' suggests, such a macro-historical phenomenon can be considered from many different perspectives and, therefore, opens up even more interpretations. This is the origin of the current debate on military revolutions, as Rogers' edited collection of 1995 proves. But many of these controversies were, in the end, not really focused on the military revolution proper but rather on its definition. At times, it has become more of a linguistic debate about terminology issues. One of these controversies revolves around the use of the word 'revolution'. Since the set of events debated above spans a period of more than three centuries, that very word seems inappropriate. A revolution is generally defined as a blunt and sudden event, lasting no more than a few years. If it lasts for a longer period of time, historians tend to consider it be something else – generally a civil war, which is slightly different. Moreover, most examples of 'revolution' refer to political history – such as the English, the French or the Russian revolutions. Besides its astronomical meaning ('the revolution of a planet around the sun', which was its primary use in the early modern period), it seems that this word should be reserved for strictly political events. But, according to the astronomical metaphor, in a revolution the planet goes back to its point of departure, a result that is anathema to revolutionaries. It would seem that the word 'revolution' has been used improperly, contrary to its original – cyclical – meaning, but the seventeenth and eighteenth centuries saw a gradual change in the sense of the word and a shift to the political field. From the 'end of a cycle', it became 'the end of an era', without any possibility of coming back. On the way, it also absorbed the meaning of 'brutal change' and, later, 'radical' and 'complete' change. But even until late in the eighteenth century, it was still more or less synonymous to coup d'état; even sometimes what is today considered as its antonym: reform. While it appears that the word 'revolution' might not be the best term to characterize the phenomenon we are talking about, the notions of 'radical and complete change' and of 'irreversibility' should be retained since they are still very appropriate to the subject of military change. Some authors argue that a 'revolution' that lasts several centuries should rather be called an 'evolution', but this is a poor descriptor for the military change of the early modern period as it implies notions of continuity, slowness, progressiveness and, above all, no time limit. As previously mentioned, an interesting synthesis came with Rogers' edited book of 1995, *The Military Revolution Debate*, which proposes the use of the concept of 'mutation', based on the works of two biologists: Niles Eldredge and Stephen Jay Gould.[19] These neo-Darwinian evolutionists had noticed that the theory of evolution as depicted by Darwin was far too gradualist and that evolution was more the product of a multitude of small transformations accumulated during millions of years that, at times, reached a critical point and/or mass where, often under external pressures, life was compelled to change radically and very quickly (on a biological scale). Rogers proposed to consider that this could be a very appropriate metaphor for a historical phenomenon such as the military revolution; hence the term 'mutation'.

In the 1990s, at the same time that scholars such as Rogers were working on the early modern period, another 'military revolution debate' was going on, this time among the American military establishment to determine if such a 'revolutionary' process should be initiated in the US armed forces. Attempting to learn lessons from the 1991 Gulf War, American soldiers, politicians, technicians and 'military intellectuals' attempted to conceptualize and drive forward major technological, tactical and operational changes within the different armed services. However, even after they published reams of material and held numerous conferences, there was still no clear conclusion. It was only at the very end of the 1990s that some papers and books were at last published in that field, trying – sometimes quite smartly and successfully – to establish connections with the 'early modern' debate. It seemed that modern strategists were beginning to understand that some broad historical perspective might be useful when dealing with such complex and fragile concepts.[20] But this debate mainly used two slightly different terms: the 'military-technical revolution' (MTR) and the 'revolution in military affairs' (RMA). Both of these concepts were never intended to be as 'broad' as the 'military revolution' proper, but rather strictly technological and tactical; both were also more or less inspired by Soviet military theoretical writings of the 1920s and 1930s (on the role of the American Civil War in the birth of industrialized warfare) and of the 1980s (on the use of electronics and 'smart' weapons). While the linguistic debate about terminology is very useful and must certainly continue, it would be a shame if it blocked research and debate on the historical phenomenon of the military revolution – or whatever it is called – particularly when it resulted in hair-splitting, as happened at times with the MTR/RMA debate.

Furthermore, such concepts appear in their turn quite fragile, mainly because they put too much emphasis on technology, when all the previous 'military revolutions' (or mutations) teach us that weapons and technology do not, in themselves, mean anything. Examples abound of technological inventions that were never – or very seldom – used. Every culture, every civilization, and every power does not automatically think according to the same principles, objectives, representations and prerequisites as modern Western states. More importantly, technological inventions become successful only when they 'meet' a large social or political demand with which they combine to become a socio-technical fact, as has been the case with plebeian infantries combining with arquebuses. Standing alone, arquebuses and guns certainly would not have been more than mere fireworks or courtly weapons for parade or guards units. Such complex combinations of social, political and economic factors alongside technological discoveries must therefore always be considered whenever a 'military revolution' is at stake. And today's 'RMA' – if there is one – is no exception. This myopia toward technology has led some authors to see a 'military revolution' whenever a major new weapon makes its first appearance. This misses the point that we must understand technological change in the light of its historical context, whether it is the early modern or contemporary age. Just as one 'decisive battle' is a mere fantasy, a single technological breakthrough does not produce a military revolution. Therefore, one can be tempted to state that all the protagonists of that historical debate – Black, Lynn, Parker, Parrott, Rogers et al. – have been right, each in his own respect. A military revolution is, therefore, best understood as a complex combination of many new technological breakthroughs, themselves combined with tactical, strategic, sociological, cultural, political, economical and even anthropological issues. Thus, the early modern military revolution is not one event, nor one moment – or period – of history, however large, but an open-ended system that the West adopted some five centuries ago. And this system is what philosophers and philosophers of history call modernity: a global phenomenon that encompasses all aspects of civilization, from family structures to art, economy, finance and politics. In this respect, the military revolution debate is nothing more than the military side of the debate that philosophers of history are having on the emergence and growth of modernity.

From this perspective, it might be possible to say that we still are in the same 'modernity process' that began at the end of the Middle Ages and saw a major turning point in the history of human civilization with radical shifts in economy (the rise of capitalism), politics (the rise of the modern state), sociology (the demise of feudal nobility and the rise of the bourgeoisie), religion (the Reformation), arts and sciences, and even geography (with the progressive colonization by the West of the rest of the world). This is not to say that today's world is the same now as 400 years ago, because within a system there will be much change and evolution, but the paradigms that rule the world began to be defined in the early modern era.

This is also partly true in the military field. Western military history of the last five centuries can be read as the development and evolution of technical, tactical and strategic paradigms that were established and developed from the fifteenth century onward. Within this broad framework, the other great military changes that happened since the end of the eighteenth century can be regarded as accelerations of the same process. For instance, while it is common to consider the French Revolutionary and Napoleonic Wars as one of the major turning points in the history of warfare, no great technological shift occurred during these conflicts and the armies continued to fight with eighteenth-century weapons. In terms of the size of armies, the wars surrounding the French Revolution simply carried on long-standing, pre-existing global trends, while the French mobilization of men and resources at the end of the war of Spanish Succession in 1712 was greater than that of 1793. The violence of combat under Napoleon was certainly no greater either, and the cruelty directed towards civilian populations during strategic campaigns carried on right through the eighteenth century. This was especially the case in eastern Europe and the colonies, although it also applied in theatres of war such as Scotland in 1745 where British-led troops massacred and suppressed Highlanders after the battle of Culloden. Even before Culloden, similar outrages occurred when the armies of Louis XIV (1638–1715) had ravaged the Palatinate and his navy had bombarded the cities of Genoa and Algiers. Even the irruption of politicized masses on the battlefields associated with the French Revolution was not a complete novelty: a very similar phenomenon had already been observed during the English Civil War of the mid seventeenth century. Finally, concerning the art of war, even Napoleon's 'genius' can be considered as the acme and point of excellence of eighteenth-century warfare.

The overemphasis on the military aspects of the French Revolution might, in some measure, be a side-effect of an ideological prejudice and bias – notably but not exclusively in the Anglo-Saxon world – of considering everything emerging from the Revolution as necessarily obscure, brutal, savage and, most of all, cataclysmic. This was evident among Tories at the time and, it could be argued, is still evident today in the unconscious mental grid embedded in many historians who transfer the momentous (or cataclysmic) political and social changes wrought by the events of 1789 to the military field, seeing a military revolution where one did not exist. A more balanced view is that the wars surrounding the French Revolution were part of a process of both continuity and change in terms of military developments, with much more emphasis on continuity stretching back into the early modern period than revolutionary change associated with the French Revolution.

A far more significant turning point occurred with the industrial revolution of the nineteenth century. It saw the absolute pre-eminence of Western military power over the rest of the world, an unbalanced situation that was completely new in history. From the middle of the century, there began the great process of industrialization and mechanization of warfare that would lead to a clear continuum of change from the steam engine and the telegraph of the nineteenth century to the machine guns, tanks, aeroplanes and radios of the twentieth. The 'nuclear revolution' can be viewed as part of this evolution, since nuclear weapons were at first developed, used and considered as no more than 'much more powerful' explosives. When rulers came to realize that they were much more than that, the 'nuclear revolution' transformed diplomacy and international relations, not military affairs. But even all these changes can also be regarded as no more than a mere brutal and geometric acceleration of the modernity process in which the true 'Copernician revolutions' have seen the transformation of the anthropological nature of courage (and fear) and the overflowing of human cognition, the never-ending quest for material superiority, the 'network-oriented' nature of power, the demise of the millennium-old paradigm of the decisive battle on a single point, and the rise of absolute Western military superiority. If there is a 'Western way of war', we must certainly look for it here rather than in Ancient Greece, as Victor Davis Hanson suggests.[21] Moreover, as Geoffrey Parker and Mark Grimsley urge, we should start thoroughly to criticize what these two authors call the 'Western military narrative'. The military history of non-Western civilizations is still in need of more research – although the writings of Geoffrey Parker, Weston F. Cook Jr and Jeremy Black provide a very solid foundation.[22] The manner in which non-European populations perceived the arrival of Europeans and experienced their take-over deserves more study. Lastly, non-Western conceptions of conflict and violence also deserve to be studied, not least as what the West calls 'war' was not the same outside of Europe, while, conversely, what Europeans call 'violence', 'banditry', 'brigandage' or 'little war' non-Europeans called 'war'.

In terms of understanding the military revolution debate, military historians would be well advised to work with colleagues in other 'sub-specialties' – such as economic history, political history, social history, cultural history, history of representations and of ideas, and the history of technology – but they should establish regular links with other disciplines, such as philosophy, sociology, anthropology, ethnology and linguistics (maybe even neuropsychiatry and cognitive sciences). Such an approach could become an opportunity to revitalize the idea of the 'total history' envisaged by Fernand Braudel. Even if such a project is never realized, attempting to tackle such big issues will inject some *longue durée* perspectives into a discipline that badly needs it: military history.

further reading

The following list of books constitutes the key texts on the subject of the military revolution: Jeremy Black, *Rethinking Military History* (London, 2004); Jeremy Black, *A Military Revolution? Military Change and European Society, 1550–1800* (London, 1991); Alfred W. Crosby, *The Measure of Reality: Quantification and Western Society, 1250–1600* (Cambridge, 1997); Alfred W. Crosby, *Throwing Fire: Projectile Technology Through History* (Cambridge, 2002); Brian M. Downing, *The Military Revolution and Political Change: Origins of Democracy and Autocracy in Early Modern Europe* (Princeton NJ, 1992); Philippe Forget and Gilles Polycarpe, *Le Réseau et l'infini: Essai d'anthropologie philosophique et stratégique* (Paris, 1997); Azar Gat, *A History of Military Thought: From the Enlightenment to the Cold War* (Oxford, 2001); Colin S. Gray, *Strategy for Chaos: Revolutions in Military Affairs and The Evidence of History* (London, 2002); J. R. Hale, *War and Society in Renaissance Europe, 1450–1620* (London, 1985); Paul Kennedy, *The Rise and Fall of the Great Powers* (London, 1988); MacGregor Knox and Williamson Murray (eds), *The Dynamics of Military Revolution, 1300–2050* (Cambridge, 2001); John Lynn, *Giant of the Grand Siècle: The French Army, 1610–1715* (Cambridge, 1997); William McNeill, *The Pursuit of Power: Technology, Armed Force, and Society since A.D. 1000* (Chicago, 1982); William McNeill, *Keeping Together in Time: Dance and Drill in Human History* (Cambridge MA, 1995); Shimon Naveh, *In Pursuit of Military Excellence: The Evolution of Operational Theory* (London, 1997); Geoffrey Parker (ed.), *The Cambridge Illustrated History of Warfare* (Cambridge, 1995); Geoffrey Parker, *The Military Revolution: Military Innovation and the Rise of the West, 1500–1800* (Cambridge, 1996); Marcus Rediker, *Between the Devil and the Deep Blue Sea: Merchant Seamen, Pirates, and the Anglo-American Maritime World, 1700–1750* (Cambridge, 1987); Clifford J. Rogers (ed.), *The Military Revolution Debate: Readings on the Military Transformation of Early Modern Europe* (Boulder CO, 1995); Merritt Roe Smith and Leo Marx (eds), *Does Technology Drive History? The Dilemma of Technological Determinism* (Cambridge MA, 1995); and Brett D. Steele and Tamera Dorland, *The Heirs of Archimedes: Science and the Art of War through the Age of Enlightenment* (Cambridge MA, 2005).

Readers should also consult the relevant entries in Thierry de Montbrial and Jean Klein (eds), *Dictionnaire de stratégie* (Paris, 2000) and the following articles: Andrew Latham, 'Warfare Transformed: A Braudelian Perspective on the Revolution in Military Affairs', *European Journal of International Relations* 8/2 (2002): 231–66; David Parrott, entry 'Military', subentries 'Armies: recruitment, organization and social composition', 'Battle tactics and campaign strategy', 'Early modern military theory', and 'Historiography', in Jonathan Dewald et al. (eds), *Europe 1450 to 1789 – Encyclopedia of the Early Modern World*, vol. 4 (New York, 2004), pp. 117–38; John Stone, 'Technology, Society, and the Infantry Revolution of the Fourteenth Century', *The Journal of Military History* 68/2 (April 2004): 361–80.

Finally, the following websites contain useful information on the military revolution debate: Mark Grimsley, 'The History of War in Global Perspective' with an answer by Geoffrey Parker, conference at the Mershon Center (University of Ohio State), 12–13 November 2004 at <http://people.cohums.ohio-state.edu/grimsley1/dialogue/mershon/global.htm> and Clifford J. Rogers, 'Revolution, Military' in *The Reader's Companion to Military History*, Houghton Mifflin, College Division, Online Studies at <http://college.hmco.com/history/readerscomp/mil/html/mh_000105_entries.htm>.

notes

1. See Kelly DeVries, *Infantry Warfare in the Early Fourteenth Century* (Woodbridge, 1996).

2. From the end of the sixteenth century, the emphasis on mass, discipline and collective action would form part of the origins of philosophical and aesthetical thought such as Cartesius' writings on 'the mechanical man', or La Mettrie's *Man A Machine*. At the turn of sixteenth and seventeenth centuries, the Dutch army of Orange-Nassau, then the most advanced infantry in Europe, was indeed thought of as a mechanical body. See William McNeill, *The Pursuit of Power: Technology, Armed Force, and Society since A.D. 1000* (Chicago, 1982) and especially *Keeping Together in Time: Dance and Drill in Human History* (Cambridge MA, 1985). See also George S. Rousseau, *Nervous Acts: Essays on Literature, Culture and Sensibility* (Basingstoke, 2004); Anson Rabinbach, *The Human Motor: Energy, Fatigue, and the Origins of Modernity* (Berkley CA, 1992); and Walter Benjamin, *The Origins of German Tragic Drama* [1974] (New York, 2003).

3. The concept of 'mental software' is developed in Alain Joxe, *Voyage aux sources de la guerre* (Paris, 1991).

4. See John Stone, 'Technology, Society, and the Infantry Revolution of the Fourteenth Century', *Journal of Military History* 68/2 (April 2004): 361–80.

5. See Robert L. O'Connell, 'Courage', *MHQ: The Quarterly Journal of Military History* 3/1 (Autumn 1990): 62–7.

6. Michel Foucault, *Discipline and Punish: The Birth of the Prison* (London, 1977), p. 168. See also Alain Ehrenberg, *Le Corps militaire: Politique et pédagogie en démocratie* (Paris, 1983).

7. Clifford J. Rogers, 'Revolution, Military' in *The Reader's Companion to Military History*, Houghton Mifflin, College Division, Online Studies at <http://college.hmco.com/history/readerscomp/mil/html/mh_000105_entries.htm>.

8. See Laurent Henninger, 'Une conséquence de la guerre de Trente Ans en Europe centrale et balkanique: le renouveau de la cavalerie dans les armées occidentales' in *Nouveaux regards sur la guerre de Trente Ans* (Paris, 1998).

9. It is very possible that Renaissance Italians and Spaniards benefited from the coming of Byzantine refugees, after the fall of Constantinople to the Turks in 1453. For instance, a large part of the Constantinople library was evacuated to Sicily during that very year. Such material helped various fields such as arts, financial and legal techniques, so it appears logical to consider it also helped with the development of military theory. After all, the Byzantines had been the only true strategists in the Christian world during all of the Middle Ages, as well as the curators and improvers of Roman military art.

10. Of these, the much overlooked Vauban might have been one of the most important. His numerous and important deeds and written works still deserve renewed and thorough studies. See, in particular, his most recent intellectual biography: Michèle Virol, *Vauban: De la gloire du roi au service de l'État* (Paris, 2003).

11. At the end of the Middle Ages and during the early modern era, the emphasis put on quantity (of infantrymen, weapons and fire) represented a real change compared to the emphasis put on quality during the Classical period and Middle Ages when the only quantitative advantage lay in better opportunities to resist strategic attrition. Indeed, at the tactical level, too many combatants on the battlefield could mean more chaos and command difficulties for commanders. However, this was not as true in Asia, where the Chinese and Indian monarchs, for instance, fielded huge armies of hundreds of thousands of men.

12. See Shimon Naveh, *In Pursuit of Military Excellence: The Evolution of Operational Theory* (London, 1997); James J. Schneider, *The Structure of Strategic Revolution: Total War and the Roots of the Soviet Warfare State* (Novato CA, 1994); B. J. C. McKercher

and Michael A. Hennessy (eds), *The Operational Art: Developments in the Theories of War* (Westport CT, 1996); and Bruce W. Menning, 'Operational Art's Origins', *Military Review* (September–October 1997) at <http://www.cgsc.army.mil/milrev/english/sepoct97/menning.htm>.

13. In my mind, 'geometrization' can be philosophically considered as much more than mere mapping of the sea-space, because it implies an intellectual process consisting in transforming actual space into a mathematical abstraction. In that respect, today's digitizing of almost anything is the perfect continuation of that process.

14. See Lesley B. Cormack, 'Mathematics and Empire: The Military Impulse and the Scientific Revolution' and Michael S. Mahoney, 'Charting the Globe and Tracking the Heavens: Navigation and the Sciences in the Early Modern Era' in Brett D. Steele and Tamera Dorland (eds), *The Heirs of Archimedes: Science and the Art of War through the Age of Enlightenment* (Cambridge MA, 2005), pp. 181–203, 221–30.

15. Flanders and the Low Countries were very important actors in the modernity process in the maritime and economic fields, if not fully on the aesthetical and philosophical ones (with the exception of the realm of painting).

16. On Dee see Ken MacMillan, 'Discourse on History, Geography, and Law: John Dee and the Limits of the British Empire, 1576–80', *Canadian Journal of History* 36/1 (April 2001): 1–25; and Amir Alexander, 'Harriot and Dee on Exploration and Mathematics: Did Scientific Imagery Make for New Scientific Practice?' in Steele and Dorland, *The Heirs of Archimedes*, pp. 205–19.

17. Carl Schmitt, *Land and Sea* (trans. Simona Draghici) (Washington DC, 1997); Carl Schmitt, *Hamlet oder Hekuba: Der Einbruch der Zeit in das Spiel* (Düsseldorf, 1956) (translated into French in 1992 by Jean-Louis Besson and Jean Jourdheuil under the title *Hamlet ou Hécube: L'irruption du temps dans le jeu*); Carl Schmitt, *The Leviathan in the State Theory of Thomas Hobbes* (trans George Schwab and Erna Hilfstein) (Westport CT, 1996); and Philippe Forget and Gilles Polycarpe, *Le Réseau et l'infini: Essai d'anthropologie philosophique et stratégique* (Paris, 1997). All these authors have no hesitation in looking for the philosophical roots of the English mastery of the seas in this period in writers such as William Shakespeare.

18. Marcus Rediker, *Between the Devil and the Deep Blue Sea: Merchant Seamen, Pirates, and the Anglo-American Maritime World, 1700–1750* (Cambridge, 1987).

19. Clifford J. Rogers, 'The Military Revolution of the Hundred Years War' in Rogers (ed.), *The Military Revolution Debate: Readings on the Military Transformation of Early Modern Europe* (Boulder CO, 1995), pp. 76–7.

20. See Colin S. Gray, *Strategy for Chaos: Revolutions in Military Affairs and the Evidence of History* (London, 2002) and MacGregor Knox and Williamson Murray (eds), *The Dynamics of Military Revolution, 1300–2050* (Cambridge, 2001).

21. Victor Davis Hanson, *The Western Way of War: Infantry Battle in Classical Greece* (New York, 1989).

22. Weston F. Cook, *The Hundred Years War for Morocco: Gunpowder and the Military Revolution in the Early Modern Muslim World* (Boulder CO, 1994).

2
warfare and the rise of the state

alan james

Michael Roberts' thesis on the military revolution has inspired, or indirectly affected, virtually all work on the history of warfare of the early modern period since his celebrated inaugural lecture of 1955. In it, he identified a number of now quite well-known developments in the conduct of war that occurred between 1560 and 1660. Although these were 'strictly technical' developments, his interest in them was specifically as agents of 'constitutional and social change' and as the origin of the international state system and the militarism that lay behind the ferocity and the scale of war witnessed in the twentieth century.[1] Light field artillery and mobile tactics by armies with infantry in shallow formations increasingly deploying firearms over the traditional pike were, in brief, the innovations mainly credited by Roberts to the Dutch and Swedes in the early seventeenth century. Among the effects of this more offensive warfare, the ever-bigger armies it required and, above all, the stricter discipline, organization, and practised drills necessary to take full advantage of the new military opportunities, was the resulting fiscal and organizational pressure felt by states. They were challenged to enforce their domestic authority as far as possible and to improve their tax-raising powers in order to mobilize as much of the available resources as they could. Thus, 'the transformation in the scale of war led inevitably to an increase in the authority of the state', with its recognizably modern domestic monopoly of violence and the institutional strength to channel a nation's resources to large-scale war abroad.[2]

Since the 1980s, the origins of the modern state has been a particularly popular subject amongst historians, political scientists and historical sociologists. For many, the clear logic and simple elegance of Michael Roberts' thesis is appealing. Certainly, in or post the 1500 period, the growth in scale of warfare broadly corresponded to the size and sophistication of European states. Yet warfare is not a simple phenomenon. By extension, its relationship to the rise of the state cannot be a simple, direct one either. Indeed, the sheer variety of different historical experiences suggests that the neat causal link in Michael Roberts' thesis is actually conceptually limited and even potentially misleading. The military historian, therefore, has a key role to play in pointing the way forward for future research on warfare and state-formation. By embracing the complexity of warfare and the wide range of social organizations from which it arose in the past, they are best placed to begin to challenge the previously unassailable assumption of the uniform effect of war as a modernizing force in history.

To illustrate the limitation of the military revolution thesis as it applies to state building, this chapter will consider the case of France particularly closely. Although Roberts himself said very little about it, France fits his model especially well. In 1598, the kingdom emerged exhausted from nearly 40 years of damaging civil war, the sixteenth-century Wars of Religion. Under the guidance of Cardinal Richelieu, the influential first-minister to Louis XIII, Catholic France formally entered the Thirty Years' War in 1635 in alliance with the United Dutch Provinces, Sweden, and other Protestant powers. In this way, Richelieu has earned a reputation as the first secular statesman, prepared to put the pragmatic interests of the state ahead of 'old-fashioned' concerns, such as confessional identity. For France, this war was long and very difficult. Indeed, its particular struggle with Spain extended well beyond the celebrated Peace of Westphalia of 1648 that ended the war in the German Empire. By 1659, when the final Peace of the Pyrenees was negotiated by Richelieu's successor, Cardinal Mazarin, France had suffered countless popular rebellions and fiscal emergencies but had nevertheless overtaken its long-time rival, Spain, and emerged as the leading military power in Europe. The elaborate court rituals and opulent display thereafter at Louis XIV's palace of Versailles were widely envied, and France's newly enlarged administration and bureaucracy, which had grown during a prolonged period of warfare, made it the epitome of modernity and the very model of royal absolutism.

Although the military revolution thesis has, therefore, always been easily accommodated by historians of France, the assumption that war was the driving force behind state growth pre-dates Michael Roberts significantly and has affected their approach especially deeply. Indeed it is Max Weber over a century ago who was primarily responsible for the idea that changes in the organization and structure of armies 'led to the establishment of the modern state'.[3] According to Otto Hintze in a lecture of 1906, waging war is the primary organizing social function, making states and armies in early civil society virtually indistinguishable institutions. Although over the centuries the purpose of states expanded, geopolitical pressures by the early modern period were such that the chief task of state financial systems was again primarily the maintenance of armed forces. Like Roberts, Hintze specifically singled out Maurice of Nassau and Gustavus Adolphus of Sweden as the 'great organizers' responsible for large, standing armies.[4] Yet due to Richelieu's domestic efforts at ruthlessly 'suppressing particularism', it was France that best fit the resulting model of coercive continental powers. According to Hintze, 'absolutism and militarism go together', and *Louis Quatorzien* France became the very embodiment of modernity because it took them both to extremes.[5] Hintze's ideas certainly reflect the traditional scholarship of France's *grand siècle* and the emphasis of nineteenth-century French nationalist historians on the state-building achievements of their iconic historical figures. Many historians have also been deeply influenced by Weberian ideas on the social effects of an emerging capitalism. From this perspective, monarchs who sought a monopoly on violence allied with an emerging, ambitious bourgeoisie against an obstructive, anachronistic nobility. This alliance with professionals not only built a growing government administration but also helped modernize the military hierarchy, creating what some might call a 'bureaucratic' absolutism.[6]

Yet it is precisely within the field of French history that some of the most serious doubts have recently been cast on Roberts' military revolution, specifically in David Parrott's painstaking research on Richelieu's army in the first half of the seventeenth century. Parrott's work makes it clear that, far from grasping opportunities afforded by the new technological and tactical innovations credited to their Dutch and Swedish contemporaries, French generals, at least, were markedly reluctant to innovate. Though the increasing military commitments of the 1630s and 1640s had indeed brought very real fiscal and administrative pressures, this did not lead to a rationalization of the conduct of war, the army, or the government. Parrott shows that the army suffered many more failures and grew much less quickly than previously thought, and as the war escalated, the government found it increasingly difficult to cajole its independent-minded regimental commanders. Fiscally, the French state lumbered from one crisis to another, alienating royal revenue as quickly as it was alienating its subjects through onerous taxation and unwanted interference.[7] Thus, neither in the sense that warfare itself was changing, nor that its scale applied a modernizing pressure on states, can Roberts' thesis be said to apply, at least to the French state of the early seventeenth century.

The military revolution debate, as it was initiated by Geoffrey Parker in 1976, has been rehearsed in a number of places already.[8] It is enough to note here that Parker passed over the issue of state-building largely in silence. He chose instead to challenge Roberts' chronology and choice of significant technological change by identifying the use of heavy cannon in the late fifteenth century and the effect that this had on siege warfare and army size as the most significant military development of the early modern period. There is little doubt, however, that Parker accepted the enormous transforming potential of military change, for he also singled out naval artillery of the early sixteenth century, and related developments in ship design, as revolutionary changes to which he largely credited European overseas expansion and 'the rise of the west'.[9] Many such changes in warfare have been identified by others, in a number of places and in different historical periods, so that the 'revolutionary' character of any one development now has to be questioned. Yet the multiplication of military transformations, on its own, has not weakened the strength of the logic of Roberts' original thesis about the rise of the modern state.

The real challenge to the thesis has come instead from a growing awareness amongst military historians that to understand transformations in warfare, we must add to our interest in tactical and technological developments the formative political forces at work in a society which bind a nation together in common purpose, and as the reflections of Jeremy Black demonstrate, in particular those in France later in the seventeenth century. Black, too, questioned the focus of Roberts' thesis, identifying different technological developments as the more important, in this case specifically the flintlock musket and socket bayonet of the late seventeenth and early eighteenth centuries. More significantly, Black claims, it was only by this time, with the raising and supporting of disciplined, professional armies on an unprecedented scale, that anything worthy of the term 'revolutionary' had occurred in European warfare since at least the late fifteenth century. In this way, he not only challenged Roberts' focus but reassessed his link between war and the state. Before France could develop a truly effective, larger, well-supported army, Black argued, the organizational capacity of the state had to have improved, as it did after 1661 under Louis XIV. By effectively reversing the causal relationship proposed by Roberts, the state is brought back into the equation, no longer simply the product, but now also a precondition of substantial military change.[10]

In some respects, Black was following in the footsteps of J. R. Hale who, in 1985, had begun to qualify the impact of technology: specifically, the effectiveness of this new, heavier artillery of the late fifteenth century which, he insisted, depended on such associated factors as 'morale, supply, defensive ingenuity, skill', and experience. Going one step further, Hale also questioned the credibility of the claim that even such profound changes in warfare could have stimulated the growth of the Renaissance state. Whilst identifying a number of changes in the scale and conduct of war over a long period (what Hale preferred to call a longer-term 'military reformation') and acknowledging that these created fiscal pressure, he argued that most states could, on the whole, cope with it. They had internal concerns and followed their own trajectories of development, which war affected but did not drive. The value of Hale's work is his sensitivity to a range of social and cultural influences on war, not least of which is the 'personal' role of monarchs and their own reasons for fighting in the first place.[11]

By privileging the relative robustness of government institutions and the cultural context of war over technology and tactics, the military historians Black and Hale are actually closer in spirit to current theorists of 'military revolutions' than Parker or even Roberts himself. This is illustrated in an important volume of essays, edited by MacGregor Knox and Williamson Murray, which taps into an intellectual tradition that arguably began much earlier in the twentieth century with the reflections of Hans Delbrück on the limited nature of eighteenth-century warfare. Delbrück attributed the sudden leap in the scale and conduct of the revolutionary wars of the early nineteenth century, as well as their strategies and tactics, to the equally dramatic intellectual and political transformations of the time.[12] Accordingly, Knox and Murray have as a defining feature of any 'military revolution' that it 'recast[s] society and the state as well as military organisations'. This is in contrast to 'revolutions in military affairs' (RMAs) which are defined as merely technological or tactical innovations in the conduct of war. The French Revolution, which 'merged mass politics and warfare', Knox and Murray agree, was one such military revolution. The first that they identify, however, was 'the creation in the seventeenth century of the modern nation-state which rested on the large-scale organisation of disciplined military power'. This was a profound, lasting change, which then spawned the associated RMAs which various historians have identified and which characterized the conduct of war until the late eighteenth century.[13] Although Knox and Murray claim to be borrowing Roberts' framework, reversing this specific causal link in the seventeenth-century context by putting such wider political and social changes before the expansion of the scale of war actually represents a significant theoretical shift. There is no such emphasis in Roberts' thesis. Indeed, he did not even acknowledge the cultural effects of the French Revolution as he linked the tactical changes of the sixteenth century to the militarism of the Second World War.

Appropriately, in a contribution to Knox and Murray's volume on the France of Louis XIV, John Lynn adopts a similar approach by playing down the effect of technology and setting out instead to identify the cultural changes that lay behind the transformation of warfare at the time. The flintlock musket and socket bayonet, he argues, despite their 'potential' to transform war, were actually adopted only very slowly by the French. Similarly, Lynn argues that new, lighter, more mobile cannon, similar to the type adopted with such great success much later in the eighteenth century, might also have changed the conduct of war, but were not adopted for a combination of political and cultural reasons. The 'cannon *de nouvelle invention*', he claims, 'remained only a *revolution manquée* because the French were not intellectually ready for such guns in an age dominated by siege warfare'.[14] By suggesting instead that a 'battle culture of forbearance', in which heavy losses could be sustained in the steadfast pursuit of victory, along with the associated assertion that drill, orderliness, and regimental community spirit led to the powerful armies of the Sun King, Lynn does well to demonstrate that 'conceptual and institutional innovation, not technological change, had a decisive impact on seventeenth-century war'. For Roberts, too, drill and discipline were key, defining features of the emerging military state, though they were the direct 'effect' of new tactical imperatives.[15] For Lynn, and others, they are presented as prerequisite societal changes to developments in warfare and, by extension, of the state. As he says elsewhere, it is this 'social technology' (army size and discipline) that 'probably mattered as much or more than material technology' in shaping history.[16]

Increasingly, therefore, military historians are stressing the importance of social and cultural expectations about the nature of warfare along with the effects of intangible political factors on its development. This certainly enriches our understanding of the past, although it does not provide any easy answers about state development, for in the process they are not necessarily choosing, nor even distinguishing, between the two related theoretical approaches to the rise of the early modern state: Roberts', based as it is on the direct formative influence of tactical and technological change, and that defined by Knox and Murray which stresses the growth of the state as a necessary catalyst of military change. Lynn's essay, for example, simultaneously challenges and reasserts the assumptions behind the Roberts thesis. Although he concludes that technology did not drive significant military or political change under Louis XIV, by making it clear that it certainly could have, he leaves such technology-driven models of change unchallenged. Indeed he positively embraces them by revisiting Parker's assertion that seafaring technology led directly to European overseas expansion and the successful exportation of a European style of war across the globe.[17] In many ways, to the extent that military historians theorize about the rise of the state at all, it is usually the very complexity of the nebulous, mutually-reinforcing relationship between it and war which they currently embrace, rather than any simple developmental formulae. Most would now probably agree with Frank Tallett that warfare did have a profound effect on the state, as 'probably the most important single factor influencing its growth', but that there was not a uniform, inevitable causal connection.[18]

In contrast to this growing sensitivity to the complexity of the relationship between warfare and the state, the direct modernizing effect of war is almost universally assumed by many political scientists and historical sociologists who are concerned primarily with elaborating state-building theories. Bruce Porter, for one, is hostile to any work which questions this link between war and the state. For him, there was a straightforward, circular pattern of state growth. The clear need to wage war in an increasingly difficult environment led governments to coerce their subjects in order to extract the necessary resources and finances, leading to larger bureaucracies, and so to ever greater wars.[19] The main challenge for him and other social scientists using this Weberian framework, of course, has been to explain the different national trajectories.

Why under this pressure did some states develop into coercive, bureaucratic absolutist states less quickly or less effectively than others? Or, more to the point for most writers, why did some, most notably Britain, not seem to do so at all? For Hintze, the answer lay in geopolitical forces. Put simply, those countries facing the greater threat from neighbouring land powers put correspondingly more effort into building appropriate resource-extracting bureaucracies and into suppressing local institutions of government. An island state like Britain did not feel the same pressure, and older constitutional arrangements could survive.

Charles Tilly declares quite categorically that 'war makes states' in the same circular, developmental pattern. National variation, according to his model, comes from the inclusion of 'capital accumulation' along with 'war-making' and 'resource extraction' in early modern state-making. This money-making could take a number of forms and depended to a large extent on the nature of the economy. In brief, Tilly agrees that governments grew in proportion to their efforts at 'extraction, state making, protection, and, especially, war making' but also in reverse proportion to the commercialization of the economy. Thus in England, with its allegedly more easily taxed commercial, maritime economy, the state grew less than its large, agrarian continental rivals.[20] Similarly, for Brian M. Downing, there is no doubting that the early modern military revolution led directly to what he calls 'military-bureaucratic absolutism'. In his aim to identify, and then openly applaud, those factors which allowed some states to avoid this pressure toward authoritarianism and to follow a specifically modern, liberal democratic pattern instead, he develops these same geographical and economic explanations.[21] A country might be relieved of some of the pressure toward domestic coercion that springs from warfare he says if, like Britain: it enjoyed natural protective frontiers; it could mobilize foreign resources to pay for war; or, if it could make profitable alliances. Similarly, an advanced economy and commercial wealth might save it, but only if this wealth was in the hands of merchants and not monarchs. Otherwise, he claims, it would just be diverted and used as an instrument of oppression, for an underlying assumption of Downing's analysis is that states, or at least monarchies, are by nature coercive or autocratic. Or, as Tilly describes it more evocatively, they acted like violent racketeers.

Despite the pains taken to explain the variety of national experiences, the problem with all of this work is that even as the nation state appears in the twenty-first century to be under assault from above (by globalization and pan-national political organizations) and from below (by revived regional nationalism), it continues to be a principal focus of study for political scientists. Although it is true that broad historically-based analyses are being written, not just to account for the rise of the nation state, but now also to predict future trends in warfare and government in its absence, the fundamental Weberian premise is in little danger, for history continues to be understood by political scientists simply as a prelude to the warring nation states that we know from the nineteenth and twentieth centuries. For example, the brave new world of the twenty-first century is presented in stark and frightening terms by Martin Van Creveld, and especially by Philip Bobbitt, in part because the future (in Bobbitt's case defined by the 'market state') is contrasted with a past that would appear to have been overwhelmingly dominated by the development of nationally defined, coercive, domestic authority and by warfare against easily identifiable, politically organized enemies.[22] Yet increasingly, historical research is tending to complicate, or even contradict, this picture.

The reaction to recent international political events by military or political historians has been more sensitive and productive. As John Elliott observed, the changes unfolding in the early 1990s awakened a new historical interest in alternative developments to that of the centralized state.[23] Increasingly, the entrenched regionalism and the informality and flexibility of constitutional arrangements in the past are seen less as anomalies or anachronisms, but as integral, defining features of early modern society. Today, continuity with the medieval past tends to be stressed by historians over 'modernizing' pressures and trends, though crucially not as a sign of weakness or of failure. No longer seen just as a group of competing, emerging nation states in various stages of development toward the ideal model of the modern liberal democracy, early modern Europe was an unashamedly complex mixture of international, personal, and dynastic political forms with its own defining interests. The most striking illustration is the patrimony of the Holy Roman Emperor, Charles V (1500–1558), whose vast collection of territories in central Europe centred on what is now modern Germany. In contrast to his power as king of Castile, the title of Emperor was a dignity with limited political authority but with tremendous prestige, for it represented the secular arm of the universalist claims of the Catholic Church. Indeed he ruled his lands in Europe and overseas in a bewildering array of other different legal capacities including 11 separate titles for his authority in the Netherlands alone.[24] Yet his fractured, disparate political power was to be neither pitied nor derided by rival monarchs, even those from superficially more centralized states like France.[25] If his authority was sometimes tenuous in places, the international pre-eminence of Charles V was never in question. Government across Europe was by nature conservative, not innovative; it respected legal traditions and was often personal or informal in practice. In war, the opportunity simply to annex territory from an enemy and eradicate its existing constitutional forms and traditions for the sake of uniformity or state-building was rarely, if ever, taken. This would have been inconsistent with the purpose of going to war in the first place. Far more usually, divinely-appointed monarchs treated each other with a certain respect, imposing terms that might have a territorial element but which were in essence designed to redefine their relative status or, through the distribution of any spoils, improve personal bonds with their nobility.[26] Similarly, a king might accept an existing, lesser title in a new territory or choose only to name a viceroy whilst otherwise maintaining local autonomy. This could be for practical reasons to do with the complications of governing at a distance, but it was also by choice because respecting legal traditions did not contradict the legitimacy of the claim (in a way that naked conquest might), and thus it satisfied better the dynastic ambitions at work. As Elliott says, constitutionally, this was, largely by preference, a Europe of 'composite', not 'absolute' monarchies. Thus current evidence of the mutability of the nation state has, in effect, liberated historians of the early modern period from the potentially distorting effect of hindsight, that is specifically the knowledge that the nation state would emerge as the dominant model of political organization in the nineteenth century. This sensitivity to the historical, cultural context of war is what is often missing from the models of social scientists.

Much recent historical work has also been done which calls into question long-held assumptions about the internal development of the instruments of state power. Within French historiography, as for other countries, former models of 'absolutism' as the successful emasculation of the nobility are today either dismissed or at least seriously qualified.[27] Louis XIV's domestic grandeur, for example, is currently seen as a more cooperative endeavour than a mere arbitrary, authoritarian one. The nobility remained the principal, defining element of society, and thus a key part of any military or political endeavour. This was universally accepted, despite whatever immediate fiscal measures might have been taken against them under the pressures of the increased scale of warfare. Thus it was through compromise and the development of a common interest with the nobility that the monarchy coordinated its military resources so effectively.[28] Equally, the fiscal pressure of war did not necessarily lead to the suppression of parliaments, estates, or other representative bodies in favour of direct, central administration and taxation. In some cases this was true, in others the desperation for money actually led to an increased dependence on them. Even those historians who insist that Louis XIV's reign ultimately was most remarkable for the extent to which he was personally able to exercise political power acknowledge the compromises and negotiations that made up the normal political process.

Such findings by historians make the task of developing state-building theories more difficult for political scientists and are therefore sometimes resisted. As an illustration, Downing says of the historian William Beik (whose very influential study of the estates of Languedoc demonstrates their continued political significance and that of the local nobility more generally under Louis XIV), that

> his emphasis on bargains between crown and local notables seems to me to shift attention unduly away from the essentially coercive and military nature of the French state after 1635. Bargains abounded, and nobles benefited from privileges and offices, as they did in the Great Elector's state [Prussia]

– absolutism was never absolute. But in neither state were such bargains defining characteristics or critical parts of the state's origins.[29]

It may well be true that these political arrangements have limited value to an understanding of the modern liberal democracies which interest Downing. Yet, with very few exceptions, political and social historians of France would nevertheless insist that these were indeed 'characteristics' of the age and 'critical parts' of the state's nature. Today, the political shape of seventeenth-century France tends to be presented as an infinitely complex pattern of overlapping kinship and clientage networks and of continued noble influence rather than as an agenda set by the crown, regardless of the administrative innovations it was forced to take. By considering 'the independence of the aristocracy' to be a 'critical shortcoming' of France's development, however, Downing betrays the teleology of his argument, treating as an unnecessary distraction current historical research on the nature of the relations between the monarchy and the nobility and the nature of the state as it actually functioned rather than what it appears, in retrospect, to have promised for the future.[30] Similarly, for Tilly, such cooperation with the nobility, though not necessarily a shortcoming was nevertheless part of a 'mixed strategy' that was essentially all about 'massive pacification and monopolization of the means of coercion'.[31]

Such assumptions by political scientists about the singular nature of early modern states seem to deny governments their historical agency and the range of organizing options open to them. Centralizing the administration of military affairs and taking a more direct role was not necessarily an obvious or desirable, nor even the most beneficial, step to take. Indeed the opposite response to the fiscal pressures of war, away from direct administration, was entirely possible, as is made most clear in the study of the early seventeenth-century Spanish government of Philip IV and Olivares by I. A. A. Thompson.[32] A state could privatize to some extent, that is to rely increasingly on mercenaries or private interests who would raise forces largely, or even entirely, at their own expense. As an example, the Holy Roman Emperor, Ferdinand II, depended to a considerable degree during the Thirty Years' War upon the private army of Albrecht Von Wallenstein. Such military 'entrepreneurship' actually represents a withdrawal from the business of army administration and finance by the state. Another option was for states simply to rely more heavily on their traditional elites to provide military services. Even in the France of Louis XIII and Richelieu, where private armies were not permitted, there was far less rationalization of government and centralization of power than once thought, and the nobility retained a tight grasp of the high command. Yet this did not necessarily lead to long-term failure. After all, despite the many failings detailed by David Parrott, the army grew over the century, and France survived to become the leading European power. Thus it seems clear that early modern military developments can only be understood if evaluated, not as either long-term 'successes' or 'failures' for the state, nor as evidence of the value of a given state-building theory, but as means to immediate political and military ends.

Needless to say, the best state-building theories incorporate as much historical work as possible and thereby consider a wider range of different types of political organization. Notable in this respect is Thomas Ertman's work which incorporates the latest historical work, including that which seeks to set the 'limits' of French absolutism.[33] Not only does seventeenth-century France appear a less powerful state than was once assumed but, Ertman concludes, the bureaucratic absolutist model which it is said to embody is clearly not appropriate. Indeed some of the most significant recent historical work has been on the financiers upon whom the crown became increasingly dependent for loans and for tax collection, or the finances and the private world of ministers of state whose personal networks of political influence monarchs required to exercise their authority effectively.[34] Not just exercises in personal aggrandisement, the private fortunes of ministers such as Richelieu and Mazarin were an essential part of the process of governing and of the representation of power. The bureaucracy itself was increasingly filled not by professionals, as we would understand the term today, through a meritocratic system of selection, but by venal office-holders who purchased their positions, holding them effectively as personal property and alienating crown control in the long run. In France, the crown often farmed out tax collection to private bidders and for centuries sold offices within its administration. Given this, and the continued significance of the nobility, Ertman insists France was more accurately a 'patrimonial' absolutist state, and in this light it developed very differently from Prussia, for example, though both were continental powers dealing with similar pressures.

This conclusion challenges the older, more simplistic dichotomy between a continental model of coercive, absolutist, and militarized states and the British one which is supposedly constitutional and commercial. The important work of the historian John Brewer, in particular, has shattered this view by challenging our understanding of the eighteenth-century British state.[35] Militarily, Britain was not a poor relation that had been spared the military pressures suffered by its continental rivals. On the contrary, it was an exceptionally militarized state with a large and sophisticated bureaucracy. Overseas trade proved more difficult to regulate than agrarian economies, and contrary to Tilly's assumption, the collection of taxes from landed wealth was actually easier to farm out to amateurs or financiers, as the case of France illustrates. The excise in Britain alone required more administrators than the entire Prussian bureaucracy. Moreover, the Royal Navy was not a pale reflection of a continental army but an enormous organizational and fiscal challenge to the state. As Ertman suggests, such recent historical judgements cast serious doubt on previous state-building theories, including the geographical and commercial variables identified by Hintze and Tilly. For him, there are more possible outcomes of the early modern state-building process than permitted by the continuum between the two poles of the absolutist, militarized state and the constitutional, commercial one. A modern state, he says, can be situated between 'constitutional' or 'absolutist' in essence, and 'bureaucratic' or 'patrimonial' in practice.

Ertman's theory of state development is based on timing. For him, the medieval origins of the process are essential. In a simplified form, it could be said that a state which began the process of modernizing early had no other model of large hierarchies to emulate than the church. This meant the monarchy operated through personal relationships with its elites. These, in turn, became entrenched and indispensable, setting a path toward 'patrimonial absolutism', as in Spain or France, whereas a state like Prussia, or Denmark, which modernized later, could benefit from the experience of others and develop a more efficient, 'bureaucratic absolutist' form of government. For Ertman, it was the timing of the effects of warfare that largely determined the path of development a state would follow. This is quite a sophisticated model, for whilst it accepts the transformative effect of warfare it suggests that it is not immediate nor uniform. As for Britain, although it experimented early with state-building, relatively long periods of peace allowed its 'strong, territorially-based representative assembly'[36] to overcome its patrimonial legacy. This peculiar 'path dependency' ensured that it developed into a 'constitutional, bureaucratic' government.[37]

Similarly, historian Jan Glete identifies the Dutch Republic, Sweden, and eighteenth-century Britain as leading, militarized, complex states. Whilst France, for example, had a large army and a bureaucracy to support it by the seventeenth century, this was an enormous country and thus on a per capita basis not nearly as militarized as many others. Whereas Tilly had recognized the differentiating effect of commercialization by which some states such as Venice and the Dutch Republic were inclined to promote capital and commercial growth within a developing, international capitalist system, the corollary was that they had relatively weak armed forces and supporting administrative organizations. For Glete, capital played a much more direct, positive role in state-formation. War-making capacity remains the measure of a state's success, yet this depends upon the extent to which a society achieves 'interest aggregration', that is to say that different social groups are able to cooperate in their mutual self-interest in complex organizations or to 'link' their various political interests to the state. Thus it is not enough to equate modernity with large bureaucracies for the collection of taxes. Dutch or English state-sponsored, armed, overseas trading companies, for example, must be considered alongside the organization of armies, navies, and state bureaucracy in those countries.[38]

By exploring different ways in which societies organized themselves to be in a position to exploit new military technology and tactics, Glete is expanding on the framework, and the more complex causal link between the state and war, that Jeremy Black introduced. Thus Glete is careful not to describe war as the unique motor of historical change as Roberts did, although it still clearly has a privileged place. It did not simply provide pressure to which states responded negatively, but opportunities which societies could embrace. The value of Glete's work is not only that it recognizes the place of different social organizations but, crucially, socially and culturally defined motives for going to war in the first place. A sensitivity to such things is essential for any worthwhile state-building theory, in order to avoid the all too common anachronistic and subjective judgement of the relative worth of states. In as much as Ertman, for example, claims states had broad aims or motivations, it was only 'to guarantee order at home and battlefield success abroad'.[39] For the fortunate few, the bureaucratic consitutional path would ensure this success in the long run. For Ertman, the obvious desirability of this, the most familiar and modern form of government, means that its strengths necessarily imply weaknesses in any alternative form of government or social organization. He clearly sees the patrimonial model embodied by France as a handicap to be overcome. Although he acknowledges that France 'operated for over three hundred years as one of Europe's greatest powers', this was despite the failings of its dysfunctional system which was inefficient, arbitrary and 'diverted substantial revenues into private hands'.[40] From this perspective, France simply had massive resources that it could draw upon, which temporarily disguised its long-term structural weaknesses.

Ertman's thesis, based on the legacy of medieval forms of local government and the 'timing' of geomilitary pressures as key variables in state development, weakens the notion of a direct, mono-causal state-building effect of warfare. Yet its effect is precisely to provide an explanation, which is still grounded in the pressures of early modern warfare, for the development of the commercially advanced and globally successful eighteenth-century British state. Categorizing France in contrast as a patrimonial absolutist state as a way of explaining its long-term weakness seems to play down the fact that it was universally acclaimed, in the late seventeenth century at least, as the leading European military power, a model of good government, and an international cultural giant. More significantly, this perspective does not seem to account for the very sudden and substantial leap in central government authority and especially in military capacity between the reigns of Louis XIII and Louis XIV, and especially from 1661. Certainly contemporaries sometimes recognized shortcomings of venal office-holding and nepotism, and they may well have been largely powerless to reform them, but as twenty-first-century analysts we should be wary because we are likely to be acutely alert to the potential abuses of such a system and thus correspondingly reluctant to acknowledge its successes.[41] The weaknesses of France are easily exaggerated. Knowing in hindsight as we do that the old system of government in France collapsed after the 1789 Revolution, it is all too easy to assume that there had been deep-rooted flaws that had led inevitably to its fall. Ertman points out that in the 'long' eighteenth century 'France was driven into bankruptcy by Britain'.[42] Yet we would do well to remember that it was not driven into the sea! After all, it was post-revolutionary France, under Napoleonic rule, that would briefly achieve military hegemony in Europe, not Britain. Whilst it is common to attribute this success to the social, political, and cultural changes of the Revolution and to the introduction of citizen armies and a new motivation, or purpose, for going to war based on the notion of national survival, it is less common to consider similar types of explanation for the sudden increase in the military capacity of Louis XIV's France, or indeed for other periods of military change. This is the key to future research into early modern warfare and the rise of the state, and it is in this regard that historical approaches will be particularly valuable.

In an early modern French context, the least valuable state-building models are those which accept the strength of the French state at face value, which is to say as a centralized, absolutist government with a well-developed bureaucracy and an enormous capacity to conduct war, and with a monarchy of which the grandeur and the pomp of Versailles were a direct reflection. Much more credible are those that accept the work of modern historians, who uncover the inherent limits of absolutism, the contradictions, the compromises, the corruption, and the desperation. The effect of warfare, in this light, is seen to be quite complex, requiring more analytical sophistication. However, as the term 'absolutism' itself is increasingly discredited by historians, what was once seen as a 'limit', or an obstacle to an otherwise assumed trajectory of modernizing change, ought to be considered simply as a natural boundary within which monarchs operated.[43] In other words, if our understanding is to improve even further, future research into the relationship between war and the French state, at least, will have to accept that, despite whatever weaknesses can be identified, the seventeenth century was nevertheless still the *grand siècle*, or golden age, of French history. Although it may be uncomfortable to those who wish to celebrate the progress of modern liberal democracy, by contemporary standards France was the most successful state, the leading power, and the envy of Europe. One reason France was not as militarized as the Dutch, is that they did not face the same threat, so it would have been impossible for the same 'interest aggregation' behind it to develop. It is not because France was relatively underdeveloped as a state (even if in hindsight it might appear to have been). The point is that this simply was not how success was measured.

Although militarization can be used as the measure of a state's development, especially in the case of Prussia, the motives and fundamental ambitions of the ruler or the political elite which defined strategic objectives is the key. Conducting war was the central, defining vocation of kings in early modern Europe, but not for its own sake.[44] Nor was it the only pre-occupation. As their authority and legitimacy was derived from God, kings of France in particular had a duty, as set out in the coronation oath, to administer justice and promote peace within their kingdom, to protect the interests of their subjects, which is to say primarily the nobility, and to protect the church and eradicate heresy.[45] For all these reasons, war had to be just and conducted in line with a king's sense of religious duty and personal dynastic interests. Even the foreign policy of the famously pragmatic Cardinal Richelieu can be seen as the expression of a deeply held concern with establishing a lasting peace within Christendom and entirely consistent with his ecclesiastical vocation.[46] Louis XIV's unusual bellicosity later in the century did not undermine the legal and religious purpose of his wars nor the related motivation of protecting the dynastic interests of the house of Bourbon.

Louis XIV's success, therefore, was not in the size of his army or the extent of his domestic political authority. These were simply the effects of his far greater accomplishment defined by his fundamental aims as an early modern monarch: as Guy Rowlands puts it that of bringing the 'dynastic state to its apogee', with himself at the centre. As Rowlands convincingly demonstrates, Louis XIV was motivated primarily by his personal dynastic ambitions, perhaps most evident in the promotion of his bastard sons. He was far more successful than his father, Louis XIII, at securing cooperation and supporting a large standing army because, rather than simply insisting on obedience or trying to introduce modern structural reforms, he recognized the importance of the personal political interests and dynastic aspirations of his leading subjects which he manipulated with exquisite political skill.[47] Far from rising above, or merely accommodating, the interests of his nobles, then, Louis XIV fully embodied them. By emphasizing the effect of the distinctly 'unmodern' motive of dynasticism on the growth of the French army and state, Rowlands provides an explanation of development that sets out to defy current modernization theory.

As Michael Braddick has shown so effectively with respect to seventeenth-century England, state-building itself was not a conscious motive. States were, more accurately, 'formed' in a number of different (sometimes seemingly contradictory) ways by a variety of forces. Braddick accepts that war created pressures that were 'modernising in the Weberian sense', yet so too did the Protestant Reformation with the state's desire for religious conformity. Moreover, forces for change did not all emanate from the state, and not all were recognizably modern. Others also competed, and Braddick insists that 'patriarchal' and 'dynastic' interests, often, though not exclusively, in the localities, worked and developed alongside the more 'autonomous' development of the 'fiscal-military' and 'confessional' state. On a methodological level, his work is a bid for the history of the state to be 'part of a wider cultural history'.[48] In this sense, it is similar to Theda Skocpol's plea of 1985 to social scientists to 'bring the state back in' to their analyses of 'social change, politics and policy making'. This plea has certainly been heeded with a great many studies of state development.[49] Yet, as Skocpol said at the time, there is clearly still much more to do with respect to the difficult process of uncovering the 'inherent historicity of socio-political structures', and in this sense historical studies have a more important role than any 'new or refurbished grand theory of "the state"'.[50] Braddick himself leads the way by identifying the diversity of culturally-defined formative forces on the state, rather than just uncovering a variety of formal outcomes of the pressures of war.

War will always be a crucial element of the history of the state and the story of its growth in sophistication and in power both at home and abroad in the modern era. Therefore, military historians have an essential role to play in explaining this development and broader social trends. However, this role is best fulfilled if we recognize that war was not a discrete force acting on states with a relentless modernizing pressure. The very ubiquity of war insists that it could never have been isolated from such other cultural considerations as religion, patriarchy, or dynasticism. Jeremy Black's recent advice to adopt a 'cultural approach' to the study of war and an increased emphasis on 'ends rather than means' is indeed the best defence against mono-causal historical explanations such as Michael Roberts' military revolution. If these ends are understood as broadly as possible, and not simply as a universal desire to improve offensive military power, we may begin to establish the intellectual context and the 'cultural specificity of particular types of warfare' along with a correspondingly more valuable appreciation of the states that exploited them.[51]

further reading

Further reading can be gleaned from the endnotes to this chapter, though as examples of the most important historical work from different national perspectives particular attention should be paid to: Michael J. Braddick, *State Formation in Early Modern England, c.1550–1700* (Cambridge, 2000); Guy Rowlands, *The Dynastic State and the Army under Louis XIV: Royal Service and Private Interest, 1661–1701* (Cambridge, 2002); and, especially, Jan Glete, *War and the State in Early Modern Europe: Spain, the Dutch Republic and Sweden as Fiscal-Military States, 1500–1600* (London, 2002). This last deals most directly with the link between warfare and the modern state, providing both an important new perspective itself and an excellent introduction to the debates and to further reading on the subject. For a general historical perspective, see the impressive work of Frank Tallett, *War and Society in Early-Modern Europe, 1495–1715* (London, 1992), especially chapter 5, 'The Impact of War', pp. 148–245. Of the social scientists, Thomas Ertman makes an attempt to incorporate the complexity of historical work on the link between war and the state. See his *Birth of the Leviathan: Building States and Regimes in Medieval and Early Modern Europe* (Cambridge, 1997), which also provides a summary of related debates amongst social scientists. A most impressive and exhilarating survey of war and states through history, with important reflections on the contemporary world and the future, can be found in Philip Bobbitt, *The Shield of Achilles: War, Peace and the Course of History* (London, 2002).

notes

1. Even those readers who believe themselves familiar with the thesis may be surprised to find in it the seventeenth-century origins of militarism, terrorism, biological warfare, the submarine, and more generally 'the abyss of the twentieth century'. Michael Roberts, 'The Military Revolution, 1560–1660' in M. Roberts, *Essays in Swedish History* (London, 1967), pp. 195–6, 218.
2. Roberts, 'Military Revolution', pp. 204–5.
3. Max Weber, *Economy and Society: An Outline of Interpretive Sociology* (edited by G. Roth and C. Wittlich) (Berkeley CA, 1978), pp. 904–8.
4. As Jan Glete has pointed out, this was actually a common observation early in the twentieth century. Jan Glete, *War and the State in Early Modern Europe* (London, 2002), p. 43.
5. Otto Hintze, 'Military Organisation and the Organisation of the State' in Felix Gilbert (ed.), *The Historical Essays of Otto Hintze* (New York, 1975), pp. 180–215.
6. John C. Rule, 'Louis XIV, Roi-Bureaucrate' in Rule (ed.), *Louis XIV and the Craft of Kingship* (Ohio, 1969), pp. 3–101.
7. David Parrott, *Richelieu's Army: War, Government and Society in France, 1624–1642* (Cambridge, 2001). See also Parrott's 'The Military Revolution in Early Modern Europe', *History Today* 42/12 (December 1992): 21–7.
8. See the collection of key essays in Clifford J. Rogers (ed.), *The Military Revolution Debate: Readings on the Military Transformation of Early Modern Europe* (Boulder CO, 1995).
9. Geoffrey Parker, 'The "Military Revolution" 1560–1660: A Myth?', *Journal of Modern History* 48/2 (1976): 195–214; Parker, *The Military Revolution: Military Innovation and the Rise of the West, 1500–1800* (Cambridge, 1988).
10. Jeremy Black, *A Military Revolution? Military Change and European Society, 1550–1800* (Basingstoke, 1991).
11. J. R. Hale, *War and Society in Renaissance Europe, 1450–1620* (London, 1985), pp. 31, 48, 245.
12. Azar Gat, *A History of Military Thought: From the Enlightenment to the Cold War* (Oxford, 2001), pp. 371–7.
13. Williamson Murray and MacGregor Knox, 'Thinking about Revolutions in Warfare' in Murray and Knox (eds), *The Dynamics of Military Revolution, 1300–2050* (Cambridge, 2001), pp. 6–14.
14. John A. Lynn, 'Forging the Western Army in Seventeenth-Century France' in Murray and Knox (eds), *Dynamics*, p. 40.
15. 'Standing armies were the product of military logic rather than of political design'. Roberts, 'Military Revolution', p. 201.
16. John A. Lynn, 'Clio in Arms: The Role of the Military Variable in Shaping History', *Journal of Military History* 55/1 (1991): 83–95, 92. Parrott, too, acknowledges the particular value of the regimental fighting spirit of veteran units. This emphasis on organization and drill as the initial cause of the rise of 'Europe's world-girdling imperial career' is found in W. H. McNeil, *The Pursuit of Power: Technology, Armed Force, and Society since A.D. 1000* (Chicago, 1982), p. 117.
17. In fact, it appears that, in France at least, the acquisition of naval gun-ships did not necessarily lead to ambitious overseas ambitions in the seventeenth century. Alan James, *The Navy and Government in Early Modern France, 1572–1661* (London, 2004).

18. Frank Tallett, *War and Society in Early-Modern Europe, 1495–1715* (London, 1992), p. 204.
19. Bruce D. Porter, *War and the Rise of the State: The Military Foundations of Modern Politics* (New York, 1994), p. 58.
20. Charles Tilly, 'War Making and State Making as Organized Crime' in P. Evans, B. Rueschemeyer and T. Skocpol (eds), *Bringing the State Back In* (Cambridge, 1985), pp. 170, 182. Tilly posits the idea of three types of development: coercion-intensive, capital-intensive and capitalized coercion. Charles Tilly, *Coercion, Capital and European States, AD 990–1990* (Oxford, 1990). A good summary of the positions of Hintze and Tilly is provided by Thomas Ertman, 'The Sinews of Power and European State-Building Theory' in Lawrence Stone (ed.), *An Imperial State at War: Britain from 1689 to 1815* (London, 1994), pp. 33–9.
21. Brian M. Downing, *The Military Revolution and Political Change: Origins of Democracy and Autocracy in Early Modern Europe* (Princeton NJ, 1991), p. 82.
22. Martin Van Creveld, *The Rise and Decline of the State* (Cambridge, 1999); Philip Bobbitt, *The Shield of Achilles: War, Peace and the Course of History* (London, 2002).
23. John Elliott, 'A Europe of Composite Monarchies', *Past and Present* 137 (November 1992): 48–71.
24. Martyn Rady, *The Emperor Charles V* (London, 1988), pp. 2–3.
25. Indeed, Francis I of France coveted Charles' title of emperor himself. R. J. Knecht, *Renaissance Warrior and Patron: The Reign of Francis I* (Cambridge, 1994), p. 165.
26. Jan Willem Honig, 'Warfare in the Middle Ages' in A. V. Hartmann and B. Heuser (eds), *War, Peace and World Orders in European History* (London, 2001), pp. 113–26.
27. H. M. Scott (ed.), *The European Nobilities in the Seventeenth and Eighteenth Centuries* (London, 1995).
28. J. Russell Major, *From Renaissance Monarchy to Absolute Monarchy: French Kings, Nobles, and Estates* (Baltimore MD, 1994); Roger Mettam, *Power and Faction in Louis XIV's France* (Oxford, 1988); Donna Bohanan, *Crown and Nobility in Early Modern France* (Basingstoke, 2001).
29. Downing, *Military Revolution*, p. 125, n. 38; William Beik, *Absolutism and Society in Seventeenth-Century France: State Power and Provincial Aristocracy in Languedoc* (Cambridge, 1985).
30. Downing, *Military Revolution*, pp. 131, 138.
31. Tilly, 'War Making', p. 175.
32. I. A. A. Thompson, 'Aspects of Spanish Military and Naval Organisation during the Ministry of Olivares' in Thompson, *War and Society in Habsburg Spain* (Aldershot, 1992).
33. Thomas Ertman, *Birth of the Leviathan: Building States and Regimes in Medieval and Early Modern Europe* (Cambridge, 1997).
34. Daniel Dessert, *Argent, pouvoir et société au grand siècle* (Paris, 1984); Joseph Bergin, *Cardinal Richelieu: Power and the Pursuit of Wealth* (New Haven CT, 1985).
35. John Brewer, *The Sinews of Power: War, Money and the English State, 1688–1783* (London, 1989).
36. Ertman, *Leviathan*, pp. 34, 156–223.
37. This is similar to Graeme Gill who identifies 'organic' state-building in the constitutionalism of Britain, properly 'embedded' in society, as the successful foil to France where the process was 'overarching'. Graeme Gill, *The Nature and Development of the Modern State* (Basingstoke, 2003).
38. Glete, *War and State*, pp. 50–66.

39. Ertman, *Leviathan*, p. 317.
40. Ibid., pp. 321–2.
41. However, for a sensible, sympathetic description of patronage, see N. A. M. Rodger *The Wooden World: An Anatomy of the Georgian Navy* (London, 1986), pp. 273–302.
42. Ertman, *Leviathan*, p. 322.
43. Alan James, *The Origins of French Absolutism* (Harlow, 2006).
44. See especially, Joël Cornette, *Le roi de guerre: Essai sur la souveraineté dans la France du Grand Siècle* (Paris, 1993); see also David Kaiser, *Politics and War: European Conflicts from Philip II to Hitler* (Cambridge MA, 2000). Kaiser does not privilege state-building, recognizes that the political causes of wars varied throughout history and realizes that Louis XIV, in particular, 'defined the political goals of war in highly subjective terms' (p. 416).
45. Richard A. Jackson, *'Vive le Roi!': A History of the French Coronation from Charles V to Charles X* (Chapel Hill NC, 1984); and Colette Beaune, *The Birth of an Ideology: Myths and Symbols of Nation in Late-Medieval France* (trans. F. Hutton, ed. F. Cheyette) (Berkeley CA, 1991).
46. Hermann Weber, '"Une Bonne Paix": Richelieu's Foreign Policy and the Peace of Christendom' in Joseph Bergin and L. W. B. Brockliss (eds), *Richelieu and His Age* (Oxford, 1992), pp. 45–69.
47. Guy Rowlands, *The Dynastic State and the Army under Louis XIV: Royal Service and Private Interest, 1661–1701* (Cambridge, 2002), p. 362.
48. Michael J. Braddick, *State Formation in Early Modern England, c.1550–1700* (Cambridge, 2000), p. 433.
49. Michael Mann, *The Sources of Social Power* (Cambridge, 1986); Anthony Giddens, *The Nation-State and Violence* (Oxford, 1985).
50. Theda Skocpol, 'Bringing the State Back In: Strategies of Analysis in Current Research' in Evans et al. (eds), *Bringing the State Back In*, p. 28.
51. Jeremy Black, *Rethinking Military History* (London, 2004), pp. 232–4.

3
war and society
michael s. neiberg

Innovative, daring, and novel in many of its approaches, the war and society method has helped to reinvigorate the study of warfare. The war and society approach springs from several of the same roots as the new military history, and thus shares with it influences, methodologies and ideas. Many of the same historians work in both fields, and numerous important works in war and society would also appear in any bibliography of the key texts in new military history. These similarities notwithstanding, new military historians are generally interested in the same questions as more traditional military historians. That is, they want to understand grand strategy and operations, how soldiers fight, how armies are recruited and maintained, and the consequences of military service on both society and the individual, to name just a few. To use a well-worn phrase, the difference between traditional and new military history is that the former is top-down, whereas the latter is bottom-up.

War and society shares the bottom-up approach of the new military history, but it addresses itself to a different set of questions. At its best, war and society literature analyses the iterative symbiotic relationship between social and cultural systems and how those systems experience war. The practitioners of the war and society approach examine such subjects as the relationships between home fronts and fighting fronts; the differences between history (what happened) and memory (a socially constructed and generally accepted version of that history); tensions between localism and nationalism; and the interactions between war, class, gender and race.

War and society scholars are generally not interested in explaining victory or defeat. Events on the battlefield and the performance of military leaders usually remain far in the background or are completely absent. Few war and society studies concern themselves with subjects like diplomacy, military organization, or tactics. Indeed the absence of such subjects has been one of the shortcomings of the field. As many critics have pointed out, some (though by no means all or even most) war and society studies have become too far detached from war to make the links to society relevant. Indeed, war and violence can become too abstract when war and society studies are more interested in society than they are in war. Some of the best of these studies, on the other hand, show an appreciation of both sides of this intellectual coin, and carefully tie the events of wartime to events in civilian society before, during and after the period of the war itself.

This chapter will explore some of the major themes of recent war and society scholarship by examining five areas: the interactions of home fronts with fighting fronts; the impact of war on civilians both far behind the front and on non-combatants caught in the direct crossfire of war; the impact of societal beliefs on the behaviour of soldiers; the influence of civilian ideas on military operations; and, finally, the nature of historical memory. This list by no means exhausts the subjects and debates of interest to war and society scholars, but it provides a rough outline of some of the major trends in the field. The chapter will conclude with some sense of the current state of war and society historiography, as well as a call for further research into some under-examined fields.

home fronts and fighting fronts

The experience of war on the home front plays a central role in war and society historiography. Wars have the power quickly and fundamentally to change patterns of civilian life. Governments (and more specifically, executive branches) generally gain more power during wartime; decisions made by central governments can produce dramatic alterations in local patterns. In other cases, wars destroy governments and produce revolutions. Finally, the departure of thousands of young men for war often produces serious disruptions in the regular social and cultural patterns of local communities. In the case of societies with local recruitment systems, military service can also mean permanent and tragic losses when a locally raised battalion or regiment goes into combat.

These themes form the focus of one of the early war and society classics, David Kennedy's *Over Here*.[1] Kennedy's analysis takes a broad view of the American home front during the First World War, focusing on economic changes and the influences of governmental decision making on local communities. Concerned about a nation unprepared for war and uncertain of the wisdom of intervention, Woodrow Wilson's administration bombarded the American people with regulations to control their behaviour and propaganda to win over their hearts and minds. Politicians and local American leaders used the international emergency created by the war as the means to achieve desired aims that had been important domestic goals from the pre-war period, including economic regulation, assimilation of immigrants, and the weakening of American socialism. The war, Kennedy contends, produced long-lasting change to American society despite the nation's relatively brief period of active belligerence.

Another of the field's most influential early books, Jean-Jacques Becker's *The Great War and the French People*, attempted to understand the collective mentality of the French people both at the outbreak of the war and during its long, tortuous course. Becker argued that the French people did not seek war in 1914, not even if war held out the prospect of recovering the provinces of Alsace and Lorraine, taken by Germany in 1871. Nevertheless, because Germany invaded France, the French people saw the war as a just conflict fought for self-defence and the rejection of unprovoked aggression. All Frenchmen could agree on these motives for fighting and thus, despite the lack of any real war aims or consensus enthusiasm for war, France entered the war united, and largely maintained that unity for four more years.[2]

As these two books demonstrate, one of the most important contributions of war and society historians has been their attempt to break the image of the home and fighting fronts as separate and distinct. People on the home front learned about the war from letters written by male relatives at the front, through the testimonies of soldiers on leave, through (heavily redacted) newspapers, and even through movies. Soldiers' letters were often lightly censored or not censored at all, allowing for a surprising degree of frankness. The correspondence between Vera Brittain and friends and relatives at the front reveals the ways by which information could be exchanged between home and fighting fronts.[3] The diary of Evelyn Blücher, an English woman who lived with her German husband in Berlin during the First World War, shows the remarkable ways that elites in belligerent nations used diplomats and people from neutral nations to exchange information, even if most of it was personal.[4]

Gerald Linderman, in his *Mirror of War*, shows how close the linkages between armies and societies could be. Using the Spanish-American War as a case study, he showed how local communities not only raised units of soldiers, but also enlisted reporters to follow the town's young men and report on their experiences. In other cases, newspapers hired a literate soldier to fulfil the same function through a column written from the front lines in an early version of the embedded reporter system used by the Americans in the two Gulf Wars (1990–91, 2003–). Thus, people at home came to learn about their soldiers and maintained close linkages between fighting front and war front.[5]

Wars also force societies to ask deep and meaningful questions about their most fundamental values. These values, of course, include the roles of women. In some states, most notably the United States and Great Britain, wars have created possibilities (at least temporarily) for women to assume economic roles they might not otherwise have played. As D'Ann Campbell and others have shown, these changes did not come without tension.[6] Propaganda images of 'Rosie the Riveter' during the Second World War notwithstanding, American economic policy and the desires of labour unions often meant that any economic changes were temporary. For example, the percentage of American women in the workforce was lower in 1920 than it had been in 1910 despite some significant changes in work patterns during 1917 and 1918. Nevertheless, wartime patterns set new precedents and opened new possibilities by breaking down gender stereotypes and images of the separate spheres of men and women.

On the political level, too, wars changed gender patterns. To cite just one example here, Nicoletta Gullace argues that the sight of male conscientious objectors refusing to serve Britain in the First World War contrasted to the sight of so many British women volunteering to serve both as industrial workers and in uniform. This contrast added significantly to the momentum that had built behind women's suffrage in Britain in the pre-war years. The war thus created the circumstances to make possible an idea – women's suffrage – that had been so hotly debated in the years before the war.[7]

The ideology of Nazi Germany produced more traditional visions of appropriate gender roles. Claudia Koonz argues that Nazi society attracted the support of German women by appealing to their desire to remain in largely traditional gender roles. Thus despite the virtual removal of women from German politics and Nazi policies that made advancement for women in middle-class professions more difficult, women came to accept both the Nazi state and their traditional role inside it.[8]

Of course, it is not only women's gender roles that experience change in wartime. Recently, the changes to men's gender definitions have come under closer scholarly examination. Men's roles often change much more fundamentally and much more quickly as they make the transition from provider of income to provider of protection. The advent of air warfare often radically changed this paradigm by placing previously distant home fronts in great peril. Non-combatants on the home front thus often faced much greater direct threats than did men serving in uniform in relatively quiet sectors of the fighting fronts. This shift in turn affected expectations of male behaviour. The change to men's gender roles is a focus of Sonya Rose's *Which People's War?* in which she argues that British men in the Second World War were expected to display a cool, controlled masculinity that was military in bearing, but not overly militaristic. Thus, British male identity was constructed in opposition both to British femininity and the excesses of Nazi male masculinity.[9]

At the risk of lumping a series of 'minorities' together, it is important to close this section by noting the important analogous work done by war and society historians on the constructions of racial, ethnic and sexual identities during wartime. As with gender, wars have the ability (again, often only temporarily) to cause radical changes in the nature of racial and ethnic relations. Joseph Glathaar provided a direct case study of this phenomenon in his examination of the interactions between white officers and black soldiers during the American Civil War. Valorous service by American blacks broke down racial stereotyping in the North and contributed greatly to support for emancipation, although it is worth pointing out that draft riots in New York City demonstrated simultaneously that the war's impacts were not all positive. In a similar vein, the service of Burmese and Indians in the British army in the Second World War made victory over Japan possible, but came at the price of post-war independence, a theme explored in a recent work by Christopher Bayly and Tim Harper.[10]

occupations and the suffering of civilians

The suffering of civilians during wartime provides an important complement to the new military history's emphasis on the suffering of soldiers. Although genocide and its links to war have long been of interest to historians, the direct impact of war on civilians is a relatively new area of examination. Peter Schrijvers's *The Unknown Dead* promises to be a groundbreaking work in this field. The book examines the misery of Belgian civilians caught between powerful armies during the 1944 Battle of the Bulge. Brutalized by the Germans for helping the Americans, yet not fully trusted by understandably wary American soldiers, civilians struggled to survive in a deteriorating environment in which food, shelter and basic services all but vanished. In a similar vein, Stephen Fritz's *Endkampf* examines the ways in which German civilians dealt with the end of the war in Europe while trying to maintain a level of humanity.[11] These two works bring together an understanding of war with an understanding of civilians as victims.

Associated with studies of civilians under fire, studies of life under occupation have become central to the war and society approach.[12] Occupied peoples experienced psychological and physical dislocations as great as those experienced by many soldiers. Food requisitioning, labour conscription, and the daily humiliation of life under conquest took its toll. In many cases, notably the Armenians in the First World War and Jews in the Second World War, occupation opened the doors to genocide. Even when occupations did not sink to such depths of dehumanization, they could still produce terrible traumas.[13]

Nevertheless, as recent studies have shown, life under enemy occupation was rarely pleasant, but it was not always murderous, either. In France and in many parts of 'Nordic' Europe, Nazi occupation could be light, especially in the early years of the war when the Germans were trying to limit the number of men they had to devote to occupation duty.[14] Many French civilians from 1940 to 1942 experienced an occupation that was more symbolic than sadistic. Theatres continued to operate, food supplies were only minimally affected, and many French civilians even found ways to make considerable fortunes out of the occupation. The occupation grew significantly more harsh in late 1942 and 1943 as the war turned against Germany and as Anglo-American forces invaded North Africa and Italy, which led to more shortages of essential goods, the deployment of more German troops to France (many of whom were veterans of the Russian Front), and more labour requisitions from French civilians. Harsher German policies in turn produced a more determined French resistance.

Historians now understand occupations as significantly more complex than heretofore. German racial ideology, for example, meant that its occupation of eastern Europe was much harsher than its occupation of western Europe.[15] Indeed, the war almost became an excuse for the occupation rather than the occupation being a result of war. Understanding the complex contingencies and contexts of occupation remains crucial to our understanding. For example, Jews living in the small part of south-eastern France occupied by Italy from 1940 to 1944 lived a much more 'normal' life and had a much greater chance of survival than Jews living in the German occupied sector or even Jews living in the Vichy French sector.

Along with this more nuanced understanding of occupation has come an equally nuanced vision of the occupied. Whereas occupied peoples had once been viewed as passive victims of an overpowering foreign military presence, the war and society approach sees them as actors capable of negotiating with and even profiting from their occupiers. While the terms of that negotiation were almost always unequal, occupied peoples nevertheless proved capable of a surprising ability to retain a modicum of local power.

The question of occupation becomes further muddled when scholars consider nations without states. For most of the period between the final partition of Poland in 1795 and the creation of an independent Poland in 1919, Poles have lacked a state. To many Poles in this period, therefore, all political control resembled an occupation. The division of the former Ottoman, Habsburg, Russian and German empires after the First World War testified not only to the prevalence of nationalism, but the extreme difficulty in defining state borders. Absent commonly accepted boundaries, occupation became a critical rhetorical device of irredentist nationalists.

Military policy toward civilians has also been the subject of several studies. Mark Grimsley is among the historians who have shown the ways that such policy adapted and changed over time. In his case, Grimsley argues that Union policy toward Confederate civilians grew progressively harsher, although it never degraded to the level that post-war critics alleged.[16] Not all occupations need be so harsh. Japan's ability to, in John Dower's phrase, 'embrace defeat', led it to accept and even learn from a six-year American occupation. Linguistic and cultural differences forced the Americans to govern indirectly, further ameliorating the potential harshness of the occupation. The result was an occupation experience that proved to be surprisingly positive, especially in light of the viciousness of the Pacific War of 1941–45.[17] Sharing some of Dower's logic, David Reynolds has advanced the argument that benign occupation is an appropriate way in which to think about the American presence in Great Britain during the Second World War in a book with a fitting title, *Rich Relations*.[18]

Militaries often dictate policy not only to enemy civilians, but toward their own citizens and subjects as well. The choices that they make can often lead to direct effects on civilians. The German people's reactions to their government's mismanagement of food policy is the subject of Belinda Davis's important book, *Home Fires Burning*.[19] She outlines the many steps taken by local and national officials in Germany in the First World War to feed a hungry population. The British blockade (which, like air war, brought suffering to civilians previously separated from fighting fronts by distance) made this task increasingly difficult, but government mismanagement added unnecessarily to civilian misery. The inability of the government to provide for the basic needs of the German people contributed to a loss of faith among Germans and, in turn, contributed to the collapse of the Second Reich.

In contrast, Jay Winter argues that carefully constructed government policy in wartime could result in positive improvements in the lives of citizens at war.[20] The First World War produced jobs and rationing that led, Winter argues, to a higher standard of living for most Britons than had been possible before the war. Owing in part to sound policy, food rationing gave working-class Britons access to more calories and a greater variety of diet than had been possible before. This combination of warfare and welfare yielded some unanticipated positive results for British citizens.

civilian values and the behaviour of soldiers

For many years, historians tended to write about militaries as if they were separate from civilian societies. Systems of recruitment, socialization and training, they argued, created a world distinct from the civilian world in important ways.[21] A civilian became a soldier through rigorous adaptation to military norms. Once adapted, soldiers retained key elements of their socialization throughout their lives. Intensely hierarchical, aggressively secretive, populated almost exclusively by men, and charged with a mission with no peacetime equivalent, the military does appear on the surface to be out of step with civil society.

Shattering these notions has been one of the greatest contributions of the war and society field. Several of the most important studies in this vein demonstrate that no matter what training programme they experience, the civilian background and upbringing of soldiers can never be entirely erased. Rather, social and cultural beliefs influence the ways in which men organize, fight and motivate themselves for war. In many cases, armies find themselves powerless to overcome these values, and instead must find ways to operate within them.

Another early war and society classic, Fred Anderson's *A People's Army*, demonstrated the power of civilian mores to set the parameters of military service.[22] Massachusetts militiamen understood themselves to be distinct from the British professionals with whom they served during the American phase of the Seven Years' War (known sometimes as the French and Indian War). Unlike British regulars, militiamen saw their roles in contractual terms. Militiamen believed that they had agreed to serve for fixed periods at fixed pay rates and in largely auxiliary operations. When the terms of that contract were violated or contested, they did not hesitate to protest, citing their rights as British subjects. Militiamen understood themselves to be citizens voluntarily taking part in emergency, part-time military service, as opposed to British regulars, most of whom had enlisted out of financial desperation. By making these distinctions, Massachusetts militiamen asserted their rights as civilians in uniform, clearly distinct from British redcoats, whom militiamen believed had surrendered away their rights when they enlisted as professional soldiers. Although the British were exasperated at American behaviour, they could not convince the militiamen to understand their military service in any other terms.

The influence of civilian values on soldiers forms the centrepiece of two studies of American combat soldiers in the Civil War. Grady McWhiney and Perry Jamieson advance the original, if not entirely unassailable, argument that the culture of manhood in the American South forced the Confederate army into battle tactics that were inappropriate to its political and strategic situation.[23] Although the Confederacy would have been well served to sit on the defensive and await attacks from Northern Armies, Southern notions of honour led to a culture that overvalued offensives and direct charges. As a result, the South suffered unnecessary losses in frontal assaults, even at the level of senior commanders, who were expected to lead these assaults personally. The authors carry this argument one step further by arguing that Southern martial culture was essentially Celtic, in contrast to the English martial culture of the North.

In contrast to this last argument, Gerald Linderman shows that a common American martial culture existed in the Civil War, influenced in North and South by the same set of values: manliness, godliness, duty, honour, and, above all, courage.[24] Nineteenth-century Americans saw war and the experience of combat as a test of these values, leading soldiers of both sides to face war with a stoicism and a willingness to expose themselves to the hazards of the battlefield. In doing so, men put their values to the ultimate test. Over time, men had to adjust these values to the cold, hard realities of the battlefield, but they never entirely gave up the values that they had held so dear.

Linderman's analysis focused on citizen armies, composed of volunteers with little pre-war military experience. As he and Gary Sheffield both show, such armies had to be governed by less formal and less official means than officers in professional armies.[25] Officers in citizen-soldier units had to accept the influence of some civilian customs such as the election of officers and handshakes replacing salutes. In the place of formal discipline came what Sheffield describes as paternalism, in which officers held their units together through visible displays of concern for their men. Punishment in such units had to be dispensed judiciously and leniently, or else the officer could lose the respect of his men. Such evidence makes clear that non-professional soldiers did not give up their civilian values and behaviours simply because they had enlisted in the army.

Much of the literature in this sub-field of war and society focuses on the ways that civilian notions of race interacted with war and the military. Omer Bartov has written two studies that show conclusively the degrading influence of civilian racial beliefs on soldiers and armies.[26] The soldiers who fought in the German army during the Second World War, he argues, were thoroughly indoctrinated by Nazi ideology to not only fight for the Fatherland, but to commit atrocities in its name. German soldiers in the east not only believed that their actions were not wrong, they believed them to be necessary to defend Germany from a supposed Russian and Jewish threat.

Christopher Browning's path-breaking *Ordinary Men* also focused on men in the Nazi state, but the subjects of his study were middle-aged policemen whose formative years occurred before the Nazi takeover.[27] As a result, Browning argues, these men acted less out of ideological motivation than practical ones. Although some of the policemen he studied were indeed anti-Semitic, their anti-Semitism does not in itself explain their actions. When read together with Bartov, a powerful portrait emerges of the ability of pre-war beliefs to dominate the ideology of armed force.

Racial hatred fuelled not only the Second World War in Europe, but the war in Asia as well. In one of the few trans-national studies of this type, John Dower explores the interactions of race and the behaviour of soldiers in both Japan and the United States.[28] Each society, he argues, held racial images of themselves and their enemies that determined the ways that their armies fought. These images combined to create a more vicious war through a dehumanization of the enemy and a mutual fear of surrender. Racial stereotyping set up images on both sides of the antagonists as polar opposites, allowing each side to claim a moral high ground.

One of the great strengths of Dower's work is his ability to show the malleability of racial stereotypes as the war developed. Before Pearl Harbor, Americans felt comfortable in dismissing the martial ability of the Japanese even in the face of Japan's astonishing recent past, which included the conquest of most of eastern China and much of Southeast Asia. American racial images were so pervasive that many Americans found it difficult to believe that the Japanese could have succeeded without massive help from Germany. After the stunning Japanese victories at Pearl Harbor, the Philippines and Singapore, images of an essentially harmless Japanese exoticism easily transferred to images of the Japanese as Asian supermen, still exotic, but now also able to fight a more vicious war with fewer resources. These images even facilitated the transition from war to peace, as the exotic Japanese superman became a savage ready to be civilized. Race, in Dower's formulation, thus fuelled war, but also became adaptable to peace.

Race also has the power to determine the ways that armies organized themselves. The segregated nature of the American military was a central feature of its official organization from colonial times until 1948.[29] In the case of the two world wars, this segregated military fought ostensibly for the promotion of democracy. Rather than using the army to underscore the common service of American males of all races to the nation, the military instead accommodated itself to racial mores by segregating the army and using African Americans disproportionately in service and labour roles. Black units were almost always commanded by white officers and 'handled' by Southern white NCOs. These roles undermined President Woodrow Wilson's claims to world moral leadership, but required minimal change in American social and cultural values.

White soldiers not only accepted these roles, they often disregarded army regulations to do so. As Jennifer Keene's research shows, white soldiers often refused to salute black soldiers who outranked them and made clear that the uniform, and by extension the service to the nation it represented, mattered little when that service conflicted with widely held beliefs on race. Black soldiers found France to be a more welcoming and less pathologically racist environment than the United States. Rather than convincing whites of the inherent contradiction in their racial beliefs, the contact of black soldiers with French civilians only reinforced white anxieties and concerns.[30]

civilian beliefs and the shaping of strategy, doctrine and operations

Keene's work goes much further, arguing that soldiers had many ways to force changes in the military's system of hierarchical discipline. Leonard V. Smith's masterful *Mutiny Amid Obedience* shows the ability of soldiers to change grand strategy through their actions.[31] Smith dissects the mutiny of the French army following the disastrous 1917 Chemin des Dames offensive and concludes that the refusal of the men to continue with futile attacks was in large part a manifestation of their frustration with French army doctrine. In effect, they saw their lives as offering only two choices: a near permanent incarceration in the miserable world of the trenches or useless sacrifice in poorly planned offensives designed to achieve the elusive rupture of the enemy lines. The mutinies were thus a demonstration of the men's unwillingness to be passive instruments in their own destruction. The mutinies forced the French army not only to improve the daily lives of the men, but to search for alternative strategies to win the war that focused on more careful planning and a more systematic use of advanced military technology.

That the mutinies were a consequence of the brutality of the First World War seems incontrovertible, but they also prove that, brutality notwithstanding, soldiers were not powerless to shape their environment. Although the suffering of soldiers during large-scale battles and extended periods of service in the trenches occupy much of the dominant imagery of front-line service in the First World War, it is not the whole story.[32] Tony Ashworth shows a different side.[33] In certain sectors of the front, soldiers on opposite sides managed to arrange informal truces that ameliorated the misery of life on the front line. As long as the men from one side, for example, refrained from shooting at ration parties, men from the other side might do the same. From these beginnings elaborate unspoken arrangements could develop. Commanders, of course, frowned on such truces and did all they could to try to stop them. Many of their efforts were in vain, as soldiers' instincts for survival and desires not to kill often overrode their willingness to obey orders.

The influence of culture on grand strategy has shaped an important debate in war and society scholarship led by Victor Davis Hanson and John Lynn. Hanson's work argues for a consistent 'western' way of war that emphasizes pitched and extremely violent battle, an emphasis on discipline, and a culture of civic militarism. Such a view of war created a special western disdain for guerrillas and partisan warfare. In Hanson's formulation, modern western societies inherited these views from the Greeks, leaving in place distinct 'western' and 'eastern' ways of war that continue to determine doctrine and operations down to the present day.[34]

Hanson's analysis of the relationship between war and culture has not gone unchallenged. Although not intended as a riposte to Hanson, John Grenier conclusively demonstrates that elements of Hanson's 'eastern' way of war have long been present in western warfare.[35] War on the American frontier in the eighteenth century, he contends, made few distinctions between soldiers and civilians. Especially when fighting Indians, Americans could engage in the sort of deceptive and guerrilla operations that Hanson categorized as essentially eastern. The style of war Grenier describes could be terribly violent, and influenced by the cultural meaning of war in Britain's American colonies. A recent work by George Satterfield makes a similar contention, arguing that partisan warfare formed a critical element of early modern European warfare, even if it was a style of war making that Europeans largely disdained.[36]

By far the most important challenge to Hanson has come from John Lynn. In *Battle*, a sweeping book that ranges from India to Egypt to the Pacific theatre of the Second World War, Lynn argues that no consistent 'eastern' or 'western' way of war exists.[37] Rather, he argues that the central importance of culture to warfare must be seen in the specific context of each society and culture. In one of the book's most important chapters, Lynn analyses the success of Indian sepoys within the army of the Raj. To the sepoy, military service represented an opportunity to fulfil crucial caste obligations and to demonstrate critical social values such as duty, honour and loyalty. The British quickly learned to adapt their way of war to Indian conditions and to use 'eastern' ways to win wars. The success of the British system in India thus depended upon a melding of 'western' and 'eastern' ways of war that defies Hanson's dichotomy.

In another section of his book, Lynn examines the ability of Egyptian armed forces to recover from the humiliation of their defeat in the Six Day War of 1967. Egyptian military culture, Lynn argues, was characterized by a lack of initiative, exaggerated patterns of deference to higher authority, and an unwillingness to face failures and shortcomings. Rather than attempting the probably impossible task of removing these cultural influences, the Egyptians instead worked to write a military doctrine that would adjust to them. The Egyptians also adjusted to what they saw as the greatest weakness of the Israeli military, its reluctance to take heavy casualties. Thus the Egyptian war plan for 1973 focused on attrition, not on manoeuvre. Egypt's relative success in the early stages of the Yom Kippur/Ramadan War, Lynn argues, was due to an ability to recognize the influence of culture on war making and adapt doctrine to those realities.

That culture can lead a military to sow the seeds of its own destruction is the subject of a powerful book by Isabel Hull.[38] She argues that pre-1914 German military culture focused exclusively on the quest for annihilating battles and total victory, as learned and experienced in Germany's imperial wars in Africa. This focus came to dominate all else, forcing Germany into a way of viewing war that was all or nothing. Because complete and total victory was the only outcome acceptable to Wilhelmine Germany, the tactics of war might change, but grand strategy could not. German military leaders thereby accepted a 'duty' to destroy Germany rather than accept changes to what they saw as the fundamental values of German society. Because the only definition of victory they understood was complete victory, large numbers of Germans could deceive themselves into believing that a lack of an Allied invasion deep into Germany meant that Germany had not truly lost the war.

Hull's work stretches the envelope considerably by making links between culture and military doctrine. Other recent works have made similar explorations, although few have done so as eloquently as Hull. In a work that received its fair share of criticism, Tami Davis Biddle attempts to explain American and British air war doctrine in the Second World War based not on military efficiency but culture.[39] British air war planners, she contends, were intensely fearful that the fragile morale of their working classes would not stand up to a sustained bombing campaign from Germany. Therefore, they decided on a bombing campaign designed to break the will of the German working classes before Germany could break the will of Britain's own working classes.

Culture can even influence the types of weapon systems a society chooses to employ. Noel Perrin detailed Japan's cultural attachment to swords in his book, *Giving Up the Gun*.[40] He argues that Japan's rejection of firearms prior to the mid-nineteenth century was due in part to a cultural preference for the symbolism that the sword brought to warfare. Swords allowed war to be more heroic, ritualistic and individual than firearms. Japan's island status and the power of the samurai also permitted Japan to reject a weapons system in wide use elsewhere, but culture played a dominant role. More recently, Linda Robertson has argued that American weapons system purchasers in the First World War emphasized fighter planes less because they were the most cost-effective ways to win the war than because they fit more neatly into an American quest to find a 'civilized' way to fight.[41]

These works share in common an emphasis on the ability of culture and society to influence the ways that militaries function. By doing so they undermine arguments that militaries operate in ways designed to maximize their efficiency. Instead, the war and society approach argues that the power of cultural and social patterns is often greater than the power of militaries to control them. War, then, appears to war and society scholars less as an extension of policy by other means than as an expression of dominant social and cultural values expressed in the crucible of national crisis.

history, memory and myth making

One of the most innovative aspects of war and society scholarship has focused on the differences between history and memory. Societies intentionally and unintentionally create constructed versions of past events that fit more easily and comfortably into national self-images or into contemporary circumstances. Thus what happened and what societies choose to remember are often dissimilar. This 'collective memory' reveals itself in works of fiction, commemoration of the dead, and the writing of history. Collective memory is conditioned not only by the past but by contemporary political, social and cultural patterns. The power of collective memory to shape visions of the past (and hence the present and future) forms an important category of analysis for war and society scholars.

Paul Fussell's *Great War and Modern Memory* deserves a great deal of the credit for shaping this field; as a result, much of the scholarship on history and memory is focused on the First World War.[42] The book has been the subject of extensive debate, but it remains as canonical a work in its field as any. Fussell argued that the Great War presented men with a tragedy far in excess of their language's ability to describe and understand it. The result was a 'myth-ridden world' with entirely new uses of language and a new 'modern' sensibility that was radically different from what had come before.[43] With the First World War, Fussell argues, the nineteenth century not only died, but came to be seen as hopelessly outdated and inappropriate to an understanding of the twentieth.

Fussell's sharp distinction between the modern world and the antediluvian world that had preceded it has not convinced all scholars. Jay Winter, for example, argues that when faced with mourning and loss on an unprecedented scale, societies and individuals fell back to what they knew best, namely organized religion and spiritualism.[44] He thus contends that the war created no sharp break between old and new beliefs, although it did force traditional belief systems to adapt to the enormous level of mourning. Spiritualism and the occult thus grew in popularity, standing alongside more traditional religions in helping people process their grief.

The meaning of the First World War to Europeans in the post-war years has also been a subject of interest to historians. As Brian Bond and Gary Sheffield both point out, Britons by-and-large have constructed an ahistorical understanding of the war, denying their nation's essential role in victory in lieu of a vision of the war as a national tragedy.[45] During the war, however, British soldiers supported the war and their nation's place in it. Even much of the anti-war literature of the immediate post-war years opposed future wars; it did not denigrate Britain's position in the First World War. Nevertheless, in the 1920s and 1930s many Britons began to accept the prevailing notion of the war as senseless as it became obvious that the post-war world would not be better for their sacrifices. Sheffield describes the decade immediately following the war as the years of numbness, but the decade before the Second World War as the years of cynicism and disillusion. It was in these years that the major elements of Britain's image of the Great War as senseless waste were born. However inaccurate it is, that image remains a major part of contemporary understandings of the war and Britain's place in it.

These myths existed outside Britain as well. Memories of the First World War in continental Europe have reshaped the war, removing many of its national elements in place of a vision of the war as shared European tragedy. Emphasizing shared suffering, mourning and loss helps Europeans to bury residual anger from the war, but it also creates a kind of intentional amnesia, allowing Europeans to forget why the soldiers of 1914–18 fought. Without an understanding of their motivations for fighting, the war appears to modern trans-national Europeans all that much more incomprehensible. In a similar vein, seeing the war as a shared tragedy allows Germany to escape responsibility for its behaviour in Belgium and occupied France, just as memories of 'poor little Belgium' have helped to erase memories of Belgium's vicious colonization of the Congo.[46] In the German case, memory helps to bury potentially dangerous sources of never-ending feuds, but at the cost of an accurate vision of the past.

Much of the scholarship on history and memory argues that societies often prefer constructed versions of the past over accurate ones. In many cases, governments contribute to the mythmaking in order to fulfil a state objective. In his study of societal responses to the beginning of the First World War in Germany, Jeffrey Verhey shows that enthusiasm for war at the outbreak was a minority view, concentrated largely among middle-class urbanites.[47] Over time, however, the myth of the 'Spirit of 1914' proved useful to German efforts to maintain civilian morale and encourage young men to join the army. The myth became reality, obscuring the actual ambivalence with which many Germans greeted the prospect of war in 1914. Even more dangerously, the myth became a crucial element of German political culture in the post-war years and a useful tool for the Nazis as they appealed to a supposedly unified German sense of consciousness and national identity.

Constructed memory also allows societies to 'forget' elements of their past that they find distasteful. French collaboration with the Germans in the Second World War provides an excellent case in point. As in Germany itself, the victorious Allies held only a few members of the French establishment directly responsible for war crimes. In doing so, they absolved the vast majority of ordinary French and Germans from any guilt. The decision made perfect sense in 1945 because it avoided the unpleasant prospect of placing hundreds of thousands of people on trial, but it also created psychological difficulties for societies trying to readjust to peacetime. Charles de Gaulle might have claimed that 'in our hearts, we were all resisters', but the French people (and undoubtedly de Gaulle himself) knew better. This gap between history and memory has had profound effects for France as it continues to deal with the impacts of large-scale collaboration.[48]

As studies of France in the Vichy period show, collective memory can also become collective forgetfulness. Peter Novick's study of Jewish memory of the Holocaust provides a powerful case study of this phenomenon.[49] American Jews, he argues, did not make the Holocaust a central part of their public discourse in the 1950s and the early 1960s. He cites three primary reasons for the surprising absence of the Holocaust in American Jewish life. First, the Holocaust was what Novick calls the 'wrong atrocity' for the Cold War era. The perpetrators (at least in West Germany) were now active American allies, making their vilification politically unpalatable. In addition, Jewish gratitude toward the Soviets for liberating many of the death camps sat uncomfortably alongside images of Jewish ties to communism, made most visible in the trial of Ethel and Julius Rosenberg. Second, asking questions about the Holocaust inevitably raised questions about the inaction of both the United States government and American Jews both in the years before the Second World War and during the Holocaust. Finally, images of Jews as victims ran counter to the dynamism of the new Israeli state.

As times change, so too does memory. In the case of American Jews and the Holocaust, the Arab–Israeli wars of 1967 and 1973 reawakened fears of the destruction of a large Jewish population. The Holocaust thus re-emerged in public discourse as a kind of warning from the past. Similarly, the First World War had always been a difficult subject for Irish historians because of its links to the Easter Rising and the Anglo-Irish Civil War. Recently, an easing of sectarian tension in Ireland has led to a reawakening in interest about Ireland's experiences in the war.[50] Memory and myth thus interact with war in ways that scholars continue to explore and analyse.

calls for further research

Most obviously, the war and society field needs more trans-national and non-western studies. Only through comparison can we begin to know how patterns in various societies over various time periods relate to one another. European history, especially, is increasingly understood in international and trans-national terms. War and society studies would do well to follow this lead as far as possible. Of course, comparative research is difficult, requiring that the researcher be familiar with several societies and, often, several languages. Associated with this need is the need to reach further into the non-western world. We still need to know more about how war and societal patterns have interacted in Africa, Asia, the Middle East and Latin America. This lacuna is not unique to war and society; it certainly exists in traditional military history as well.

Perhaps most importantly, future research into war and society patterns must maintain careful links with military history. Subjects such as leadership, doctrine, tactics and operations must be brought into war and society studies where appropriate. Scholars of both 'new' and 'old' schools of military history must realize that they have much to learn from one another. Too often, historians of the war and society approach and traditional military historians fail to see the synergistic relationship between their two fields. War and society scholars ignore military history at their peril. They ought never to forget that war, the socially sanctioned act of killing, lies at the heart of their analysis. When they do so, they can make great contributions to our understanding of how societies operate and function in the extraordinary circumstances of wartime.

further reading

This section will not attempt full coverage of the field, nor will it repeat works mentioned in the text. The following list is therefore simply a starting point. For broad surveys of war and society see Brian Bond, *War and Society in Europe, 1870–1970* (Guernsey, 1984); J. R. Hale, *War and Society in Renaissance Europe, 1450–1620* (Baltimore MD, 1985); Geoffrey Wawro, *Warfare and Society in Europe, 1792–1914* (London, 2000); and Michael Neiberg, *Warfare and Society in Europe, 1898 to the Present* (London, 2004). For the United States, see Fred Anderson and Andrew Cayton, *The Dominion of War: Empire and Liberty in North America, 1500–2000* (London, 2005).

Notable nation-specific case studies include Peter Karsten (ed.), *The Military in America from the Colonial Times to the Present* (New York, 1986); Richard J. Smethurst, *A Social Basis for Prewar Japanese Militarism: The Army and Rural Community* (Berkeley CA, 1974); Harry Ward, *The War for American Independence and the Transformation of American Society* (London, 1999); Jeffrey A. Keshen, *Saints, Sinners, and Soldiers: Canada's Second World War* (Vancouver, 2004); Ute Frevert, *A Nation in Barracks: Modern Germany, Military Conscription, and Civil Society* (Oxford, 2004); Daniel Moran (ed.), *The People in Arms: Military Myth and National Mobilization since the French Revolution* (Cambridge, 2002); John Gooch, *Army, State, and Society in Italy, 1870–1915* (New York, 1989); Charles Patrick

Neimeyer, *America Goes to War: A Social History of the Continental Army* (New York, 1995); Leonard V. Smith, Stéphane Audoin-Rouzeau and Annette Becker, *France and the Great War, 1914–1918* (Cambridge, 2003); and Roger Chickering, *Imperial Germany and the Great War, 1914–1918* (Cambridge, 2004).

Important local studies include: Harold Selesky, *War and Society in Colonial Connecticut* (New Haven, 1990); Jacqueline Carr, *After the Siege: A Social History of Boston, 1775–1800* (Boston, 2005); Richard Melvoin, *New England Outpost: War and Society in Colonial Deerfield* (New York, 1989); Maureen Healy, *Vienna and the Fall of the Habsburg Empire: Total War and Daily Life in the First World War* (Cambridge, 2004); and Ian Hugh Maclean Miller, *Our Glory and Our Grief: Torontonians and the Great War* (Toronto, 2002). Three history and memory studies not mentioned in the text are Carol Reardon, *Pickett's Charge in History and Memory* (Chapel Hill NC, 1997); Jenny Macleod, *Reconsidering Gallipoli* (Manchester, 2004); and Janet S. K. Watson, *Fighting Different Wars: Experience, Memory, and the First World War in Britain* (Cambridge, 2004).

In addition to the works in the further reading section in the new military history chapter of this book, gender and sexuality are covered in Linda Grant de Pauw, *Battle Cries and Lullabies: Women in War from Prehistory to the Present* (Norman OK, 1998); Mary Beth Norton, *Liberty's Daughters: The Revolutionary Experience of American Women, 1750–1800* (Boston, 1980); Frances Early, *A World Without War: How U.S. Feminists and Pacifists Resisted World War I* (Syracuse NY, 1997); Myna Trustram, *Women of the Regiment: Marriage and the Victorian Army* (Cambridge, 1984); Meredith Turshen and Clotilde Twagiramariya (eds), *What Women do in Wartime: Gender and Conflict in Africa* (London, 1998); Tammy Proctor, *Female Intelligence: Women and Espionage in the First World War* (New York, 2003); Alan Bérubé, *Coming Out Under Fire: The History of Gay Men and Women in World War Two* (New York, 1991); and Paul Jackson, *One of the Boys: Homosexuality in the Military During the First World War* (Montreal, 2004).

notes

1. David Kennedy, *Over Here: The First World War and American Society* (Oxford, 1980).
2. Jean-Jacques Becker, *Les français dans la grande guerre* (Paris, 1983). Translated by Arnold Pomerans as *The Great War and the French People* (Oxford, 1985).
3. See Alan Bishop and Mark Bostridge (eds), *Letters from a Lost Generation: The First World War Letters of Vera Brittain and Four Friends: Roland Leighton, Edward Brittain, Victor Richardson, and Geoffrey Thurlow* (Boston, 1998).
4. Evelyn Blücher, *An English Wife in Berlin* (New York, 1920).
5. Gerald Linderman, *The Mirror of War: American Society and the Spanish-American War* (Ann Arbor MI, 1974).
6. D'Ann Campbell, *Women at War with America: Private Lives in a Patriotic Era* (Cambridge MA, 1984). See also Maureen Honey, *Creating Rosie the Riveter: Class, Gender, and Propaganda in World War I* (Amherst MA, 1984).
7. Nicoletta Gullace, *Blood of Our Sons: Men, Women, and Renegotiation of British Citizenship in the Great War* (London, 2004).
8. Claudia Koonz, *Mothers in the Fatherland: Women, the Family, and Nazi Politics* (New York, 1998).
9. Sonya Rose, *Which People's War? National Identity and Citizenship in Wartime Britain 1939–1945* (Oxford, 2003).
10. Joseph Glathaar, *Forged in Battle: The Civil War Alliance of Black Soldiers and White Officers* (New York, 1990); Christopher Bayly and Tim Harper, *Forgotten Armies: The Fall of British Asia, 1941–1945* (Cambridge MA, 2005).

11. Peter Schrijvers, *The Unknown Dead: Civilians in the Battle of the Bulge* (Lexington KY, 2005); Stephen Fritz, *Endkampf: Soldiers, Civilians, and the Death of the Third Reich* (Lexington KY, 2004).

12. See for example several of the essays in Aviel Rohwald and Richard Stites (eds), *European Culture and the Great War* (Cambridge, 1999), especially those by Harold Segel, Aviel Roshwald, Evelina Kelbetcheva, Maria Bucur and Sophie de Schaepdrijver. As another indication of the dynamism of this field, a recent conference on the First World War held at Trinity College, Dublin hosted a panel with three papers by post-graduate students on occupation: Lisa Myerhofer's on the relationship of occupiers and occupied in Romania; Jovana Knežević's on Belgrade; and Aurore François's on joint Belgian–German efforts to control child prostitution in Brussels.

13. On the agonies of occupation, see among others, Larry Zuckerman, *The Rape of Belgium: The Untold Story of the First World War* (New York, 2004); Leonard V. Smith, Stéphane Audoin-Rouzeau and Annette Becker, *France in the Great War, 1914–1918* (Cambridge, 2003); and Philip Snow, *The Fall of Hong Kong: Britain, China, and the Japanese Occupation* (New Haven CT, 2003).

14. Robert Gildea, *Marianne in Chains: Daily Life in the Heart of France During the Occupation* (New York, 2004); Ian Ousby, *Occupation* (New York, 2000); Julian Jackson, *France: The Dark Years, 1940–1944* (Oxford, 2003); and Philippe Burin, *France under the Germans: Collaboration and Compromise* (New York, 1998).

15. Ben Shepherd, *War in the Wild East: The German Army and Soviet Partisans* (Cambridge MA, 2004); Omer Bartov, *The Eastern Front, 1941–1945: German Troops and the Barbarization of Warfare* (London, 2001); Robert Abzug, *Inside the Vicious Heart: Americans and the Liberation of Nazi Concentration Camps* (New York, 1985); and, more controversially, Daniel Jonah Goldhagen, *Hitler's Willing Executioners: Ordinary Germans and the Holocaust* (New York, 1997).

16. Mark Grimsley, *The Hard Hand of War: Union Policy toward Southern Civilians, 1861–1865* (Cambridge, 1997).

17. John Dower, *Embracing Defeat: Japan in the Wake of World War I* (New York, 2000).

18. David Reynolds, *Rich Relations: The American Occupation of Britain, 1942–1945* (New York, 1995).

19. Belinda Davis, *Home Fires Burning: Food, Politics, and Everyday Life in Berlin* (Chapel Hill NC, 2000).

20. Jay Winter, *The Great War and the British People* (London, 2003).

21. An extreme example on the Vietnam period is chapter 3 of Christian Appy, *Working-Class War: American Combat Soldiers and Vietnam* (Chapel Hill NC, 1993).

22. Fred Anderson, *A People's Army: Massachusetts Soldiers and Society in the Seven Years War* (Chapel Hill NC, 1984). See also John Shy, *A People Numerous and Armed: Reflections on the Military Struggle for American Independence* (Ann Arbor MI, 1990).

23. Grady McWhiney and Perry D. Jamieson, *Attack and Die: Civil War Military Tactics and the Southern Heritage* (Tuscaloosa AL, 1982).

24. Gerald Linderman, *Embattled Courage: The Experience of Combat in the American Civil War* (New York, 1987).

25. Gary Sheffield, *Leadership in the Trenches: Officer-Man Relations, Morale and Discipline in the British army in the Era of the First World War* (New York, 2000).

26. Omer Bartov, *Hitler's Army: Soldiers, Nazis and War in the Third Reich* (Oxford, 1992) and Bartov, *The Eastern Front, 1941–1945*.

27. Christopher Browning, *Ordinary Men: Reserve Police Battalion 101 and the Final Solution in Poland* (New York, 1993).

28. John Dower, *War Without Mercy: Race and Power in the Pacific War* (New York, 1986).
29. It is worth noting, however, that many fighting units strayed from official policy and integrated themselves, especially on the American frontier.
30. Jennifer D. Keene, *Doughboys, the Great War, and the Remaking of Modern America* (Baltimore MD, 2001). For a work that shows how the military experience could lead to an attenuation of racism, see Leo Bogart, *Social Research and the Desegregation of the U.S. Army* (Chicago, 1969).
31. Leonard V. Smith, *Mutiny Amid Obedience: The Case of the French Fifth Infantry Division During the First World War* (Princeton NJ, 1994).
32. See for example John Keegan, *The Face of Battle: A Study of Agincourt, Waterloo, and the Somme* (London, 1983); John Ellis, *Eye Deep in Hell: Trench Warfare in the First World War* (Baltimore MD, 1976); and Denis Winter, *Death's Men: Soldiers of the Great War* (London, 1993).
33. Tony Ashworth, *Trench Warfare: The Live and Let Live System* (New York, 1980).
34. Davis is a particularly prolific author. See among his works *Carnage and Culture: Landmark Battles in the Rise of Western Power* (New York, 2001) and *The Western Way of War: Infantry Battle in Classical Greece* (New York, 1989).
35. John Grenier, *The First Way of War: American War Making on the Frontier* (Cambridge, 2005).
36. George Satterfield, *Princes, Posts, and Partisans: The Army of Louis XIV and Partisan Warfare in the Netherlands (1673–1678)* (Leiden, 2003).
37. John Lynn, *Battle: A History of Combat and Culture from Ancient Greece to Modern America* (New York, 2003).
38. Isabel V. Hull, *Absolute Destruction: Military Culture and the Practices of War in Imperial Germany* (Ithaca NY, 2004).
39. Tami Davis Biddle, *Rhetoric and Reality in Air Warfare: The Evolution of British and American Ideas about Strategic Bombing, 1941–1945* (Princeton NJ, 2004).
40. Noel Perrin, *Giving Up the Gun: Japan's Reversion to the Sword, 1543–1879* (Boston, 1979).
41. Linda Robertson, *The Dream of Civilized Warfare: The First World War Flying Aces and the American Imagination* (Minneapolis MN, 2003).
42. Paul Fussell, *The Great War and Modern Memory* (Oxford, 1975).
43. Ibid., p. 115.
44. Jay Winter, *Sites of Memory, Sites of Mourning: The Great War in European Cultural History* (Cambridge, 1996).
45. Gary Sheffield, *Forgotten Victory: The First World War, Myths and Realities* (London, 2001) and Brian Bond, *The Unquiet Western Front: Britain's Role in Literature and History* (Cambridge, 2002).
46. See Stéphane Audoin-Rouzeau and Annette Becker, *14–18: Understanding the Great War* (New York, 2003); John Horne and Alan Kramer, *German Atrocities 1914: A History of Denial* (New Haven CT, 2001); and Adam Hochschild, *King Leopold's Ghost: A Story of Greed, Terror, and Heroism in Colonial Africa* (New York, 1999).
47. Jeffrey Verhey, *The Spirit of 1914: Militarism, Myth, and Mobilization in Germany* (Cambridge, 2000).
48. Henry Rousso, *The Vichy Syndrome: History and Memory in France since 1944* (Cambridge MA, 2004) and Eric Conan and Henry Rousso (eds), *Vichy: An Ever-Present Past* (Hanover, 1998).
49. Peter Novick, *The Holocaust in American Life* (Boston, 1999).
50. See, for example, Keith Jeffery, *Ireland in the Great War* (Cambridge, 2000) and Timothy Bowman, *The Irish Regiments in the Great War: Discipline and Morale* (Manchester, 2003).

4

military thought from machiavelli to liddell hart

nikolas gardner

Since the advent of armed conflict, soldiers and scholars have attempted to understand warfare and devise methods to secure victory on a consistent basis. This chapter will introduce some of the most prominent and enduring theories regarding the nature and conduct of war that have emerged in the modern period. It will shed light on the individuals who developed them and the historical context in which they were created. It will highlight their key similarities and differences, as well as identify unique insights and limitations of particular theories. Given the number and complexity of such concepts, it is impossible to provide a comprehensive discussion of military thought within the confines of a relatively short essay. It is therefore necessary to exclude specifically focused strategies and tactical concepts, such as theories of siegecraft, guerrilla warfare, counterinsurgency and nuclear warfare. The chapter will consider instead those theories that attempt to explain in general terms the nature and conduct of war, on land, at sea, and in the air. Furthermore, not every theory under scrutiny will receive equal attention. Concepts that are susceptible to misinterpretation, as well as complicated ideas that yield particularly rich insights, will be examined in greater depth. Thus, the ideas of Carl von Clausewitz, which are profound yet easy to misunderstand, will be subject to a relatively detailed analysis.

This chapter will examine theories of warfare in chronological fashion, beginning with the ideas of Niccolo Machiavelli and the military thinkers of the European Enlightenment. It will then consider two key theorists of the nineteenth century, Jomini and Clausewitz. This will be followed by a discussion of the principal theories of 'seapower' and 'airpower', which emerged in the late nineteenth and early twentieth centuries. Finally, the chapter will examine the ideas developed by two British theorists, J. F. C. Fuller and Sir Basil Liddell Hart, after the First World War. In the process, two main themes will emerge. The first is the historically specific nature of military thought. Theories of warfare are a product of the unique historical circumstances in which they are developed. They reflect the prevalent form of conflict and the intellectual fashions of a given period, as well as the personal biases of their creators. Consequently, no theory can serve as a universally applicable intellectual tool that will explain warfare regardless of time and place. The second key theme is the commonality of certain ideas about the nature and conduct of war. Despite the considerable historical and intellectual distances separating the most prominent military theorists, they have nonetheless come to similar conclusions about particular aspects of warfare. Thus, it is possible to identify basic ideas and assumptions that unite even the most disparate theories.[1]

machiavelli: the foundation of modern military thought

Niccolo Machiavelli (1469–1521) is best known today as a political philosopher. His ideas about the organization of armies and the conduct of war, however, serve as the basis of military thought in the modern period. Machiavelli revived the classical notion that the study of historical conflicts could yield lessons, or universal principles, to guide the conduct of war in the present and future. Machiavelli was a civil servant in the Florentine republic from 1498 until 1512, when the former ruling family of Florence, the Medici, resumed their control over the Italian city-state. He was relieved of his duties and briefly imprisoned, after which he began writing on politics and statecraft, at least partly with the intent of gaining favour with the Medici and returning to public life. The three principal works in which Machiavelli discussed conflict were *The Prince*, the *Discourses*, and *The Art of War*. It is in the latter book that military matters are addressed in the most detail.

Machiavelli developed his ideas in a period when educated Europeans looked to the classical period for the greatest examples of achievement in all aspects of human life. It was thus natural that he looked to ancient Rome to gain insights into the conduct of war. He was at no loss, however, for contemporary examples of warfare. Machiavelli lived and wrote against a background of endemic political upheaval and conflict, as Italian city-states attempted to expand at each other's expense, often enlisting the support of external powers such as France and Spain. The widespread employment of foreign mercenaries added a chaotic element to these conflicts, as hired soldiers often deserted their employers and even switched sides.

Machiavelli's historical studies and observations of contemporary Italy led him to the conclusion that war was essential in order to enable a state to survive in a dangerous and unpredictable world. He argued that control of the army should be placed in the hands of a single commander with the authority to conduct a rapid campaign culminating in a decisive battle. Given the intensity of such a battle, Machiavelli emphasized the importance of strict discipline in order to maintain the cohesion of the troops involved. Discipline alone, however, was not sufficient. A fundamental argument in all of Machiavelli's discussions of warfare is that an army should be made up of inhabitants of the state it defends. He supported this argument by highlighting the effectiveness of the armies of the Roman republic as well as the unreliability of the mercenaries employed by Italian city-states in his own time.[2] Machiavelli recognized that the readiness of ordinary citizens to die in battle was dependent on their commitment to the state for which they were asked to fight. Thus he argued that by fostering the loyalty of its constituents, a good government would enhance the effectiveness of its army.

Machiavelli's ideas were limited in their depth and their predictive power. In comparison to later theorists, his discussion of the conduct of battle and the exercise of command is relatively brief. In addition, while his call for a citizen-army appears to be a prophetic vision of the conscript armies of the nineteenth and twentieth centuries, he never imagined the mass mobilization that took place during the French Revolutionary Wars, much less the world wars. He had in mind only a part-time militia on the pattern of the classical city-states. He also failed to recognize the impact of firearms on the composition of armies in his own time. Well into the eighteenth century, the operation of artillery and handheld weapons required a degree of expertise that encouraged the employment of the mercenaries that Machiavelli abhorred.[3]

Nevertheless, Machiavelli set the stage for the subsequent development of military thought in several ways. His advocacy of training and discipline influenced military reformers of the sixteenth and seventeenth centuries such as Gustavus Adolphus and Maurice of Nassau. In the aftermath of the Napoleonic Wars, Clausewitz expanded upon Machiavelli's observations regarding the relationship between the character of the state and the commitment of its citizens to defend it. More generally, numerous prominent soldiers followed his example in the seventeenth and eighteenth centuries, attempting to distil universal principles of warfare from the study of the classical period.

towards a science of war:
military thought in the seventeenth and eighteenth centuries

The 1600s and 1700s saw the emergence of what the historian Azar Gat has termed 'the military school of the Enlightenment'.[4] Like scholars in other fields of study, military thinkers in this period sought to illuminate the conduct of war through the application of reason. These theorists are too numerous to consider individually, and most have faded into obscurity. Their ideas are nonetheless worthy of general discussion for two reasons. First, extending Machiavelli's notion of 'principles' of war, they conceived of conflict as susceptible to scientific analysis, identifying laws and even mathematical equations to guide the conduct of campaigns. Elements of this approach remain a component of military thought today. Secondly, Enlightenment-era theorists advocated reforms that France and Napoleon Bonaparte would use to transform the conduct of war at the turn of the nineteenth century. Following the example of intellectuals in other fields, military thinkers in this period used the natural sciences as a model for their enquiries into the nature and conduct of war. The work of Raimondo Montecuccoli (1609–1680), the most prominent military theorist of the seventeenth century, exemplified this approach. A commander in the Habsburg army, Montecuccoli had an avid interest in the scientific thought of his time, citing the work of numerous natural scientists in his own books. He considered knowledge of arithmetic and trigonometry to be essential for the conduct of war. His goal was to summarize the vast historical experience of warfare into universal rules that could be applied by commanders in future conflicts. Similarly, the British mercenary Henry Lloyd (c.1729–1783) attempted to develop a universal theory of war from the study of history. His objective was to derive scientific principles that 'governed war and existed in nature like Newton's laws of gravity and physics'.[5]

Most military thinkers of this era acknowledged that the conduct of war was not wholly susceptible to scientific explanation. They believed that the correct application of military rules and principles in the changing circumstances of a conflict required the creative genius of the commander. In 1799, however, the Prussian officer, Adam Heinrich Dietrich von Bulow (1757–1807) advanced a geometrical model that purported to remove the necessity of sublime calculations in war. According to Bulow's theory, the success of a military campaign depended upon the distance of the attacker's advance in relation to the width of his base of supplies. If the attacking army attempted to penetrate deeply into enemy territory without a sufficiently broad base from which to draw provisions and reinforcements, it would be cut off by the defending force. Bulow expressed these ideas in a geometric model that ostensibly offered a means of calculating mathematically the feasibility of any given campaign. Thus, victory no longer required a commander of genius.

Unfortunately for Bulow, the publication of his model coincided with the French Revolutionary and Napoleonic Wars, a series of conflicts that underlined the importance of non-quantifiable factors such as patriotic sentiment. At the same time, Napoleon Bonaparte demonstrated the ample scope that remained for a talented general. More generally, the scale and intensity of the French Revolutionary and Napoleonic Wars cast doubt on many of the 'universal' theories of the seventeenth and eighteenth centuries. These ideas, based on classical and modern conflicts that had been limited in their size, duration and objectives, seemed largely antiquated. Nonetheless, subsequent theorists followed the 'military school of the Enlightenment' in attempting to establish enduring principles of war. Even today, military organizations employ such precepts to help cope with the complexity of modern conflicts. The United

States army, for example, recognizes nine ostensibly unchanging principles of war.

In addition to influencing the study of warfare in subsequent centuries, military thinkers of the Enlightenment advocated a variety of practical reforms that contributed directly to the increased effectiveness of armies from the 1790s onwards. In 1772, the Comte de Guibert (1743–1790) encouraged France to raise a citizen army. Guibert argued that such a force, inspired by national pride, would prove far more potent than the mercenary armies that predominated in eighteenth-century Europe. He also advocated the organization of the army into divisions. While the unwieldy armies of the period remained shackled to lengthy supply lines, smaller divisions could support themselves by requisitions while on campaign, thus restoring a greater degree of mobility to warfare.[6] In addition, Henry Lloyd developed the concept of lines of operations, later popularized by Jomini. Lloyd also suggested operational manoeuvres that closely resembled methods used by Napoleon. Ultimately, it was Bonaparte who saw the potential in all of these innovations and combined them to devastating effect in the late 1790s and early 1800s. Nonetheless, the theorists of the seventeenth and eighteenth centuries left a legacy that was evident in the methods Napoleon used to transform the map of Europe.

jomini: interpreter of napoleonic warfare

Following in the intellectual footsteps of Enlightenment-era theorists, Antoine-Henri Jomini (1779–1869) attempted to develop timeless principles to guide the conduct of war. Influenced significantly by the Napoleonic Wars and the exploits of Bonaparte himself, Jomini's theory proved to be no more 'universal' than those of his predecessors. Despite its limitations, however, Jomini's relatively simple approach to warfare proved appealing to subsequent generations of soldiers.

Born and raised in Switzerland, Jomini reached adulthood as revolution spilled out of neighbouring France. Inspired by the momentous political and military developments that had transpired since 1789, he joined the French-backed revolution in Switzerland in 1798. After helping organize the militia of the new Helvetic Republic, he travelled to Paris in 1802. There he began to write on military history under the patronage of the cavalry commander Michel Ney. While producing a continuous flow of publications, Jomini served as a staff officer to Ney and Napoleon over the next decade. In 1813, however, obstacles to the further progression of his career led him to defect to the Russian army at an opportune moment in the Napoleonic Wars. Jomini subsequently reached the rank of general under the Tsars, whom he served as late as the Crimean War of 1853–56. Following Napoleon's defeat, however, he devoted the bulk of his time to writing on military history and theory.

Jomini's ideas were shaped by his involvement in some of the bloodiest and most decisive engagements of the Napoleonic Wars. He served at Austerlitz, Jena and Eylau, and participated in the French campaigns in Spain and Russia. Throughout his career, he viewed events from the elevated perspective of a senior staff officer at the side of his commander, largely removed from the chaos of the battlefield. This vantage point had a dramatic impact on his conception of war. According to John Shy: 'War, at least the only part of it that truly interested him concerned the supreme commander, the Frederick or Napoleon who played the great bloody game, who by sheer intellect and will dominated the men who served him and used them to defeat his enemies.'[7]

Throughout his career, Jomini emphasized that strategy was the key to warfare.[8] More important than morale, logistics or a myriad of other factors was the ability of the army commander to formulate a plan to defeat the enemy on the battlefield. This victory was achieved through the destruction of the enemy army. Jomini dismissed the comparatively indecisive campaigns of the eighteenth century, and theorists such as Lloyd and Bulow who developed flawed precepts based on their conduct. In his view, Napoleon's greatest victories revealed the true principles of warfare. Foremost among these was the concentration of force to achieve local superiority at a decisive point. By 'decisive point', Jomini meant a position on or near the battlefield at which the enemy was especially vulnerable. A successful attack on this position would threaten the safety or cohesion of the enemy force. The location of the decisive point was dependent on the nature of the battlefield and the armies involved in the engagement, and Jomini argued that it required a talented commander to discern it. He nonetheless identified enemy flanks and supply lines as particularly susceptible to attack.

In order to achieve superiority at the decisive point, the commander must manoeuvre his army into an advantageous position in relation to the enemy force. To explain the most effective means of achieving this, Jomini used the concept of 'lines of operations'. This term had been used by Lloyd and Bulow to describe the routes linking armies to their supply depots and magazines. Jomini employed a broader definition, conceiving of lines of operations as an army's supply lines, its potential routes of retreat, and its communication links with allied forces. He also attempted to define specific types of lines of operations, but the majority of his definitions proved imprecise and confusing. Jomini produced one particularly effective explanatory tool, however, when he developed the notion of interior lines of operations. If an army occupies a central position between two or more separate enemy forces, it possesses the advantage of interior lines, as it can move quickly to concentrate against each force in turn. In contrast, the dispersed enemy forces are compelled to operate on exterior lines, with relatively large distances inhibiting their ability to communicate and concentrate. Thus, Jomini argued that an army could use interior lines of operation to defeat separated enemy forces in succession, even when the combined strength of those forces was greater than its own.[9]

Jomini identified these basic principles relatively early in his career. By 1813, when he left the French army, he had gained international renown for his insights regarding the concentration of force and lines of operations. His theories contained limitations, however, that he was never able to overcome. While Jomini's ideas shed light on the effective deployment of armed forces on the battlefield, he largely ignored qualitative differences between these forces in areas such as morale, training and armament. In addition, despite his experiences in Spain and Russia, Jomini struggled to apply his principles to popular insurrections and guerrilla wars, in which the enemy refused to reveal its dispositions and provide the opposing army commander with a 'decisive point' to attack.

Like the theorists who preceded him, Jomini failed to devise a set of universal principles to guide the conduct of war. It is more accurate to say that he simply revealed the principles behind Napoleon's greatest victories. Nonetheless, Jomini's ideas retained remarkable appeal in the nineteenth and twentieth centuries. In the aftermath of the Napoleonic Wars, his theory proved comforting to European elites as it provided a relatively simple explanation for a prolonged period of violence and political upheaval. According to Jomini, France's military victories resulted from the application of basic principles by a gifted commander. The popular nationalism unleashed by the French Revolution could therefore be disregarded. For soldiers, Jomini reduced the chaos of war by prescribing straightforward methods of achieving a decisive victory. The principal wars of the nineteenth century – the American Civil War and the German Wars of Unification – did not appear to discredit these methods entirely. Thus, as late as 1914, Jomini still exerted a strong influence on military thought. The First World War, however, revealed the folly of concentrating forces for offensive action when weapons technology favoured the defensive. While Jomini's ideas never regained their popularity afterwards, inter-war theorists such as Giulio Douhet, J. F. C. Fuller and Sir Basil Liddell Hart retained his general approach, placing a similar emphasis on striking at a decisive point. Ultimately, despite its shortcomings, Jomini's quest for decisive victory struck a chord among professional soldiers.[10] It was his rival Clausewitz, however, who provided a more compelling explanation of warfare as a phenomenon.

carl von clausewitz (1780–1831)

Clausewitz's *On War* invariably frustrates its first-time readers. While his theories are widely hailed for their profundity, the complexity of his ideas and the manner in which they are expressed renders them all but indecipherable to the uninitiated. The Prussian theorist's insights are certainly worthy of careful consideration. While his contemporaries offered simple principles that proved limited in their applicability, Clausewitz provided a detailed study of the dynamics of warfare that transcended the period in which it was written. In order to grasp *On War* fully, however, it is imperative to understand the context in which it was produced. Thus, before discussing Clausewitz's key ideas, it is first necessary to consider his military career, the ideas that influenced his explanation of conflict, as well as the process by which he developed his theory of war.

Clausewitz and Jomini served in the same conflicts, but their experiences were very different. Born in 1780, Clausewitz joined the Prussian army and first saw combat at the age of 12. He served through the 1790s before entering the Institute for Young Officers in Berlin in 1801. Three years later he graduated and joined the staff of Prince August of Prussia. Clausewitz was captured during Napoleon's destruction of the Prussian army at Auerstadt in 1806. He returned to Prussia in 1807, but became dismayed by Kaiser Frederick William III's acquiescence as Napoleon prepared for his invasion of Russia. As a result, for rather more patriotic reasons than Jomini, Clausewitz absconded to Russia in 1812. He later rejoined the Prussian army, serving as a senior staff officer in 1815. Subsequently, however, he proved unable to shake off the reputation for disloyalty that clung to him following his defection. Thus, in 1818, Clausewitz was shunted into an administrative position as director of the Prussian war college. Although he did not welcome this appointment, it afforded him time to develop his theory of warfare. This extended sabbatical only ended in 1830 when he was appointed to command an artillery division. He died suddenly of cholera in 1831. Significantly, while he was not blessed with Jomini's longevity, Clausewitz's military career was much more varied. In addition to serving both in combat and as a staff officer, he had savoured victory and endured defeat. The diversity of his military experiences in comparison to his Swiss counterpart undoubtedly contributed to the relative complexity of Clausewitz's ideas about warfare.

Clausewitz also developed these ideas in a different intellectual context than other military thinkers. Theorists such as Lloyd, Bulow and Jomini were products of the Enlightenment, which sought to identify the universal principles underlying human behaviour. By the early nineteenth century, however, a growing chorus of voices was emerging in opposition to this worldview, particularly in Germany. Known as the 'Counter-Enlightenment' or the 'German Movement', this broad school of thought emphasized the diversity and unpredictability of human behaviour. It also advocated historicism, the notion that historical actors and societies were unique products of the values and circumstances prevalent in their own time, and therefore could not be judged by the standards of the present. These criticisms of Enlightenment thought shaped Clausewitz's opinion of existing military theories. In the early 1800s, he chided theorists such as Jomini and Bulow for simplifying warfare and ignoring the unique conditions that had influenced the conduct of past conflicts.

From 1810 to 1812, however, Clausewitz served as an instructor at the Prussian war college and tutor to the crown prince. As a teacher, he discovered the utility of theory in rendering a chaotic phenomenon such as war more comprehensible to his students. Nonetheless, he remained convinced that the prescriptive formulae of Jomini, Bulow and others were inherently flawed. Given the infinite complexity of warfare, it was impossible to devise a set of principles that would be applicable to any conflict at any time. Clausewitz's expectations of theory were more modest. While it could not provide explicit instructions to enable soldiers to respond to any situation in war, a good theory could serve as an organizational tool to help soldiers understand the situations they encountered. As he explained in *On War*: 'Theory cannot equip the mind with formulas for solving problems, nor can it mark the narrow path on which the sole solution is supposed to lie by planting a hedge of principles on either side. But it can give insight into the great mass of phenomena and of their relationships, then leave it free to rise into the higher realms of action.'[11]

From 1819 to 1826, Clausewitz continued to develop his ideas, completing the bulk of *On War*. Despite his recognition of the great diversity of conflicts throughout history, Clausewitz was influenced profoundly by his own experiences. This led him to define warfare in Napoleonic terms. Thus, throughout this period, he emphasized that the ultimate objective was the total defeat of the enemy state, achieved through the destruction of its army on the battlefield. Military strategies and tactics that did not contribute to the achievement of this end were therefore a wasteful and dangerous diversion. In 1827, however, Clausewitz experienced an intellectual crisis. His study of history showed him that armies had often fought wars without the intention of destroying their enemies completely. More generally, he realized that prior to the French Revolution wars had often been fought using limited means to achieve limited ends. For the next four years, Clausewitz began revising *On War* to reflect this revelation. Unfortunately, he died in 1831 with the process only partially complete, and it was left to his wife to publish the book in its existing form. As a result, Clausewitz's pre-1827 emphasis on the annihilation of the enemy army on the battlefield appears in *On War* alongside his later recognition of the legitimacy of a broad spectrum of strategies and tactics. Beatrice Heuser has characterized these conflicting arguments as two faces of the same theorist. According to Heuser, 'Clausewitz the Idealist' saw the decisive battle as central to war, while 'Clausewitz the Realist' subsequently recognized that conflicts took a variety of forms, depending on their aims and intensity.[12] Thus, when reading Clausewitz, it is important to recognize the diverse nature of his military service, his conception of theory, and the fact that his ideas evolved significantly as he struggled to write a book that was never completed to his satisfaction.

Nonetheless, by 1831, Clausewitz had made significant changes to his study of war. By the time of his death, it seems that he intended to make only minor revisions to the book.[13] But how did Clausewitz modify his ideas to encompass very different types of war in one unified theory? He found his solution in the process of dialectical reasoning, a method of argument that aims to reconcile conflicting points of view. The process begins with the statement of a position, or thesis. Evidence is then introduced to support and to challenge the thesis, after which an opposing argument, or antithesis is posited. Finally, the thesis and antithesis are brought together in a conclusion, or synthesis. In addition to acknowledging Clausewitz's military experiences, his intellectual background, and the unfinished status of his work, it is essential to be aware of this pattern of argument in order to understand *On War*.

This dialectical process can be discerned in Chapter 1 of Book I, in which Clausewitz introduces the general framework of his theory of war. Among the last chapters revised before his death, it represents his ideas at their most mature. It is also the chapter in which Clausewitz explains the nature of conflict in broad terms. As Michael Handel has commented: 'had Clausewitz written only this chapter and nothing else, his place as the most important theorist of war would still remain unchallenged'.[14] An examination of Chapter 1 of Book I therefore provides an essential introduction to Clausewitz's conception of war.

In the opening sections of the chapter, Clausewitz develops his initial thesis. He takes the position that in theory, war is prone to escalate to the maximum intensity possible. He then explains why this tendency towards escalation should exist. War, argues Clausewitz, is an interactive process, in which each side must calibrate its efforts with only partial knowledge of the capabilities and fervour of its opponent. It is also a zero-sum game, from which only one side can emerge victorious. Therefore, as each side increases its efforts in order to ensure that they surpass those of its enemy, the intensity of the war should escalate. This process will continue until the conflict culminates in the total defeat of one side by the other.

Having posited this thesis in Sections 1–5, Clausewitz then begins to challenge it, explaining why in reality war often does not escalate to this extreme. He points out that the enemy is never a completely unknown entity. Therefore, it is possible for a state to limit its exertions based on its knowledge of its opponent. He also notes that it is impracticable for any state to mobilize all of its resources at one time, as the training of soldiers, the production of war materials and the enlistment of allies are ongoing processes. In addition, Clausewitz observes that military means alone are seldom sufficient to bring a conflict to its final conclusion. As he comments in Section 9: 'The defeated state often considers the outcome merely as a transitory evil, for which a remedy may still be found in political conditions at some later date.'[15] This encourages both sides in any conflict to husband their resources. In light of these factors, Clausewitz argues that leaders must use their judgement when deciding the extent to which they will mobilize the resources of their state. He makes the important point that this decision reflects the political objective that the war is intended to achieve. Thus, in Section 11 he contends: 'it follows that without any inconsistency wars can have all degrees of importance and intensity, ranging from a war of extermination down to simple armed observation'.[16]

After identifying factors that restrain a state's mobilization of resources in a given conflict, Clausewitz explains how the dynamics of military action also limit the intensity of war. He observes that in any conflict it is less difficult to sit on the defensive than to take the offensive. Thus, in order to attack, one side must have an advantage over its opponent sufficient to outweigh the greater strength inherent in taking up a defensive position. If the two sides are evenly matched, or nearly so, then it is in the interest of neither to take the offensive and military action will therefore be suspended until this situation changes. Clausewitz also maintains that imperfect intelligence, or what he calls elsewhere the 'fog of war', can encourage the suspension of military action. Based on limited or inaccurate information, a commander may overestimate the enemy's strength and delay attacking as a result.

These tendencies, combined with the play of chance throughout military operations, make warfare an activity pervaded by uncertainty. As Clausewitz comments in Section 21: 'From the very start there is an interplay of possibilities, probabilities, good luck and bad that weaves its way throughout the length and breadth of the tapestry. In the whole range of human activities, war most closely resembles a game of cards.'[17] Clausewitz maintains that a commander must possess courage and self-confidence in order to cope with the uncertainties of conflict. Therefore, rather than prescribing explicit principles, a theory of warfare should recognize these qualities and their impact on human decisions. Clausewitz is quick to make clear, however, that war is not simply a game. At basis, he argues, a society goes to war to achieve a political objective. The magnitude of that objective will determine the scale and intensity of the war effort. Thus, in Section 24 Clausewitz makes one of his most famous assertions. War, he argues, 'is a continuation of political intercourse, carried on with other means'.[18]

This statement is effectively the antithesis of his original argument that there is no logical limit to the intensity of war. Clausewitz then attempts a synthesis of these two positions, outlining a conceptual model to assist in determining the specific nature of any conflict. As a whole, Clausewitz argues, war is a 'paradoxical trinity' composed of three tendencies: the power of emotions such as hatred; the play of chance in battle; and the dominance of the political objective. These three tendencies are associated with the people of a society, its armed forces, and its political leadership, respectively. As Clausewitz explains in Section 28: 'The passions that are to be kindled in war must already be inherent in the people; the scope which the play of courage and talent will enjoy in the realm of probability and chance depends on the particular character of the commander and the army; but the political aims are the business of government alone.'[19]

In order to understand the character of a war, it is necessary to analyse the interaction of these three dimensions in each society involved. Their relative importance will vary in different societies and different conflicts. Clausewitz concludes, however, that it is essential to develop a theory that acknowledges the changing influence of these three tendencies, 'like an object hanging between three magnets'.[20] Such a theory will help reveal what Clausewitz elsewhere referred to as the 'centre of gravity' of each society in question. This term refers to the focal point of the society's war effort. It may be an armed force, an individual leader, or even an idea or widely-held belief. Regardless of its location, a successful strike against the centre of gravity will destabilize the war effort or even produce its collapse.[21] Thus, by focusing on the relationship between the three dominant tendencies in any conflict, the 'Clausewitzian Trinity' illuminates the overall nature of that war as well as suggesting potential routes to victory.

Scholars have questioned the value of *On War* as a tool for understanding contemporary conflicts. John Keegan has criticized Clausewitz for interpreting war in eighteenth-century terms, as a purely rational pursuit of political objectives.[22] Martin van Creveld has dismissed *On War* as inapplicable to low-intensity conflicts, in which the belligerents are not both conventional armies fighting on behalf of sovereign states.[23] A careful reading of the first chapter of *On War*, however, reveals that Clausewitz recognized clearly the power of irrational considerations such as emotion in war. Moreover, his 'paradoxical trinity' is sufficiently flexible to be applied to conflicts involving guerrilla armies, terrorist groups, or any other entity seeking to obtain an objective through violence. A more enduring criticism of Clausewitz is that the laborious manner in which he expressed his arguments has left them vulnerable to misinterpretation. Nevertheless, his book yields unsurpassed insights to readers with the patience to navigate the intellectual thicket of *On War*. Rather than a series of simple maxims that ostensibly lead to victory, Clausewitz provided a detailed analysis of the nature of conflict that influenced later theorists and retains its relevance even today.

alfred thayer mahan and julian corbett: theorists of naval warfare

The late nineteenth century saw a flurry of colonial expansion by Western states, primarily in Africa and Asia. This 'race for empire' fuelled widespread interest in naval power, which was essential for any state with imperial ambitions overseas. In this context, the two most prominent theorists of naval warfare, Alfred Thayer Mahan and Julian Corbett, advanced divergent ideas about naval power and its application. For obvious reasons, both Corbett and Mahan viewed conflict from a different perspective than theorists concerned primarily with land warfare. Nonetheless, their ideas shared common themes with existing theories of war.

Alfred Thayer Mahan (1840–1914) joined the United States navy just prior to the American Civil War. He had a largely unremarkable record of service until 1886, when he accepted a lectureship in naval history at the newly created Naval War College. Mahan had shown no great promise as a strategist or historian prior to this appointment. Quickly, however, he revealed a strong grasp of naval history and the common themes running through it. In 1890, he published his first book, *The Influence of Sea Power upon History, 1660–1783*. Two years later, he published its sequel, *The Influence of Sea Power upon the French Revolution and Empire, 1793–1812*.[24] These books rapidly established Mahan's reputation as a naval theorist, particularly in Britain, where his arguments regarding the importance of naval power and his praise of the Royal Navy struck an appreciative chord.[25] In 1896, Mahan retired from the Naval War College to devote himself to writing. He subsequently published 20 books and over 130 articles. When he died in 1914, he was one of the best known historians in the Western world.

Despite his prolific record of publication, Mahan is best known for his first two books on 'sea power'. While he devised this term as a means of attracting attention to his work, he never defined it precisely. Throughout his books, Mahan employed two related but distinct definitions of sea power. Primarily, he meant the ability to establish command of the seas by force. In addition, however, Mahan referred to sea power as the economic activity associated with overseas possessions and seaborne trade.[26] Notwithstanding his ambiguous use of the term, Mahan was clear about its influence. In his first two books, Mahan developed a simple argument that had important implications for an age in which naval power was seen to be an instrumental factor in international relations. Focusing on conflicts between Britain and its continental enemies in the period 1660–1812, Mahan maintained that command of the sea had determined the outcome throughout. Thus, sea power had been vital to Britain's ability to best France during the Seven Years' War, the Napoleonic Wars, and other conflicts of the period.

Mahan argued that command of the sea should be achieved by neutralizing the enemy battle fleet. If the enemy did not seek a confrontation, this could be accomplished through a blockade. Ideally, however, the enemy fleet should be destroyed in battle. Mahan's conception of tactics reflected his heavy intellectual debt to Jomini. He argued that the most effective way to destroy the opposing fleet was to concentrate one's own fleet against a decisive point in the enemy line. This might require breaking through the enemy line of battle and then using the naval equivalent of 'interior lines' to attack the remaining fragments in turn. Alternatively, it could be achieved simply by concentrating against one point in the enemy line while holding the remainder with a screening force.[27]

In addition to adapting Jomini's tactical ideas to maritime warfare, Mahan also emulated the Swiss theorist's prescriptive approach. Like Jomini, Mahan advocated relatively straightforward methods that would ostensibly secure decisive victory. These methods could be reduced to simple principles, such as Mahan's famous admonition: 'never divide the fleet'. Also like Jomini, however, Mahan devised a theory of war with significant limitations. In arguing the decisive importance of command of the sea in international history, he discounted other factors, such as land operations, which were clearly crucial. At the operational and tactical levels, Mahan's emphasis on concentration of force for offensive purposes led him to disregard defensive measures as well as attacks on enemy commerce and amphibious operations, both of which required the dispersion of the fleet. In addition, while Mahan assumed that his principles of naval warfare were timeless, their validity was in fact undermined by technological changes in his own lifetime. The advent of torpedoes, for example, rendered Mahan's battle fleet vulnerable to much smaller vessels, while the submarine revolutionized the conduct of commerce warfare, which he had dismissed. Thus, like many of the theorists examined in this chapter, Mahan's insights into the significance and conduct of naval warfare were limited in their applicability.[28]

One of Mahan's most effective critics was the British theorist Julian Corbett (1854–1922). Originally a barrister, Corbett began writing naval history in the 1890s. In 1902, his growing reputation as a historian and naval strategist earned him a position at the Royal Naval College at Greenwich. He also became a civilian adviser to the Admiralty, a position he held throughout the First World War. After the war, Corbett wrote the official history of British naval operations in the conflict. By the time Corbett began his career as a naval historian, Alfred Thayer Mahan was recognized as the foremost authority in the field. Corbett's early work, however, posed a challenge to Mahan's arguments. Examining the conflict between England and Spain in the late sixteenth century, Corbett noted that the war had dragged on for years after the decisive defeat of the Spanish Armada in 1588. Similarly, despite the destruction of the French fleet at Trafalgar in 1805, Napoleon defeated his principal continental enemies, Austria, Prussia and Russia, and established control over virtually all of Europe by 1807. It was only in 1813 that the French Empire crumbled. Thus, Corbett's research indicated that command of the sea did not have the decisive importance that Mahan suggested.

Corbett's understanding of warfare grew more sophisticated in the early 1900s when he read Clausewitz's *On War*. The impact of the Prussian theorist is evident in Corbett's most famous book, *Some Principles of Maritime Strategy*, published in 1911.[29] As discussed above, Clausewitz made the important observation that war was a means of achieving a political end. Corbett adapted this notion to naval warfare. Rather than being an end in itself, he maintained that naval warfare was just one way in which a state might pursue its overall political objective. Nor was it necessarily the most direct route to this goal. Corbett pointed out that naval operations were inherently less decisive than operations on land, simply because people live on land rather than on water. While a naval force could implement blockades, attack enemy commerce and even destroy the enemy fleet, its impact on the people of the opposing state was much less immediate than that of an army, which could control or destroy the actual land on which those people lived.

If naval warfare was just one means to a political end, then it followed that the most effective way of utilizing a state's navy was dependent on the political objective to be achieved. This revelation led Corbett to challenge other aspects of Mahan's arguments. Addressing Mahan's fixation with the destruction of the enemy fleet, Corbett suggested that there were other, equally legitimate ways of using naval power. In some cases, he contended, the concentration of force for offensive purposes was neither necessary nor advisable. It might in fact be prudent for a weaker navy to disperse its forces, forcing its stronger enemy to do the same and thereby creating opportunities to win localized battles, rather than engaging the entire enemy fleet at once. Corbett even suggested that command of the sea is not always necessary for victory. Given that naval warfare is only one means of achieving a larger political goal, victory in war might still be possible when command of the sea is disputed.

Corbett often received a cool reception from professional naval officers. Unlike Mahan's theory of sea power, his ideas did little to advertise the importance of navies as instruments of state policy. Nevertheless, Corbett's approach was largely vindicated by the world wars, which saw naval forces engaged in a wide range of activities including commerce warfare and amphibious operations. More generally, Corbett proved more successful than his American counterpart in providing a versatile and enduring explanation of war at sea. Mahan followed Jomini in offering a recipe for decisive victory that applied only to certain types of naval operations with certain types of weapons. Corbett, however, placed naval warfare as a whole within the broader context of conflict and statecraft.[30]

giulio douhet: theorist and advocate of air power

Public interest in sea power at the turn of the twentieth century was followed by a growing fascination with winged aircraft. In the decade following Orville Wright's inaugural 12-second flight in 1903, the capabilities of airplanes developed rapidly. By 1914, they had crossed the English Channel, served as a means of commercial transport, and even aided in Italy's 1911 eviction of Ottoman forces from Libya. The First World War saw the widespread use of airplanes for military purposes, including reconnaissance, the achievement of air superiority, and even long-range bombing raids. The increasing versatility and potency of military aircraft, as well as the appalling human and economic costs of land warfare from 1914 to 1918, fuelled interest in the potential of 'air power' in the aftermath of the war. In Europe, this interest was stimulated further by the rise of fascism, an ideology that exalted new technologies as a means to national unity and conquest. While recognition of the military potential of aircraft was by no means limited to those with fascist sympathies, fascism provided a hospitable context for the development of theories regarding air warfare.[31]

All of these factors influenced Giulio Douhet (1869–1930), a staff officer in the Italian army. Douhet developed an interest in the military potential of aircraft as early as 1908, but it was the First World War that convinced him that aerial operations could be truly decisive. As early as 1915, he began advocating massive bombing raids directed at enemy production centres well behind the front lines. His ideas continued to develop after the conflict. In 1921, Douhet published *The Command of the Air*, in which he presented air power as the decisive weapon of the future.[32] After observing the inconclusive land campaigns of the First World War, Douhet recognized that modern weaponry conferred a considerable advantage to the defensive. He believed, however, that aircraft had the ability to bypass the resulting stalemate. Writing before the invention of radar, he argued that there existed almost no means of defending against an attack by a fleet of bombers accompanied by fighter escorts. The only effective way of thwarting such an assault was a pre-emptive strike against the enemy air force before it left the ground. Therefore, rather than devoting resources to supporting indecisive land and naval operations, Douhet advocated an air force comprised primarily of bombers. At the outset of a conflict, this force would attack enemy population centres, which had traditionally been spared from destruction. Douhet believed that in modern warfare, the distinction between combatants and non-combatants was largely irrelevant, as civilians were both economic assets and potential soldiers. Air attacks aimed at them would quickly destroy their morale and force their leaders to sue for peace, thus averting the prolonged carnage of the First World War.

Following Mussolini's seizure of power in 1922, Douhet served as an adviser to the new Italian government while continuing to promote air power through a series of publications. His growing celebrity in Italy attracted the attention of military thinkers elsewhere. By the late 1920s, Douhet's work was subject to considerable debate in the Luftwaffe. In addition, it had a significant impact on Billy Mitchell, a proponent of an independent United States Air Force in the inter-war period. Although Mitchell had originally envisioned multiple roles for aircraft, he became an increasingly fervent supporter of strategic bombing after exposure to Douhet's ideas. Certainly, not all advocates of the bomber were Douhet's disciples. Sir Hugh Trenchard, Chief of the British Air Staff from 1919 to 1929, independently discerned the potential of strategic bombing. Nonetheless, the Italian theorist's association with the notion that air power could independently achieve decisive victory is evident in the use of the term 'Douhetism' to describe it.

Douhet's hopes for strategic bombing were not realized in the Second World War. Contrary to his predictions, most of the belligerents eschewed chemical weapons for fear of retaliation. In addition, radar enabled defensive measures against bombing raids, thereby reducing their impact. Moreover, civilian morale proved more durable than Douhet expected. Thus, while bombing caused immense damage throughout the war, it did not bring it to a rapid and decisive conclusion. Nor has it lived entirely up to Douhet's lofty expectations in any conflict since 1945. Nevertheless, even though the deliberate targeting of civilians has fallen out of favour, Douhet's belief in the decisive potential of air power has retained a strong appeal, particularly among air force officers. This is in part due to its value in justifying a strong and independent air force. More generally, however, Douhet followed in the footsteps of Jomini, proposing a formula for rapid and decisive victory achieved by striking at a decisive point. Given the increasing aversion to war casualties in Western societies since 1945, such an approach remains attractive to soldiers and political leaders alike.

theorists of limited war: j. f. c. fuller and sir basil liddell hart

Douhet was not alone in his reaction to the catastrophic costs of the First World War. During the inter-war period, military thinkers also sought ways to restore mobility to land operations in the hope of achieving decisive victory. Among the most prolific were the British theorists J. F. C. Fuller (1878–1966) and Sir Basil Liddell Hart (1895–1970). Disillusioned by the conduct of the First World War, Fuller and Liddell Hart emphasized the potential of mechanized warfare as a means of averting stalemate. Liddell Hart went further, incorporating mechanized operations into a broader strategic approach that promised victory with limited expenditure. While both theorists were disappointed with the reception of their ideas by the British army, they did have an impact on the conduct of the Second World War. Moreover, the value of Liddell Hart's strategic ideas was evident in the relative success of American strategy during the Cold War.

With a wide range of interests that included history, philosophy and mysticism, Fuller stood out in the British officer corps of the early twentieth century. His military career remained undistinguished, however, until he was assigned to the newly formed Tank Corps in 1917. Convinced of the revolutionary potential of tanks, Fuller soon became instrumental in the development of early armoured tactics. After helping orchestrate the first successful use of British tanks to penetrate enemy lines at Cambrai in November 1917, he devised Plan 1919, a scheme to defeat the German army through a massive armoured attack. Fuller's plan called for a three-wave assault involving 5,000 tanks supported by aircraft. The first wave, the Breaking Force, would pierce the German line at separate points, surprising the enemy. The second wave, the Disorganizing Force, would break through the enemy's defensive system and strike at its command, control and communications infrastructure. Finally, a Pursuing Force would take advantage of the resulting chaos, carrying out a sustained advance over a period of five days that would bring about the collapse of the enemy army.

It is debatable whether the tanks of the First World War were capable of achieving these ambitious aims. In any case, Germany surrendered before Plan

1919 came to fruition. Nonetheless, in the aftermath of the First World War Fuller continued to advocate the use of armour to penetrate fortified defensive positions and disrupt what he called the enemy's brain and nervous system. He also argued that the advent of armoured warfare marked the beginning of a new cycle in the history of conflict, in which mass armies equipped with projectile weapons would be replaced by small, highly-trained forces employing shock weapons such as aircraft and tanks to achieve rapid, decisive, and less costly victories.[33] Despite Fuller's recommendations, however, the inter-war British army never embraced armour to his satisfaction. Frustrated with its lack of progress, he retired from the army in 1933. He continued to write until his death in 1966.

The British failure to embrace Fuller's ideas resulted in part from economic constraints, the unsuitability of armour for colonial operations, and organizational resistance to innovation. It was also a consequence, however, of Fuller's own lack of clarity and tact. From 1918 until he died in 1966, Fuller published dozens of books and hundreds of articles that articulated a dizzying array of ideas, often in an abstruse manner that confused many readers. He also had little patience with those who did not appreciate his insights. It was ultimately Fuller's associate, Liddell Hart, who communicated these ideas to a wider audience. Seventeen years younger than Fuller, Liddell Hart served on the Western Front in 1916 until a German gas attack left him unfit for front-line service. He subsequently took up a training post, and after the war he published an infantry training manual that incorporated the lessons of the conflict. When poor health necessitated his discharge from the British army in 1924, he turned to journalism.

Liddell Hart developed his ideas on warfare as a columnist for the *Daily Telegraph* and *The Times*, as well as in a series of books published in the 1920s and 1930s. By the mid 1920s, he had become disenchanted by the strategies and tactics of the First World War, an attitude nurtured through his acquaintance with the acerbic Fuller. Thus, his articles and books criticized the conduct of the war on the Western Front. The immense costs of the conflict, he argued, stemmed from the obsession of commanders on all sides with the destruction of the enemy army in the main theatre of battle, an outdated notion that he attributed to Clausewitz. In place of this misguided and bloody means of making war, Liddell Hart advocated what he called the 'indirect approach'. Ironically, given his criticism of Clausewitz, this approach was based on the recognition that all acts of war and diplomacy are simply a means to a political end. Liddell Hart maintained that this end should be pursued according to a 'grand strategy'.[34] While the term strategy had previously been used to refer to military planning, he argued that a state could pursue its objective through diplomatic, economic or military means.

The key, Liddell Hart emphasized, was to devise a grand strategy that would enable the achievement of a political objective at as little cost as possible. As he explained: 'The perfection of strategy would be... to produce a decision without any serious fighting.'[35] Therefore, a state seeking to coerce an opponent should first employ non-military methods such as the formation of alliances, economic blockade, and deterrence. If military operations were necessary, Liddell Hart advocated targeting of the enemy's weak points. Thus, he argued for air strikes against the enemy civilian population using weapons such as poison gas. If operations against the enemy armed forces were unavoidable, Liddell Hart called for the use of armour and motor vehicles to break through enemy lines, bypass strong points, and attack the enemy's vulnerable command and control systems.

Liddell Hart's ideas bore strong similarities to those of earlier theorists, even those he criticized. His view of armoured warfare as a means of achieving rapid and decisive victory was derived directly from Fuller's work. In addition, in their discussion of armoured tactics, both he and Fuller placed an emphasis on concentration against a decisive point that Jomini would have recognized. More generally, Liddell Hart's advocacy of victory without bloodshed strongly resembled a similar admonition by the ancient Chinese theorist Sunzi, although Liddell Hart claimed to have developed it independently. Finally, notwithstanding his castigation of Clausewitz as the 'Mahdi of mass and mutual massacre', Liddell Hart's conception of war as a means to achieving a political objective reflected the influence of Corbett and the Prussian theorist.

Despite their lack of originality, Liddell Hart's ideas proved popular in inter-war Britain, where economic constraints and public disillusionment with the First World War created a receptive audience for strategies that promised to limit the nation's sacrifices in future conflicts. His reputation suffered a damaging blow in the late 1930s, however, when he advocated coexistence with Germany even after the scale of the Nazi threat became evident to the vast majority of the British public. After the Second World War, Liddell Hart never regained his earlier stature, despite his rather crude efforts to publicize the influence of his ideas on the development of German armoured tactics.[36] Nonetheless, German officers did draw heavily upon the ideas of both Liddell Hart and Fuller in devising the doctrine of armoured warfare that proved so effective against Poland, France and the Soviet Union from 1939 to 1941.[37] Moreover, Liddell Hart's indirect approach, emphasizing alliances, deterrence and economic blockade, bore a strong resemblance to the strategy adopted by the United States and its allies against the Soviet Union after 1945. Although there is no evidence that Liddell Hart influenced the formulation of this strategy, its relative success suggests the merit of his ideas.[38]

conclusion

Since 1945 the study of armed conflict has become increasingly specialized, as scholars have examined particular aspects of warfare from a variety of disciplinary perspectives. As a result, there now exists a multitude of studies focusing on a wide range of specific topics, such as logistics, intelligence, counterinsurgency, and combat motivation among ordinary soldiers. During the Cold War, there also emerged an extensive body of scholarship on nuclear strategy, which grappled with the problem of devising credible methods for the use of nuclear weapons. It would be impossible to summarize this vast and diverse post-1945 literature in a single essay. It is significant, however, that much of this research has drawn heavily on the canon of concepts and theories examined in this chapter. This canon thus forms an essential foundation for the contemporary study of warfare and strategy.

The diversity of the theories and concepts examined in this chapter is considerable. This range is primarily a reflection of the transformation of warfare in the modern period. The mass armies and global conflict that provoked the ideas of Liddell Hart would likely have been incomprehensible to Machiavelli. It is therefore hardly surprising that their ideas about warfare share little in common. The disparate nature of the canon of military thought also results from the various intellectual trends that have shaped it. Disagreements between Jomini and his contemporary Clausewitz, for example, can be traced in part to the influence of the Enlightenment and Counter-Enlightenment on their respective ideas. In addition, the particular goals and agendas of military thinkers have shaped the development of their theories. Thus, Douhet's optimistic predictions for air power likely stemmed partly from his desire to secure a strong and independent Italian air force. Therefore, in order to understand the insights and limitations of any military theory, it is essential to appreciate the historical and intellectual context in which it was developed.

The diversity of military thought notwithstanding, the theorists examined in this chapter share certain ideas and assumptions about conflict. At basis, they agree that warfare is an essential and unavoidable element in international relations. They also concur that rather than an entirely chaotic phenomenon, war is susceptible to analysis. Military thinkers have disagreed over the extent to which analysis will lead to comprehension and mastery of warfare. A majority, including Machiavelli and the theorists of the Enlightenment, as well as Jomini, Mahan, Douhet, Fuller and Liddell Hart, have argued that the conduct of war is reducible to principles, the correct application of which will lead to victory. Thus, they have developed what may be termed *prescriptive* theories, which offer a series of maxims to guide the intelligent political or military leader to a successful outcome. Given the complexity of war, Clausewitz and Corbett are less convinced of the predictive power of theory. Consequently, they have developed largely *descriptive* theories that attempt to explain the phenomenon of warfare and identify recurring patterns within it. Without exception, however, the military thinkers examined in this chapter favour the attainment of victory without disproportionate human and economic costs. Certain theorists are more explicit than others in their advocacy of this principle. Writing in the aftermath of the First World War, Douhet, Fuller and Liddell Hart made no secret of their desire to avoid a repetition of its prolonged carnage. Nonetheless, even Clausewitz, who has been accused of taking a needlessly bloody approach to war, recognized that conflicts vary in their intensity depending on the objectives at stake. He also offered his readers a tool to help reduce the costs of war in the form of his 'trinitarian analysis'. By identifying the enemy's centre of gravity, the Prussian theorist suggested that victory might be expedited. Thus, despite considerable differences in their theories, the most prominent military thinkers of the modern period have agreed on the inevitability of war, and the desirability of limiting its costs.

further reading

An excellent point of departure for the student of military and strategic thought is Peter Paret (ed.), *Makers of Modern Strategy: From Machiavelli to the Nuclear Age* (Princeton NJ, 1986). An updated version of Edward Mead Earle's book of the same title published in 1944, Paret's volume contains chapters introducing a wide range of strategic thinkers and ideas, including Machiavelli, the theorists of the Enlightenment, Jomini, Clausewitz, Mahan, the theorists of air power, revolutionary warfare and nuclear strategy, all written by pre-eminent scholars in the field. Also essential is Azar Gat, *A History of Military Thought: From the Enlightenment to the Cold War* (Oxford, 2001). Comprising three of Gat's earlier books, it offers a survey of military thought from Machiavelli to Sir Basil Liddell Hart, placing theories of war firmly in the context of broader intellectual trends prevalent at the time of their development. Michael Handel differs from Gat's historicist approach in *Masters of War: Classical Strategic Thought* (London, 2001). Rather than emphasizing the specific historical context that nurtured particular military and strategic ideas, Handel identifies common threads uniting the ideas of Clausewitz, Jomini, Corbett, Sunzi and other theorists.

Studies of individual theories and theorists are too numerous to mention, but several will be of particular use to students of military thought in general. Soldiers and scholars have dismissed the military thought of the Enlightenment as simplistic and barren of enduring insights into the nature of war. Patrick Speelman, *Henry Lloyd and the Military Enlightenment of Eighteenth-Century Europe* (Westport CT, 2002) casts new light on the ideas of the relatively obscure British thinker Lloyd, and offers important new insights into the military thought of the period. Studies of Clausewitz are justifiably more numerous. Although there exist abundant English translations of *On War*, the translation by Michael Howard and Peter Paret (Princeton NJ, 1976) is still recognized as the most authoritative. In addition to Clausewitz's own ideas, the volume contains insightful essays on their origins and influence. While it is not a substitute for tackling *On War* itself, Beatrice Heuser, *Reading Clausewitz* (London, 2002) offers a helpful guide to understanding the Prussian theorist's writings. Two of the harshest modern critiques of Clausewitz are Martin van Creveld, *The Transformation of War* (New York, 1991), and John Keegan, *A History of Warfare* (London, 1993). Although both books contain important insights, their attempts to discredit Clausewitz have been subject to scathing criticisms from other scholars. Christopher Bassford articulates some of these criticisms in, 'John Keegan and the Grand Tradition of Trashing Clausewitz', *War in History* 1/3 (November 1994). Equally contentious to the scholarly debate over the continuing relevance of Clausewitz is that regarding the influence of British military theorists on the German army in the inter-war period. Azar Gat, *British Armour Theory and the Rise of the Panzer Arm: Revising the Revisionists* (London, 2000), offers a useful synopsis of this debate while attempting to end it conclusively.

notes

1. For a discussion of the similarities between the best known theories of war, see Michael Handel, *Masters of War: Classical Strategic Thought* (London, 2001).
2. See Niccolo Machiavelli, *The Art of War* (trans. Neal Wood) (Cambridge MA, 2001), book 1.
3. Felix Gilbert, 'Machiavelli: The Renaissance of the Art of War' in Peter Paret (ed.), *Makers of Modern Strategy: From Machiavelli to the Nuclear Age* (Princeton NJ, 1986), p. 28.
4. Azar Gat, *A History of Military Thought: From the Enlightenment to the Cold War* (Oxford, 2001).
5. Patrick J. Speelman, *Henry Lloyd and the Military Enlightenment of Eighteenth-Century Europe* (Westport CT, 2002), p. 47.
6. On Bulow and Guibert, see R. R. Palmer, 'Frederick the Great, Guibert, Bulow: From Dynastic to National War' in Paret, *Makers of Modern Strategy*, pp. 91–119.
7. John Shy, 'Jomini' in Paret, *Makers of Modern Strategy*, p. 157.
8. See for example Antoine-Henri Jomini, *Summary of the Art of War* (New York, 1854).
9. Gat, *A History of Military Thought*, p. 117; Shy, 'Jomini', pp. 167–9.
10. Shy, 'Jomini', pp. 176–85.
11. Carl von Clausewitz, *On War* (trans. and ed. Michael Howard and Peter Paret) (Princeton NJ, 1976), p. 578.
12. Beatrice Heuser, *Reading Clausewitz* (London, 2002), ch. 2.
13. Gat, *A History of Military Thought*, p. 265.
14. Michael Handel, 'Who is Afraid of Carl von Clausewitz? A Guide to the Perplexed', Courseware, United States Naval War College (February 1996), p. 2.
15. Clausewitz, *On War*, p. 80.
16. Ibid., p. 81.
17. Ibid., p. 86.
18. Ibid., p. 87.
19. Ibid., p. 89.
20. Ibid.
21. Anatulio Echevarria, 'Clausewitz's Centre of Gravity: It's Not What We Thought', *Naval War College Review* 56/1 (Winter 2003): 108–23.
22. John Keegan, *A History of Warfare* (London, 1993).
23. Martin van Creveld, *The Transformation of War* (New York, 1991).
24. Alfred Thayer Mahan, *The Influence of Sea Power upon History, 1660–1783* (Boston, 1890); Mahan, *The Influence of Sea Power upon the French Revolution and Empire, 1793–1812* (Boston, 1892).
25. Phillip A. Crowl, 'Mahan' in Paret, *Makers of Modern Strategy*, p. 444.
26. Mahan, *The Influence of Sea Power upon History*, pp. 138, 71.
27. Crowl, 'Jomini', pp. 455–62.
28. Gat, *A History of Military Thought*, pp. 467–72.
29. Julian Corbett, *Some Principles of Maritime Strategy* (Annapolis MD, 1988).
30. Gat, *A History of Military Thought*, pp. 480–93.
31. Ibid., pp. 561–88.

32. Giulio Douhet, *The Command of the Air* (London, 1943). Originally published in 1921 as *Il Dominio dell'aria*.
33. J. F. C. Fuller, *The Dragon's Teeth: A Study of War and Peace* (London, 1932).
34. Christopher Bassford, 'John Keegan and the Grand Tradition of Trashing Clausewitz', *War in History* 1/3 (November 1994): 319–36.
35. B. H. Liddell Hart, *Strategy: The Indirect Approach* (London, 1954), p. 338.
36. John J. Mearsheimer, *Liddell Hart and the Weight of History* (Ithaca NY, 1988).
37. Azar Gat, *British Armour Theory and the Rise of the Panzer Arm: Revising the Revisionists* (London, 2000).
38. Gat, *A History of Military Thought*, pp. 806–23.

5

land warfare from machiavelli to desert storm

warren chin

The history of land warfare obviously pre-dates the era of Machiavelli.[1] At the same time there is no doubt that Desert Storm in 1991 did not signal the end of this most brutal dimension of conflict. An important question to ask is: why is the timeframe of this chapter confined to a period of little more than five centuries, when the history of land warfare covers a span of some 14,000 years? The simple answer is that this timeframe captures the rise, apotheosis and possible decline of the concept of modern war. According to Charles Townshend, the term modern war was a product of three sources of change: technological, administrative, and ideological.[2] The combined effect of these changes was to transform battle, the conduct of operations and strategy. Equally important, it apparently also played an instrumental role in creating a new political structure that came to dominate European politics: the nation state.[3] Within the context of war the most important aspect of this development was that the state assumed an unassailable monopoly on the use of force. However, it now seems that this model of war is threatened by technological, economic, political and social forces that are bringing about profound changes in the ownership, organization, and use of force as an instrument of policy.[4] The aim of this chapter is to explain the birth, apotheosis and possible decline of modern war.

Warfare in the period before Machiavelli is portrayed as being fixed both in its nature and conduct. Technology was limited to that of edged and missile weapons which relied on both human and animal muscle power. The dominant 'weapon system', at least in medieval Europe, was the armoured knight who relied on the shock charge to break the enemy. Battle was a ritualistic affair and knights fought more often to capture than to kill because of the importance of ransom. As such, there was a strict code that governed the conduct of fighting. Moreover, the cost of armies and the related problems of supplying them ensured that armies were small and possessed a limited range and endurance because most kingdoms lacked the bureaucratic skill needed to organize a sound logistical base and because peasant levies were usually needed for the harvest. Equally important, battle itself was infrequent and raids, skirmishing and sieges tended to dominate campaigns.[5]

Technological, economic, political and social changes occurred in the later medieval period that were to have a profound impact on both the tactics and strategy of war.[6] However, during the time of Machiavelli, it was not clear what impact such change was going to have on the conduct of war. Consequently, it was hardly surprising that some of his more notable judgements about the conduct of war were to prove inaccurate. Two particular errors stand out. The first was his belief that militia armies were far superior to mercenary forces.[7] The second was his failure to appreciate the impact that firearms would have on the battlefield.[8] It is unclear why Machiavelli failed to appreciate the significance of firearms and yet this technology was to have far reaching effects on all aspects of the art of war.[9] In fact, one could argue that in Europe the discovery of gunpowder provided the single most important spark that started a chain reaction of innovation in the military domain.[10]

The potential of gunpowder took time to mature and its effectiveness depended on a number of related developments, particularly in the field of metallurgy. It seems that the substance was first discovered in China in the eleventh century and the knowledge of how to manufacture it arrived in Europe one hundred years later. A further 150 years passed before it was used as an explosive propellant in European warfare. Even then the correlation between size and weight of cannons, and the firepower they produced meant that gunpowder did not play a major role on the battlefield until much later. At this time the guns were simply too big and heavy to be of any practical use and it was not until the 1490s, when the French began manufacturing lighter bronze cannon, that guns were sufficiently mobile and powerful enough to be useful in this environment. In the early days, gunpowder and cannons exerted the greatest impact at the strategic level of war within the domain of siege warfare.[11]

In strategic and political terms siege artillery caused a profound change in the relationship between the monarchy and their nobles. In the period between the eighth and the fourteenth centuries warfare was dominated by the castle which tipped the scales between offence and defence firmly in favour of the latter. It also ensured that political power was decentralized because besieging operations required a massive investment in terms of time and resources.[12] The development of siege artillery changed the political and military landscape dramatically. By the 1430s the Burgundians possessed a siege train capable of destroying most castle walls.[13] However, it was the French who demonstrated the potential of this technology most clearly. Thus, whereas it took Henry V ten years to conquer Normandy after Agincourt in 1415, the French monarch, Charles VII, re-conquered these lands in a year. The fall of Constantinople in 1453 and with it the collapse of the Byzantine Empire, reaffirmed the power of artillery and the power of offence.[14] The strategic consequences of siege artillery were also demonstrated in Spain. In a period of ten years the Christian monarchs Ferdinand and Isabella were able to conquer the Muslim region of Granada (1482–92). According to Machiavelli, no wall now existed that was strong enough to resist the power of the new artillery.[15]

As Parker explains, this pessimism was ill founded and almost immediately military architects tried to improve the design of fortresses so that they were able to resist cannon. The first man to design such a system was Leon Battista Alberti who created a new system of fortifications which could withstand the effects of bombardment and made use of elaborate interlocking zones of fire that made it virtually impossible for assaulting infantry to storm the position without suffering heavy loss.

The nature of this new defensive system meant that besieging operations against these fortifications proved to be labour intensive and protracted. This process required digging massive entrenched lines around the fortress at a distance of one mile or more to ensure that the work was out of the range of the enemy's guns on the walls. A town with walls of 1,500 metres in length might need a system of 40,000 metres of entrenchments.[16] In addition, two sets of circumvallation were required, one to keep the enemy within the fort, the second to prevent a relief force from getting into the fortified town. It is not surprising that the period witnessed a significant increase in the size of armies and it was estimated that at least 20,000 men were now needed to conduct a siege.[17]

The development of the *trace italienne*, as it was known, created a strategic problem in that a heavily fortified town could not be left in the rear of an advancing army. This made battles all but irrelevant in areas where the new fortifications existed. The exception to this was where battle took place between the besieging army and the relief force so that the result decided the outcome of the siege. Consequently, siege warfare became the norm from the sixteenth until the late eighteenth century. Thus, during the Seven Years' War, Marlborough fought four battles but conducted over 30 sieges during his ten campaigns.

gunpowder and the battlefield

What impact did the gunpowder revolution have on the battlefield? The earliest handguns were developed at the same time as cannons. They were simple tubes of iron or brass with a hole in the top. Powder and ball were placed in the tube and the powder was ignited by placing a red-hot iron over the touchhole which caused the powder to explode and propel the ball from the tube. Improvements were made in the fifteenth century to improve the general utility of small arms: the touchhole was moved from the top to the side; a pan was added to hold priming powder; and a cord soaked in saltpetre was used to ignite the weapon. Reliability was improved further with the development of the matchlock. These innovations were introduced only very gradually. Consequently, the impact of the musket on the battlefield was slow and armies tended to use firearms as part of a combination of weapons which contained pikes, crossbows and musketeers. Although the musket was cumbersome and dangerous to use it was relatively easy to train the soldier to employ the weapon, which ensured that, in spite of its many faults, armies used it ever more frequently.[18]

The most demanding aspect of training lay in organizing these weapons so that they could be combined in massed formations that achieved a balance between firepower, mobility and protection. Whilst it was relatively easy to use a musket, the need to achieve these tactical goals resulted in the creation of a system that had far reaching implications for armies. Initially, the Spanish were the first to develop an effective tactical unit that integrated the firepower of the musket with the defensive power of the pike in the form of the *tercio*. This formation was first used in Italy in the 1550s and comprised a pike phalanx which was 50 ranks deep and protected by two companies of musketeers deployed on the fringe of the formation. Each *tercio* contained approximately 2,000 pikemen and 1,000 troops armed either with muskets or the more primitive arquebuses.[19]

The problem with the *tercio* was that it created large tactical formations of 3,000 troops or more which were difficult to manoeuvre and the firepower of muskets was not used effectively. In the 1590s, in the midst of the Dutch revolt against Spain, Counts Maurice and William of Nassau devised a solution to the problem of increasing the firepower of muskets by adapting the tactical system of the Roman army. Their aim was to create and sustain a rolling volley of fire from their infantry. This was to be achieved through the adoption of complex methods of drill which required infantry to be organized in a series of long lines ten ranks deep, the first rank firing and then marching to the rear. The second and succeeding ranks then repeated this process. One of the most immediate consequences of this tactical evolution was that it resulted in an expansion of the battlefield. Medieval battlefields tended to be one kilometre across the front and usually contained 10,000 men or more, organized in close order formations. The new system made it important to deploy troops in less dense formations across as wide a front as possible so that the maximum number of muskets could be brought to bear on the enemy. A wider pattern of dispersal also reduced the vulnerability of a unit to the impact of the opposing army's muskets. Such changes created new challenges in terms of coordinating the movement within units and between them and this required the breakdown of infantry units into smaller and more manageable formations.[20]

In essence, the reforms of Maurice reversed the decline in quality of infantry. The introduction of small manoeuvrable units placed a premium on drill so that formations could move quickly and flexibly. It also meant that many more officers were needed to lead these formations. According to Roberts, during this time the size of the standard infantry unit fell from 3,000 to around 30 men and there was a pronounced increase in the technical and organizational competence of infantry formations.[21]

This tactical system was subsequently modified and improved by Gustavus Adolphus of Sweden. A new training regime meant that only six ranks, rather than ten, were needed to sustain a rolling volley of musket fire. Even more impressive was the fact that the Swedish infantry could march and fire whilst moving forward to attack. More complex manoeuvres required more training and discipline and this in turn resulted in the establishment of permanent professional forces. Equally important, much greater use was made of field artillery. Gustavus Adolphus's goal was to combine infantry, cavalry and artillery attacks and this required artillery that was light enough to move around the battlefield. To this end the Swedes standardized their artillery at three calibres: twenty-four, twelve and three pounders. New manufacturing processes were also introduced to make these guns as light as possible: for example, the three pounder weighed 625 lbs and could fire 24 rounds in an hour. The role of cavalry was also changed from skirmishing with handguns to charging the enemy with sabres.

The effectiveness of the Swedish military system was demonstrated most clearly in the Thirty Years' War (1618–48). Swedish armies achieved victories at Breitenfeld (1631), Lutzen (1632), Wittstock (1636), Breitenfeld II (1642) and Jankow (1645). In effect, the changes wrought by Gustavus indicated that decisive battle was possible and that it was also possible to secure a strategic victory via this medium. As a result, other states quickly began to emulate the Swedish military system and this had important consequences for the conduct of war. The most immediate of these consequences was a drive to increase the size of armies and to maintain a permanent force.[22] Initially these changes were wrought through mercenary armies. This was because of the prolonged period needed to drill and train soldiers, which meant that a citizen militia was not suitable. However, the cost of such forces and the many disadvantages associated with them eventually forced states to raise and train their own national armies organized on the lines of the Swedish model.[23]

warfare in the period of absolutism

The rise of Absolutism witnessed the rapid centralization of political and military power in the hands of the monarchy. This process was caused in part by the impact of changes in the military realm, which brought about a phenomenal increase in the cost of military power. Only the nation state possessed the means to pay for the forces required to defend the kingdom, which effectively meant the monarchy achieved a monopoly on the use of force. Equally important, the period also witnessed the creation of a modern bureaucracy capable of taxing the population and providing the means needed to create and sustain the armed forces. According to Black, this period is significant because the expansion of the state system, and the political stability that stemmed from it, permitted a pronounced increase in both the size and quality of armies.[24] Ironically, although Absolutism improved the capability of the nation to wage war, it also resulted in the imposition of political constraints which paradoxically meant that monarchs actually possessed an increased means to wage war, but lacked the will to use it. Absolutism created a fragile social and political system which excluded the mass of the population from the process of governance. The military implications of this were that the monarch could not mobilize the vast potential of the nation state to fight a war; to do so jeopardized the internal stability of the regime. Consequently, the imperative of political survival drove Europe's monarchs to conduct what became known as 'cabinet wars'. These were limited conflicts, fought by small professional armies, which because of the cost to acquire them, were used sparingly for fear that they might be lost.[25]

Political constraints were reinforced by the problems of waging war with armies recruited from the least productive members of society. As a result, the quality and fighting spirit of these forces was usually low. In the absence of any other source of motivation coercion became the only way to keep soldiers under control. This style of command had important consequences in terms of what such troops could do during campaigns. For example, armies could not forage because it was feared that soldiers would desert. Because of this it became imperative for armies to ensure that they carried their supplies, which entailed the creation of a large and cumbersome supply train. It also required the creation of storage depots on the line of march. In essence, supply problems ensured that the speed and tempo of operations were conducted at a snail's pace. Equally important an unwillingness to conduct reconnaissance, skirmishing or pursuit for fear that soldiers allowed to do these things would desert meant that battle was characterized by indecisiveness.[26]

napoleonic wars

The French Revolution brought about a fundamental change in the relationship between the state and the individual. The establishment of democratic nationalism meant that all citizens faced an unlimited liability to protect the state from harm. As a result, war was now a matter for the entire nation and this had important consequences for the conduct of war. The simplest, but most significant of these changes was that the nation in arms created a massive manpower pool. Equally important, the moral quality of the French army also improved. These developments affected the conduct of battle, campaigns and strategy. Most obviously it meant that armies were now much larger and losses were easier to replace: indeed, Napoleon boasted that he could afford to lose 30,000 men per month during a campaign.[27] This allowed greater emphasis to be placed on battle, which exposed a critical weakness in the armies of the monarchies opposed to the French Republic. As a result, the destruction of the enemy army became the principal means through which the French sought to achieve their strategic aim. The increased size of the French army also placed a premium on the creation of new command and control systems that allowed forces to march separately when on campaign but combine into an effective whole at the critical moment when it was required. The creation of the division and the corps represented an effective organizational structure which gave the French an important advantage in terms of speed and flexibility. These were combined arms formations which cooperated to fix and hold the enemy in place before other corps closed in on the flanks and rear of the enemy army. Because of its size and organization the corps could fight independently for a day or more. As a result, the army had an organizational framework that limited the possibility of collapse and provided new operational possibilities. Thus in 1805, the French *Grande Armée* deployed on a front of 150 miles and surrounded the Austrians at the battle of Ulm. Similar results were achieved at the twin battles of Jena-Auerstadt.[28]

The Napoleonic Wars resulted in the expansion of armies on a scale that was unprecedented in the history of war. The success of the French military system resulted in the defeated nations emulating this new way of war. Consequently, by 1809, the French were facing a mirror version of their military organization. As Epstein points out, the most important consequence of this development was that battle became more attritional and less decisive. Thus, in the battle of Wagram Napoleon clashed with a reorganized and vastly improved Austrian army. The result was not a battle of manoeuvre but one of attrition. At the end of the battle, both armies were exhausted, the French suffered 32,000 casualties and the Austrians 40,000. There was also no pursuit after the battle.[29] Both sides lost heavily, but in the end, Austria could not afford losses on this scale. In this campaign victory was a product of successive battles and engagements. Battles were so big that each now took days to fight. The structure of these armies caused a wider distribution of front, which produced continuous operations: four days around Ratisbon, two each at Aspern-Essling and Wagram.[30]

The problem would repeat itself in the campaign of 1812–13. The *Grande Armée* stood at 670,000 men with 1,393 guns. Again, Napoleon thought he could create another victory like 1805, but this was unlikely because the Russians had adapted. Their military forces were increased to 409,000 troops with 1,344 guns and they had also adopted the corps system.[31] The results of these changes were demonstrated at the battle of Borodino, an encounter that caused heavy casualties, but failed to produce a decisive outcome. The War of Liberation in 1813 was also characterized by indecisive outcomes in battle. The Grand Coalition operating in Germany in August 1813 contained four armies deployed on a front of 360 miles. This arc stretched from Brandenburg to Bohemia. Facing this force was Napoleon's army of 240,000. Using his central position in Saxony, he hoped to defeat the enemy in detail. However, it was not possible for Napoleon to destroy an army in the same way that he had corps sized formations in earlier battles. The size of these armies and the massed artillery available made the offensive extremely costly and breakthrough very unlikely. Success was only possible if a field army could be surrounded, which because of the scale of operations was virtually impossible to achieve, except in the case of the French army which was operating on interior lines and which was therefore exposed to the risk of concentric and simultaneous attack. This was the situation he faced in the battle of Leipzig. At the battle, 200,000 French soldiers with 799 guns engaged four allied armies totalling 361,000 men with 1,456 guns. The battle was fought across a front of 16 miles. Although the French lost, casualties on both sides were heavy: 73,000 French and 54,000 allied soldiers. The French were able to withdraw and pursuit was minimal. Although Napoleon escaped he was not able to replace his losses while the allies could and the campaign of 1814 marked the victory of mass and attrition.[32]

Although the campaign of 1815 was short and the battle of Waterloo was decisive, it also reflected many of the characteristics associated with later evolution of warfare in Europe. The course of the campaign (15–18 June) consisted of continuous and sequential operations. Battles were fought on 15, 16 and 18 June at Charleroi, Quatre Bras and Ligny, and Waterloo. Though the French were outnumbered 2:1, Napoleon hoped to defeat the enemy in detail. But even though he inflicted 25,000 losses on the Prussians they were still able to support the British at Waterloo. The result was the envelopment of the French by two armies. An interesting statistic was that although the French were defeated decisively the losses for the campaign were almost equal: 63,000 French versus 61,000 allied troops. This ratio of 1:1 happened even though the French were outnumbered by 2:1 in the theatre of operations.[33]

impact of the industrial revolution

The French Revolution released the political and institutional constraints that had served to limit war. In the immediate aftermath of that war the victorious monarchies attempted to turn the clock back to the 'cabinet wars' that prevailed in the eighteenth century. However, Clausewitz warned that re-imposing such control over war would prove virtually impossible.[34] Ultimately this prescience was proved right with material changes, caused by the process of industrialization, resulting in governments having access to a vast fiscal and productive capacity with which to wage war. When these changes in the material domain of war were joined to the political concepts of nationalism and democracy the resulting outcome was a vast expansion in the scale and complexity of war.

the american civil war

The American Civil War (1861–65) provides one of the clearest illustrations of how such forces affected the conduct of war. No one believed that the secession of slave owning states from the Union in 1861 would result in a war that would last four years, and result in over a million dead. According to Hagerman: 'the American Civil War ushered in a new era in land warfare', which was brought about by the combined impact of technology and the particular ideological, social and geographical factors peculiar to the United States. These factors shaped tactical and strategic responses to the challenges of war. The result was the creation of new forms of tactical and strategic organization that 'made the Civil War arguably the first modern war'.[35]

Although this argument is overstated, the American Civil War represents an example of how existing tactical doctrine and strategy was made obsolete by changes in technology both on and off the battlefield. Both Union and Confederate armies were organized and trained to fight in the Napoleonic way of war. Indeed, the size, scale and character of American Civil War battlefields were similar to those of the Napoleonic Wars. However, the strategic impact of battle during the American Civil War was very different from the Napoleonic ideal. The first and most important detail was that battle achieved less than the desired strategic effect.

This failure to realize the political potential of battle in the American Civil War stemmed from three sources. First, in the early stages of the war, both Union and Confederate armies were inexperienced and, as a result, the opportunity to destroy the enemy failed to arise or when it did the commander was unable or unwilling to seize the moment. Second, even though the tactical proficiency of the forces improved so too did the armament available to them and this also induced tactical stalemate. In the early stages of the war both armies relied heavily on smooth bore muskets and cannons which were no different to those used during the Napoleonic Wars. However, within a year this changed and rifled muskets became the standard weapon of war. As a result, the range, rate of fire, and accuracy of the infantryman's rifle increased in theory by at least a factor of three. Under these new conditions, the tactical organization espoused by Napoleon and his successors simply resulted in the attacker suffering large casualties. The best illustration of the impact of this weapon was the battle of Fredericksburg in December 1862. In this engagement an entrenched Confederate army inflicted 13,500 casualties against assaulting Union forces, but suffered only 5,500 casualties.[36]

In fact, the casualties of the victor in these battles were frequently similar to those of the defeated army. This was important because it meant that the victorious army was often too exhausted to pursue their defeated opponent and this prevented tactical success from being translated into strategic and political success. What is also interesting is that although new and more accurate artillery and small arms were increasingly used there was no noticeable change in tactical doctrine, which remained embedded in the Napoleonic paradigm.

Third, even when stunning victories, like Fredericksburg, were achieved, it did not result in the defeated nation ending the war. In the first two years of the war the Union suffered a succession of defeats in the Eastern theatre, they were defeated at First Bull Run, driven out of the Peninsula during the Seven Days' Battles, outmanoeuvred and outfought in Jackson's Valley campaign, very nearly destroyed at Second Bull Run and humiliated at Chancellorsville. But this only made the Union more determined to win. Part of this determination stemmed from the recognition that, even when defeated, they had the means to replace their manpower and material resources. Even the Confederacy, with an industrial base only one-tenth the size of its opponent, was able to keep fielding forces until near the end of the war. This ability to replace losses revealed how the political and economic system, especially in the Union, was able to match the political will to continue the fight.

the prussians

The American Civil War demonstrated that social, political, economic and technological conditions combined to make warfare more protracted and more total in character. However, what is interesting is that although the Prussians operated within a similar environment to that of the Americans, their military system was able to realize the goal of achieving short, sharp decisive victories. There are basically two ways of explaining this difference in performance. The first is to compare the professional competence of the respective armies and conclude that the failure of the American military system was due to the absence of skill needed to fight modern war.[37]

The second and more persuasive explanation is that the Prussians created a military system that was so superior to that of its counterparts both in Europe and the United States that it created an asymmetry that made it possible for the Prussians to achieve the strategic goal of decisive victory via the medium of battle. This appears to offer a more persuasive explanation of Prussian success, but how is this success to be explained? On paper at least, Prussia was the weakest of the great European powers, it possessed only a small population, a limited economy and its borders were indefensible. Its problems were compounded by an army that relied heavily on reservists and militia to supplement it in time of war and as a result mobilization was a slow and inefficient process. In an attempt to address these weaknesses, Showalter argues that the Prussians introduced a variety of innovations that were designed to overcome these shortcomings. For example, the Prussians attempted to use technology as a force multiplier. The first and most important of these developments was the introduction of the first breach-loading rifle, the Dreyse needle gun. This rifle was accurate, had a high rate of fire and allowed the soldier to fire and load without having to stand. As such, it represented an important increase in capability.

The Prussians were also forced to take note of developments in firepower on the battlefield following the Crimean War (1853–56) and the war in Northern Italy (1859). The available evidence suggests that their troops did not possess the skills needed to deal with the new weapons being used. Most worrying was the low calibre of the reservists and the *Landwehr*. Of course, in theory there was the option of using force defensively, but Prussia's poor strategic position called for quick offensive action to resolve the challenge that it might have to face and this meant taking the offensive. As a result, in 1859 the Prussians introduced radical changes that had far reaching consequences both within Prussia's political system and beyond. The most important of these developments was the introduction of a three-year term of conscription and an increase in the length of time men served in the reserves and the militia. This not only increased the numbers of troops immediately available in time of war, it also ensured there was sufficient time to train soldiers.

The second important development in the Prussian military system was the use of the telegraph and rail. Two factors drove Moltke's concept of strategic planning and the use of the railways. First, Prussia's need for a short sharp war in which battle was decisive in terms of its effect. Moltke was convinced that a swift decision was most likely to be achieved in the earliest stages of war and that it was best achieved by seizing the initiative. The key problem was that the battlefield itself offered only limited prospects for a quick and decisive resolution. The most obvious solution was to use flank and encircling movements, but these were tactically demanding manoeuvres and were beyond the skill of the ordinary Prussian infantry. In the first instance, the solution was to use the railways to manoeuvre forces strategically.[38]

The railway offered opportunities at the operational and strategic level of war. The first railway to appear in Prussia was in 1832, but their first significant military use came in 1850 when the Prussians tried to mobilize 500,000 men and deploy them by rail. The result was a complete disaster and it was clear that the Prussians lacked any preparation for such a movement of force. In the aftermath of the 1850 fiasco the Prussian General Staff began to develop systems for the large-scale transport of men and supplies by rail. Interestingly, at this stage the rail was still seen as a defensive tool; it was not until Moltke became Chief of Staff that railroads became the central part of an offensive mode of operation. Underlying this was meticulous organization and planning within a newly created department within the General Staff. Mobilization orders now went out by telegraph, reducing notification time from five days to just one.[39] By 1870, the time taken to move an army by rail had been reduced from 30 to 20 days. Such speed ensured that the Prussians achieved a decisive concentration before their French counterparts in the Franco-Prussian War (1870–71).

Thus, by the fourteenth day of the war, the French were supposed to have over 385,000 men at the frontier, but in fact only 200,000 were in place. In contrast, by the eighteenth day of the war the Prussians had over 1 million men ready for battle. These forces were organized in 15 corps. Within six weeks, the Prussians destroyed the best army in Europe. The main reason for this success was good administration and good staff work. The Prussian system of mobilization and the use of the railways gave Moltke an advantage that he never lost.

These technologies accelerated the mobilization, speed of movement and distance covered by armies. They also allowed forces to deploy across a wide front. In 1866, Moltke deployed three separate armies on a front of 190 miles. Napoleon would have marched such an army as a concentrated mass. By the time of the Franco-Prussian War we began to see the emergence of what has been termed 'linear strategy'. This phenomenon reflected the impact of the railway and the opportunities created by the telegraph. Both developments allowed for an increase in the size of armies and a parallel increase in the geographical spread of operations. In addition, the need for greater dispersal to avoid the effect of firepower also reinforced the geographical expansion of the battlefield and operations. As a result of these developments corps and armies advancing on a linear front found that they were engaging in battle simultaneously at different points across the front. Victory in war was no longer dependent upon the concentration of force on a single battlefield. Now military operations took the form of a series of consecutive and mutually related actions across the front. Now strategic goals could only be attained by achieving success in operations as a whole.

mass industrialized warfare 1914–45

The Franco-Prussian War set a new standard in the conduct of war and all the major continental European powers sought to adopt the Prussian model. What this meant in practical terms was that Prussia lost those advantages that ensured success in campaigns fought in the 1860s and 1870s. An added complication was the impact of the unrelenting progression in weapons development, which resulted in further improvements in range, accuracy and rate of fire of artillery and small arms. These trends were to combine to produce the bloody battlefields of the First World War.

At the outbreak of war in August 1914, all the principal belligerents mobilized and deployed multi-million man armies, equipped with modern weapons, and manoeuvred them via the telegraph and the railway. War became literally a rail timetable as each side tried to steal a march against its opponent and get their forces into an advantageous position for the expected great climactic battle. The increasing lethality of war did not induce a sense of restraint and the common feature of all military plans in 1914 was the importance of offensive action, which it was hoped would result in a swift and decisive victory.[40]

Contrary to popular opinion this was not the product of incompetence of the general staff, but rather the fear that modern industrial societies could not withstand the pressures of fighting a protracted war.[41]

Unfortunately the material and political conditions of war made it impossible to realize the goal of a quick and victorious campaign. Mass armies equipped with modern firepower meant that these forces could now cover the entire West European continent and what started as a war of manoeuvre quickly degenerated into stalemate and eventually trench deadlock as each side ran out of space in which to move.[42] In an effort to achieve some respite from the effects of modern firepower and stabilize the front line armies built an elaborate system of fortifications that stretched across the Western and Eastern fronts. These defensive systems were formidable and reinforced the power of the defence. For example, the German defensive system on the Western Front was 400 miles long and between six and ten miles deep. Within this system there were successive belts of barbed wire, trenches, machine gun posts and heavily fortified positions.

As a result, of these innovations both the temporal and physical dimensions of the battlefield changed and the scale of violence unleashed within it was unprecedented. Battle now involved hundreds of thousands of troops attacking across a front of between ten and sometimes as much as 70 miles supported by hundreds, and by the latter stages of the war, thousands of pieces of artillery. Most important was the human cost of these battles, which sometimes must have seemed almost incomprehensible to contemporaries of the war. Thus, in the battle for Verdun (February–November 1916), the French and Germans each suffered over 330,000 casualties.[43] Similarly, in the case of the battle of the Somme (July–November 1916), the Allied forces suffered over 623,000 casualties and the Germans 680,000 killed and wounded.[44]

Technology created a battlefield where the advantage lay clearly with the defence. Thus, entrenchments were largely immune to the effects of a prolonged artillery bombardment and the first waves of an assault, even if successful, were often badly disorganized and depleted after suffering heavy casualties crossing no-mans-land. Although efforts were made to cover the advance of attacking infantry with the provision of a creeping barrage, a curtain of artillery shells placed in front of an advancing force as it marched forward, it proved difficult to coordinate the movement of the artillery's barrage with that of the marching infantry and frequently the infantry were left behind as the barrage swept quickly across no-man's-land. The absence of radio communications made it impossible to call the barrage back and it also made it impossible to call for rapid reinforcement once in the enemy's defences. In the absence of such technology, attacking forces relied on a variety of measures: flags, flares, pigeons and runners. In contrast the defender's telephone lines were usually intact and they were able to summon reserves forward to plug any gaps and call for extensive artillery support to bombard the attacker.

Trench deadlock was eventually broken through the deployment of new technologies in the form of the tank and improvements in existing platforms like aeroplanes. Equally important, wireless communications improved command and control and experience resulted in the creation of new strategies and tactics designed to unravel a trench system. However, of fundamental importance to the neutralization of this system of defence were improvements in artillery and especially the skill of providing indirect fire support to infantry in defence or attack.[45] When these measures were combined with improvements in air power, artillery and the tank, the result was a change in the balance between offence and defence in favour of the former. The Germans clearly demonstrated this in the 'Michael' Offensive of March 1918 and so, too, did the British and French in the summer of 1918. By November 1918 the Allies had driven the Germans from virtually all of occupied France and liberated the Belgian coast.

It was during the inter-war period that the experience of the First World War was assimilated, and new operational concepts emerged that were to shape the character and conduct of battle during the Second World War. The most fertile and productive thinking on this issue recognized that a future major European war would quickly replicate the conditions of the First World War. In fact, it was predicted that the next war would be even more protracted and costly because of continuing improvements in firepower and the creation of new fortifications like the Maginot Line in France.[46]

In spite of this pessimism, new strategies were created to avoid a repeat experience of the First World War. The most famous of these was the emergence of the German concept of 'Blitzkrieg' warfare which achieved stunning success in the first two years of the Second World War. The strength of the German system lay in the fusion of tanks, self-propelled artillery, mechanized infantry, engineers and logistic elements into a combined arms formation in the form of the Panzer division. These formations formed the spearhead of an attack and were heavily supported by the air force. Strategically and operationally German doctrine focused on fixing the enemy across the front before finding a weakness in the line. When such a weakness was found, the Panzer divisions and the Luftwaffe were able to fight through the enemy's defensive system using mobile artillery and air power to suppress the enemy's artillery, engineers to neutralize any defensive barriers and infantry to break into the enemy's first zone of defence. The tanks then worked with air power attacking deeper into the enemy defence. Their function was to harass and delay the arrival of reinforcements until the forward defence collapsed. The Panzers then broke out and linked up with other Panzer attacks which produced tactical encirclements of enemy forces that were then crushed.[47]

This style of operation achieved stunning results against France in 1940 but was to unravel in the Soviet Union. Battle and the conduct of operations within the Soviet Union were conducted on a scale that cannot easily be grasped in today's world. The initial German invasion force against Russia involved over 3.5 million soldiers organized in 190 divisions and led by 3,250 tanks and 2,770 aircraft.[48] The lion's share of this force was committed to a massive battle of annihilation in the region of Belor Russia. The Germans anticipated that the bulk of the Soviet army could be destroyed in the region between the border and the Divina and Dneper rivers and that the Soviet Union would quickly collapse. In contrast, Soviet military thinking operated on the assumption that modern war meant fighting a prolonged total war. As such, the enormous size of modern armies and the ability of states to generate new formations on an unprecedented scale made it impossible for an attacker to defeat a state in a single decisive operation in the way envisaged by the Germans.

In the subsequent clash of these military ideologies it was the Soviet view that proved the most prescient. Thus, although the opening phase of the German assault was very successful the sheer size of the Soviet forces in the region made the rapid collapse of the Soviet Union unlikely. The Soviets deployed over 170 divisions in three successive lines and behind these were approximately 20 mechanized corps. Moreover, unknown to the Germans was the deployment of a reserve of five armies which was located in the vicinity of the Dneper and Divina and stood on the principal German line of advance towards Moscow. Although the Germans were able to destroy these forces, their rate of advance slowed considerably. This gave the Soviet system of mobilization the time needed to generate the forces to repel the attacker and between June and December 1941 the Russians raised 194 new divisions to replace those lost in battle. The Germans thought the Russians would be able to field about 300 divisions, but they actually deployed over 600 divisions in the first six months of the war.[49]

In the first two years of the war on the Eastern Front, the Soviets relied on a strategy that was defensive in nature, trading space for time, stymieing German attacks and then launching localized counter-attacks with overwhelming superiority of force. The frequency and scale of operations was to increase by another order of magnitude as the Soviets went over to the offensive against the Germans in summer 1943. The German reaction to this onslaught was to increase the physical dimensions of the battle zone from about seven miles in depth to 75 miles in depth by the time the Russians entered eastern Europe. However, this proved insufficient to stop the advance of the Red Army. To some extent this was due to the fact that the Soviets enjoyed approximately a 2:1 superiority in manpower and equipment over their German counterparts. However, a more important reason underlying Soviet success was their use of strategic deception and surprise to cause the Germans to misallocate their forces. Through such action the Soviets frequently achieved a local superiority of as much as 40:1 in tanks and equally favourable ratios in manpower and artillery.

Typically a Soviet operation would involve over a million men, up to 5,000 tanks, 30,000 to 40,000 guns and between 4,000 and 5,000 aircraft. The initial attack might be on a front of 190 miles, which was big enough to ensure the enemy could not plug a gap of this size. Once through the defensive zone mobile reserves would then be committed to exploit by as much as 250–310 miles deep behind enemy lines. These mobile forces took the form of tank armies each of which consisted of over 500 tanks. The size of these formations, the fact that there were usually two or three of them involved in the exploitation phase, and that they were supported by tank corps moving ahead and on their flanks, ensured they were able to move deep into the enemy rear and destroy the enemy's ability to reorganize. At the same time, trapped enemy units were encircled and destroyed by combined-arms armies. This mode of operation provided the template for the 'Ten Strategic Victories' in 1944, which drove the Germans out of the Soviet Union and much of eastern Europe, and provided the platform from which they were able to launch their invasion against the German homeland. The legacy of the war on the Eastern Front was to have important consequences for the future of land warfare during the Cold War and inspired not just the Soviets, but also American and British military thought.

warfare in the nuclear age

The detonation of the atomic bomb in 1945 had a profound impact on the evolution of land warfare. In the first instance, it threatened to make war obsolete.[50] Writing in 1946 Brodie commented that, whereas in the past the main purpose of the military establishment was to win wars, with the advent of the atomic age its primary purpose was to avert them. In essence the rationale of force was no longer to fight, but to deter war.[51] However, this new strategic context did not stop the Soviets or Americans trying to devise ways of using nuclear weapons on the battlefield and both states developed nuclear artillery shells, free fall nuclear bombs and missiles that were intended to be used in battle. However, the practical problems of dealing with the effects of nuclear weapons and the fear that their use would cause war to escalate limited the integration of these weapons into a fully functional battle plan. Consequently, the battlefield became a fusion of tried and tested ideas that stemmed from the experience of the Second World War and half-baked notions of how nuclear weapons might be used.

Developments in land warfare did take place, but in the more unorthodox context of low-intensity conflict operations which occurred primarily in the Third World. The clearest illustration of these changes was the American intervention in the Vietnam War. This conflict had an important impact on the conduct of war because the technology used marked the beginning of a military revolution that continues today. Within the context of the Vietnam War new technology served two important functions. First, it acted as a force multiplier, which allowed the USA to limit the numbers of troops committed to operations. Second, technology was also seen as a way of preventing casualties and consequently a great reliance was placed on the generation of systems capable of creating unprecedented levels of mobility and firepower. The most obvious example of this was the development of the helicopter and the doctrine of air mobility. This capability extended an infantry unit's control at least threefold. Its importance in terms of allowing fewer troops to cover more ground can be seen in the battle of the Ia Drang in 1965. The 1st Air Cavalry Division fought on a battlefield which stretched over an area of 1,500 square miles.[52]

Another important innovation was the electronic battlefield. Although its track record was rather patchy, it is interesting that Griffiths compares its development to that of the tank in the First World War. It had great potential – which was clearly demonstrated during the Gulf War – but in Vietnam it suffered from being in its first experimental generation.[53] The first significant evidence of this endeavour was the decision to construct the 'McNamara Line'. This anti-infiltration system was envisioned as a 25-mile long physical barrier to be deployed on the border between North and South Vietnam. This was to consist of electronic sensors that detected movement and even human odours. If any of these were activated then artillery fire and air strikes were initiated in the vicinity of the activated sensor. The great advantage of this system was that it allowed US forces to monitor large areas of the jungle without having to commit troops to provide garrisons. The McNamara line was never constructed. Instead the sensors were used to fulfil two functions; first enhancing tactical security around their garrisons, and second, to assist the American interdiction campaign. Called Igloo White, the programme cost over $3 billion by 1971 and represented an incredibly ambitious project. Sensors were supposed to detect the movement of North Vietnamese forces moving down the Ho Chi Minh Trail; they would then send a signal to a computer based in Thailand and a fighter or fighters would be dispatched to bomb the area in question. The problem with Igloo White was that it proved easy to counter and within a year it was deemed to have failed and was replaced by more conventional methods of interdiction.

Increased mobility and transparency over the battlefield was matched by the emergence of precision guided munitions (PGMs). Of particular importance was the development of air launched guided weapons – designed to destroy armour and other vehicles, enemy radar and missile batteries – and smart bombs. The classic example cited to illustrate the effectiveness of these weapons was the destruction of the Thanh Hoa Bridge. By 1972, 871 sorties had been flown against the bridge, without success. Eleven aircraft had also been lost in these attacks with dumb bombs. In the end, the Americans destroyed the bridge using four laser-guided Paveway bombs.[54]

The impact of these new technologies on the conventional battlefield first became apparent in the Yom Kippur/Ramadan War of 1973, and was demonstrated again in the Israeli invasion of Lebanon in 1982. By this time the development of more powerful information systems and PGMs had reached a point where the Soviets believed that a military technical revolution had taken place.[55] However, it was the First Gulf War in 1991 that signalled a possible paradigm shift in the nature and conduct of land warfare.

the gulf war, 1990–91

The Gulf War was a war of contrasting operational concepts. In the case of the Iraqis they were determined to fight a classic battle of attrition. To this end, their forces were deployed in a linear in-depth defence. Such a plan played to the strengths of the Iraqi military which lay in the sheer size of their forces. After eight years of war with Iran the Iraqi army contained over 1 million troops, 7,000 tanks, and over 12,000 pieces of artillery. The army was organized into 66 divisions which were trained and organized to fight according to the principles of Soviet military doctrine. As such, the Iraqis focused their energies on constructing a powerful defence that extended across the border between Saudi Arabia and Kuwait and contained minefields, barbed wire, strong points and entrenchments. Supporting this were artillery and tanks that were to contain any breakthrough. Deep in the operational depth of the position the Republican Guard acted as the main reserve for any planned counter-attack. Military experts predicted that the liberation of Kuwait through a land war would result in heavy Coalition casualties. Figures ranged from the mildly pessimistic, 20,000–30,000 killed and wounded, to the outright depressing – as many as 100,000 dead. In actual fact, out of force of over 540,000, only 900 soldiers in the Coalition force were killed in the campaign. In contrast, Iraqi military losses were estimated to be over 20,000 killed, 60,000 wounded and 86,000 prisoners of war taken.[56]

This victory was the product of a variety of factors and of key importance was the low quality of much of the Iraqi army. The open terrain also made target acquisition by US sensors and missiles systems relatively easy and this made the aerial destruction of their forces straightforward. That said, it is also clear that the technological capability of the US ground and air forces and the operational concepts devised to exploit this capability resulted in a mode of operation that represented the start of a shift in the conduct of land warfare. The Iraqis expected to engage the Coalition in a classic Second World War battle in which mass armies were deployed along a linear front extending over several hundred miles. Battle, at least initially, would be attritional and it was expected that Iraqi firepower would stop the advance of a Coalition attack. However, the campaign unfolded in a very different way to that anticipated by the Iraqis. Of critical importance to the success of the US campaign was the utilization of space and aerial surveillance systems that generated a clear picture of the battle space.

At the same time, the Americans were able to blind and jam virtually all radars and other sensors being used by the Iraqis to monitor the movement of Coalition forces. The extensive use of precision guided munitions was also of critical importance in destroying Iraqi command, control and communications networks, the extensive air defence system and the physical infrastructure needed to ensure that the Iraqi army remained able to react to any attack. As a result of such actions the Americans were able to neutralize Iraq's impressive air defence system within the first 24 hours of the war and establish complete control over the skies of the theatre of operations which was of critical importance to the land war.

US air power also played a critical role in preparing the enemy for an attack. In the run up to the ground war, air power destroyed over 1,400 Iraqi tanks, 1,100 pieces of artillery and 900 other armoured vehicles. Apparently, the intensity of the air campaign also led to the desertion of over 80,000 Iraqi troops and between 17 January and 24 February 1991 Iraqi forces fell from 336,000 men to 200,000. The systemic organization of the Iraqi army was also seriously disrupted, 70 per cent of the communications infrastructure was destroyed and up to 75 per cent of the electrical power system was put out of action. The flow of supplies into Kuwait was also reduced to only one-tenth what it had been before the air campaign started. It is also believed that air power had a decisive impact on the conduct of the land war. Between 24 and 27 February, Coalition air power destroyed another 450 tanks, 224 armoured vehicles, 353 pieces of artillery and nearly 1,000 trucks. Although the Iraqi army still possessed sufficient force to resist the subsequent ground campaign, even where they demonstrated a will and capability to fight they were overrun and destroyed by US ground forces supported by air power.[57]

To the Soviets, the Gulf War demonstrated that air power combined with powerful surveillance systems and extremely accurate long-range weaponry could bring about the virtual collapse of the enemy's political and economic system. Most important, this outcome could be achieved without becoming embroiled in a prolonged campaign.[58] In their view, Operation Desert Storm served as a paradigm for future military operations. Speaking in 1993, Russian Defence Minister Grachev noted that future wars will begin with an offensive air space operation by both sides. In such a war there will be no front and space will emerge as an independent theatre of operations. Most important was the belief that since strategic objectives could be destroyed through massed aerospace attack, victory would be achieved without the seizure and occupation of territory by ground forces.[59] Subsequent operations in Kosovo in 1999, Afghanistan in 2001 and Iraq in 2003 clearly demonstrate the importance of space and air power. However, it is also clear that both the latent and actual use of land power was of critical importance in achieving a favourable resolution in each of these wars and that in the case of Kosovo and Afghanistan a more robust deployment of land forces might have achieved an even faster and more decisive outcome. What this demonstrates is that land warfare remains as important today as in the time of Machiavelli, but that the configuration and scale of land operations is changing in subtle but important ways. The most important of these changes is that the unrelenting expansion of land warfare, which in the case of Europe began in the lifetime of Machiavelli, and which was an important source of change in the period in question, is now at an end. In the post-modern era, land war is no longer about the generation of mass and attrition, but the production of strategic effect through the application of widely dispersed forces fighting in a non-linear fashion utilizing a wide variety of advanced conventional munitions that are intended to bring about the moral rather than the physical destruction of the enemy's forces.

further reading

For those interested in the history of land warfare it is recommended that they begin by first looking at more general texts on the development of war. Easily accessible sources that focus heavily on land warfare include the following: Lyn Montross, *War Through the Ages* (New York, 1960); J. F. C. Fuller's *A Military History of the Western World* (Jersey City, 1987); John Keegan's *History of Warfare* (New York, 1993); and William McNeill's *The Pursuit of Power: Technology, Armed Force and Society Since AD 1000* (Oxford, 1983). This last study is particularly important because it demonstrates how politics, economics, market structures and technology changed the conduct of war from the Middle Ages to the twentieth century. In addition, it is one of the few books on the development of war that looks beyond the European experience. Charles Townshend's *The Oxford History of Modern War* (Oxford, 2000) also provides a broad survey of the evolution of war from the early modern period to the present and contains essays written by experts in each of the main periods of war.

   The single best survey of land warfare is presented in Hans Delbrück's four-volume study: *The History of the Art of War Within the Framework of Political History* (Westport CT, 1975–82). This massive study covers warfare from the period of antiquity until the end of the Napoleonic Wars. Delbrück demonstrates a mastery of the subject and his analysis of the evolution and conduct of war is unsurpassed. Particularly impressive is his methodology and the extreme effort made to develop a theory of war based on solid and meticulous research. Michael Howard's *War in European History* (Oxford, 2001) is small, but actually provides a superb analysis of the major influences on warfare from the Dark Ages through to the twentieth century and emphasizes the relationship between war and society.

   More limited in scope, but still very useful is Hew Strachan's *European Armies and the Conduct of War* (London, 1983). This provides a concise, but insightful, overview of the chief influences on warfare in Europe from the time of Marlborough until the Second World War. Russell Weigley's study, *The Age of Battles: The Quest for Decisive Warfare from Breitenfeld to Waterloo* (Bloomington IL, 1991) demonstrates that advances in tactics, organization and the size of armies resulted in battles that were less decisive and more attritional in character. Shimon Naveh's *In Pursuit of Military Excellence* (London, 1997) marks an important contribution to the study of land warfare. The book addresses two important questions: why did the operational level of war emerge and why did it take so long for military commanders in the nineteenth and twentieth centuries to recognize this change and act upon it in terms of developing new tactical and operational doctrine.

   Texts covering specific periods of warfare are numerous. Philip Contamine's *War in the Middle Ages* (New York, 1984) provides one of the best overviews of warfare from the collapse of the Western Roman Empire in the fifth century to the formation of permanent armies at the end of the fifteenth century. Contamine demonstrates that, contrary to popular opinion, warfare in this period was marked by innovation in the use of intelligent strategies and considerable skill on the battlefield. Another useful source on this period is Sir Charles Oman's *The Art of War in the Middle Ages, A.D. 378–1515* (Ithaca NY, 1953). Although some of his views are now dated he still provides some interesting insights on warfare in this period.

Geoffrey Parker's *The Military Revolution: Military Innovation and the Rise of the West* (Cambridge, 2003) provides an interesting examination of warfare in the early modern period of the fifteenth, sixteenth and seventeenth centuries. David Chandler's *The Art of War in the Age of Marlborough* (New York, 1976) provides a granular picture of the military organization, training and tactics used by late seventeenth-century and early eighteenth-century European armies. Christopher Duffy's *The Military Life of Frederick the Great* (New York, 1986) and *The Army of Maria Theresa: The Armed Forces of Imperial Austria, 1740–1780* (New York, 1977) provides a complete history of the warfare during the Seven Years' War in the mid eighteenth century.

Charles Esdaile's *The Wars of Napoleon* (London, 1995) provides an interesting interpretation of the factors that determined the success of the French military system and the reasons for its demise. For a more orthodox view of the Napoleonic Wars see David Chandler's *Campaigns of Napoleon* (London, 1967). For those interested in the American Civil War, two studies stand out and in fact complement each other. The first is Herman Hattaway and Archer Jones's, *How the North Won: A Military History of the Civil War* (Urbana IL, 1983). This study provides a strategic analysis of the war and focuses on logistics, communications, command and control and tactics. In addition, the study also contains an appendix on how to study military operations. The second of these books is Richard Berlinger et al. (eds), *Why the South Lost the Civil War* (Athens GA, 1986). The authors question the most frequently cited reasons for Southern defeat and conclude that the fundamental problem was the weakness of nationalism within the Confederacy.

Moving on to the First World War Richard Prior and Trevor Wilson's *Command on the Western Front* (Barnsley, 2004) and Paddy Griffith's *Battle Tactics on the Western Front* (New Haven CT, 1994) provide a revisionist interpretation of the military history of the First World War and shows how armies became increasingly skilled in fighting a modern industrialized war. If interested in the Second World War, Ned Wilmot's *The Great Crusade* (London, 1989) and Gerhard Weinberg's *A World at Arms: A Global History of World War II* (Cambridge, 1994) provide good single-volume histories of this conflict. Wilmot's study is packed with fascinating facts, details and insights on strategy, operations and tactics in all the main theatres of operation. Weinberg's study is based on access to more recent documentation research to produce a fascinating narrative of German and Allied strategy and operations during this conflict.

In terms of conventional wars since 1945, the single best source covering the Arab–Israeli Wars from 1948 until 1973 is A. Bregman's *Israel's Wars* (London, 2000). Phillip Davidson's *Vietnam at War: The History, 1946–75* (London, 1988) presents a complete military history of the conflict and questions why first the French and then subsequently the United States failed to defeat the Vietnamese. For those interested in the First Gulf War see Michael Gordon and Bernard Trainor's *The Generals War: The Inside Story of the Conflict in the Gulf* (Boston, 1995). Gordon and Trainor provide a detailed inside story of the planning and execution of the campaign. A detailed operational and tactical history of the Gulf War is provided by Brigadier General Robert Scales in *Certain Victory: The US Army in the Gulf* (London, 1994). Also recommended is the Lessons of Modern War series by A. Cordesman and H. Wagner. This multi-volume study covers the 1973 Arab–Israeli War, the Falklands Conflict, the Iran–Iraq War and the First Gulf War.

notes

1. See A. Ferrill, *The Origins of War: From the Stone Age to Alexander the Great* (London, 1986).
2. C. Townshend, *The Oxford History of Modern War* (Oxford, 2000), p. 3.
3. See J. F. C. Fuller, *The Conduct of Modern War* (London, 1972).
4. See M. van Creveld, *The Transformation of War* (New York, 1991); M. Kaldor, *New and Old Wars: Organised Violence in the Global Era* (Cambridge, 1999); C. Hables Gray, *Postmodern War: The New Politics of Conflict* (London, 1997); S. Woodward, 'Failed States: Warlordism and Tribal Warfare', *Naval War College Review* 52/2 (Spring 1999): 55–68; and Mark Duffield, 'Post-Modern Conflict: Warlords Post-Adjustment States and Private Protection', *Journal of Civil Wars* 1/1 (Spring 1998).
5. See P. Contamine, *War in the Middle Ages* (Oxford, 1999) and Sir Charles Oman, *A History of the Art of War in the Middle Ages. Volume II* (London, 1924).
6. C. J. Rogers, 'The Military Revolutions of the Hundred Years' War', *Journal of Military History* 57/2 (April 1993): 241–78.
7. Michael Roberts, 'The Military Revolution, 1560–1660' in Clifford J. Rogers (ed.), *The Military Revolution Debate: Readings on the Military Transformation of Early Modern Europe* (Oxford, 1995), p. 77.
8. N. Machiavelli, *The Art of War* (Cambridge MA, 1956), p. xxxviii.
9. See A. Gat, *A History of Military Thought: From the Enlightenment to the Cold War* (Oxford, 2001), p. 8.
10. G. Parker, *The Military Revolution: Military Innovation and the Rise of the West 1500–1800* (Cambridge, 1988), pp. 6–44.
11. Rogers, 'Military Revolutions', pp. 268–9.
12. R. Bean, 'War and the Birth of the Nation State', *Journal of Economic History* 32/1 (March 1973): 203–21.
13. Ibid.
14. Ibid., p. 207.
15. Parker, *The Military Revolution*, p. 10.
16. J. A. Lynn, 'The *trace italienne* and the Growth of Armies' in Rogers (ed.), *The Military Revolution Debate*, p. 176.
17. Parker, *The Military Revolution*, p. 24.
18. Rogers (ed.), *The Military Revolution Debate*, p. 14.
19. Parker, *The Military Revolution*, p. 154.
20. Ibid., p. 20.
21. In Rogers (ed.), *The Military Revolution Debate*, p. 15.
22. Ibid., p. 19.
23. Ibid., p. 17.
24. See J. Black, *European Warfare: 1600–1815* (London, 1994).
25. See H. Strachan, *European Armies and the Conduct of War* (London, 1983), pp. 8–22, and C. Duffy, *The Military Experience in the Age of Reason* (Ware, 1998), pp. 151–89.
26. Strachan, *European Armies*, p. 20.
27. H. Smith, *On Clausewitz: A Study of Political and Military Ideas* (Basingstoke, 2005), p. 29.
28. R. M. Epstein, 'Patterns of Change and Continuity in Nineteenth-Century Warfare', *Journal of Military History* 56/3 (1992): 375–88, 377.
29. Ibid., 379.
30. Ibid., 381.

31. Ibid., 382.
32. Ibid., 383–5.
33. Ibid., 385.
34. C. von Clausewitz, *On War* (trans. and ed. Michael Howard and Peter Paret) (Princeton NJ, 1976), p. 610.
35. E. Hagerman, *The American Civil War and the Origins of Modern Warfare: Ideas, Organisation, and Field Command* (Indianapolis IN, 1988), pp. x–xiii.
36. See G. W. Gallagher (ed.), *The Fredericksburg Campaign: Decision on the Rappahannock* (London, 1995).
37. See P. Griffith, *Battle Tactics of the American Civil War* (Marlborough, 1999).
38. See D. E. Showalter, 'The Prusso-German RMA, 1840–1871' in M. Knox and W. Murray (eds), *The Dynamics of Military Revolution, 1300–2050* (Cambridge, 2001), pp. 101–8.
39. Ibid., p. 103.
40. See J. Snyder, *The Ideology of the Offensive: Military Decision-Making and the Disasters of 1914* (London, 1989).
41. Strachan, *European Armies*, pp. 108–29.
42. P. Griffith, *Battle Tactics of the Western Front: The British Army's Art of Attack 1916–18* (London, 1994).
43. A. Horne, *The Price of Glory: Verdun 1916* (London, 1962).
44. Gary Sheffield, *The Somme* (London, 2003), p. 151.
45. J. Bailey, 'Deep Battle 1914–41: The Birth of the Modern Style of Warfare and the Century of Firepower', *British Army Review* 120 (December 1998): 3–18.
46. V. K. Triandafillov, *The Nature of Operations of Modern Armies* (London, 1994).
47. H. Guderian, *Achtung Panzer: The Development of Armoured Forces, Their Tactics and Operational Potential* (London, 1992).
48. H. P. Wilmott, *The Great Crusade: A New Complete History of the Second World War* (London, 1992), pp. 133–46.
49. D. Glantz, *When Titans Clashed: How the Red Army Stopped Hitler* (Lawrence KA, 1995), pp. 63–7.
50. B. Brodie, *The Absolute Weapon: Atomic Power and World Order* (New York, 1946), p. 25.
51. Ibid., p. 76.
52. John Hay, *Tactical and Material Innovations in Vietnam* (Washington DC, 1973), pp. 6–11.
53. P. Griffiths, *Forward into Battle: Fighting Tactics from Waterloo to Vietnam* (Chichester, 1981), p. 111.
54. J. Dunnigan, *Digital Soldiers: The Evolution of High Tech Weaponry and Tomorrow's Brave New Battlefield* (New York, 1996), p. 129.
55. M. Fitzgerald, *The New Revolution in Military Affairs* (London, 1994), p. 1.
56. A. H. Cordesman and A. R. Wagner, *Lessons in Modern War Volume IV: The Gulf War* (Oxford, 1996), p. 650.
57. Ibid., ch. 7.
58. Fitzgerald, *The New Revolution*, pp. 12–18.
59. C. Bellamy, *Expert Witness: A Defence Correspondent's Gulf War* (London, 1993) p. 232.

6
low-intensity conflict, insurgency, terrorism and revolutionary war

john p. cann

Low-intensity conflict, insurgency, guerrilla and revolutionary war are terms used to describe the limited politico-military struggle of an aggrieved group against recognized authority with the aim of achieving certain political, social, economic or psychological objectives. It is a conflict in which one or more parties are prepared to limit their political will and resources, and it falls in intensity between peacetime competition and conventional war. Such conflicts are generally protracted affairs and require inglorious, patient day-to-day work on both sides. They are usually confined to the Third World, and are characterized by constraints on weaponry, tactics and violence. This form of conflict dominates the modern spectrum in that while there have been few conventional wars in the recent past, there have been numerous unconventional or irregular wars.

Over the years, campaigns against irregular opponents have been termed small wars, colonial warfare, guerrilla war, imperial policing, revolutionary warfare, wars of the third kind, low-intensity conflict, counterinsurgency, peacekeeping, and the awkward term 'MOOTW' or military operations other than war. In the future such wars may be termed 'complex contingency operations' or revert to 'small wars'. Names change because these wars are not considered 'real wars' to conventionally minded military professionals, however lethal they may be. Never quite dignified as 'real fighting', especially by military historians and theorists, who prefer to talk about organized wars between formed armies, the genre remains a controversial topic. This controversy is fanned by the fact that the combatants involved have seldom been recognized as lawful. Writers have described them as bandits, criminals, terrorists, and the like, whether they are the aggrieved group or the recognized authority.

It is for this reason that the topic is so important and yet the genre remains so mysterious. Its development can be divided into two phases, that of the initial theorist-practitioners of the colonial period and that of the analysts of the post-Second World War era. This chapter will offer insight into the modern development of 'small wars' from both perspectives and provide an appreciation of its complexity and solutions.

the first theorists-practitioners

By the late nineteenth century irregular warfare was the norm for the European powers as well as the United States. The last three decades of the century saw the European empires expand rapidly into the non-Western world. There European armies, or locally recruited European-led armies, regularly confronted hostile tribesmen, bandits, peasant uprisings, and sometimes proto-nationalist movements, such as the Taiping rebels or the 'Boxers' of China. With the exception of the South African (or Boer) War (1899–1902), in which the British fought the Dutch settlers of South Africa, colonial warfare generally pitted Europeans against non-Europeans. With rare exceptions, the Europeans handily triumphed over their adversaries. The classic theoretical work to encapsulate the lessons of this warfare is Charles E. Callwell's *Small Wars*, first published in 1896 and reprinted several times during the author's lifetime (1859–1928).[1] Since then, it has seldom been out of print. Callwell was widely read in a variety of late nineteenth-century conflicts ranging from India, Afghanistan and Burma to North America, South Africa, North Africa, and Southeast Asia, and distilled a number of lessons, both strategic and tactical.

Callwell defines 'small wars' as any military campaign in which organized armies are fighting forces that are not organized along European army lines. Today we would update Callwell to say that the term small wars refers to 'illegal combatants', warriors organized as militias, or some form of combatants who operate outside the conventions of lawful warfare, as traditionally defined by Hugo Grotius in his 1625 *Law of War and Peace*.[2]

Callwell offers several thoughts on his colonial wars that continue to be useful. He constantly warns against 'exasperating' the civilian population through pointless destruction of crops, herds, housing, and the like. He observes, as every other writer on the topic has done subsequently, that armies operating in this kind of warfare rely on the goodwill, or at least not the open animosity, of the host population.[3] Current operations in Iraq following the 2003 invasion are a case in point, although this observation would hold true for any number of similar circumstances.

Callwell's views abound in Victorian attitudes towards non-Western peoples. Although we may smile at his talk of 'uncivilized peoples' or 'lower races', his attitudes appear throughout his writings on this kind of warfare. Events in Iraq have abundantly demonstrated the problems with such a view and the mischief that it spawns. Probably the most important leadership challenge that organized armies face today in irregular warfare is keeping such attitudes in check and thereby avoiding episodes that will discredit the effort and worsen the problems faced by troops in the field.[4]

Finally, Callwell recognizes that logistics and intelligence are central to irregular warfare. Every case study that he cites turns on the ability or inability of the military to develop intelligence, often too late, and to maintain supply lines in the face of hostile climate, terrain and population.[5]

Armies fighting in unfamiliar theatres can get into serious trouble by underestimating supply requirements, the effects of disease, and the nature of their opponents. It is exceedingly difficult to estimate the strength of the opposition, especially when neighbouring tribes or clans may or may not join the fighting. A central issue is that irregular opponents lack the same requirements as organized armies and thus act independently of normal military procedures. Armies accustomed to fighting other organized armies experience great difficulties when confronting 'savages', as Callwell puts it. The indigenous population knows the countryside well and is surprisingly observant of an army's movements, vulnerabilities, and methods of fighting. By contrast, an army has great difficulty finding indigenous peoples who will give honest information. A further hindrance is that army intelligence officers often cannot operate safely in pursuing local intelligence.

Human intelligence, or HUMINT, was crucial in the primitive environments of Callwell's time and remains so today in places where there are few paved roads or telephones. Modern forces typically will have comparatively few personnel fluent in the local language. Their sophisticated modern intelligence collection methods are only moderately useful. Thus the language barrier and the time needed to establish a reliable and useful HUMINT network make intelligence collection extremely difficult, particularly in this type of conflict in which intelligence drives successful offences.

The difficulties of supply in the Third World are enormous and have scarcely changed in the past century. Just as the transportation options available to modern armies have grown more sophisticated, so has the infrastructure of the Third World. However, relative to North America and Europe, the typical Third World setting has poor or non-existent roads, little available transportation, poorly developed ports and railways, limited airports, sparse petroleum-oil-lubricants stores, and a limited number of mechanics and spare parts. Nearly everything will have to be brought to the scene of the campaign, just as it was in Callwell's day. When US marines, for instance, went to Somalia in 1991, for them it was like going to the moon.[6] Everything that they needed had to be carried with them. In many cases local Third World infrastructure today is worse than it was 50 years ago when the Europeans began to abandon their empires.

Callwell further observes that non-European peoples are easily overawed by regular armies. As he puts it, 'The lower races are impressionable.'[7] Operational and tactical delays are thus a bad idea, and given a choice, a commander should always assume the offensive. This advice, of course, is based on the assumption that he has accurate intelligence and secure lines of supply. Adversaries under these conditions tend to increase or shrink according to the perceived might and dangerousness of the army. Military vigour and success bring waverers to the army's side. Passivity, by contrast, encourages doubtful tribes or clans to join the rebels. Successes need to be pressed to advantage, as unorganized opponents lack the ability to reconstitute themselves.

Callwell correctly points out that the ultimate object of all campaigns is to secure a lasting peace. Although the destruction of crops and villages and the taking of livestock might be necessary to deal with certain kinds of guerrillas or to reprovision one's own forces, such activities had to be minimized. He cautions explicitly against 'exasperating' the rebels lest they become embittered. All this said, Callwell certainly says nothing about rebuilding societies. While he is wise and humble enough to avoid laying down anything hard and fast, he does emphasize that warriors understand battle far better than the destruction of their livelihoods. As we shall see, the French *tâche d'huile* or oil spot method stands in marked contrast to Callwell's 'big gun' approach with its destruction and intimidation.

As one French colonial expert put it, 'While the British Empire was being built by businessmen wanting to make money, the French Empire was built by bored officers looking for excitement.'[8] Francophone acquisitions began with the conquest of Algiers in 1830 and ended with the final pacification of Morocco in 1934. Throughout these campaigns money was an issue in that Paris was never excited about funding expeditions into some unknown land for adventurous colonial officers. The 'real' army in the *métropole* always drew the bulk of any funds distributed. The aim, therefore, of French colonial warfare was not the destruction of the enemy, but his organization and the integration of his territory into the 'imperial' whole both economically and politically. Thus, the most important goal was not necessarily the decisive defeat of the enemy, as in the Callwellian manner, but to subordinate him at the lowest cost and in a way that would guarantee permanent pacification. This philosophy meant that destruction of the people and their territory must be avoided for two reasons. First, the French expedition needed local supplies because of Parisian parsimony, and operations that precluded foraging were too expensive and thus counterproductive. Second, a destroyed land without the means to contribute to the empire would also likely become a burden with a starving and disaffected population needing support and reconstruction and perhaps further pacification. The methods for expanding the French Empire, which began in 1830, were developed by three great men: Marshals Thomas

Bugeaud (1784–1849), Joseph Galliéni (1849–1916) and the most brilliant, Hubert Lyautey (1854–1934).[9] Their thinking was linked together, and the impact on their pupils, enormous. It did not, however, come together easily, as there was much 'learning while doing'.

The French initially operated in the classic Napoleonic style of mass manoeuvre, sending heavy columns with artillery deep into the remote Algerian countryside or *bled*. This did not work, as it played into the strength of an enemy who was comfortable in harsh terrain and used mobility to defend itself and limit its opponent. This desert foe would regularly surprise the French and would wreak havoc on their exposed and vulnerable columns. In 1840, Bugeaud was appointed governor-general and commander-in-chief and in his six years in this post extended French rule over most of the country using quite different methods.

Bugeaud immediately recognized that the primary advantage of his enemy was its light and fast fighting units and their consequent mobility. He thus abandoned the series of isolated fixed forts and the French defensive posture and copied his foe. He made French units equally as light and mobile and threw fear into enemy hearts by appearing unexpectedly when his foe was unprepared and vulnerable. His army gained confidence, and the war of pacification became one of movement. With their strong suit trumped, tribe after tribe submitted to French rule. Bugeaud solidified his position by building a network of mutually supporting blockhouses commanding his lines of communication and serving as warehouses and bases for continued operations over yet recalcitrant tribes. When Bugeaud began to penetrate the mountainous area of Algeria, his light forces again encountered problems and found that the mobility enjoyed in the open country was no longer available. To counter this difficulty he used several mutually supporting columns to reduce the enemy in his stronghold. In order to prevent enemy reconstitution, he sought to break his will and did this by disrupting not only his armies but also his economy. As much as possible, Bugeaud used surprise to weaken the enemy's resistance, and his newly deployed, light, and mobile columns with practice and good intelligence were able to appear in the mountains where and when they were unexpected.[10]

Another of his techniques was to create internal dissention within the tribal ranks and thereby weaken his enemy. He played on the antagonisms between the various enemy factions much as, for instance, the Portuguese did in their later colonial wars of 1961 to 1974. In the case of the nationalist movements in the Portuguese colonies, dissention was so great that the Portuguese intelligence service was able to exploit the fissures and persuade disaffected elements in Mozambique to assassinate their leader Eduardo Mondlane in February 1969, and in the case of Guinea-Bissau, their leader Amílcar Cabral in January 1973.[11] This was particularly effective in the midst of military failure when the factions were blaming each other for their reverses. Bugeaud thus set in motion the break with Napoleonic teaching. His successful methods needed to be adapted to modern armies and to widely expanded theatres, and this new school found its leader in Galliéni, a purely colonial officer.

Galliéni may be best known for his role in the Battle of the Marne in 1914 and for his inspired fighting as a junior officer in the Franco-Prussian War; however, his real career was that of empire builder.[12] He served in a number of assignments in French West Africa, Réunion and the Caribbean before being assigned to Tonkin in Indochina as a colonel in 1892. In his brief four-year stay there, he achieved amazing results in pacification and development work. Galliéni saw the army's task as one of improving the existing conditions of local life and civilization through education, construction of infrastructure, medical support, and the like. He worked to create conditions of enduring peace and prosperity, to avoid bloodshed, and to align such progress with France and thereby increase the prestige of the mother country.[13]

Galliéni's companion in Tonkin was a young officer serving a sort of exile to the colonial army for his controversial views on the role of the army, and particularly its officers, in the education and intellectual development of French youth, almost all of whom spent a few years in military service. This man was Lyautey, who was 40 at the time and potentially faced a ruined career. Galliéni and Lyautey were fortuitously of like mind, and after their tour in Tonkin together, were assigned to Madagascar, the Great Island of the Indian Ocean. It was here that the new General Galliéni and his chief of staff Lyautey would apply the new and developing French concept of colonization.

One of the guiding principles in this concept was the notion of the 'right man for the job', whether he be military or civilian. There was great competition between the military and civilian arms of the colonial government as to which should take the lead. Galliéni and Lyautey believed that it did not matter, as each colonial pioneer must organize his own security and the security of the land around him through not only military means but also economic and social initiatives. This meant that the armed forces would now seek to replace the column with progressive occupation, a regularly progressing tide of well-organized administration. The need for troops, of course, would not disappear, as initial and continuing operations would be necessary to gain and maintain control, but military means alone were no longer seen as the way ahead, and thus military men no longer had a higher claim to the colonial portfolio. Instead, military operations would be seen as an organizing effort behind the actively advancing front. A French network would be imposed by personnel trained and thoroughly prepared in civil administration skills and would secure the occupied territory and the lines of communication of the advancing front. The counter-argument was that hostile forces would be pushed ahead of the advance, never fully annihilated, and thus always pose a problem. Lyautey argued that the establishment of a functioning society with its markets, roads and encircling protective belt would isolate the troublemakers and eventually they too would be transformed into useful citizens or be banished to the sparse countryside.[14]

In Madagascar, it developed that political action was as much a factor of progress as force. The population was treated with consideration as a policy, for its support was required in imposing French rule and in developing the colony. Any required force against a village was immediately followed by its reconstitution, the creation of a market, the establishment of a school, and the obvious help needed to return its population to a functioning society. Galliéni and Lyautey obtained amazing results in Madagascar with this process of progressive occupation and organization despite the fact that it was the only real means at their disposal with their small force.[15] In the classic words of Sun Tzu, these two subdued the enemy without fighting.[16]

France undertook its final colonial conquest in Morocco, the only one in the twentieth century. Here Lyautey applied the theory developed under Galliéni in Indochina and Madagascar on a grand scale with dramatic results. The interest in Morocco developed because it was being used as a sanctuary by Algerian rebels, so in October 1903 Lyautey was sent there as a newly appointed brigadier general to apply the new doctrine of pacific occupation. His primary conflict was with his superiors in the North African army who disapproved of his and Galliéni's methods. Lyautey overcame this obstacle by developing a direct reporting arrangement with the governor-general in Algiers. Next he established a political link in a loyal alliance with the sultan's government and took no action without its approval and support. This was the basis for the special protectorate status within the French Empire. Finally, he acknowledged that this system of protection would be accomplished gradually and that no date for its realization could be set. Lyautey did not envision advancing by columns or great victories, but rather as a metaphoric patch of oil. He would progress slowly and play local conditions to his advantage. Over the next seven years he brought peace and prosperity to the occupied regions and contributed to the progressive reshaping of the North African army. He departed from Morocco in 1910 as a lieutenant general, and his oil spot or *tâche d'huile* method would, as a result of his success there, take its place in history as a proven method of pacifying a population and of bringing security and relative prosperity to it.

Unfortunately after Lyautey's departure the situation in Morocco deteriorated into complete revolt, and in 1912 he was ordered to resume command there. Lyautey remained in Morocco on and off until 1925 and during that period unified and developed the country into what was reputed to be the 'masterpiece of French colonisation'.[17] Lyautey and the regime that he conceived, organized and administered was immensely popular, so much so that for much of the twentieth century the city of Kenitra on the Atlantic was named Port Lyautey. Elevated to the rank of marshal, Lyautey continued to expound his ideas for another nine years until his death.

The last of the pre-war theorist practitioners to be considered here is Mao Zedong. Mao's writings on warfare emerged amidst a three-way struggle for power in China that dominated the first half of the twentieth century. From the collapse of the Manchu dynasty in 1912 until the Japanese invasion of 1937, China was wracked by intermittent civil war. In the early years of the Chinese Communist Party, Mao sought simply to survive and in doing so developed his notions of revolutionary war. Later under the pressure of Japanese aggression, the Guomindang (GMD) or Nationalist Party and the Communist Party sometimes fought beside each other, but just as often disdained the common cause and fought each other while ignoring the Japanese. Both planned ahead for the acquisition of political power over all of China in a post-war world. Thus, with both parties having been well armed by their allies to fight the Japanese between 1937 and 1945, the Chinese Civil War was ultimately fought as a conventional struggle between 1945 and 1949 and bore little resemblance to Mao's 'guerrilla war'.[18]

The ground that would nurture Mao's theory can be traced to the people's operations in Spain between 1808 and 1813. The Spanish population that was forced to supply Napoleon's invading army was composed of patriots loyal to their ruler whose crown had been usurped by the French. They were not revolutionists and did not desire a change of government. Their objectives were simply to survive in the face of a marauding army foraging in an area of subsistence agriculture, and later to help Wellington force the French armies from Spain.[19]

Again, insurgents contributed to Napoleon's sound defeat in his 1812 invasion of Russia, where thousands of Cossacks and peasants harried his *Grande Armée* on its retreat from Moscow over the frozen countryside in a bitterly cold winter. He had crossed the Niémen River in June with 422,000 men and reached Moscow in September with his numbers reduced to 100,000. During his retreat, the army was further reduced not only by the weather but also by the force of a people's war that was waged without rules or fine distinctions until the surviving 10,000 men re-crossed the Niémen in December. In neither the Spanish nor the Russian case was the population that wielded the cudgel composed of revolutionists. They were simply patriots. Such warfare would have to wait for the arrival of later revolutionaries, such as V. I. Lenin, to give it the potent political injection that would radically alter its character. It would remain for Mao, however, to produce the first systematic study of the subject and to lead the most radical revolution in history.

After graduating from normal school in 1917, Mao accepted a job at Peking (Beijing) University library, where he associated with Marxist study groups and discovered the writings of Lenin, Trotsky, Marx and Engels.[20] By 1920, he was a convinced communist and had begun his mission to create a new China based on what he had learned over the last three years. China at the time was a chaotic assembly of 400 million peasants, all struggling to survive in the face of natural and man-made adversity. In 1926, Mao went to Hunan to wage a campaign for land reform in what was then a semi-colonial and feudal society. He immediately clashed with the GMD, which backed the landed gentry who had historically been seen as the stabilizing element in Chinese society. Mao was viewed as a political troublemaker, and by March 1927 his honeymoon period was over. He fled south with other political dissidents into a rugged mountain area in the Fujian-Jiangxi borderlands and in April 1928 began to mould an army. Over the next two years, Mao and his associates would reach the conclusion that their organization must be based on the rural peasant and not on the traditional industrial proletariat of Marxist dogma. This decision led to a break with Moscow and remains the source of the Chinese challenge to Kremlin infallibility on Communist doctrine. In 1930 the GMD began its campaign against the new armies of the Chinese Communist Party, and in 1933 Mao and his followers were forced to flee on their now celebrated 6,000-mile Long March to shelter in the caves of Pao An in western Shaanxi province, situated on the north bank of the Wei River.

During this trip and in its aftermath, Mao refined his theory of warfare. Mao believed that his agrarian-based revolutionary war would pass through a series of merging phases: firstly, organization, consolidation and preservation; secondly, progressive expansion; and thirdly, decision, or destruction of the enemy. The initial phase was to be devoted to establishing a regional base area that should be situated in isolated and difficult terrain. This remoteness was necessary to keep the activity of recruiting and indoctrinating volunteers and turning them into effective agitators and propagandists sufficiently private from the government's prying eyes. These trained volunteers would be formed into groups or sent singly to proselytize in the surrounding countryside and enlist support. This process would operate much like Lyautey's *tâche d'huile* in that the base area would be surrounded by an expanding protective belt. Samuel B. Griffith describes this process as 'conspiratorial, clandestine, methodical, and progressive'.[21] Military operations would not play a significant role in this phase. One of the primary objectives, however, would be to generate as much support as possible by persuasively recruiting a significant portion of the population to develop a 'mass'. Further, the infrastructure of intelligence networks, tax collectors, kidnappers and assassination squads would be formed with the job of protecting the revolution.[22]

The second phase, on the other hand, would emphasize direct action, and this element would confront and openly challenge accepted government authority. Acts of sabotage and terrorism would become commonplace, and vulnerable opponents, such as tribal chiefs, local government officials or unsuspecting and under-strength military units, would be liquidated. Soft, isolated targets with little risk were logical favourites. The primary purpose of this activity would be to acquire important supplies of war material and to throw the government off balance. As revolutionary forces became better equipped and gained experience, their capabilities would improve. The threat to government forces and consequent insurgent credibility would increase, and the insurgents would progressively secure and expand their 'liberated areas' with increasingly battle-hardened troops.[23]

The third phase was to be characterized by negotiation with the government to gain time. These would not be good faith negotiations in that revolutions rarely compromise, but would rather be designed to frustrate, reduce and harass the government. Meanwhile, insurgent forces would complete their transformation into an orthodox army capable of successfully engaging government forces in conventional war. This substantially strengthened force and the attritional negotiations were designed to give the insurgents a 'victorious situation'.[24]

In Mao's vision intelligence would always drive both insurgent and counterinsurgent operations. Successful insurgent intelligence networks were to be tightly organized and all-pervasive. Every individual would be considered an intelligence agent. Local insurgent cadres were to pressure everyone under their sway to produce every conceivable piece of information. Their methods were rarely pretty but always effective. Conversely, the insurgents would work to deny the government any useful information on themselves and be effective in this process through intimidation. Any individual found cooperating with the government would be virtually assured of being tortured to death.

The insurgents generally engaged their enemy under favourable circumstances because of their superior intelligence, knowledge of local conditions, and military inferiority. If events took a bad turn, then they simply withdrew. Their attacks were 'hit and run' in nature and aimed more at targeting the will of government leaders than in inflicting large numbers of casualties. Their primary motivation was one of self-preservation, and with this they were able to preserve the momentum of the revolution. It would generally be suicidal for them to attempt direct confrontation with the enemy in any conventional setting. Mao once remarked slightly facetiously that guerrillas were experts at running away because they did it so often.[25]

While Mao used his theory first to survive and later to combat the Japanese invaders, his struggle became progressively conventional. As in similar circumstances observed by Callwell's waverers, the Chinese peasants increasingly aligned themselves with Mao, the perceived winner. Entire GMD units defected to the Communists with their US-supplied equipment. These defectors numbered in the tens of thousands and brought with them jeeps, tanks, artillery, radios and small arms. This experience caused Mao to observe that he had a claim on the arsenals of London as well as Hanyang.[26] Moreover, the arms were to be delivered by the enemy's own transport corps. This is the sober truth, not a joke.[27] These surrendered weapons later appeared in Indochina and Korea.

The lasting impact of the Chinese Communist victory in 1949, although important, has not been as great as Mao's acolytes had anticipated. Mao's methods of war, however, were implemented to one degree or another and with varying degrees of success in countries as diverse as Malaya, Algeria, Vietnam, Angola and Peru, for he had established a potentially successful system for rural peasant revolt. While it is usual for social scientists to stress the differences between such nations and the particular character of each of their wars, the basis of these conflicts is Maoist theory, and one cannot understand the methods of the various revolutionary groups without understanding Mao. While Vo Nguyen Giap, Che Guevara, and others have added their refinements, all is essentially a derivative of the original scholar.[28]

post-war developments

Mao's campaign to capture state power in China has long served as the model for revolutionary warfare. Indeed the vast scope of the Chinese Civil War (1927–49) dwarfs possible rivals and remains the inspiration for would-be revolutionaries. Mao's formula is a technique for deliberate action, a means to an end. That end is the seizure of political power with the avowed purpose of overthrowing the existing regime and installing the Party as the governing power.[29] This is a ruling party that cannot and will not tolerate competitors. It does not intend to be an alternative form of democratic governance. In fact, as we shall see, democracy offers the only realistic counter to the Maoist approach.

In contrast to the post-war period revolutionaries, much work has been devoted to developing an antidote to Mao. The suffering and destruction of revolutionary war can be as great or greater than that of conventional war and, equally, contributes nothing to human well-being. In virtually all cases in which a government has been overthrown, a bitter legacy remains, and all prospects for any peaceful political and economic advancement are either delayed or halted. The atrocities perpetrated on the population continue long after hostilities have formally ended, and the damage is incalculable. Cambodia, for instance, lost about 1.7 million people or 21 per cent of its population to Pol Pot and his Khmer Rouge regime, and the population, both refugee and internal, remains traumatized long after the genocide tragedy.[30] China has taken 50 years to begin even its economic development and in the interim has left a legacy of mass murders and executions rivalling those of the Soviet Union. The countries of austral Africa, which followed the Maoist insurrectionary model, particularly Angola, Mozambique, Guinea-Bissau and most of West Africa, have regressed amid civil wars and uncountable deaths. Vietnam after 30 years remains on the Chinese road in its glacial progress. In every case, the true intention of the insurgency, regardless of the faux-idealistic anti-colonialist or nationalist banner, was to decide succession by force in favour of a ruthless minority intent on implementing a utopian ideology. On the surface, the utopian notion sounds remarkably attractive, particularly to peasants who have been marginalized and have little to lose. The insurgents, after all, can develop their political momentum exclusively on promises, while the government is under pressure to deliver on those promises. In truth, however, no matter how authoritarian or oppressive a government may be, it is a false assumption that successful insurgents will be any better, even when their ostensible aim is to overthrow colonialism.[31] They can and have been defeated, but there are more naysayers than positive advocates for counterinsurgency.

Robert Taber argues in his work *War of the Flea* that an insurgency cannot be overcome by military means because it is a war of the people among whom the insurgent fights.[32] The record of governments successfully fighting insurgencies is indeed poor. Military action alone rarely suffices, as the conflict is foremost political. Taber largely misses this notion, and a more useful study is that of Andy Krepinevich. In his book he analyses the failure of US forces in Vietnam in light of the requirements of counterinsurgency and reaches the conclusion that the insurgents can be beaten, but not by fighting the US army way.[33] Taber's theme of legitimacy, although he does not identify it as such, is the key. The government frequently wins militarily, such as the French in Algeria or the USA in Vietnam; however, the political legitimacy of the government was either lost, as in the former case, or never established, as in the latter. The clear question then arises as to how a government can best counter such people's revolutions.

Britain, France and others were faced with a series of colonial wars, disturbances or threats to legitimate authority and each in turn developed its own style of addressing the problem. Between 1945 and 1960 Britain conducted campaigns in Palestine, Malaya, Kenya and Cyprus. Except for Palestine, these post-Second World War campaigns were successful.[34] The conduct of these operations was not based on formal doctrine but rather on certain principles of English common law and policing experience: firstly, disorders were suppressed with a minimum of force; secondly, successful counterinsurgency had depended on a close cooperation between all branches of the civil government and the military, and this coordination had been the responsibility of a single individual; thirdly, successful counterinsurgency had depended on good intelligence, and its gathering and collation had been coordinated under a single authority; and lastly, successful counterinsurgency had called for the adoption of highly decentralized, small unit tactics to defeat irregulars.[35]

Eventually these principles were brought together in a comprehensive strategy in 1960, when all were incorporated into a formal doctrine.[36] But until that time doctrine was individually crafted for each campaign after a lengthy apprenticeship. The British theatre doctrine for Malaya (1952) and Kenya (1954) became key references.[37] These doctrines embodied the principles of minimum force, civil–military cooperation, intelligence coordination, and small unit operations that had proved so successful in British imperial policing over the years. These principles fit an effective and inexpensive approach to counterinsurgency that was appropriate both to its means and to the circumstances in Britain's colonies.

The suppression of the Communist-led insurgency in Malaya between 1948 and 1960 is the classic example of British counterinsurgency doctrine in practice.[38] Malaya, comprising what is today Singapore and Malaysia, was the most prosperous British colony after India. Conquered by the Japanese in 1942, it returned to British rule in 1945. Malaya was an ethnically divided society, with approximately 45 per cent Chinese, 45 per cent Malay, and another 10 per cent Indian, European or Eurasian. The insurgency, however, was nearly entirely a Chinese-led affair. From its inception in 1948, an ethnically Chinese Communist, Chin Peng, led the uprising. The initial British response was to declare an 'emergency', meaning that the colonial government assumed emergency powers and reinforced the garrison with additional British and Ghurkha forces. Later on, both Australian and New Zealand forces contributed substantially. However, at no time did the total British military strength in Malaya exceed 17,000. The rebels adopted a campaign of Maoist terror against their opponents. In particular, they targeted European planters living in isolated rubber plantations in the back country, but they also targeted representatives of the government, Chinese who remained loyal to the British, and Malays who refused to cooperate.

The insurgents, known by the British as communist terrorists or 'CTs', achieved their greatest success in 1951 when a small party of insurgents ambushed and killed the High Commissioner, Sir Henry Gurney, while he was en route to the summer capital. Gurney's death galvanized the government in London into appointing a military governor, General Sir Gerald Templer, and giving him full powers, meaning a single person commanded the military, the police and all aspects of civil administration. Under Templer, the British adopted an imaginative plan devised by a staff officer, Brigadier General Sir Harold Briggs. The so-called Briggs Plan embraced a number of strategies. Briggs identified an element of the Chinese population, specifically landless 'squatters', as the insurgents' centre of gravity. Separating these elements from the guerrillas by relocating them to 'new villages' (basically fortified hamlets under British control) would deprive the insurgents of support, food and shelter. Beginning in 1952, the British and their Malayan allies proceeded to resettle approximately 600,000 Chinese squatters. At the same time, the British employed a strengthened Special Branch of the Police (comparable to the FBI or MI5) to penetrate and to break the Communists' urban as well as rural cell organization. This tedious police work proved decisive in the end, allowing the British to identify and detain Communists and those suspected of sympathizing with them. Finally, Templer himself determined that counterinsurgency by itself would not be enough; rather, the Malays and loyal Chinese needed a positive aim. This aim was independence, and Templer announced in 1953 that Britain would grant Malaya its independence as soon as the Emergency was under control. By 1957, the British felt confident that they had the situation in hand, and Malaya became an independent nation and member of the British Commonwealth.

Since 1960, the British success in the Malaya Emergency has suggested that the British possessed some extraordinary skill in counterinsurgency. Compared

with the dismal results achieved by the French in Indochina during essentially
the same period, the British experience appealed to Americans eager for a
textbook approach to dealing with revolutionary war. Sir Robert Thompson,
the former Permanent Secretary of Defence for Malaya, did much to propagate
this belief, writing a series of well-received books in the 1960s.[39] Foremost
among these was *Defeating Communist Insurgency*, wherein he propounded his
'five principles': positive objective, need for an overall plan, need to follow the
law, priority of political as against military objectives, and need to secure base
areas first. His contemporary, General Sir Richard Clutterbuck, likewise a highly
regarded expert on terrorism, wrote extensively on the British experience.[40]
Certainly, the USA eagerly embraced the Malayan practice of establishing
fortified hamlets during the Vietnam War, and the Marine Corps Combined
Action Program (CAP) was clearly derived from the Malayan experience.[41]

In recent years, however, this admiration has faded. In part, Communist
revolutionary war no longer seems the worldwide threat that it did in the early
years of the Kennedy administration. Further study of the French and British
experience has shown that the British enjoyed two significant advantages
not present in Indochina. In Malaya, the Communists lacked sanctuary areas
across international frontiers. Additionally, the insurgency was for practical
purposes confined to one ethnic group, the Chinese, and then to the 'squatter
Chinese', in a multi-ethnic society. As a result, the British could rely on the
support of ethnic groups, notably the Malays but also the urban Chinese,
Indians, and Eurasians of Singapore, to defeat the Communist insurgents
without a major military effort. The overwhelming majority of Malays had
no desire to be ruled by Communist Chinese and supported the British. The
insurgency was consequently contained, both in terms of its popular base
and in terms of the area in which guerrillas operated. At its most intense, the
Malayan insurgency cost government lives at a rate only a fraction of the
losses experienced by the South Vietnamese and the United States. Then, too,
the British have employed similar techniques in Northern Ireland since 1969,
and results have proved far more difficult to achieve. Compared with the
contemporary French experience in Indochina, the British counterinsurgency
impressed many Americans as pointing the way to successful operations in
Southeast Asia. Some of the British practices, notably the construction of
fortified hamlets and the relocation of suspect populations, were employed
in Vietnam beginning in the early 1960s. Other British practices, notably the
use of minimum force, proved difficult for the United States to follow. Lastly,
when it was all said and done, the American experience in Vietnam shook the
confidence of its policymakers and military alike that counterinsurgency, or
whatever it was labelled, could be readily solved by the adoption of merely a
set of techniques. On balance, Malaya provides an excellent example of how
a communist insurgency was beaten through a judicious blend of military
coercion, solid police work, sensible political concessions, and population
control. It holds valuable lessons, but is not the ultimate template.

The French like the British had had a successful history of pacification before the Second World War, but since then counterinsurgency doctrine had been built on lessons of defeat. Following France's debacle in Indochina (1946–54), the concept of revolutionary war or *guerre révolutionnaire* was formulated by a group of officers whose experiences there led them to seek methods of countering anti-colonial wars. This list included the prominent commanders and senior staff officers in General Lionel-Max Chassin, Colonel Lacheroy and General Nemo, and noteworthy junior officers in Hogard, Poirier and Souyris.[42] These officers wrote prolifically on the topic, and their theories were widely debated but not readily accepted in the French staffs or service schools that wrote and taught doctrine.

The central idea of *guerre révolutionnaire* theory was that an inferior force could defeat a conventional army if it could gain the tacit support of the population in the contested area – clearly a Maoist notion. These theorists had also witnessed the strength that a truly unified politico-military command gave to the enemy Viet-Minh insurgents and argued that this structure must also exist in a counterinsurgent force. These assertions were reinforced by their own experiences with civil–military responsibilities in Indochina. These officers had also felt the impact of psychological warfare and had become convinced that this dimension could be exploited to reinforce the ideological cohesion of government civil and military forces and to counter the enemy's ideology. The French doctrine also addressed intelligence coordination and small unit operations, but omitted the British principle of minimum force. Although the French, too, had limited resources, the cost sensitivity of the British was not a conscious part of their doctrinal thinking. With this concept of *guerre révolutionnaire*, modern counterinsurgency reverted to the *tâche d'huile* principle that Lyautey and his predecessors had successfully applied over half a century earlier. The only difference was that the political techniques and military solutions to the problem of civil–military cooperation had been revised for modern times. From the mid 1950s this doctrine provided the theoretical framework for France's effort to retain Algeria.

The Algerian War (1954–62) was 'France's Vietnam', not that it was fought in Indochina but for being the most divisive, bloody and ultimately futile war in recent French history. In 1954, Algeria was formally an organic part of France, not a colony. Its citizens enjoyed the rights of Frenchmen, including the right to elect members of the French parliament. By 1962, armed insurrection had cost approximately 1 million Algerian lives out of a population of 10 million and had convinced the French to give Algeria its independence. Throughout the conflict, however, the French military enjoyed substantial success in suppressing terrorism in Algerian cities, in interdicting foreign support for the rebels, and in crushing armed rebels in a series of well executed 'search and destroy' missions. Most frustratingly, the French government under President Charles de Gaulle (President of the Fifth Republic, 1958–69) elected to negotiate with the rebels whom the army had beaten. In the end, army successes went for nothing, and it became discredited in the eyes of the world and of the French, too, when dissident Algeria-based generals attempted a coup in April 1961.[43]

The French had acquired Algeria in 1830, largely to deal with local pirates who had threatened European trade in the Mediterranean for decades. This 'peace-enforcement' action became permanent administration, and in 1848 Algeria became a part of France proper with its European residents and a small, select number of Arabs exercising the rights of French citizenship. The scantily populated interior of the country remained lawless and provided a training ground for generations of French colonial soldiers. With its equable Mediterranean climate, Algeria attracted substantial European settlement, including many Jews, Corsicans, Italians and Spaniards. Called the *pieds noirs*, literally 'black feet' because the initial colonists worked the land in bare feet, these European settlers were a major factor in the Algerian War.

In the early 1950s, France ruled Algeria in the same fashion as the USA currently rules Hawaii, Puerto Rico or Alaska. France also administered neighbouring Morocco and Tunisia as protectorates. Under the impact of pan-Arab sentiment, rebellions broke out in the latter two countries at the same time as the French were fighting in Indochina. France thus gave both countries their independence in 1956 and 1957 respectively, while vowing to keep Algeria. Although Algeria had never been completely pacified, French rule remained substantially secure until 1954. In the wake of the French disaster at Dien Bien Phu and the evacuation from Indochina, pan-Arabist leaders in Algeria initiated a campaign of selective assassination, bombings and banditry against the French.[44] Supported by sympathizers in Tunisia and Morocco, the rebels enjoyed highly vocal political support from Egyptian president Jamal Abd al-Nasir. Indeed, one of the major reasons behind the French effort to overthrow Nasir in the Suez Expedition of 1956 was to silence Radio Cairo, the voice of Pan-Arabism and anti-Imperialism.

Convinced that the rebels were Communists and that they were following an articulate strategy derived from the ideas of Mao Zedong, the army developed a succession of techniques to combat 'revolutionary war'. The French army interpreted the goals of revolutionary war as nothing less than the overthrow of Western civilization and came to believe that only the army stood between France and barbarism. The operational methods developed and expanded by the French included the construction of sophisticated anti-infiltration barriers, such as the Morice Line, use of helicopters for search and destroy missions, psychological warfare, nation-building activities, and such familiar methods as *quadrillage*, sectioning the country and putting it under military management.[45]

The army in Algeria precipitated the political crisis that brought down the Fourth Republic in May 1958 and that installed General Charles de Gaulle as President of the new Fifth Republic with greatly expanded presidential powers. Both the army and the European settlers believed de Gaulle would stand by

them, but he did not. De Gaulle, always a believer in modernizing France's armed forces, came to see the Algerian War as counter-productive. After the successful Challe Offensive of 1959, de Gaulle opened negotiations with the rebels. He hoped that the insurgents in the *Front de Libération Nationale* (FLN) would accept some kind of voluntary association with France short of complete independence, but the FLN held out. Realizing that de Gaulle meant to end the French role in Algeria, portions of the army there attempted to overthrow him in April 1961, but its soldiers in France held firm, and the attempted coup came to nothing. Its leaders were hunted down and imprisoned or executed, and Algeria received its complete independence in 1962. The *pieds noirs* fled Algeria for France, and many of the Muslims who had collaborated with the French paid with their lives.[46]

Algeria provides an excellent example of how a major military power dealt with an Arab nationalist revolt in the 1950s and how the French military developed a theory of operations that shaped United States practice in Vietnam as well as current joint doctrine. Of the several cases cited, the Algerian War provides the closest analogy and most direct applicability to the current American 'war on terror'. Not only were the French fighting in the Middle East and against Arabs, but they were engaged in a prolonged struggle against adversaries who were predominantly 'illegal combatants', terrorists enjoying the protection of civilian status while waging war against armed forces and police hamstrung by the laws of war and the norms of European society. The FLN was not inspired by religious fervour as much as by Pan-Arabism, the widespread anti-Western sentiment that guided nationalist rebels throughout the Middle East. FLN leaders, if not exactly Communists, were secular socialists sympathetic to the Soviet Union and its allies but also united by a determination to evict the European presence from the Middle East and North Africa in particular. Movements today, such as al Qaeda, have militant Islam as their ideology and seek to evict Western influences from their societies, whether Israeli, American, or European. Additionally, al Qaeda seeks to overturn Arab and other regimes deemed too deferential to Western influences.

For the United States military of the 1960s, counterinsurgency was the 'small war' of the times. Counterinsurgency doctrine was formulated in response to the Wars of National Liberation doctrine of Communist China and the Soviet Union, first formulated by Mao Zedong and popularized by Nikita Khrushchev, as a means of exploiting the decolonization movement of the 1950s and 1960s to bring more countries into the socialist fold. Given that the Soviet Union and the United States had rough parity in nuclear weapons, it appeared that the Soviets and the Chinese were shifting their focus from conventional war, which might readily lead to a nuclear exchange, to unconventional war in the Third World, the non-aligned nations that had recently become independent. In the view of American strategists, the Soviets were preparing to go on the offensive in Latin America, in Africa, and in Southeast Asia.

Vietnam was a natural place to put counterinsurgency into practice as a means of defeating Communist-led revolutionary war. The United States had become involved in the ongoing Vietnamese conflict in the 1950s, supplying the French with materiel support after 1950.[47] Subsequently, the Eisenhower administration backed the authoritarian, but non-Communist, Ngo Dinh Diem, who was President of the Republic of Vietnam from 1955 to 1963. In 1959, the North Vietnamese decided that the time was ripe to renew the war in the South and to reunite both Vietnams under Communist rule from Hanoi. Diem received increasing amounts of American aid, advice, equipment and advisers but was unable to quell the Viet Cong guerrillas. Convinced that Diem was no longer 'the Churchill of Asia', as Vice-President Lyndon Johnson had dubbed him in 1961, the Kennedy administration acquiesced in a coup in November 1963 that deposed and murdered Diem. A succession of unstable military and civilian regimes followed, and it appeared in 1965 that South Vietnam was about to collapse. At this point, American policymakers decided that counterinsurgency could take a back seat to full-scale military involvement, first with bombing of North Vietnam, then with large-scale deployments of combat troops.

For the next three years, American forces first supported and then largely supplanted the South Vietnamese, taking over an increasing share of combat operations. By the autumn of 1967, it appeared that the US armed forces had at last reached the 'crossover', that point at which enemy casualties exceeded the level of replacements reaching their forces from the North. The Communists in Hanoi did not think they were losing and launched a full-scale general uprising during the Tet ceasefire in January–February 1968.[48] This epochal offensive failed to destroy the South Vietnamese regime or its army and cost the Communists heavily. Yet the Tet Offensive proved a watershed. While a significant military victory for United States forces, now fighting the type of stand-up fight they had always wanted to wage against the guerrillas, Tet proved a political plus for the Communists. The American public was shocked at the scale of the offensive and the number of casualties, and opinion began to turn against the war. American public opinion had not been part of the original plan, though North Vietnamese General Vo Nguyen Giap later took credit for the Tet effect on United States morale. After Tet the United States made the political decision to move towards a process of Vietnamization, 'nation assistance' in current terminology, and ultimately to withdraw as soon as decently possible.

It was during the four long years of disengagement (1968–73) that well-known atrocities by Americans took place. Given that these events reflected the growing indiscipline of American forces in an enervating and substantially faceless war fought by illegal combatants, such events are not surprising. The infamous My Lai massacre of 1968 came to light a year later. The Son Thang massacre, 'the Marine My Lai' as the *Washington Post* put it, occurred in 1970 and was swiftly uncovered. Prosecution by courts-martial led to mixed

verdicts with the most culpable escaping and their subordinates receiving prison sentences. In general, the American public, much as it had soured on the war as a whole, supported servicemen accused of war crimes. To the public and many of their comrades, they were 'doing their duty'. Even though army Lieutenant William Calley was convicted and sentenced to prison for the My Lai massacre, public pressure led to his being pardoned by President Nixon.

This much-analysed war had an incalculable impact on nearly every aspect of American military and strategic culture with the exception of perhaps nuclear strategy. The last American forces pulled out in 1973, and South Vietnam staggered on for another two years before collapsing in April 1975. Although American forces avoided direct defeat, the memories of the war followed United States forces for many years. In 1991, President George H. W. Bush made a point of claiming that its memories had finally and decisively been expunged in Operation Desert Storm, but this is improbable. Vietnam was a case in which the United States did not prevail. Conventionally, the military has blamed the unsatisfactory outcome on strategic blunders at the highest level rather than execution in the field. Two books, widely read in the military, have made this case persuasively: Harry Summers's *On Strategy* in 1982 and H. R. McMaster's more recent *Dereliction of Duty* in 1997.[49] An alternative view, put forward most cogently in Andrew Krepinevich's *The Army in Vietnam* in 1986 and in Mark Clodfelter's *The Limits of Air Power* in 1989, is that the military attempted to fight the war with techniques developed for conventional war in a European or Korean setting, the sort of war with which the four services were most comfortable.[50] These books do not rehabilitate the national command authority but instead suggest that the blame for 'losing' Vietnam should be apportioned differently. To what extent the military itself mishandled the war is the central question we will seek to answer.

The message seems to be that the US politico-military establishment did not have a clear understanding of how or why they would carry out the intervention. Krepinevich criticized the United States for failing to incorporate native South Vietnamese forces into the counterinsurgency effort. The United States, with its airmobile forces, was 'flitting when it should have been sitting'. This manoeuvre concept aggravated the problem, since US units were never in one place long enough to obtain a feel for the culture or local geography. Thus, American forces ignored 'presence', a basic tenet of counterinsurgency, as the civilian population became vulnerable. While United States forces were roaming around in search of targets for their superior firepower, the Viet Cong, usually by night, were mobilizing the civilian population, the real centre of gravity. Krepinevich also questions US policies regarding body counts, one-year rotations, and a bias toward large-unit conventional operations. The United States tended to dwell on the more comfortable technical and logistical elements of strategy, such as sensors, radar, herbicides and helicopter gunships. As was also the case with the Russians in Afghanistan and Chechnya, and the Germans in Yugoslavia during the Second World War, a seemingly inferior enemy was able to surround and ambush United States forces possessing superior firepower.

Krepinevich argues that pacification was successful to the extent that it was implemented. For the most part, however, the army as well as the Marine Corps clung to 'the concept', employing firepower lavishly and in the process creating additional refugees, losing hearts and minds, and employing intelligence resources to locate enemy main force units instead of the more insidious Viet Cong insurgents. After Tet, most of the Viet Cong were eliminated. This opened the way for effective pacification. The problem was that Tet also signalled the beginning of the end for United States troop involvement. When the North Vietnamese regulars launched their massive conventional attack in 1975, it did not matter that the hamlets had been pacified because there were inadequate conventional forces to resist the onslaught. This highlights the recurring theme of the two simultaneous wars that the United States fought in Vietnam, a conventional and an unconventional one. Krepinevich suggests that while the USA lost the conventional war, it won the unconventional one.

It is evident from these varied experiences that there is no formula, as in Thompson's five principles; however, there are adequate proven weapons to counter revolutionary war and its derivatives successfully. Primary in opening such an offence is the establishment of a strong politico-military foundation before starting any large-scale operation to gain or regain control of the countryside or urban terrain and its population. Because of the inevitable limit on resources, a strategy of incremental advance in the tradition of the *tâche d'huile* is most appropriate. Within this context strategic bases must be built around population concentrations on which support can be relied. This active assistance provides vital intelligence and a psychological boost to the process. Patient counter-organization under a constant and protective government presence is vital, as it was in Lyautey's time. This presence should be bolstered by population support measures in the form of fresh drinking water, regular sewage and waste removal, reliable electricity, tailored medical attention, basic education, local markets, wash houses and the like. Ultimately and patiently the entire country can be reclaimed.

The ongoing US counterinsurgency campaign in Iraq that began in 2003 has put these theories to the test. There, for instance, the USA has a goal of relinquishing responsibility for the country to a properly elected local democratic government that is supported by trained security forces to ensure its survival and a continuing rule of law. The strategy to realize this goal, however, is lacking in that the coalition forces move constantly in large sweeps reminiscent of Vietnam and fail to create a presence that can bring security to the population and counter-organize it against the insurgents. Infrastructure projects are constantly disrupted, and the population remains fearful and insecure. Public safety cannot be assured. The key intelligence necessary to prevent terror and intimidation is thus not forthcoming. A classic example is the still insecure 11-mile highway between Baghdad and its airport, a key piece of infrastructure immediately under the government nose. While the coalition is thus not losing, it is not winning either. Winning in Iraq and in any similar war will require extraordinary organization, dedication, sacrifice and time to defeat the enemy on the revolutionary battlefield, particularly on this one where the people will have to be taught a new form of government and then their society rebuilt around it. Half-measures, misguided actions and ineffective plans in this type of fight can lead only to protracted and costly defeats, as in Vietnam and Algeria. It is thus this Maoist 'people's war' that remains the inspiration for the insurgents of today, and yet in a final irony such a war can only be met successfully through a democratic response, a true people's war, as the USA is attempting in Iraq.[51]

further reading

Robert Asprey, *War in the Shadows: The Guerrilla in History* (Garden City NY, 1975): the author handles the overall subject of guerrilla warfare in one of the most comprehensive manners of any survey volume from the eighteenth century through to the Vietnam War. D. S. Blaufarb and George K. Tanham, *Who Will Win? A Key to the Puzzle of Revolutionary War* (London, 1989): the authors seek to define insurgency and then to prescribe antidotes for it. Max Boot, *The Savage Wars of Peace: Small Wars and the Rise of American Power* (New York, 2002): the book treats the American background in small wars, arguing that such conflicts have been the norm for the US military rather than the exceptions. Brian Crozier, *The Rebels, A Study of Post-War Insurrections* (Boston, 1960): the author explores the origins of outbreaks, the techniques of rebellion and repression, and the background and character of the typical rebel leader, shedding new light on the personalities who have captured the headlines over the past decades. Régis Debray, *Revolution in the Revolution* (trans. Bobbye Ortiz) (New York, 1967): a radical French look at insurgency and its vulnerabilities. David Galula, *Counter-Insurgency Warfare, Theory and Practice* (London, 2005): the author first published this book in 1964 after serving as a French officer in Greece, China, Southeast Asia and Algeria. His observations stand the test of time: treat prisoners well, protect innocent civilians, and convince the population that the counterinsurgent will win. Charles Gwynn, *Imperial Policing* (London, 1934): a classic that includes the general principles of internal security operations and a series of case studies from the British inter-war experience, for example, India, Burma, China, Palestine and Egypt. Janie J. Geldenhuys, 'Rural Insurgency and Counter-Measures' in M. Hough (ed.), *Revolutionary Warfare and Counter-Insurgency* (Pretoria, Institute for Strategic Studies, 1984): a South African perspective on insurgency in Southern Africa and successful ways to defeat it. T. N. Green (ed.), *The Guerrilla and How to Fight Him* (New York, 1962): a compendium of case studies on methods and an appraisal of their successes. Frank Kitson, *Low Intensity Operations: Subversion, Insurgency and Peacekeeping* (London, 1971): Kitson's prescription for fighting insurgency envisioned aggressive use of a government's armed force to counter insurgency. T. E. Lawrence, *Seven Pillars of Wisdom* (London, 1935): Lawrence's classic account of his role in the 1916–18 Arab Revolt. He concludes that military might alone will not win an unconventional war. John McCuen, *The Art of Counter-Revolutionary War* (London, 1966): this book is one of the best works in English analysing the military methods of revolution Chinese-style. Roger Trinquier, *Modern Warfare: A French View of Counterinsurgency* (trans. Daniel Lee) (New York, 1964): the author develops the idea that military hardware and tactics are all well and good, but they are really quite useless if one has lost the confidence of the population among whom one is fighting. US Marine Corps, *Small Wars Manual* (Washington, 1940): practical, relevant thoughts on conducting small wars from the strategic level to the tactical.

notes

1. C. E. Callwell, *Small Wars, A Tactical Textbook for Imperial Soldiers* (London, 1896).
2. Hugo Grotius (Huig de Groot), *De Jure Belli ac Pacis* [On the Law of War and Peace] (trans. from 1625 original) (Cambridge, 1853).
3. Callwell, *Small Wars*, p. 147.
4. Charles W. Gwynn, *Imperial Policing* (London, 1936), p. 25; Max Boot, *The Savage Wars of Peace: Small Wars and the Rise of American Power* (New York, 2002), p. 284.
5. Callwell, *Small Wars*, pp. 115–24, 143–4.
6. John P. Cann, 'Somalia: The Limits of Military Power' in *L'Afrique politique* (Paris, 2000), p. 168.
7. Callwell, *Small Wars*, p. 72.
8. Jean Gottman, 'Bugeaud, Galliéni, Lyautey: The Development of French Colonial Warfare' in Edward Mead Earle (ed.), *Makers of Modern Strategy* (Princeton NJ, 1944), p. 234.
9. Pascal Venier, *Lyautey avant Lyautey* (Paris, 1997).
10. General Yusuf, *De la guerre en Afrique* (Paris, 1851), pp. 11–138; and General Bugeaud, *Par l'epée et par la charrue: ecrits et discourse de Bugeaud* (Paris, 1948).
11. John P. Cann, *Counterinsurgency in Africa: The Portuguese Way of War, 1961–1974* (Westport CT, 1997), pp. 7, 122.
12. Joseph Galliéni, *Mémoires du Maréchal Galliéni: Défense de Paris, 25 août–11 septembre 1914* (Paris, 1926).
13. Joseph Galliéni, *Trois colonnes au Tonkin (1894–1895)* (Paris, 1999).
14. Hubert Lyautey, *Lettres du Tonkin et de Madagascar, 1884–1899* (Paris, 1942).
15. Albert Ditte, *Observations sur la guerre dans les colonies* (Paris, 1905).
16. Sun Tzu, *The Art of War* (trans. Samuel B. Griffith) (London, 1963), p. 77.
17. Gottman, 'Bugeaud, Galliéni, Lyautey', p. 249.
18. Edgar Snow, *Red Star over China* (New York, 1961).
19. John L. Tone, *The Fatal Knot: The Guerrilla War in Navarre and the Defeat of Napoleon in Spain* (Chapel Hill NC, 1994); and Don Alexander, *Rod of Iron: French Counterinsurgency Policy in Aragon during the Peninsular War* (Wilmington DE, 1985).
20. A normal school is an institution for training teachers.
21. Mao Tse-tung, *On Guerrilla Warfare* (trans. Samuel B. Griffith) (Baltimore MD, 1992), p. 48.
22. Mao Tse-tung, *On Protracted War. Volume 2. Selected Works* (New York, 1954), pp. 157–243; *Strategic Problems of China's Revolutionary War. Volume 1. Selected Works* (New York, 1954), pp. 175–253; and *The Struggle in the Chingkang Mountains. Volume 1. Selected Works* (New York, 1954), pp. 71–104.
23. Mao Tse-tung, *On Guerrilla Warfare*, pp. 47–9.
24. Ibid.
25. Ibid., p. 51.

26. Mao was arming himself with weapons either stolen or brought to him by surrendering GMD troops. These weapons were, moreover, made not only in the arsenals of the foreign powers supporting the GMD (or, figuratively, any other government power fighting guerrillas), such as London, but in China itself at its largest and most famous arsenal in the industrial city of Hanyang. The reference is a very famous one and often cited in any explanation of the Maoist model of guerrilla war.

27. Ibid.

28. Vo Nguyen Giap, *People's War People's Army* (Hanoi, 1961); and Che Guevara, *Guerrilla Warfare* (New York, 1961).

29. Thomas A. Marks, *Maoist Insurgency Since Vietnam* (London, 1996), pp. 1–2.

30. Philip Short, *Pol Pot: Anatomy of a Nightmare* (New York, 2005).

31. John J. McCuen, *The Art of Counter-Revolutionary War* (London, 1966), p. 16.

32. Robert Taber, *War of the Flea* (New York, 1965).

33. Andrew F. Krepinevich, *The Army and Vietnam* (Baltimore MD, 1986), pp. 7–15.

34. Thomas R. Mockaitis, *British Counterinsurgency, 1919–1960* (London, 1990), p. 12.

35. Bruce Hoffman and Jennifer M. Taw, *Defense Policy and Low-Intensity Conflict: The Development of Britain's 'Small Wars' Doctrine During the 1950s* (Santa Barbara CA, 1991), pp. vi, vii; and Mockaitis, *British Counterinsurgency*, pp. 13–14.

36. *Army Field Manual* (British Army General Staff, 1960).

37. *The Conduct of Anti-Terrorist Operations in Malaya* (Kuala Lumpur, 1952); and *A Handbook of Anti-Mau Mau Operations* (Nairobi, 1954).

38. Gene Z. Hanrahan, *The Communist Struggle in Malaya* (New York, 1954).

39. Robert Thompson, *Defeating Communist Insurgency: Experiences in Malaya and Vietnam* (London, 1966); *No Exit From Vietnam* (New York, 1969); *Revolutionary Warfare in World Strategy* (London, 1970); *Peace Is Not At Hand* (New York, 1974); and *Make for the Hills* (London, 1989).

40. Richard Clutterbuck, *The Long Long War: The Emergency in Malaya 1948–1960* (London, 1967); and *Riot and Revolution in Singapore and Malaya, 1945–1963* (London, 1973).

41. William R. Corson, *The Betrayal* (New York, 1968); F. J. West, *The Village* (New York, 1972); and Al Hemingway, *Our War Was Different* (Annapolis MD, 1994).

42. Peter Paret, *French Revolutionary Warfare from Indochina to Algeria: The Analysis of a Political and Military Doctrine* (London, 1964), p. 7; Lionel-Max Chassin, 'The War in Indo-China can be Won' in *France Actuelle* (Washington DC) 2/32 (31 August 1953); Charles Lacheroy et al., 'La Guerre du Viet-Minh', *Revue Militaire d'Information* 281 (February–March 1957): 25–41; J. Hogard, 'Guerre Révolutionnaire et Pacification', *Revue Militaire d'Information* 280 (January 1957): 7–14; and Captain André Souyris, 'Les Conditions de la Parade et de la Riposte à la Guerre Révolutionnaire', *Revue Militaire d'Information* 281 (February–March 1957): 93–111.

43. Alistair Horne, *A Savage War of Peace: Algeria 1954–1962* (New York, 1987), pp. 436–60.

44. Bernard Fall, *Street Without Joy* (Harrisburg PA, 1961); *Hell in a Very Small Place: The Siege of Dien Bien Phu* (New York, 1967); and *The Two Vietnams* (New York, 1963).

45. Horne, *A Savage War of Peace*, pp. 251–70.

46. Ibid., pp. 480–534.

47. Ronald H. Spector, *Advice and Support: The Early Years, 1941–1960* (Washington, 1983); and Archimedes L. A. Patti, *Why Viet Nam? Prelude to America's Albatross* (Berkeley CA, 1980).

48. Marc Jason Gilbert and William Head (eds), *The Tet Offensive* (Westport CT, 1996).

49. Harry Summers, *On Strategy* (Novato CA, 1982); and H. R. McMaster, *Dereliction of Duty* (New York, 1997).

50. Andrew F. Krepinevitch, *The Army and Vietnam* (Baltimore MD, 1986); and Mark Clodfelter, *The Limits of Air Power* (New York, 1989).

51. Marks, *Maoist Insurgency*, p. 289.

7
total war

william j. philpott

The two world wars of the first half of the twentieth century gave rise to a new classification of war: 'total war', an expression supposedly first coined in the last year of the First World War by a Frenchman, Léon Daudet, in his 'summons to national mobilization', *La Guerre Totale*.[1] Such conflicts are characteristic of the age of industrial capitalism, imperialism and mass politics, and are typified by the mobilization of society's (in practice an empire's) full resources – economic, diplomatic, scientific, technological, and above all population – for the 'total' war effort. Thus, such conflicts take place both on fighting and home fronts, and the distinction between the two becomes increasingly blurred. The destruction of civilian property and morale becomes as much an objective as the defeat of the enemy's armed forces, and victory is determined by the productivity of the industrial economy and the resilience of civilian morale as much as the size and effectiveness of the armed forces.[2]

General Erich Ludendorff, former first Quartermaster of the Imperial German Army, popularized the phrase 'total war' in his 1935 treatise of the same name, *Der Totale Krieg*.[3] Ludendorff asserted that he was not writing a theory of warfare, merely setting down the reality of war: 'succinct and accessible explanations' which derived from his personal experience.[4] 'The war of 1914', he wrote, 'had not been waged solely by the armed forces of the belligerent nations, which strove to destroy and annihilate themselves mutually. The nations themselves enlisted in the service of warfare, and the War being directed against the nations themselves, involved the latter very deeply.' Rejecting Carl von Clausewitz's idea of 'Cabinet war', Ludendorff contended, in oblique acknowledgement of Clausewitz's fundamental understanding of the nature of war, that war had ceased to be the continuation of politics by other means; it had become absolute, the passions of the people had become involved, and war had become 'totalitarian'. The new style of war, characterized by universal conscription and the use of new means of warfare, 'directly touches the life and soul of every single member of the belligerent nations', and total means are employed for absolute ends: 'the preservation of the nation'.[5] Thus, Ludendorff provided a clear, informed summary of the new style of warfare, and a blueprint for the war effort (and peacetime preparation) of Nazi Germany.

Although Ludendorff was offering a practical treatise, rather than a Clausewitzian hypothesis for academic evaluation, prior and subsequent events have inevitably led scholars to investigate the concept and impact of this early twentieth-century phenomenon, to assess the validity or otherwise of Ludendorff's typology of total war, and to relate it to broader theories of the nature of conflict. Beyond the theoretical, the nature and practical implications of the new form of totalitarian war for armed forces and the societies from which they are sprung has been the focus of much scholarship. Nevertheless, the intense scrutiny of industrial-age warfare has generated more heat than light. The most thorough academic investigation of the phenomenon to date – a series of conferences organized under the auspices of the German Historical Institute in Washington DC, and subsequently published under the editorship of Roger Chickering and Stig Förster[6] – noted during the course of their investigations:

Participants found it hard to agree on the dimensions of total war, the origins of the phenomenon, the conflicts that might lay claim to the label, and whether total war ever fully materialised. In fact, doubts have lingered over whether the concept of total war has occasioned more confusion than insight and ought to be abandoned.[7]

This plaint reinforces the paradigm that historical concepts are better defined and judged by their range and complexity than their simplicity. In part, the difficulty lies in the great range of phenomena encompassed by nineteenth- and twentieth-century war, especially the blurring of the distinction between armed forces and societies, fighting and home fronts. The solution, Chickering and Förster have posited, taking their cue from Keith Neilson, lies in 'total history': that the history of war should be written by more than specialist military historians.[8]

the elements of total war

Any attempt to define and assess total war as a concept has to reconcile a philosophical conception with actual practice. Before the 'total war' of the twentieth century there was 'absolute war', Clausewitz's conception of the supreme form which war would take if unrestrained by his famous 'frictions':

although for Clausewitz war would never in practice obtain this ultimate form, as political considerations, military methods and social mores would impose limitations upon its conduct. This philosophical juxtaposition has animated scholars of Clausewitz and of war ever since.

While generally associated with the industrial age, the philosophical roots of total war go back to the revolutionary age, Clausewitz's source material, when the stirrings of the 'passions of the people' of France after 1789 removed many of the limitations on the methods and objects of war which had characterized the Age of Enlightenment, unleashing a quarter century of almost uninterrupted, world-changing conflict on Europe. What Clausewitz did establish firmly was the link between war and society, although here he took his cue from the Comte de Guibert, whose late eighteenth-century tactical writings, from which Napoleon and his commanders were to draw inspiration, were underpinned philosophically by the as yet embryonic and untried concept of the 'nation in arms'.[9] The first stirrings of mass mobilization, first in France's 1792 *leveé en masse*, but later matched by Clausewitz's Prussia, defined the fundamental change in the nature of conflict. France went to war in 1792 for her very existence, and she, if not her early enemies, was fighting for all or nothing; to save her new polity, and extirpate the monarchies, with their dynastic, clericalist philosophies, which threatened the future.[10] Thus, total war always has an ideological dimension; a clash of cultures is fundamental to its purpose and conduct. Its methods reflect this extreme object. Mass armies, political centralization and state control of public life appeared as the means of fighting total war. Lazare Carnot's *levée en masse*, Joseph Fouché's police state, and Maximilien Robespierre's 'Terror' furnished the models for future revolutionary regimes. With these means at her disposal France would overthrow thrones and redraw national borders more or less at will between 1793 and 1812.

As well as means, aims became more total, a key difference between the European wars of the pre-revolutionary and pre-industrial age and those which followed. While a number of wars before 1789 brought about death and destruction over a prolonged period on a scale comparable to that of the modern era (the Thirty Years' War being the most obvious example), essentially these wars were limited in their aims. While these wars sometimes had an 'ideological' dimension, schismatic or contrary religion underpinning them and often furnishing their moral justification, these were not wars for 'the preservation of the nation', or the extirpation of another culture, merely the imposition of a set of values or advantages within the prevailing Christian tradition: although here one should make a clear distinction between these wars and earlier spiritual 'crusades' against Muslim powers or heretical sects. But perhaps the pragmatic outcome of these interminable, gruelling dogmatic struggles, the Peace of Westphalia (1648) and the modern state system which it established, underpinned the new forms of international war: struggles for hegemony between imperial powers. While these remained fights over

material possessions or commercial advantages they might be limited, but if they became struggles over principles or ideology they became once more 'spiritual and therefore infinite', Hew Strachan's defining characteristic of total war in any age.[11] Ends, more than means, are paramount in the characterization of total war.

Yet in France, although her society was fully mobilized and ideologically motivated, certain elements of the 'total war' paradigm, those associated with the industrialized capitalist economy, were missing. With her own embryonic capitalist development actually hindered by prolonged war, Revolutionary and Imperial France funded their ideological wars by tribute and plunder, and supplied them from the farms and workshops of the pre-industrial economy. Across the English Channel, France's one undefeated rival for hegemony, the British Empire, founded its long-term strategy on a modern financial system underpinned by the products and profits of trade, industry and empire. Taxation, credit and commercial profit, in time supplemented by judicious political reform, brought Britain both victory over France and global economic pre-eminence without political fracture. In the first 'total war', Britain had preserved and enhanced her nation, while France had crippled hers. And on the basis of this capitalist revolution Britain would facilitate the final element of 'modern' total war, industrial mass production and mass-killing technology – magazine rifles, smokeless powder, machine guns, quick-firing artillery, aeroplanes, tanks, bombs and gas, the weapons of total war – which developed slowly during the relatively peaceful century between the two prolonged struggles against French and German hegemony.

Although France's bid for hegemony after 1792 had been defeated, her model of mass warfare would not go away. After 1815, Austrian Chancellor Prince Metternich's continent-wide surveillance regime could only contain the phenomenon of popular ideological war for so long; Metternich himself was to be the first casualty of the revolutionary explosion that devastated Europe in 1848. The victors of 1815 had been more effective in restraining wars between Great Powers, and almost 40 years of relative international peace ensued until the pressures of industrialization forced a belligerent readjustment of the hierarchy of states in the middle decades of the century. Yet, these 'Wars of Unification', bloody though they were, were brief, and their protagonists appeared to adhere to Clausewitz's dictum that war should be limited by its political purpose. In his redrawing of the map of central Europe, Germany's Iron Chancellor, Otto von Bismarck, struck a better balance between economic growth, social progressiveness and political conservatism, using nationalism and war as a means of promoting national unity and international success. The relative limitation of the wars of the second half of the nineteenth century lured Europe's governments into a false sense of security. War seemed to have reverted once more to 'politics by other means', yet the American Civil War and the forcible suppression of the 1871 Paris Commune both indicated to thoughtful observers that long, bloody, ideological war had not been expunged.

However, such disagreeable lessons seemed to be lost on the military. In the late nineteenth and early twentieth centuries, the real ideologues of total war were to be found on the political Left. In 1848, Karl Marx and Friedrich Engels had given the world the Communist Manifesto, and both went on to study the events of the mid nineteenth century in terms of the struggle between classes which had arisen out of the rise of industrial capitalism. Herein lay the philosophical roots of much of the total war which was fought out between the adherents of Marx and Engels and their class enemies in the twentieth century. Lenin and Trotsky (and later, with a particular Chinese slant, Mao Zedong), welded socialist thinking, military doctrine, industrial manufacture and state power into Communism, a millenarian philosophy predicated upon the waging of total war against capitalism in all its forms. The Soviet Red Army, the armed force of an industrialized, centrally-controlled, one-party state, represented the epitome of total war military might. Moreover, as a result of the spread of this new war-driven creed, total war in the twentieth century became as much a domestic as an international phenomenon, in which modern creeds such as 'War Communism' and 'Cultural Revolution' – and not forgetting the nationalistic and racialist causes of their bastard right-wing offspring fascism – turned the resources of the centralized state against their ideological enemies at home and abroad.

armed forces, national mobilization and the origins of total wars

But all this was in the future. In the decades before the first of the twentieth-century's total wars, when socialism still appeared a worrying but containable threat, and armed class struggle merely the marginal doctrine of its most extreme faction, military professionals and early academic military historians struggled with the concept of modern war between empires, and its practice on the battlefield and home front. General Staffs' preoccupations with the next war, and the resulting phenomena of arms races and rigid military planning, have ever since been a rich and controversial seam mined by historians in their attempts to explain how and why in the first half of the twentieth century Europe plunged the world into two massive conflicts within 30 years.

Before 1914, planners' conceptions of the 'nation in arms' were narrowly focused on the number of men who could be put into uniform and rushed to the front for the first massive, and potentially decisive, battles. In the 1990s, two studies of the pre-1914 arms races, focusing particularly on the previously neglected land arms race, by David Hermann and David Stevenson, appeared in quick succession. As well as detailing the armaments policies of the two rival Great Power alliances, these studies emphasized the general destabilization of pre-1914 Europe by a runaway arms trade interacting with regular international crises and Balkan wars to militarize societies and harden political attitudes.[12] Everyone expected war, and so when a third Balkan War threatened the brakes were taken off the wound-up military machines. Industrial societies had created mechanical war machines ready to deliver A. J. P. Taylor's famous 'war by timetable'. The militaristic societies which supported these practices, and evinced little surprise or hostility when war broke out, are the final element of the pre-war machine. A collection of essays published in the 1980s delineated the mood for war in the belligerents in 1914,[13] but the broader phenomenon of early twentieth-century militarism is worthy of deeper investigation.

War plans were an integral part of this early twentieth-century military confrontation, and have in themselves attracted much attention, none more so than Germany's famous (even infamous) 'Schlieffen Plan', an issue which has provoked considerable academic controversy. The 'Fischer debate', sparked by Fritz Fischer's famous 1961 book on pre-1914 German policy,[14] has been one of the longest running and convoluted historiographical debates of recent times.[15] Subsumed into the wider diplomatic and socio-political arguments, analyses of German armaments policy – both naval and military arms races – and war planning have been deployed to support or oppose Fischer's thesis of premeditated aggressive war. It is certainly true that after the 1871 victory over France, the German Great General Staff closely analysed the reasons for Moltke the Elder's decisive triumphs in the Wars of Unification. Against a background of growing international isolation and national crisis, German military thinkers took Clausewitz's ideas and von Moltke's methods and sought to mould them into a viable strategy for Germany in the great power war which appeared inevitable, and in which Germany, fighting on two fronts, was expected to be at a disadvantage.[16] Hence the 'Schlieffen Plan', for a rapid attack on France through Belgium, was conceived to defeat one of Germany's enemies quickly.[17] In recent years this plan itself, and the intellectual context in which it was prepared, has been one of the liveliest and most bitter themes of the ongoing debate, and much light has been thrown on the complexities of planning and the mindset of the pre-war German army. The debate was ignited by Terence Zuber's denial of the Schlieffen plan, and hence German war guilt, in the pages of the journal *War in History*,[18] a stance subsequently challenged by Terence Holmes, Robert Foley, Annika Mombauer and others in their own articles and books. The details are abstruse and involved, and cannot be summarized here,[19] but the very intensity of this debate attests to the liveliness of the controversy, and the continued fascination with the phenomenon of war planning.

In contrast, the debate on the Entente's preparations before 1914 is less intricate and advanced than that over Germany's war planning, although revision is ongoing.[20] For Britain and France the discussion focuses on joint planning, and for France itself on the 'cult of the offensive' and General Joseph Joffre's resulting disastrous 'Plan XVII'.[21] Russia's plans are far less well known.[22]

The role of military planning and arms races in causing war are themes which are taken up once more in the debate on the origins of the Second World War. As well as the discussion of arms races in all three elements (land, sea and air) scholars also develop a new theme, that of economic preparation – not just absolute numbers of armed forces and weapons, but also the means to increase and sustain them after the outbreak of war. Things could only intensify after the first experience of industrial mass war, with its false starts, improvisations and mistakes in the mobilization of society for war. States were unwilling to be caught short again as 'the experience of mass industrial warfare transformed the accepted standard of national strength and erased the distinction between armies and societies'. In preparing a second time 'the yardstick of power had become a nation's ability to mobilise its whole economy and population for total war', and this has added a new complexity to the analysis.[23]

Once again, the focus is on Germany, and the Nazis' planning, preparation and intentions for the war they were to unleash on Europe in 1939, and the response of the Democracies. Subsumed in the complicated debates about appeasement and Nazi war aims is a controversy over the nature of German rearmament and preparation for her second total war. The crux of the dispute is whether National Socialist Germany was gearing up for blitzkrieg ('lightning war'), and rearming 'in breadth' – concentrating on weapons production rather than creating the economic infrastructure to sustain a long war and harming the civilian economy in the process – and adopting military plans and methods which reflected this idea of short, decisive war. Or alternatively, Germany was rearming 'in depth' – creating through the 1937 Four Year Plan the infrastructure for Ludendorff's 'totalitarian war' – in anticipation of a total war for hegemony against her liberal and communist ideological enemies. Richard Overy has been the principal proponent of the revisionist view that, rather than planning for a blitzkrieg in 1939, Hitler was preparing and rearming in depth for a longer war, but at a later date. It was foreign policy failures which initiated war prematurely, and structural weaknesses in the German economy which restricted 'total war' mobilization subsequently.[24] Recently, Jurgen Förster has reviewed the issues surrounding Germany's attitude to total war, concluding that while Germany's war aims were 'total', her mobilization effort did not match that intention until the last year of the war.[25]

In contrast, analysis of British and French rearmament focuses on the limitations imposed upon military preparations by pacifistic public opinion and economic constraints.[26] Its main feature is a stark contrast between the cooperation and preparedness of Britain and France to fight together in 1914, with their belated, half-hearted and incomplete preparations before 1939. The British army was not ready for war in 1939, coordination was problematic, and France's 'Maginot-line mentality' planning reflected her First World War trials and inter-war domestic paralysis rather than the realities of modern war. The Democracies inevitably lost the rearmament race with Germany, and in this lay the seeds of the disaster of 1940.[27] In contrast, they were much better prepared economically for a long war, although in this dimension policies contributed to the early defeat of France. Britain's policy of prioritization in defence spending delayed her creation of a mass army capable of intervening effectively in a continental war until it was almost too late. France, in contrast, failed to take her antediluvian aircraft industry in hand and found herself at a severe disadvantage in this sphere of war when war broke out. However, in the long haul which followed, Britain's pre-war foresight enabled her to catch up with and overtake Germany's war machine by 1941.[28]

More recently, with the opening of Soviet archives following the fall of the Iron Curtain, the military preparations of the Soviet Union, the other totalitarian behemoth of the inter-war years, have been studied in detail. Once more, insecurity was the driving force in military planning. In the intense climate of ideological debate which defined the proletariat's newly won freedom, and the party apparatchiks' jockeying for power, General Michael Frunze and Marshal Mikhail Tukhachevsky promulgated a 'total war' strategy, predicated on the defence of Communism from hostile capitalism both within and without Russia. Their dynamic offensive operational and tactical theories of large scale attack with masses of tanks, guns and aeroplanes (judged appropriate for a young, vigorous, mass society),[29] combining the lessons of world war and civil war, coupled with Stalin's planned economic system designed to deliver the wherewithal of national defence, exemplify the extreme measures which totalitarian societies were able to pursue in their own defence. The combination of the huge Red Army itself, the rapidly-expandable military industrial complex of Soviet heavy industry created through successive centrally managed Five Year Plans, and the thorough militarization of Soviet society, represent the extreme response to the challenge of total war.[30] So in the inevitable struggle for hegemony, while Germany's blitzkrieg military methods were effective in breaking the Eastern Front in 1941, the Nazis' economic and social policies proved inadequate for the prolonged attritional total war imposed upon them by Soviet military thinking and armaments policy between 1942 and 1945.[31] Whether by design or default, blitzkrieg had met its match in a true 'totalitarian' war machine.

armed forces and the conduct of total war

The 'total history' paradigm is certainly evident in the great volume of literature on the world wars themselves. Inevitably, the actions of armed forces in the total war situation take centre stage. The military aspects of both conflicts – battles, campaigns, weaponry, generals, tactics, strategy – have been endlessly reviewed, and indeed are starting to attract historiographical surveys, bibliographies and encyclopaedias of their own.[32] Much of this work is narrative and popular, and a lot of it is repetitive. Certain themes dominate.

For the First World War, 'generalship' (now, more properly being referred to as 'command and control') – how the high command approached the new challenges of industrial warfare on the battlefield, and how the strategic conduct of the war led to clashes between soldiers and civilian politicians – has been the staple of British historiography since the war itself, a row ignited initially by the outpouring of antagonistic memoirs by both the generals themselves and their political detractors after the war.[33] Detailed research into official and private papers since the 1980s has established a more objective view of the problems of the new industrial battlefield, and the effectiveness of the solutions found. A new paradigm, of a high command 'learning curve', has been established in which, by a process of trial and frequently error, but also careful reflection on professional experience, the new weapons of modern war were absorbed into the armed forces, which went through a fundamental culture and organizational shift between 1914 and 1918. This produced new, so-called 'combined-arms' tactical theories that broke the battlefield stalemate and delivered military victory in 1918.[34] It has taken a practising soldier, Jonathan Bailey, to summarize these changes – what today might be defined as a Revolution in Military Affairs – as the onset of 'three-dimensional modern deep battle'.[35] Although this paradigm is by no means universally accepted, it is becoming the prevailing orthodoxy, although qualified on occasion. Gary Sheffield's work in particular has championed the concept of the learning curve, which is echoed in Paddy Griffith's work on British tactics.[36] On the other side of the divide, Tim Travers has dwelt on the problems of the British high command, largely derived from the pre-war army's institutional weaknesses,[37] and Simon Robbins's 2005 monograph entitled *British Generalship on the Western Front* points out faults as well as progress.[38] Despite the great progress made in understanding how total war works on the battlefield, it looks as if the long-running debate on the war on the Western Front will continue; there are still many who refuse to give the generals much, if any, credit for mastering the new methods of industrial warfare in the relatively short time span of four years. For example, Robin Prior and Trevor Wilson's 2005 study of the Somme, a polemic against the British high command, contrasts oddly with their earlier balanced and ground-breaking study of the career of General Sir Henry Rawlinson, which began the detailed analysis of the nature of command and control on the Western Front.[39] Many of the studies of subsidiary aspects of the campaign have advanced our understanding of the subject. For example, Ian Malcolm Brown's monograph on the British army's logistics on the Western Front was a worthy Templer Medal prize winner, opening up an unexplored area of research which needs to be repeated for the other belligerents.[40]

This is indeed a more general problem. Since other countries' historians do not share the British obsession with their experience on the Western Front, the parallel 'learning curve' of the French and German armies is yet to be thoroughly studied: indeed the existing English-language literature assumes an innate German professionalism and superiority over their adversaries which is not always borne out by detailed examination of the sources.[41] Anthony Clayton's *Paths of Glory* surveys the French army's experience, but adds little to our understanding of how that army worked, a gap which Robert Doughty's *Pyrrhic Victory* begins to fill.[42] In the United States, the debate is further forward; after decades of assumed competence, the operational failings of the American Expeditionary Force in France in 1918 are starting to be recognized.[43]

The debate on the strategic conduct of military operation in the First World War is, like the Western Front itself, stalemated. The innate assumption that the generals could and should have done better, and the endless repetition of the point that their old methods did not work in the new circumstances of industrial-war,[44] has not allowed more objective analysis of how the generals actually thought about the new war, and how they put their theories into practice, to become the new orthodoxy. Popular but controversial books, such as John Mosier's recent *The Myth of the Great War*,[45] and Gordon Corrigan's *Mud, Blood and Poppycock*,[46] keep the debate raging, and any agreed consensus seems some way off.

In contrast, the controversies about the nature of military operations in the Second World War, if no less studied, are more muted, although a younger generation of scholars may ignite new debates which will be in their turn as lively as those about the First World War. For example, high command is again coming in for scrutiny, with Bernard Montgomery being a particular focus of interest amongst British scholars, although as yet not as controversial a figure as Douglas Haig.[47] Significant anniversaries tend to provoke reassessments and evaluations; the 50th anniversary of the fall of France in 1940 was one such which led to a range of new writing.[48] The more long-running debates focus on the new ways of war: the nature and effectiveness of 'blitzkrieg', the merits and effectiveness of strategic bombing, and the significance of partisan warfare are all topics which have attracted interest.[49] More recently, Robert Citino has attempted to relate the military developments of the two world wars.[50]

Debate on higher strategy in the two world wars also show this dichotomy, the First World War generating more controversy than the second, where the official history has set a more balanced tone. For the First World War, David French's two-volume study of British strategy delivered a thoroughly researched and well-balanced survey which set the standard for such analysis, putting to the sword the long-standing paradigm of a struggle between 'easterners' and 'westerners' over the strategic conduct of the war.[51] French's analysis has subsequently been challenged by Brock Millman, who detected a current of pessimism setting in amongst British political leaders after the Somme, which led to their reorientation of British strategy away from the Western Front towards a 'new eastern strategy'.[52] Since the 1980s, the study of British strategy has become more nuanced, focusing more deeply on the alliance context in which Britain developed her policy and military operations, and addressing the economic context in which Britain's war effort was conducted.[53] This in turn has generated controversy of its own over the strategic independence which Britain was able to exercise in a coalition war.[54] Equivalent studies of the strategic policies of Britain's principal allies, France, Italy and Russia, are less developed,[55] and an overall synthesis of the Entente's war effort still remains some way off. Key strategic themes also need further work. Carter Malkasian's study of attrition, while a ground-breaking work, is by no means thorough or convincing enough to be definitive, although more specific studies of the phenomenon are now appearing.[56]

Controversies about the Allies' strategic conduct of the Second World War have yet to be revisited in the same way that those of the First World War have been in the last two decades, although it is only a matter of time before they too are reignited. Partly this is because the official histories of the conflict covered the theme of 'Grand Strategy' for the first time. Such long-running controversies as there are relate to the relationship between the separate fronts – whether a second front in Europe should have been opened by the western allies before 1944, and whether the Italian campaign was a strategic backwater for example.[57] Equally, the role of strategic bombing in the defeat of Germany has been subjected to intense scrutiny.[58] The liveliest new debate, ignited by the revelation of the 'Ultra' secret in 1974, has been on the role of strategic intelligence in planning and decision making during the war.[59] Here scholarship on the Second World War has taken a lead over that of the first, in which the contribution of strategic intelligence remains to be fully investigated.[60] German strategy, and in particular the influence – pernickety and malign – of Adolf Hitler on command decision-making, have been more thoroughly analysed.[61] The ten-volume official history produced by the German Military History Institute, recently available in English translation, is providing a thorough and balanced, if not universally accepted, survey of Germany's military and political strategies.[62]

economy and society in total war

The other dimension of total war, the home front experience, has an equally extensive literature, addressing both political and economic management and war experience in the context of total mobilization and the blurring of distinctions between fighting and home fronts. Paralleling the military's attempts to grapple with the conduct of total war even before it had occurred, social scientists before 1914 were addressing questions of popular involvement in, and the likely political and social consequences of, war between industrial societies. Many of the most influential and accurate predictions of the nature and impact of total war come from the speculations of those mainly left-wing social theorists who, as capitalist society developed in the nineteenth century, mused on the impact of industrialization, population growth and the development of class consciousness upon the nature of warfare. Their prescience ensured that many – Marx, Engels, Lenin, Trostsky and Weber

– were to become household names in the twentieth century as their theories about social structure and class conflict played out on the street as well as the battlefield.

They had many wars to study, from the recent lengthy revolutionary and Napoleonic struggles of the past, through the revolutionary, civil and national wars of the mid-century, to the colonial conflicts endemic outside Europe. In *The Manifesto of the Communist Party*, first published in 1848, Karl Marx set out his new utopian ideology, and the methodology for its realization, the armed struggle. Premature in the circumstances of mid-nineteenth-century Europe – witness the brutal suppression of the Paris Commune in 1871 – it was to come into its own in Europe because of the social dislocations occasioned by the First World War. If unable to bring about their dream, Marx and his long-term collaborator, Friedrich Engels, never ceased to study and to plot. Their voluminous historical and social writings give interesting insights into the nature of future war. Engels, for example, wrote in 1887 of 'world war with never before seen extension and intensity ... eight to ten million soldiers will slaughter each other ... collapse of old states and their traditional wisdom in such a way that the crown will roll in the gutter': all of course with the teleological end, 'general exhaustion and the creation of circumstances for the final victory of the working class'.[63] More successful were their Russian disciples, Lenin and Trostsky, who in their long years of political exile studied carefully the nature and impact of industrialization on warfare and the workers who would be required to wage it. Their models were the failed French social revolutions of 1789, 1848 and 1871, and their object was to organize and arm the proletariat for the class struggle so that these mistakes would not be repeated. Trotsky himself made his living as a war correspondent in the Balkans and elsewhere, and was well versed in the practicalities of combat and mobilization.[64] When the opportunity came after 1917 to put theory in practice he was ready: his theory of 'permanent revolution', and its realization in the 'War Communism' years, 1918–21, represent the apogee of total war mobilization.

Other theorists of the Left and Right also wrestled with the idea of popular war in the years before 1914, although their premise was the strengthening of the nation state rather than its overthrow. In Germany, Baron Colmar von der Goltz studied carefully the principles of national mobilization, summarized in his book, *The Nation in Arms*, first published in 1883 and revised frequently thereafter. Drawing on his experience in France in 1870, von der Goltz wrote of the 'totality' of warfare, and that future wars would go on until one nation had exhausted the resources of the other. As Robert Foley has suggested, such ideas of long war and national struggle were more prevalent and influential in German pre-war thinking than has hitherto been acknowledged by those whose gaze focuses on the detailed pre-1914 mobilization and attack plans.[65] The response was universal military training, so that all able-bodied men would be able to contribute to national defence. Across the border, and at the other end of the political spectrum, French socialist leader Jean Jaures had reached a similar conclusion in his 1911 book *L'armée nouvelle*, if for different reasons. Only the 'nation in arms' could guarantee popular security against the enemy without and the foe within. What these social scientists of the Left and Right had in common was that they predicted that society would be put under a great strain if war occurred between industrialized empires, and their institutions and social structures might not be strong enough to take the strain. The Polish banker Ivan Bloch's infamous prediction that the capitalist international economy would not be able to survive the strains of prolonged war proved erroneous, despite the massive dislocations which the outbreak of hostilities in 1914 occasioned. Hence, 'total war' became a reality, and the subject for historical analysis.

By the mid twentieth century, totalitarian theorists had done their best to merge the two into a seamless whole. The '-isms' of the Second World War era – Communism, Fascism, National Socialism – were all millenarian political creeds based on the principle of inherent conflict within and between societies, whether it be over differences of class, nation or race. Inevitably, the class-focused approaches of pre-1914 and inter-war thinkers furnished many twentieth-century scholars with their theoretical template and agenda for studying total war on the home front.

Since total war involves civilians on the home front to a great degree, for social historians mobilization is not simply a military event, but a socio-political phenomenon worthy of study in its own right. Examining this civilian experience of total war proved to be the catalyst for the development of the broader 'war and society' genre which emerged after the Second World War.[66]

Arthur Marwick, in his 1974 comparative study of the twentieth-century war experiences of Britain, France, Germany, Russia and the United States, *War and Social Change in the Twentieth Century*, following on from earlier work on the impact of total war on Great Britain, set the parameters for the debate on the impact of total war on the civilian population. In this influential work, Marwick posited that the principal effects of total war can be categorized in a 'four-tier model': firstly, 'disruption and destruction on an unprecedented scale'; secondly, the testing of existing social and political structures in the belligerent states; thirdly, the participation of previously disadvantaged groups in the war effort as a consequence of total mobilization; fourthly, a 'colossal psychological experience'.[67] Marwick's model, while not watertight, has proved highly influential in determining the parameters of future debate. Moreover, Marwick's influence, through the Open University course *War Peace and Social Change: Europe 1900–1955*, which he headed up during the 1980s and 1990s, has been prolonged and permanent.[68]

The Open University approach has been to assume that war brings about social change, and total war the most profound and lasting change. In itself, few would dispute this contention, although the nature of this change, its extent and duration, and its permanency, have all been subject to critical assessment. Taking the analysis deeper, the changes of the early twentieth century have to be evaluated in relation to 'the other social forces, which, entirely independently of war, were making for social change'.[69] Take for example the impact of total war on the social status, political power and economic role of women, one of the 'previously disadvantaged groups' mobilized for the total war effort. This argument, 'whether or not twentieth-century wars have, or have not, resulted in improvements in the conditions and status of women is one of the most intense in the whole area of war and society studies'.[70] Originally women's penetration of traditionally male occupations during wartime, and even their serving in uniform for the first time, their increased earning power, wider social opportunities and increasing political power were all identified as positives which resulted from female participation in total war mobilization. Subsequently, the debate became more nuanced, with permanent gains being contrasted with those temporary advances which were achieved only 'for the duration', bringing out the complexity of the dynamic of women's rise in the twentieth century. While none would deny the profound changes in women's economic and social status and political influence, and that their wartime role was instrumental in these changes, no-one would now argue in favour of a simple linear correlation between the two.

In studying the nature and impact of total war on society the focus has been on how civilians are mobilized, physically and mentally (such themes as industrial relations, military recruitment, the growth of government power, home front economic conditions, and propaganda are all well covered); how they experience war; and how societies – mentalities, social relations and social structure within them – change as a consequence of their war experience. One recent trend, developed principally by Jay Winter and the French historians Annette Becker and Stephane Audoin-Rouzeau, has been to focus on the impact of total war on society through examination of such 'new military history' themes as memory, mourning, and remembrance – Marwick's 'colossal psychological experience'.[71] Becker and Audoin-Rouzeau's recent synthesis of this new approach to the study of the First World War in particular, raises interesting new insights into the mobilization – or, according to their argument, remobilization to fight a new kind of war as the conflict dragged on – of societies, and the motivation of soldiers and civilians during such an all-pervading struggle. Their sholarship represents one of the more vibrant and innovate approaches to the study of total war of recent years.[72] This approach takes the discussion beyond the key debates which emerged during the class-riven Cold War era: firstly about whether total war experience levelled or heightened class distinctions; secondly about how the state mediated a 'corporate social partnership' between capital and organized labour to meet the needs of national mobilization and peaceful demobilization, especially in the First World War period; and, finally, how 'social democracy' eventually emerged from the traumatic 'thirty years' war' of the first half of the twentieth century as a means of maintaining a viable domestic consensus.[73] Although the world has moved on, such classic studies of labour relations, such as Gerd Feldman's *Army, Industry and Labour in Germany*, or post-war social reconstruction, such as Charles Maier's *Recasting Bourgeois Europe*, are still worth reading.[74]

In this chapter, it is only possible to give a sample of the many and varied themes which have been taken up in the discussion of the impact of total war on society. For both world wars, themes of manpower policy, economic management, diplomatic strategy, and social organization are all investigated, normally with the purpose of assessing their contribution to the war effort and their input into success or failure. Almost all the great powers, and many of the lesser, have been examined and re-examined, in depth and in breadth, in general national studies and more focused particular examinations. The volume of works is huge, the quality generally good, but the focus often narrow, either geographically or thematically. Understandably, perhaps, because although total war supposedly needs 'total history' the constraints of the journal article or academic monograph discourage the broad sweep. What has until recently been lacking is much effective comparative study, either within or between rival alliances, or between the two world wars, to bring out the range and complexity of the total war experience. Happily, the trend in recent years has been to move from the micro to the macro, and synthesize the mass of work into a single, accessible narrative. For example, Germany and Austria-Hungary's First World War experience has been masterfully surveyed by Holger Herwig, furnishing a model for the writing of 'total history', and bringing out in particular the complex symbiotic relationship between the two allies, Germany 'shackled to a corpse', with the corpse unable to break free.[75] Similar treatments for other nations, which link the home-front experience closely to events at the front, are still needed. If one of the principal effects of total war is to blur the distinction between the home and fighting fronts, historians need to address their own tendency to compartmentalize and treat battlefield events separately from domestic developments, and vice versa.

writing on total wars

Of course, where this happens best is in the grand narrative, the synthesis which attempts to address a world war as a whole. In this respect, the judgement that the study of total war requires total history is validated. Clearly, the writing of the military history of the first half of the twentieth century must range over many facets of both military and civilian action and experience, not just the events on the battlefield. Histories of the world wars themselves have been forced to address these vast fields of human experience, and to synthesize them into a coherent, accessible whole. With such a difficult task, the results are inevitably mixed. Of the numerous general histories of the First World War, for brevity and clarity Michael Howard's *The First World War* is unlikely to be bettered.[76] Hew Strachan's projected three-volume history, of which the first volume *To Arms!* was published in 2001 to critical acclaim, has the potential to become the definitive account.[77] Until the other two volumes are published, Strachan's *The First World War: A New Illustrated History* will stand as one of the best single-volume histories of the conflict.[78] A. J. P. Taylor's widely read and influential *The First World War*, first published in 1960, is deeply flawed, like many works of history embodying the prejudices and preoccupations of its author rather than balanced judgement of its material; the same can be said of John Keegan's *The First World War*, and John Morrow's recent *The First World War: An Imperial History*.[79] David Stevenson's 2004 volume *1914–1918: The History of the First World War* is perhaps the most thorough and balanced of the single-volume histories of the war which have multiplied in recent years.[80] Inevitably, the First World War will continue to attract scholarly interest, and the ground-breaking books on aspects of the war, such as John Terraine's *White Heat: The New Way in Warfare* published in 1982,[81] and wide-ranging 'total history' treatments such as the 1996 collection of essays *Facing Armageddon*,[82] will continue to appear side-by-side with the more fanciful, popular analyses, such as John Mosier's *The Myth of the Great War*, which are an inevitable part of such a controversial and multi-faceted subject.

For the Second World War, the events are less controversial, and the studies more monolithic. The eponymous *Total War*, first published in 1972 and now available in a revised second edition, holds centre stage, although it is dominated by the narrative of military affairs.[83] Gordon Wright's 1968 narrative, *The Ordeal of Total War* integrates domestic and military matters more effectively, although it is brief and now rather dated.[84] Perhaps it is only possible to cover such a huge human experience in a multi-authored, multi volume-work: the collection *The Great World War*, relating the two world wars across both military and socio-political themes, represents a worthy attempt to link these two total conflicts, total history in its fullest sense.[85]

conclusion

The nature and impact of total war remains one of the most active fields of research in military history: it often seems that as much is written about the two world wars, and the early twentieth century more generally, as about the many wars which went before. Inevitably, it was the subject of wide-ranging and often intense debate in the second half of that century, although more recently there have been both attempts to compare and synthesize, and also more fragmentation and detailed engagement with novel themes, as the major controversies generated by long-standing ideological confrontation and its inevitable intellectual fall-out have died down. Analysis of the nature and impact of total war spawned a series of subsidiary debates, informed by the prevailing socio-political or cultural historical paradigms of the time, such as that on the levelling of class, and more recently the growing body of literature on the phenomena of memory and mourning. This has taken our understanding of total war and its impact, and of the place of warfare in human history, in new directions.

Now, in the early twenty-first century, historians are able to ask larger questions, which put total war in its place: 'Was total war a momentary aberration in the long history of warfare? Did it emerge in specific historical circumstances during the nineteenth century, come to fruition in the early twentieth century, and then disappear?'[86] Is total war defined by its ends, means, or scale, or by a combination of two, or three of these?[87] Total war ends were established as early as 1792, although the means lagged behind. Political and social structures were adaptable from the start, but the economic, productive and technological capabilities which define war in the industrial age did not reach their zenith till 1939–45. Although there were early manifestations of certain defining phenomena of total war between 1914 and 1918 – global geographical reach, domestic and military mobilization, propaganda, unrestricted submarine warfare, strategic bombing, atrocities against civilians, even genocide, phenomena distinguishable for their intensity and extremity – the First World War was merely a dress rehearsal between partially-industrialized societies for a second which was to follow in the age of mass production, and to become the archetype of 'total war' if not the reality.[88]

This is because the crux of the problem of effective analysis of 'total war' as a definable historical commodity lies in the matter of 'totality'. Is this 'absolute war' state actually obtainable and viable, or merely a hypothetical 'ideal type'?[89] If one accepts the latter, then all analysis of war is of limited war; or more precisely of the limitations on war. Moreover, the teleological assumptions of the 'total war' narrative, the inevitable progression from 'revolutionary war' through 'people's war' via 'modern war' to 'world war', falls into the trap of so-called 'retroactive foreshadowing'.[90]

In the early years of the twenty-first century, total war as a human experience is perhaps a thing of the past, a historical phenomenon which we shall not see again, from a particular age in which industrialization, mass politics and fervent nationalism combined in a volatile yet transitory mixture. Michael Howard summed up the First World War: 'That [the Great War's] course should have been so terrible, and its consequences so catastrophic, was the result not so much of its global scale as of a combination of military technology and the culture of the peoples who fought it.'[91] While war today maintains its global reach, and technology remains central to armed conflict, perhaps (in the West at least) the overriding universal economic and cultural imperatives that underpinned the era of total war are no longer quite the motivating force that they were at the start of the last century, and future conflicts will return to the limited conflict of earlier ages, geographically, ideologically and materially.

further reading

The starting point for considering aspects of total war should be the five volumes published by the German Historical Institute addressing the phenomenon between the American Civil War and the Second World War. Their individual chapters summarize many of the key themes and debates, while the introductions assess the theoretical problems associated with the concept. S. Förster et al. (eds), *On the Road to Total War: The American Civil War and the German Wars of Unification; Anticipating Total War: The American and German Experiences, 1827–1914; Great War, Total War: Combat and Mobilization on the Western Front, 1914–1918; The Shadows of Total War: Europe, East Asia and the United States, 1919–39; A World at Total War: Europe, Global Conflict and the Politics of Destruction, 1937–45* (Cambridge, 1997–2005). Hew Strachan's article 'On Total War and Modern War', *International History Review* 22/2 (June 2002), 341–69 considers the important distinction between these two often-confused concepts. For the social impact of total war, the Open University's *War, Peace and Social Change: Europe 1900–55* course texts and readers by Arthur Marwick et al. (Milton Keynes, 1989–90) survey many key themes within a structured analytical framework. Marwick's own *War and Social Change in the Twentieth Century: A Comparative Study of Britain, France, Germany, Russia and the United States* (London, 1974), set the agenda for much of what was to follow. More recently, A. Becker and S. Audoin-Rouzeau's *1914–1918: Understanding the Great War* (London, 2002) has moved that agenda on from the social to the cultural.

notes

1. H. Strachan, 'On Total War and Modern War', *International History Review* 22/2 (2000): 341–70, 349.
2. Although the application of industrial technology to the battlefield has also been a key feature of the wars of the early twentieth century, this on its own does not determine whether a war is total. Rather Strachan distinguishes this as the primary characteristic of 'modern' war. Ibid., 350–1.
3. General Ludendorff, *Der Totale Krieg* (Munich, 1935). Translated into English as *The Nation at War* (trans. A. S. Rappoport) (London, 1936).
4. *The Nation at War*, p. 11.
5. Ibid., pp. 11–19. Strachan suggests ('On Total War and Modern War', 349) that Ludendorff's theme was '"totalitarian war"'... the book was less about the means of war, and more about the structure of the state designed to conduct it'.
6. S. Förster and J. Nagler (eds), *On the Road to Total War: The American Civil War and the German Wars of Unification* (Cambridge, 1997); M. F. Boemeke, R. Chickering and S. Förster (eds), *Anticipating Total War: The American and German Experiences, 1827–1914* (Cambridge, 1999); R. Chickering and S. Förster (eds), *Great War, Total War: Combat and Mobilization on the Western Front, 1914–1918* (Cambridge, 2000); R. Chickering and S. Förster (eds), *The Shadows of Total War: Europe, East Asia and the United States, 1919–39* (Cambridge, 2003); and R. Chickering, S. Förster and B. Greiner (eds), *A World at Total War: Europe, Global Conflict and the Politics of Destruction, 1937–45* (Cambridge, 2005).
7. Chickering and Förster, 'Introduction', *Shadows of Total War*, p. 3.
8. Ibid.
9. B. Heuser, *Reading Clausewitz* (London, 2002), p. 25.
10. T. C. W. Blanning, *The Origins of the French Revolutionary Wars* (London, 1986).
11. Strachan, 'On Total War and Modern War', 350.

12. D. Hermann, *The Arming of Europe and the Making of the First World War* (Princeton NJ, 1996); D. Stevenson, *Armaments and the Coming of War: Europe, 1904–1914* (Oxford, 1996).
13. R. J. Evans and H. Pogge von Strandmann, *The Coming of the First World War* (Oxford, 1988).
14. Published in English as F. Fischer, *Germany's Aims in the First World War* (London, 1967).
15. For a wider analysis of Germany's role, inspired by Fischer's argument, see H. W. Koch (ed.), *The Origins of the First World War: Great Power Rivalry and German War Aims* (Basingstoke, 1972). For a general introduction to the debates on the origins of the First World War, see J. Joll, *The Origins of the First World War* (London, 2004).
16. H. Herwig, *The First World War: Germany and Austria-Hungary, 1914–1918* (London, 1997), pp. 6–61 *passim*.
17. G. Ritter, *The Schlieffen Plan: Critique of a Myth* (London, 1958).
18. T. Zuber, 'The Schlieffen Plan Reconsidered', *War in History* 6/3 (1999): 262–305.
19. A good evaluation is provided by A. Mombauer, 'Of War Plans and War Guilt: The Debate Surrounding the Schlieffen Plan', *The Journal of Strategic Studies* 28/5 (2005): 857–85.
20. See W. Philpott, 'More than a "Single Private Soldier": France and the Prospect of British Military Support Before 1914' in J. F. V. Keiger and P. R. A. Venier (eds), *Defence and Diplomacy from the Entente Cordiale to the First World War* (London, 2007) and W. Philpott, 'The General Staff and the Paradoxes of Continental War' in D. French and B. Holden Reid (eds), *The British General Staff: Reform and Innovation, 1880–1939* (London, 2002), pp. 95–111.
21. The standard work on the subject is S. R. Williamson's *The Politics of Grand Strategy: Britain and France Prepare for War, 1904–14* (Cambridge MA, 1969). See also K. M. Wilson, *The Policy of the Entente: Essays on the Determinants of British Foreign Policy, 1904–14* (Cambridge, 1985). D. Porch, *The March to the Marne: The French Army, 1871–1914* (Cambridge, 1981) looks at French military preparations for the war.
22. D. C. B. Lieven, *Russia and the Origins of the First World War* (London, 1983) remains the standard account, although it predates the opening of the Russian archives after the fall of the Iron Curtain.
23. For an introduction see J. A. Maiolo, 'Armaments Competition' in R. Boyce and J. A. Maiolo (eds), *The Origins of the Second World War: The Debate Continues* (Basingstoke, 2003), pp. 289–90.
24. R. J. Overy, 'Hitler's War and the German Economy: A Reinterpretation', *Economic History Review* 35 (1982): 272–91. His arguments are further developed in R. J. Overy, *War and Economy in the Third Reich* (Oxford, 1994). For the earlier view, see A. S. Milward, *The German Economy at War* (London, 1965).
25. J. Förster, 'From "Blitzkrieg" to "Total War": Germany's War in Europe' in Chickering et al. (eds), *A World at Total War*, pp. 89–108.
26. G. C. Peden, *British Rearmament and the Treasury, 1932–1939* (Edinburgh, 1979).
27. M. S. Alexander, *The Republic in Danger: General Maurice Gamelin and the Politics of French Defence, 1933–40* (Cambridge, 1993); M. S. Alexander and W. Philpott (eds), *Anglo-French Defence Relations Between the Wars* (Basingstoke, 2002); R. A. Doughty, *The Seeds of Disaster: The Development of French Army Doctrine, 1919–39* (Hamden CT, 1985); and E. C. Kiesling, *Arming Against Hitler: France and the Limits of Military Planning* (Lawrence KS, 1996).
28. For a comparative investigation of the economies of the rival alliances, see R. J. Overy, *Why the Allies Won* (London, 1995).
29. See the chapter on Land Warfare in this volume.

30. S. Stoecker, *Forging Stalin's Army: Marshal Tukhachevskii and the Politics of Military Innovation* (Boulder CO, 1998); M. von Hagen, *Soldiers in the Proletarian Dictatorship: The Red Army and the Soviet Socialist State, 1917–30* (Ithaca NY, 1990); D. R. Stone, *Hammer and Rifle: The Militarization of the Soviet Union, 1926–33* (Lawrence KS, 2000); and E. F. Ziemke, *The Red Army, 1918–41: From Vanguard of World Revolution to US Ally* (London, 2004).

31. M. Harrison, 'The USSR and Total War: Why Didn't the Soviet Economy Collapse in 1942?' in Chickering et al. (eds), *A World at Total War*, pp. 137–56.

32. Of note in this genre are B. J. Bond (ed.), *The First World War and British Military History* (Oxford, 1991) and J. Keegan, *The Battle for History: Re-fighting World War Two* (Toronto, 1995).

33. See Part II: 'The Battle of the Memoirs' in Bond (ed.), *The First World War*.

34. R. Prior and T. Wilson, 'Conflict, Technology and the Impact of Industrialisation: The Great War, 1914–1918', *The Journal of Strategic Studies* 24/3 (2001): 128–57 provides a succinct introduction to the nature of the industrial battlefield.

35. J. B. A. Bailey, 'The First Word War and the Birth of Modern Warfare' in M. Knox and W. Murray (eds), *The Dynamics of Military Revolution, 1300–2050* (Cambridge, 2001), pp. 132–53.

36. G. D. Sheffield, *Forgotten Victory: The First Word War, Myths and Realities* (London, 2001); G. D. Sheffield and D. Todman (eds), *Command and Control on the Western Front: The British Army's Experience, 1914–1918* (Staplehurst, 2004); P. Griffith, *Battle Tactics of the Western Front: The British Army's Art of Attack, 1916–18* (New Haven CT, 1994); and P. Griffith (ed.), *British Fighting Methods in the Great War* (London, 1996).

37. T. Travers, *The Killing Ground: The British Army, the Western Front and the Emergence of Modern Warfare, 1900–1918* (London, 1987); T. Travers, *How the War Was Won: Command and Technology in the British Army on the Western Front* (London, 1992); and T. Travers, 'The Offensive and the Problem of Innovation in British Military Thought', *Journal of Contemporary History* 13/3 (1978): 531–3.

38. S. Robbins, *British Generalship on the Western Front, 1914–18* (London, 2005).

39. R. Prior and T. Wilson, *Command on the Western Front: The Military Career of Sir Henry Rawlinson, 1914–18* (Oxford, 1992); R. Prior and T. Wilson, *The Somme* (New Haven CT, 2005).

40. I. M. Brown, *British Logistics on the Western Front* (Westport CT, 1998).

41. M. Samuels, *Doctrine and Dogma: German and British Infantry Tactics in the First World War* (Westport CT, 1992) and M. Samuels, *Command or Control? Command, Training and Tactics in the British and German Armies, 1888–1918* (London, 1996).

42. A. Clayton, *Paths of Glory: The French Army, 1914–18* (London, 2003); R. Doughty, *Pyrrhic Victory: French Strategy and Operations in the Great War* (Cambridge MA, 2005).

43. See for example, D. Trask, *The AEF and Coalition Warmaking, 1917–18* (Lawrence KS, 1993).

44. For example, British commander-in-chief Sir Douglas Haig's reputation is still the subject of much analysis. See B. J. Bond and N. Cave (eds), *Douglas Haig: A Reassessment after 70 Years* (Barnsley, 1999).

45. J. Mosier, *The Myth of the Great War: A New Military History of World War One* (London, 2001).

46. G. Corrigan, *Mud, Blood and Poppycock: Britain and the First World War* (London, 2003).

47. Most recently, S. Hart, *Montgomery and 'Colossal Cracks': 21st Army Group in Northwest Europe, 1944–5* (Westport CT, 2000) and N. Barr, *Pendulum of War: The Three Battles of El Alamein* (London, 2004).

48. See J. Blatt (ed.), *The French Defeat of 1940: Reassessments* (Oxford, 1998).

49. These are among the topics reviewed in C. McInnes and G. Sheffield (eds), *Warfare in the Twentieth Century* (London, 1988).

50. R. M. Citino, *Quest for Decisive Victory: From Stalemate to Blitzkrieg in Europe, 1899–1940* (Lawrence KS, 2002).

51. D. French, *The Strategy of the Lloyd George Coalition* (Oxford, 1995); D. French, *British Strategy and War Aims, 1914–16* (London, 1986).

52. B. Millman, *Pessimism and British War Policy, 1916–18* (London, 2001).

53. K. Burk, *Britain, America and the Sinews of War, 1914–18* (London, 1985); K. Neilson, *Strategy and Supply: The Anglo-Russian Alliance, 1914–17* (London, 1984); W. J. Philpott, *Anglo-French Relations and Strategy on the Western Front, 1914–18* (London, 1996); and G. Cassar, *The Forgotten Front: The British Campaign in Italy, 1917–18* (London, 1998).

54. E. Greenhalgh, 'What the British Were on the Somme in 1916', *War in History* 6/2 (1999): 147–73; W. J. Philpott, 'Why the British Were Really on the Somme: A Reply to Elizabeth Greenhalgh', *War in History* 9/4 (2002): 446–71; and E. Greenhalgh, 'Flames over the Somme: A Retort to William Philpott', *War in History* 10/3 (2003): 335–42.

55. Doughty's *Pyrrhic Victory* will begin to fill that gap for France. N. Stone's dated *The Eastern Front, 1914–17* (London, 1975) remains the standard work on the Russian Front.

56. C. Malkasian, *A History of Modern Wars of Attrition* (Westport CT, 2002); R. T. Foley, *German Strategy and the Path to Verdun: Erich von Falkenhayn and the Development of Attrition, 1870–1916* (Cambridge, 2005).

57. See for example, G. Kolko, *The Politics of War, The World, and United States Foreign Policy, 1943–45* (New York, 1990). For a recent revisionist overview, see P. P. O'Brien, 'East Versus West in the Defeat of Germany', *The Journal of Strategic Studies* 23/2 (2000): 89–113.

58. See the chapter on Air Power in this volume.

59. F. W. Winterbotham, *The Ultra Secret* (London, 1974).

60. The main works to date are P. Beesly, *Room 40: British Naval Intelligence, 1914–1918* (London, 1982) and M. Occleshaw, *Armour Against Fate: British Military Intelligence in the First World War* (London, 1989).

61. See for example B. H. Liddell Hart, *The Other Side of the Hill: Germany's Generals, Their Rise and Fall* (London, 1948); G. P. Megargee, *Inside Hitler's High Command* (Lawrence KS, 2000).

62. W. Deist et al. (eds), *Germany and the Second World War* (Oxford, 1990–2006). The first six volumes have been translated into English. Volume seven will be available in English later in 2006.

63. Quoted in S. Förster, 'Dreams and Nightmares: German Military Leadership and the Images of Future Warfare, 1871–1914' in Boemeke et al. (eds), *Anticipating Total War*, pp. 343–7.

64. H. H. Nelson, *Leon Trotsky and the Art of Insurrection, 1905–17* (London, 1988); I. D. Thatcher, *Leon Trostsky and World War One: August 1914 to February 1917* (Basingstoke, 2000); M. Liebman, *Leninism under Lenin* (London, 1975); and N. Harding, *Leninism* (Basingstoke, 1996).

65. Foley, *German Strategy and the Path to Verdun, passim.* See also Förster, 'Dreams and Nightmares: German Military Leadership and the Images of Future Warfare, 1871–1914' in Boemeke et al. (eds), *Anticipating Total War.*

66. For example A. Calder, *The People's War: Britain 1939–45* (London: 1969) was a defining study of the phenomenon.

67. A. Marwick, *War and Social Change in the Twentieth Century: A Comparative Study of Britain, France, Germany, Russia and the United States* (London, 1974). For a succinct review of the value of Marwick's model see I. F. W. Beckett, 'Total War' in McInnes and Sheffield (eds), *Warfare in the Twentieth Century*, pp. 1–23.

68. A. Marwick et al., *War Peace and Social Change: Europe 1900–1955* (Milton Keynes, 1989–90).

69. C. Emsley, A. Marwick and W. Simpson (eds), *War, Peace and Social Change in Twentieth Century Europe* (Milton Keynes, 1989), p. 2.

70. Ibid., p. 11.

71. J. M. Winter, *Sites of Memory, Sites of Mourning* (Cambridge, 1995).

72. A. Becker and S. Audoin-Rouzeau, *1914–1918: Understanding the Great War* (London, 2002).

73. Such debates are addressed in Marwick, *War Peace and Social Change.* Further more recent debates, such as the impact of demobilization and the motivation for genocide, are addressed in the updated Open University course reader by Marwick et al. (eds), *Total War and Historical Change, 1914–55* (Milton Keynes, 2001).

74. G. D. Feldman, *Army, Industry and Labour in Germany, 1914–1918* (Princeton NJ, 1966); C. Maier, *Recasting Bourgeois Europe: Stabilization in France, Germany and Italy after World War I* (Princeton NJ, 1988).

75. Herwig, *The First World War: Germany and Austria-Hungary.*

76. M. Howard, *The First World War* (Oxford, 2002).

77. H. Strachan, *The First World War: Vol. 1: To Arms!* (Oxford, 2001).

78. H. Strachan, *The First World War: A New Illustrated History* (London, 2003).

79. John H. Morrow, *The Great War: An Imperial History* (London, 2004); J. Keegan, *The First Word War* (London, 1998).

80. D. Stevenson, *1914–1918: The History of the First World War* (London, 2004).

81. J. Terraine, *White Heat: The New Way in Warfare* (London, 1982).

82. H. Cecil and P. Liddle (eds), *Facing Armageddon: The First World War Experienced* (London, 1996).

83. P. Calvocoressi, G. Wint and J. Pritchard, *Total War: Causes and Courses of the Second World War* (London, 1989).

84. G. Wright, *The Ordeal of Total War, 1939–45* (New York, 1968).

85. P. Liddle, I. Whitehead and J. Bourne (eds), *The Great World War, 1914–1945: Vol. 1: Lighting Strikes Twice* and *Vol. 2 Who Won? Who Lost?* (London, 2000–2). In this genre, see also, 'Total War: Total Defence, 1789–2000', *Proceedings of the 26th Congress of the International Commission for Military History* (Stockholm, Swedish Commission on Military History, 2001).

86. Chickering and Förster, 'Introduction' in Chickering et al. (eds), *The Shadow of Total War*, p. 2.

87. See the discussion in ibid., pp. 8–12.

88. Chickering and Förster, 'Are We There Yet? World War II and the Theory of Total War' in Chickering et al. (eds), *A World at Total War*, pp. 1–16.

89. Chickering et al. (eds), *The Shadow of Total War*, pp. 6–7.

90. Chickering and Förster, 'Are We There Yet?' in Chickering et al. (eds), *A World at Total War*, p. 5.

91. Howard, *The First World War*, p. 1.

8
air power

john buckley

Of any modern military technological innovation, there can be little doubt that the aeroplane has had one of the most profound effects on the conduct and nature of war. In just a few decades air power has come to dominate war to such a degree that nations are now compelled to incorporate employment of, or defence against, air forces in planning to an extent that would have seemed fantastic to the first airmen. Indeed, it is remarkable that even though the first military use of flimsy and clumsy aeroplanes dates back only to the second decade of the twentieth century, we have now entered an age when military operations and national strategies are often entirely dependent on the ability to deploy air forces. Moreover, for the industrial world, air power has opened up wholly new approaches to conflict, including the possibility of fighting wars without ever having to put soldiers on the ground, or indeed without ever having to set foot outside home territory. In the early twenty-first century, for the USA at least, military aviation now offers truly global reach, capable of delivering destruction upon an enemy within a few hours, or with missiles, in just minutes.

The growth of war into the third dimension has had many profound consequences. The first and most obvious impact has been the expansion of the battle area into the skies above the field of battle, and further still into the rear zones of armies far beyond the range of artillery. Supply dumps and lines of communication have been exposed to air attack, whilst ground troops themselves have become increasingly vulnerable to aerial bombardment, particularly when inadequately shielded by protective air cover. This use of air power became known as tactical, or latterly, conventional air power.

153

Secondly, as the range and capability of bomber aircraft grew, so enemy centres of industry and population came to be threatened from the air, expanding still further the scope and intensity of the war experience, bringing home to civilians the destruction and devastation of war that hitherto had rarely or only indirectly affected them. By the Cold War era, air attack presented the possibility of whole cities being razed to the ground and millions of civilian casualties inflicted in just a few hours. The use of air forces to wage war against an enemy state, largely independent of other arms, became labelled as strategic air power, and many air forces have emphasized strategic role in an effort to gain and then maintain independence from the older services, such as armies or navies.

Air power has also deepened the demands of war on societies in quite specific ways, adding considerably to the exponential increase in the burden of war during the industrial age. The maintenance of first class air power status made near ruinous demands on economies absorbing huge resources, specifically technological assets. In order to compete in air campaigns, states had successfully to manage and integrate advanced industries, the training of personnel, and technological innovation, in the knowledge that air warfare frittered away such valuable resources in a quite profligate manner.

Air power has also had a major impact on the relationship between modern industrial powers and the wider world. The military capability of developed nations has grown at a rapid rate since the late nineteenth century leading to a chasm which could no longer be bridged by traditional military effort. Air power increased still further this growing divide between the industrial powers and the rest of the world, in part precipitating the development, with some success, of new modes of warfare, such as guerrilla or terrorist tactics, intended to evade the overwhelming military strength of the industrial powers. Thus, the inherent strengths and advantages brought by air supremacy over the past hundred years may well have been partially obviated in the early twenty-first century.

global air power and national strategy

Over the last hundred years or so much has been written about the vital importance of air power to a nation's military strength and security, but the development of air power and its place within strategic planning has been more complex than a simple measure against theoretical models can provide. Although fully independent air forces appeared to advocates to be both logical and necessary for the unhindered development of air power, the history of the twentieth century demonstrates that this was not necessarily so. States usually, though by no means always, developed air forces in conjunction with prevailing national strategies, which often did not require or suit the creation of strategic bombing fleets or independent air forces. In Germany in the late 1930s and early 1940s, strategic bombing fell from the agenda and factors such as technological shortcomings and a weak aero-industrial base were instrumental in this. Equally, however, when the war began and Germany was drawn into shorter campaigns there was little room or apparent need for long-range heavy strategic bombers.[1] This is not to argue that the Luftwaffe did not desire strategic bombing forces, for they clearly did, but national strategic priorities lay elsewhere. For Japan and the USA the notion of an independent air force was less important in the inter-war era. Neither nation was confronted by the immediate threat of a nearby air power, for which an independent air force might offer a superior form of defence, and greater emphasis was therefore placed on close co-operation with naval forces, for example. In part this explains why the USA did not create a separate, independent air force until 1947.

For the Americans and Japanese, facing each other across the Pacific Ocean, the development of strong naval air forces, principally based on aircraft carriers, was a clear priority, in a way that it was not for the British, tied in as they were to continental European affairs. For Britain, threatened by air bombardment since the airship and bomber raids of the First World War, an independent air force to provide strategic defence and mount similar offensives against continental opponents was considered vitally important. Yet again this contrasted with France where, like Germany, although the air force dabbled with notions of strategic bombing, national strategy placed much greater emphasis on support of the army in its defensive posture behind the Maginot Line.[2] The USSR invested heavily in strategic bombing fleets in the 1920s and early 1930s, but when war came the Voyenno Voznushnyye Sily (VVS or Soviet Air Force) became tightly enmeshed with the army's pivotal war against the Wehrmacht and consequently devoted little effort to long-range air bombardment.[3]

However, although air forces often dovetailed neatly with national strategic needs, this was not always so. Trade defence was a vital requirement for the survival of maritime powers such as Britain and Japan, yet neither invested heavily in this field of air power in the inter-war era, resulting in difficult and painful learning periods in the Second World War. Britain was able to adapt, but Japan was not.[4] For the USA, the Cold War period saw the stagnation of tactical-conventional air forces, as greater emphasis was placed on strategic nuclear capability: thus when intervention was required in Vietnam, American air assets were exposed as weak and inappropriately trained and equipped. Low-level operational capability, without resorting to nuclear response, caused a major strategic problem for the US forces in Europe if faced with a Soviet attack in the 1960s and 1970s. Conventional defence lacked credibility, and thus reliance was placed on nuclear weaponry to deter attack; but this also lacked credibility as any use of nuclear weapons was likely to escalate into a strategic level exchange of missiles, something neither side wanted. Would the USA risk nuclear holocaust to save Europe? The perceived inability of the West's conventional forces – including air forces – to resist a Warsaw Pact assault provoked only vacillation until, in the aftermath of the Vietnam War, US analysts began to develop the Air–Land Battle concept, in which it was envisaged that in the near future increasingly sophisticated technologically based air and land forces would develop the ability to defeat a Soviet-led attack on the West. By the 1980s, therefore, a more realistic and credible NATO strategy had been established, one in which air power was to play a key role.[5]

The broader global strategic requirements of the great or superpowers have also been met in a variety of ways by air power. In the early twentieth century imperial powers regularly deployed air forces to bolster their grip on their dominions and possessions. Indeed, against insurgents and dissident groups, aircraft have often proved to be very effective, helping in quelling rebellions and supporting imperial strategies. The British used aircraft in the Third Afghan War in 1919, and with great success against an uprising in Iraq from 1922 onwards. The Spanish and French employed air forces in the Riff War (1921–26) in Morocco, and the USA employed air units in Central America between 1927 and 1933. Furthermore, the Italians infamously bombed Emperor Haille Salassie's troops in the 1935 invasion of Ethiopia, even employing poison gas. [6]

However, although air forces were relatively successful in some cases, in other examples of counterinsurgency operations they were obviously less so. In the dense jungle and difficult terrain of Southeast Asia aircraft were much less useful, especially when opposed by troops and guerrillas employing appropriate defensive measures. For the French in 1953–54 at Dien Bien Phu, US forces in Vietnam, and the Soviets in Afghanistan, limitations on the effectiveness of air power were amply exposed. Post-Cold War campaigns in the Balkans and the Middle East have yet to rectify the impression that air power can provide only a limited answer in certain asymmetric scenarios. Moreover, it can be argued that in response to the overwhelming conventional military might of the industrial powers, opposing forces – guerrilla, terrorist or insurgent based – have further evolved to counter or at least evade much of the firepower and support afforded to military operations by air forces.

air power and technology

The search for success in the employment of air power, particularly in late twentieth- and early twenty-first-century conflicts, has increasingly rested on the development and introduction of ever more sophisticated technologies, offering highly accurate firepower, correspondingly resulting in fewer civilian or collateral casualties and, even more importantly, fewer friendly combat losses. Such efforts have been responses to the desire to maintain the ability to employ military action as an acceptable method of meeting political aims. In a world increasingly governed by a judgemental world media, squeamish about avoidable civilian deaths, and with national public opinion vital for support of military action carried out in democratic states, this desire is understandable and rational.

However, too often in air power history, technologically based explanations of highly complex issues have been employed, to the detriment of greater understanding of why and how air campaigns have been decided. Equipment or 'kit-based' explanations of success and failure abound in the literature of air power, precipitating a degree of technological determinism – that air war is essentially shaped and defined by the input of new technology. This view has come to dominate ever more since the end of the Cold War and the growth of the high-tech world. Examples have been culled from history to underpin this interpretation: the British won the Battle of Britain because of the Spitfire fighter aircraft and radar; the Luftwaffe lost control of the skies over Europe in 1944 because of the mismatch between the P-51 Mustang and available German interceptors; and that the underlying cause of the shortcomings of American air power over Vietnam lay in the vulnerability of their aircraft to SAMs (surface-to-air missiles) and in the weaknesses of their air superiority aeroplanes.

Yet these are profoundly dissatisfying and often misleading interpretations. Technology is obviously important in explaining the outcome of air campaigns, but it has only intermittently proved in any way decisive in its own right. The differences between respective combat aircraft capabilities were rarely enough to prove pivotal, often being only one of a number of important factors in determining victory or defeat. Indeed, even quantum leaps such as the introduction of jet fighters by Germany in the Second World War had little effect because of pilot and fuel shortages. These were the real causes of the collapse in the Luftwaffe in 1944 and the introduction of the Messerschmitt Me 262 jet fighter could do little to prevent this.

Even in the very narrow field of air-to-air combat, technology does not necessarily confer success on one side. In the 1960s missiles were gradually introduced into the inventory of weapons carried by aircraft, but had less impact than had been hoped, despite the obvious combat advantages theoretically gained. Aircrew were in fact unwilling to fire on a target they could not see or identify and often closed to visual range before attacking, thus much negating the advantages conferred by missile technology. Moreover, combat experience and situation awareness proved to be more crucial factors in determining success or failure in aerial dog fighting.[7]

Nevertheless, the edge potentially provided by technological superiority could mix with other factors to tilt the balance of air power one way and it naturally made sense for technologically advanced powers to attempt to seize and hold superiority in this field. The problem remains, however, that Western powers in particular, have and continue to rely too heavily on technological interpretations of success and failure in air war. Indeed, in 1994 one air power analyst claimed that the USAF had 'long worshipped at the altar of technology' and that policy, doctrine and operational art were too often driven by technological determinism.[8]

strategic air power

Of greatest interest to theorists writing and speculating about air power has been the concept of the knockout attack from the air, what was to become known as strategic bombing. It was predicted that air bombardment of major urban centres would be devastating, that there would be no viable defence against such attack, and that offensives of this type would encapsulate the future of air war, and indeed war more generally. The novelist H. G. Wells popularized these ideas before the First World War and the apocalyptic imagery of savage air attacks being launched against civilian populations has continued to flourish in fiction and film ever since.[9] However, it was to take some 40 years from the birth of controlled powered flight for such notions to become reality.

Although serious speculation and thinking about strategic air power began before 1914, it was only in the First World War that such concepts could be put into practice. Both the Allies and the Central Powers devised plans for the use of long-range aerial bombardment to derive strategic benefits. Germany's efforts initially centred upon the use of airships, then long-range heavy bombers to drive Britain out of the war. However, the theory proved easier than the practice. Long-range navigation, in poor weather, over hostile territory, when confronted by stout resistance all seriously compromised the effectiveness of such campaigns and when increasing loss rates forced operations to switch to night-time, accuracy declined still further. However, German strategy partly rested on the assumption that even if specific targets could not be hit, random bombing of urban areas was likely to damage civilian morale to a greater or lesser degree and that this could prove effective. Such thinking presaged the concept of area bombing employed to such devastating effect in the Second World War. Despite considerable investment in time, resources and effort, strategic bombing in the First World War achieved very little. Material damage was slight and the initial shock value was soon matched by civilian stoicism and improvements in defensive techniques which reduced the bombing raids to the level of mere nuisance.

The decisive air attack concept nevertheless became more relevant to political leaders in the aftermath of the First World War and all its associated butchery, slaughter and attritional trench warfare. It was imperative to many after 1918 that a new method of fighting wars, should it again become necessary to wage them in the future, was required; a method which would be quick and decisive and would avoid years of stalemate and agony. Aerial bombardment, however tentative and ineffective in the Great War itself, seemed to offer a strategy for winning wars quickly. A series of heavy air attacks on enemy cities over a few days or possibly weeks would be enough to decide the war, it was contended: losses would be heavy and the conflict intense, but total casualties compared to the First World War would be lower and the fighting concluded comparatively quickly.[10]

Because strategic bombing in the First World War caused little material damage, post-war analysts focused upon the supposed impact of bombing on civilian morale, though modern analysis has demonstrated that there was little real evidence of this also.[11] However, the assumption that civilian morale was highly vulnerable to sustained and concerted aerial bombardment persisted throughout the inter-war era. Such notions were most famously encapsulated in the work of Giulio Douhet (1869–1930), an Italian writer of the 1920s. More than any other, Douhet's name has come to be linked with air warfare, even though in reality he was little read outside of Italy until the 1940s, and his direct influence on the development of air power theory may in truth have been negligible.[12] In terms of theorizing the principles of strategic air war, Douhet had little new to say, but as a propagandist and prophet Douhet proved important, even if retrospectively so. In *The Command of the Air* (1921, revised 1927), Douhet's most famous work, he argued that there was no defence against massed bombing raids and that in order to ensure that a war was concluded quickly, an air offensive had to be as savage and brutal as possible to ensure the decisiveness of the knockout blow. He even argued for the liberal use of poisoned gas.

Although Douhet's vision of an unstoppable bomber fleet was later to be heavily criticized as being simplistic – to say nothing of it being profoundly amoral – he did write in a time before radar, when a surprise raid was much more likely to be successful, and secondly, he did always argue for the destruction of the enemy's air forces as a priority, in order to win command of the air. This last point was too easily ignored when air forces later attempted to put into practice the concepts of strategic bombing in the 1940s.

There were also air power publicists who worked hard to cajole and persuade governments into investment in air power in the inter-war era. In the USA, Billy Mitchell (1879–1936) lobbied throughout the 1920s and early 1930s for resources to be poured into American air power. At one point he criticized his superiors in the American military so openly that he was court-martialled and ejected from the US army.[13] In the 1940s Alexander de Seversky (1894–1974), an expatriate Russian who was a leading figure in the American aero-industry in the twenties and thirties, extolled the virtues of an air based national strategy for the USA, most famously in his book of 1942 *Victory Through Air Power*. Curiously, by the following year the book had been transformed into a Disney produced cartoon, in which de Seversky also appeared in several live action sequences. The film attempted to demonstrate that America's route to victory in the Second World War lay in the development of a long-range heavy bomber force. It is now difficult to gauge the impact of the film on the public, but it clearly set out the arch air power advocates' case and President Roosevelt made it required viewing for his chiefs of staff.

Prior to the Second World War a more technical and scientific approach to strategic bombing emerged, particularly in the USA where the USAAF (United States Army Air Force) developed concepts of precision bombing with defensive formations of aircraft equipped with an array of machine guns and cannon. The RAF, the only other force that by 1939 had maintained an interest in strategic bombing since the First World War, was more haphazard in its planning and thinking. Although it had thrown off many of the morale-oriented approaches to bombing embedded in the 1920s by Marshal of the RAF Hugh Trenchard, the RAF still had few clear ideas on precisely how a bombing campaign could be prosecuted.[14]

Paradoxically, the Luftwaffe was the most accurate bombing force in the early stages of the Second World War, but strategic circumstance and infrastructural weaknesses drew the German air force away from strategic bombing, despite some plans for very-long-range bombers – such as the *Uralbomber* and *Amerikabomber*.[15] German attempts to blitz Britain in the 1940–41 period foundered quickly as their aircraft were unsuitable and ill equipped for such a campaign, while the Luftwaffe was too weak to build and maintain the air strength necessary to support such an effort. In a similar fashion to the First World War, German efforts switched to bombing at night, but still came to grief against organized defences. Operations were further hindered by poor weather and shifting operational objectives.

However, the British were determined to press on with their own bombing campaign especially as from the summer of 1940 onwards it was the only realistic and obvious method Churchill's government had of striking back at Germany. The RAF, however, encountered the same problems as the Luftwaffe; doctrine and equipment were exposed as flawed and inadequate and heavy losses ensued. A switch to night-time raiding followed, but this had further deleterious effects on bombing accuracy.[16] With little to show for its costly efforts, by the end of 1941 RAF Bomber Command was on the point of being put out of business.

Three factors saved the bomber offensive: first, the entry of the USA opened up the possibility of linking the RAF's efforts with those of the USAAF; second, the RAF appointed Air Marshal Arthur Harris to lead Bomber Command; and third, the Air Staff (not Harris) decided upon a policy of night-time area bombing of urban centres, rather than persisting with precision bombing. Although area bombing was less accurate it would cause sufficient damage and disruption to justify the shift in policy towards, in effect, targeting civilians. It would also keep RAF losses to manageable proportions. Harris was an enthusiastic supporter of the policy – though he did not subscribe to the notion that undermining German morale could be achieved – and prosecuted it with single-minded vigour. He also pulled Bomber Command together and despite many setbacks transformed its effectiveness.

The USAAF's initial doctrine of precision, daytime raids by box formations of mutually supporting heavy bombers was ruthlessly exposed during much of 1942 and 1943, with losses reaching levels even the Americans could not endure.[17] Harris's area campaign was also stalling, and redemption only came when the USAAF began employing long-range escort fighters in large numbers to battle with German interceptors over Europe.[18] From the spring of 1944, P-51 Mustangs equipped with fuel-filled drop tanks and capable of operating over Germany for sufficient time, broke the back of the Luftwaffe and seized control of the skies over Europe. It was a costly campaign and one which made little sense unless supported by a resource rich alliance, but in the strategic environment of 1943–44 it yielded great rewards. When the USA began a major bombing campaign against Japan in 1944 the effects were devastating, as the Japanese were in no position to offer the level of resistance as provided by the Germans until the summer of 1944. In the spring of 1945 the USAAF switched to a programme of area bombing Japanese cities with quite horrific results. Firestorms had previously been caused in Europe on occasion, following the increased use of incendiary or firebombs during heavy raids. Whole areas of cities were destroyed in such operations in which temperatures at the centre of the firestorms reached 1,000 degrees Celsius. In July 1943 in Hamburg around 35,000 civilians were killed, while at Dresden in February 1945 over 80,000 died. Japan suffered more, with 100,000 killed in one night in Tokyo alone in March 1945 while many other cities were systematically burnt out even before the atomic bombings in August. By the cessation of hostilities some 40 per cent of the urban areas of Japan's cities had been laid waste.[19]

The strategic effectiveness of the bombing campaign remains hotly contested and in moral terms the deaths of around 1 million civilians at the hands of Allied bombers when the war still had to be won with ground offensives seems quite indefensible. The surveys of the bombing campaigns carried out by Allied investigators and analysts in the post-war period implied that the effects of bombing had not been as dramatic as initially thought, and that the RAF's area bombing campaign in particular had contributed little to Allied victory in the war. Moral indignation at the deaths of so many civilians for little strategic benefit grew in the 1960s as anti-war sentiment flourished in the age of the Vietnam War. More recently writers such as Michael Sherry, Steven Garrett and Robert Pape have been savage in their condemnation of Allied bombing policy in the Second World War on both moral and strategic grounds.[20]

However, although the bombers alone did not bring about the defeat of either Germany or Japan, there is strong evidence that they contributed significantly to the Allied victory. Richard Overy and Tami Biddle have both put forward strong cases that in strategic terms the bombing campaign yielded great rewards to the Allies.[21] In Europe, Allied bombers hindered the expansion of the German economy, drew dwindling enemy resources away from other fronts, and imposed severe attrition on the Luftwaffe, effectively breaking it prior to the D-Day landings in June 1944. The impact of the bombing on Japan's war effort is more debatable, as the destruction of Japanese cities began only when the economy was already crumbling, largely as a result of the blockade. Moreover, it is by no means clear that the deaths of hundreds of thousands of civilians had a significant impact on the Japanese military's consent to surrender in August. There is even great dissent over the degree to which the atomic bombings directly caused Japan's capitulation.[22]

The ultimate realization of Douhet's vision finally appeared to come with the emergence of nuclear weaponry in the post-1945 period. Long-range bombers equipped with atom bombs had the ability, it seemed, to blast an opponent into submission in a few hours, and thus prove Douhet correct. By the 1950s there is little doubt that both the USA and the Soviet Union had the capacity to inflict enormous damage on each other, amounting to a potential knockout blow. Yet, few benefits were to accrue from this power. Strategic air forces had attained such potency that there was no political capital to be made and by the 1960s notions of mutually assured destruction consigned nuclear air power to the level of a politico-strategic deterrent, with little practical military use. In many ways, strategic air power had reached a dead-end.

Little of substance emerged to change this until 1988 when Colonel John Warden III, USAF (United States Air Force), put forward a theoretical model for the employment of air forces in a conventional non-nuclear scenario, a model he claimed offered many virtues. He contended that an enemy state's centre of gravity, and therefore most obvious primary target, was the leadership. Although very difficult to hit and eliminate, doing so would yield great rewards if successful. Other parts of the enemy state offered fewer immediate benefits if targeted, but would prove easier to hit, though would take progressively longer to cripple, the further one moved from the enemy state's true centre of gravity: its leadership.[23] However, Warden's theory only became workable if the capacity to hit and destroy the enemy leadership existed. Prior to the 1990s it did not, but with the employment of emerging technologies such as satellite navigation, cruise missiles and smart weaponry, the possibility began to emerge of delivering a knockout blow, tolerable in civilian casualties, which could end a war quickly and without the commitment of huge ground forces. Moreover, such methods could provide a potent political policing tool against rogue powers. Clearly, much of this thinking was conditioned by the American failure in Vietnam when the blunt instrument of air power had been unable to deliver much of worth to the US government, certainly not until restraints on bombing were supposedly eased in 1972, and arguably not even then.[24] Succeeding US administrations were desperate to avoid such entanglements and faith in military intervention and air power had been badly shaken by the experience.[25]

Nevertheless, despite the importance and influence of Warden's writing in developing air power theory, his ultimate vision of crippling a state through precision air attacks on its leadership has yet to be fully tested. The First Gulf War in 1991 demonstrated that air operations could paralyse an enemy field army's command and control structure preparatory to attack but there was no concerted attempt to eliminate the Iraqi leadership, whilst subsequent operations in the Balkans until 1999 clearly did not aim to put the theory of a focused strike against an enemy leadership into practice. The Kosovo Crisis in that year appeared to offer such an opportunity, but political constraints and shifting strategic objectives resulted in air power being applied incrementally and this thus put paid to notions of putting Warden's grand vision to the test. The predominantly US invasion of Iraq in 2003 has thus far provided the best example of this new theoretical approach, but the supposed 'shock and awe' concept did not reap great rewards and attempts at decapitating Saddam Hussein's regime from the air palpably failed. It took a traditional and conventional ground force invasion and occupation to drive the regime from power, though air power played a key role in this.

Theories of air power over the last century have therefore generated a dichotomy. Much of the theorizing and literature has focused on the potential of air power and has offered a near panacea-like answer to the problems of war: cleaner, decisive and politically acceptable. Yet, the capabilities of the world's air forces have trailed behind such visions, invariably unable to meet the exacting claims, demands and objectives set for them. Consequently, because of this mismatch between theory and reality, when measured against the more excessive claims, air forces have often been seen to fail, certainly on a strategic level. Nevertheless, when the progress and impact of air power is measured against what was actually practical and possible at given points in the history of air operations, it can be seen to have had a major and decisive influence upon the conduct and outcome of wars.

tactical and operational air power

Although strategic air power has largely dominated discussion of air operations since the First World War, tactical and operational air support has in reality played a greater role in shaping and changing the face of warfare and battle. Although the earliest such air operations focused largely on reconnaissance and observation, it was an obvious and logical progression to contesting control of the airspace over a battlefield, and then using such command to influence directly the ebb and flow of battle on the ground. By the Second World War the links between air and ground forces had strengthened considerably, though subsequently air support doctrine and forces in the West arguably stagnated relatively for much of the Cold War. During the late 1970s and early 1980s, however, the close integration of ground and air forces, precipitated by the development and potential of new computer and communication technologies, forced tactical-conventional air power to the top of the military agenda again, with consequent strategic implications.

A key factor hindering the development of battlefield air support capability for much of the twentieth century was the unwillingness of air forces to embrace the role. In the First World War, it quickly became apparent that ground support operations imposed the highest levels of attrition on nascent air forces: even air combat caused fewer losses than battlefield support operations. As pilots, aircrew and aircraft represented heavy investments, air commanders were loath to commit them to such duties lightly. Yet, the development of the war in Europe demonstrated the important role that ground support air operations could play. Initially, reconnaissance and observation aircraft – balloons as well as aeroplanes – dominated the skies in 1914–15 directing artillery fire and providing valuable intelligence on the enemy's forces.[26] Denying such advantages to the enemy led inexorably to air-to-air combat to wrest and maintain control of the airspace over the battlefield – air superiority. The first true fighter aircraft, such as the revolutionary Fokker Eindekker of 1915, emerged as a result of this development. Large-scale air superiority battles soon followed, from Verdun in 1916 onwards. During such campaigns both sides also recognized the potential of employing aircraft to attack enemy ground forces directly – machine gunning (to become known as strafing) and bombing. The Allies employed dual-purpose fighter-bomber aircraft in this role, though the Germans plumped for specialized ground attack aircraft. More importantly, the Allies began to link aircraft with infantry, tanks and artillery more closely and by 1918 this combined arms approach proved remarkably successful, helping to reintroduce manoeuvre and movement on to the Great War battlefield.

However, air force loss rates on these operations remained high, and when the war came to an end, many air power experts sought ways to eschew such ruinously costly and wasteful duties in the future. By 1939 air–ground support doctrine and equipment had suffered from 20 years of marginalization as air forces largely devoted their attention to strategic or maritime air power.[27] In the early stages of the Second World War however, the Luftwaffe indicated what was possible with air support of land operations. The Germans had learned significant lessons in the Spanish Civil War (1936–39) and this edge on their rivals was to prove invaluable. Even though in 1939 the Luftwaffe was relatively ill equipped for close-air support duties (less than 10 per cent of the force being designed for this role), the seizure of air superiority and the employment of general-purpose bombers against enemy rearzones and communications networks proved highly successful, contributing to the so-called blitzkrieg of 1939–41.[28] However, attrition rates were still very high even in successful campaigns, and when the Luftwaffe was drawn further towards direct battlefield air support operations in Russia in 1941, the limitations of an under-prepared and medium sized air force were ruthlessly exposed.[29]

By 1942 the Luftwaffe was crumbling and air superiority began to swing towards the Soviet and Western Allied air forces. The Red Air Force remained tied closely to the Soviet army and employed the bulk of its air power to support ground operations directly. Large numbers of fighters would seize localized air superiority, facilitating air attack operations by dedicated ground support aircraft. The Western Allies developed the idea further, investing heavily in air superiority fighters to sweep the Germans from the sky, resulting not just in air superiority, but air supremacy. From 1944 onwards the German army in the west had to operate with negligible air support and under threat of near constant attack by enemy aircraft, predominantly fighter-bombers. Such air support aided the Allied ground forces considerably with swarms of Republic P-47 Thunderbolts and Hawker Typhoons providing near instantaneous air support for Allied units, and more importantly interdicting the German lines of supply and communication. However, the actual physical potency of such air attacks should not be exaggerated; the accuracy of air-to-ground weaponry, particularly rockets and free fall bombs, was low and equated more closely to area suppression weapons. Indeed, proportionally very few tanks were destroyed by direct air attack and analysis showed that some 140 rockets were required to secure even a 50 per cent chance of a direct lethal hit.[30]

Nevertheless, the Allied air forces in 1944–45 demonstrated that, within certain limitations imposed by the prevailing level of technology, air power could markedly influence the outcome of land operations. It was also clear from the Second World War that seizing control of the airspace over the battlefield was essential; indeed, it was preferable to eliminate all possible threat from an enemy air force to create the circumstances in which air assets could most favourably influence and shape the outcome of battle.

However, the period after the Second World War witnessed a stagnation of tactical air power, most notably in the ground support role. Strategic air power predominated for much of the Cold War and though the Korean War (1950–53) demonstrated that tactical air power had already declined somewhat since 1945, little was done to address the problem, as in theory large-scale conventional war had been consigned to the past by the emergence of nuclear deterrence. The Vietnam War (1965–73) exposed the weaknesses in this policy when US air forces were dragged into an asymmetrical confrontation in Southeast Asia in which tactical air units were required to support American and South Vietnamese ground forces. Although constrained by political directives, the campaign illustrated that US air power was incapable of imposing itself upon military operations as effectively as it might due to deficiencies in doctrine and equipment. Losses to surface-to-air missiles and other types of ground fire illustrated both a worrying trend and once again emphasized that suppression of the enemy's anti-aircraft capability was crucial to the maintenance of effective ground support operations. In Southeast Asia the USA lost a staggering 2,561 aeroplanes and 3,587 helicopters, and losses on this scale threatened to undermine any future military response to perceived threats by being politically much too costly. The Soviet Union encountered similar problems in Afghanistan when air assets began to suffer heavy and embarrassing levels of attrition to ground fire, notably surface-to-air missiles. Unwillingness to endure high loss rates coupled with a lack of desire to pump in the huge ground forces necessary to impose Soviet will upon the country demonstrated the inherent weakness of air power against a guerrilla-insurgent based persisting strategy.

The one significant theatre of operations where air power did markedly influence the outcome of major land campaigns was the Middle East. The Arab–Israeli conflicts demonstrated clearly that the effective integration of air assets into strategic planning could prove fruitful. This proved to be most obvious in the Six Day War of 1967 when the Israeli Air Force scored a great success against their Arab counterparts, particularly the Egyptians, who lost some 300 aircraft out of a force of 340. Seizing air superiority provided the Israeli ground forces with considerable latitude for offensive action. In the Yom Kippur/Ramadan War of 1973 the Egyptians, in an effort to evade the Israeli Air Force's continuing superiority, relied heavily on SAM protection, and only came seriously unstuck when they ventured beyond this protective umbrella. A ground force's vulnerability to enemy air attack when in open terrain and largely unprotected was once again demonstrated.

However, positive analysis of Israeli success should be tempered by the advantages conferred by military aid and finance provided by the USA and indeed, since the 1950s, the Israeli Air Force has maintained a significant qualitative advantage over its neighbouring Arabs opponents. Nevertheless, their success demonstrated vividly what could be achieved by properly integrated air and land forces.[31]

In the USA, by the late 1970s and early 1980s the lessons of Vietnam and the desire to confront Soviet conventional military superiority in Europe with non-nuclear response options, fused with concepts of incorporating emerging computer technologies into the integrated Air–Land Battle concept. The US military proposed dealing with the whole battlefield area in its entirety rather than having ground and air forces working largely separately, only coming together at specific points and moments of the battle. In addition, the concept of Follow-On Force Attack – precision air attack directed by satellite guidance and smart weaponry – offered the opportunity to strangle Warsaw Pact offensives by crippling support structures and the vital second wave forces, considered essential in Soviet operational doctrine to exploit the inroads made by first wave assaults. The Air–Land Battle concept was in its infancy when the Soviet Union began to collapse, but its near future potential added to the growing burden felt by the USSR's political and military leadership in the mid-to-late 1980s.[32]

The integrated air–land battlefield notion was supposedly eventually put to the test in the First Gulf War (1991). Apparently sophisticated tactical air forces put the Iraqi ground forces to the sword, allowing the coalition ground forces to achieve their operational objectives relatively painlessly. However, it should be noted that the great majority of ordnance dropped in 1991 was 'dumb' rather than 'smart' weaponry – by a ratio of some 10 to 1 – and that in both Gulf Wars (1991 and 2003), American air power has effectively demonstrated its high capability against a clear and identifiable target in straightforward and initially conventional scenarios.[33] It remains to be seen whether such campaigns will constitute the majority of Western military activity in the future.

It is quite possible that although increasingly potent and decisive against conventional military force structures, technologically based Western air power is still unable to provide a decisive contribution in asymmetric warfare against guerrillas and insurgent forces. In such scenarios, complex political problems and delicate international balances remain, and when so constrained, tactical air forces, even when backed by the latest technological gadgetry, are found wanting, unless allied to sizeable supporting ground forces. This is not to argue that air power is impotent or unimportant in such operations, but that it must be viewed as part of a mixed military and political force structure. Indeed, it will be of little value in the future if air forces are constituted and trained to fight high-intensity wars simply because they are most effective at it, when the more likely scenarios are low-intensity operations requiring flexible responses.

The role of air power in maritime affairs has to a degree mirrored the experience of its land-based cousin. In the age of so-called total war, maritime operations were markedly influenced by air power, reaching an apogee in the Second World War. Aircraft had played an important part in protecting convoys and shipping in the Great War, but in the Second World War, they were pivotal to success. Indeed, inability or unwillingness to deploy air forces in defensive roles around sea lines of communication was to court disaster. The Allies in the Atlantic were able to muster enough resources to solve the problem, but in the Pacific, the Japanese were not and suffered accordingly. It became axiomatic in the Second World War that where aircraft were operating enemy commerce raiders, including submarines, only did so at great risk.[34]

In the Pacific War (1941–45) American and Japanese air-maritime forces battled to and fro employing aircraft as the principal method of attack and defence. Aviation dominated the campaign, and the aircraft carrier rapidly supplanted the big gun battleship as the capital weapon of the world's navies. Indeed, a key factor behind Japan's ultimate defeat lay in her inability to produce enough pilots, aircraft and carriers to compete with the US navy. Once Japan had lost control of the seas, she became blockaded by American air-naval forces (submarines and air-dropped mines) and the war was lost.[35]

However, although aircraft carrier battlegroups and task forces dominated naval operations in the Pacific, they were much less effective in inshore continental waters against properly organized land-based air forces, and in the Cold War NATO was facing just such a threat in the shape of the Soviet Union. Although air-maritime forces allowed the USA to project conventional forces around the globe, and maintain control of the seas, this had only limited benefit in any potential confrontation with the USSR. Moreover, even though the Soviets began a major naval construction programme in the 1960s in an effort to expand their global presence, NATO air-naval power remained dominant at the operational and conventional level, and there was no radical shift in the balance of air-maritime power.

The real weakness of air-maritime naval power in the Cold War era was the inherent vulnerability of carrier centred naval taskforces to nuclear attack. A carrier battlegroup could offer little defence against a tactical nuclear weapon, and thus in high-intensity conflict against major enemy powers, the viability of hugely expensive aircraft carrier battlegroups was seriously open to question.

For conventional power projection around the globe, however, air-naval power remained useful and in the post-Cold War strategic environment, where the USA has been required to provide localized conventional air power for peace-keeping/implementation operations, or in asymmetric scenarios, the aircraft carrier has proved effective. The carrier force certainly offers a considerable degree of flexibility and independence of action, as seen when the British fought to recover control of the Falkland Islands in 1982. For the USA since 1991, the aircraft carrier battlegroup has provided a means of global power projection without recourse to occasionally compromising political deals with allied nations in order to secure land air bases. Carrier groups have also proved useful as a political tool, emphasizing American policy, presence and dominance in a region, without a permanent commitment.

conclusions

There can be little doubt that air power has had an immense impact on war since its first use in the years prior to the First World War. In just a few decades air forces have developed the ability to shape and influence land and maritime conflict to such a degree that military strategy invariably now incorporates air power into all levels of planning. In the Second World War victory was in large part dependent on the successful incorporation of fully supported air power into an integrated strategy. The Allies, especially the USA and Britain, were willing and able to accomplish this and were correspondingly successful; the Axis powers were not and thus suffered the consequences.

Air power has also greatly expanded the scope of war to civilian populations, drawing them into direct confrontation both in a strategic and physical sense. By the Second World War, urban areas had become obvious targets, legitimized by circumstance and necessity, while throughout the Cold War, even though both sides refused to acknowledge openly that civilian populations were being targeted, the consequences of an aircraft or missile projected nuclear war would be a holocaust.

Yet, because of the appalling carnage inflicted in the Second World War and the unacceptability of mass civilian casualties in the modern world, nations employing air forces have attempted to meet the challenge and provide a means of air based force projection politically acceptable to a sceptical and scrutinizing world. The poor levels of accuracy and precision that resulted in the often indiscriminate bombing of civilians in the Second World War and Southeast Asia are clearly no longer acceptable. The search for precision and supposedly clinically efficient air attack is therefore a crucial ongoing issue. Very largely this has been based on increasingly sophisticated levels of aero-technology – aircraft, ordnance and guidance/targeting systems.

To some degree this has been successful, but in the post-Cold War world new challenges now face air forces, other than direct and open confrontation in high-intensity conflicts. The necessity and effectiveness of employing air forces in counterinsurgency, policing or peace-implementation duties, backed by surgical or precision strikes, is now perhaps the most pressing demand made of modern air forces and, when previous failures in this field are recalled, its greatest challenge in the twenty-first century.

further reading

The most useful and accessible single-volume histories of air power are Robin Higham's *A Concise History of Air Power* (New York, 1972), Tony Mason's excellent *Air Power: A Centennial Appraisal* (London, 1995), and this author's more recent *Air Power in the Age of Total War* (London, 1999). Sebastian Cox and Peter Gray's edited collection *Air Power History: Turning Points from Kitty Hawk to Kosovo* (London, 2002) is also valuable in that it deals with key issues and debates in the development of air power. The First World War is best served by Lee Kennett's concise and clear *The First Air War, 1914–1918* (New York, 1991) and John H. Morrow's larger and more detailed *The Great War in the Air, 1909–1921* (Washington DC, 1993), while for the Second World War *The Air War, 1939–1945* by Richard Overy is still unsurpassed. There is a great deal on strategic bombing in the Second World War but *Rhetoric and Reality in Air Warfare: The Evolution of British and American Ideas about Strategic Bombing, 1914–1945* (Princeton NJ, 2002) by Tami Davis Biddle is the best single volume on the subject. Robert Pape's *Bombing to Win: Air Power and Coercion in War* (Ithaca NY, 1996) is provocative and thought provoking, but should not be read in isolation from other material on the subject of bombing and strategy. Mark Clodfelter's *The Limits of Air Power: The American Bombing of North Vietnam* (London, 1989) is an excellent introduction to air power in Southeast Asia in the 1960s and 1970s while more contemporary air power matters are dealt with in Richard Hallion (ed.), *Air Power Confronts an Unstable World* (London, 1997) and John Olsen, *Strategic Air Power and the Gulf War* (London, 2003).

notes

1. Matthew Cooper, *The German Air Force, 1933–45* (London, 1981), pp. 34–43; see also Williamson Murray, *Luftwaffe: Strategy for Defeat* (Washington DC, 1985).
2. Pascal Vennesson, 'Institution and Airpower: The Making of the French Air Force' in John Gooch (ed.), *Airpower: Theory and Practice* (London, 1995) and L. Robineau, 'French Air Policy in the Interwar Period and the Conduct of the Air War Against Germany, September 1939–June 1940' in Horst Boog (ed.), *The Conduct of the Air War in the Second World War* (Oxford, 1992).
3. K. R. Whiting, 'Soviet Aviation and Air Power under Stalin, 1928–41' in Robin Higham and J. W. Kipp (eds), *Soviet Aviation: A Historical View* (Boulder CO, 1977), pp. 51–2, 58.

4. Contrast John Buckley, *The RAF and Trade Defence, 1919–1945* (Keele, 1995) with Mark Parillo, *The Japanese Merchant Marine in World War Two* (Annapolis MD, 1993).

5. Tony Mason, *Air Power: A Centennial Appraisal* (London, 1995), pp. 97–104; B. Rogers, 'Greater Flexibility for NATO's Flexible Response', *Strategic Review* (Spring 1983): 11–19.

6. David Omissi, *Air Power and Colonial Control: The RAF, 1919–1939* (Manchester, 1990), p. 37. See also Richard Hallion, *Strike from the Sky: The History of Battlefield Air Attack, 1911–1945* (Washington DC, 1989), chs 6, 7.

7. C. A. Robinson, 'Fighter, Missile Gains Pressed', *Aviation Week and Space Technology* (4 April 1977): 11–14 and 'Aerial Combat Test to Advance', *Aviation Week and Space Technology* (25 April 1977): 28–30.

8. C. H. Builder, *The Icarus Syndrome: The Role of Air Power Theory in the Evolution and Fate of the US Air Force* (London, 1994), p. 155.

9. See H. G. Wells, *The War in the Air* (London, 1908).

10. Frederick Lanchester was the most important theorist on this area in the period up to and including the First World War. See Frederick Sykes, *From Many Angles* (London, 1942), pp. 558–74.

11. See Tami Davis Biddle, *Rhetoric and Reality in Air Warfare: The Evolution of British and American Ideas about Strategic Bombing, 1914–1945* (Princeton NJ, 2002) on the development of strategic bombing concepts in this period.

12. On Douhet see Giulio Douhet, *The Command of the Air* (London, 1942); Claudio Segre, 'Giulio Douhet: Strategist, Theorist, Prophet?', *Journal of Strategic Studies* 15/3 (1992): 351–66; and Azar Gat, *Fascist and Liberal Visions of War: Fuller, Liddell Hart, Douhet et al* (Oxford, 1998).

13. Douglas C. Waller, *A Question of Loyalty: General Billy Mitchell and the Court-martial that Gripped a Nation* (London, 2004). See also William Mitchell, *Winged Defense* (London, 1925).

14. Tami Davis Biddle, 'British and American Approaches to Strategic Bombing' in Gooch (ed.), *Airpower: Theory and Practice.*

15. Richard Overy, 'From *Uralbomber* to *Amerikabomber*: The Luftwaffe and Strategic Bombing', *Journal of Strategic Studies* 1/2 (1978): 154–78.

16. The Butt Report of 1941 indicated that only 20 per cent of bombers were delivering their payloads within five miles of their targets.

17. The two raids on Schweinfurt in 1943 cost the US 8th Air Force some two-thirds of its frontline bomber strength.

18. See Stephen McFarland, 'The Evolution of the American Strategic Fighter in Europe, 1942–44', *Journal of Strategic Studies* 10/2 (1987): 189–208.

19. Conrad Crane, *Bombs, Cities and Civilians: American Airpower Strategy in World War Two* (Lawrence KS, 1993), pp. 120–43; Kenneth P. Werrell, *Blankets of Fire: US Bombers over Japan during World War Two* (Washington DC, 1996), chs 6, 7.

20. Michael Sherry, *The Rise of American Air Power – The Creation of Armageddon* (New Haven, 1987); Stephen Garrett, *Ethics and Airpower in World War Two* (New York, 1993); and Robert Pape, *Bombing to Win: Air Power and Coercion in War* (New York, 1996).

21. Tami Davis Biddle, *Rhetoric and Reality*; and Richard Overy, *Bomber Command, 1939–45: Reaping the Whirlwind* (London, 1997).

22. See Pape, *Bombing to Win* for a critical discussion of the effects of Allied bombing in the Second World War upon enemy governments. The debate on the atomic bombings remains contentious to say the least; see, for example, the work of Gar

Alperovitz on the topic, particularly his book, *The Decision to Use the Atomic Bomb* (London, 1995).

23. John A. Warden, *The Air Campaign: Planning for Combat* (Washington DC, 1989). See also John A. Warden, 'The Enemy as a System', *Airpower Journal* 9 (Spring 1995): 40–55.

24. A. L. Gropman, 'The Air War in Vietnam, 1961–73' in R. A. Mason (ed.), *War in the Third Dimension: Essays in Contemporary Air Power* (London, 1986).

25. Harry G. Summers, *On Strategy: A Critical Analysis of the Vietnam War* (Novato CA, 1982).

26. Peter Mead, *The Eye in the Air* (London, 1983), ch. 1.

27. See Richard Muller, 'Close Air Support: The German, British and American Experiences, 1918–41' in Williamson Murray and Allan Millett (eds), *Military Innovation in the Interwar Period* (Cambridge, 1996).

28. See James Corum, *Creating the Operational Air War, 1918–40* (Lawrence KS, 1997).

29. On the decline of the Luftwaffe, see Williamson Murray, *Luftwaffe: Strategy for Defeat* (Washington DC, 1985).

30. Ian Gooderson, *Air Power at the Battlefront: Allied Close Air Support in Europe, 1943–5* (London, 1998), chs 3, 5.

31. Tony Mason, *Airpower: A Centennial Appraisal* (London, 1994), pp. 66–79.

32. See Robert Leonhard, *The Art of Maneuver: Maneuver-Warfare Theory and AirLand Battle* (New York, 1991), chs 5, 6, 7, pp. 135–8.

33. Richard Hallion, 'Precision Air Attack in the Modern Era' in Richard Hallion, *Air Power Confronts an Unstable World* (London, 1997), pp. 119–23.

34. On the two campaigns, see John Buckley, *The RAF and Trade Defence 1919–1945: Constant Endeavour* (Keele, 1995) and Marc Parillo, *The Japanese Merchant Marine in World War Two* (Annapolis MD, 1993).

35. On the development of carrier aviation, see Clark Reynolds, *The Fast Carriers: The Forging of an Air Navy* (New York, 1968).

9
naval warfare

andrew lambert

Conventionally naval warfare has been treated as a distinct subject, set apart by specialist knowledge and essentially concerned with fighting between navies. This reflects the origins of academic naval history in the naval educational needs of an age of profound technological transformation without conflict (1865–95), rather than its connection with the newly professional discipline of history.[1] The influence of navies on their history has favoured the production of highly detailed narratives which rarely extend their scope beyond the maritime dimension. This history of naval warfare is filled with inconclusive engagements between fleets of essentially identical configuration, technological advantage being perhaps the most transitory of all advantages, rarely lasting long enough to decide a war, even if the initial impact was significant. The famous *Monitor–Virginia* action of 1862 is typical. While most accounts focus on the fighting the real impact was the effect this drawn action had on Union General George McClellan's Peninsula Campaign. This example suggests the important questions for naval history address the balance between land and sea power, and the ability of navies to influence the result of conflicts.

In 1911 the brilliant maritime strategist Sir Julian Corbett (1854–1922) wrote:

> Since men live upon the land and not upon the sea, great issues between nations at war have always been decided – except in the rarest cases – either by what your army can do against your enemy's territory and national life, or else by what the fear of the fleet makes it possible for your army to do.[2]

His argument was directed at those who followed a simplified version of the case advanced by Alfred T. Mahan (1840–1914) that securing command of the sea would ensure victory in war. Corbett stressed that *naval warfare* settled control of oceanic communications, enabling *maritime strategy* to project power against the enemy, while securing the territory and trade of the dominant naval power. For Corbett, and all strategists of the sea, the real measure of naval power is the impact it can produce on a conflict ashore.[3]

However, narrowly focused historical studies also require revision. Modern scholarship has demonstrated that naval writing in previous eras was largely driven by contemporary agendas, adjusting the past for contemporary audiences, rather than helping those audiences to understand the past. Historians happily ascribed modern ideas and capabilities to ancient fleets, antedating key tactical developments and homogenizing the very different issues that determined the role of navies in war across the centuries. This older literature, developed to educate contemporary naval officers, focused on future prospects, teaching strategy by example,[4] at the expense of scholarship.[5] The tension between academic concerns and pedagogic imperatives has dominated the development of naval history.[6] One consequence of the limited scale and pedagogic impulse of so much naval history has been a lack of large-scale debates among practitioners. Such debates as have emerged tend to reflect personal rivalries rather than intellectual exchange. Naval history is more effective when it joins in wider historical debates.

Navies have always been costly, resource intensive organizations demanding professional skills and experience that cannot be acquired as easily, and more significantly as quickly, as those of contemporary armies. It has been far easier for great naval powers to create armies than vice-versa. If a nation is to sustain the costly long-term commitment to naval power the body politic must be convinced there is a real need. This conviction has most often come from the commercial sector. Defence against invasion, and imperial ambition also prompted the creation of fleets, but they have rarely endured beyond a generation. The navies of oligarchic or democratic maritime commercial states have proved more durable than those merely seeking military power at sea. The navies of Venice, Holland and Britain in the period under review easily outlasted various Russian and Soviet, French and German fleets. Even the United States, which began life a maritime state, has frequently questioned the future of its navy, and reduced vital long-term funding.[7]

The role of the sea in war and strategy has a long history, and a solid body of analytical literature. Naval missions have been relatively constant since the dawn of organized states: invasion and counter-invasion, military logistics, economic warfare, deterrence, constabulary action to control the illegal use of force at sea and revenue collection. The question is how significant naval power can be in warfare at any period, as compared to military and latterly aerial power, and how that relationship has changed over time.

The threat posed by naval power to nation states differs considerably. Whereas food importing, insular Britain has been potentially extremely vulnerable to naval warfare since the mid nineteenth century other states have appeared impervious to maritime suasion. Similarly the ability of navies to impact on land has been greatly affected by technological development.

the sea and strategy before 1500

From classical times most sea fighting was essentially infantry combat, on slippery, moving platforms. The introduction of gunpowder weapons at sea in the fifteenth century, combined with three-masted caravel built wooden sailing ships or existing Mediterranean galleys, produced warships that could have an impact on land. Large guns firing heavy stone shot could bombard castles. Consequently castles were rebuilt as artillery platforms, beginning a cycle of competitive ship and fort development that would last 400 years.

By the late sixteenth century sailing warships had acquired the endurance and firepower to provide insular defence against invasion. In 1588 the English fleet kept the Spanish Armada from landing or collecting reinforcements. Naval power enabled a small, isolated offshore kingdom, beset by enemies within and without, to defeat the mightiest land empire of the age. However, the subsequent attempt to destroy Spain by economic blockade merely exposed the limitations of the sailing ship and the maritime systems of the age. Spanish treasure would be a delusion for two centuries, distracting strategists from less profitable, but more useful missions.[8]

ideas, roles and potential

Elizabethan English writers and navigators dreamt of a maritime empire. John Dee,[9] Walter Raleigh and Francis Bacon propounded the basic tenets of sea power and empire long before the practical problems of using large fleets at sea had been addressed. Naval power was useful, but it remained the Queen's policy of last resort. Despite the success of 1588 naval power possessed only limited strategic value. Tudor ships could not defeat a continental rival.

By the 1650s warships were larger and more heavily armed, and naval tactics followed those ashore. Fleets fought in line ahead, employing broadside fire to break up enemy formations, before closing in for the kill. The three Anglo-Dutch Wars (1652–74) marked a watershed. England built a battlefleet for defence, but used it to secure trade and territory from the hitherto dominant maritime power. In 1654 the Dutch were forced to make peace by naval action alone. When Bourbon France, the military colossus of the era, acquired a large fleet she forced England and Holland to ally in defence of liberty and commerce. Naval power played a critical role in defeating Louis XIV's drive for European hegemony, breaking his economy and opening his seaward flanks to powerful diversions. By 1714 the British fleet was the most potent power political instrument in Europe, able to discipline Spain and Russia in the same season, suppress piracy and open new markets. The capture of Gibraltar by amphibious assault in 1704 demonstrated that a well-manned fleet could apply power ashore, forcing many nations to invest heavily in fixed shore defences. Tsar Peter the Great's great fortress at Cronstadt, defending the sea approaches to St Petersburg was only one demonstration of the strategic power of the English battlefleet.

By 1660 costly purpose-built warships had replaced armed merchant vessels in the line of battle. Naval power required money and infrastructure, which could only be provided over the long term by a modern bureaucratic fiscal military state. Such states could sustain war long enough for the slow grinding action of economic blockade to defeat rivals. Britain took the decisive step in 1688–1701, creating a new political structure where merchants shared power with noblemen. The National Debt, set up to fund the navy, gave both groups a vested interest in the Revolution settlement of 1688, while the Bank of England handled the transactions. This structural reform was the key to British success in the eighteenth century: Britain had access to far more money than France.[10]

Navies were built to serve the specific interests of states, and revealed more differences of shape and scale than contemporary armies. Spain and Portugal tried to control imperial communications, while Holland and then England tried to carve out new empires. By contrast France was more concerned with European power, land frontiers and dynastic expansion. The link with trade and colonies was made by Colbert, but his immense battlefleet of the 1670s–90s proved impossible to sustain when his King's land campaigns faltered. When it failed to restore Louis's ally James II to the British throne in 1692 the French battlefleet lost political utility, and was subsumed into a commerce destroying strategy that attacked the economic lineaments of England and Holland as a useful adjunct to the land war.[11] The contest between strategies of sea control and commerce destruction would be replayed many times over the next 250 years. Commerce destroying preyed on the economic power that funded maritime states at war, and distracted sea control navies from offensive strategies. It was also cost effective: it made a profit for the state. By contrast sea power annihilated commerce and secured overseas territories, but it drained the exchequer in the process.

The tactical and technical stability of the period 1670–1793 saw Britain, France and Spain fight for the rich sugar islands of the West Indies, and the trade settlements of Asia. In each war as France saw her economy sliding into bankruptcy, and her land operations bogged down, the attraction of an invasion of Britain came to the fore, either with local support, or simply in overwhelming military force. Each time the Royal Navy countered the move, and usually wiped out the fleet intended to escort the transports. The defensive dreams of 1588 had become reality: a well handled blockading fleet could destroy hostile merchant shipping and deny the seas to an enemy. However this strategy was only effective in the long term. It took seven years (1756–63) to ruin the French economy because Britain and her allies lacked the military power to win on land.

To make the blockade more effective the British constantly tightened up their legal position to bear down harshly on neutral powers. However, the limited wars of the eighteenth century were not the occasion for the full development of this policy.[12] Britain also captured overseas possessions for exchange at the peace table. Expeditionary warfare was restricted by the limited supply of ocean going ships, and the difficulty of landing armies in row boats.[13] Horses and artillery were peculiarly difficult to land across a beach, but without them no serious operations were possible. Much of Britain's success in the western hemisphere from Quebec to Havana between 1700 and 1763 was based on American manpower and supplies. The attempt to sustain military power across the Atlantic between 1776 and 1782 failed: contemporary maritime logistics simply could not support the war.[14]

In the eighteenth century Britain relied on European allies to keep France tied down in Europe, and was careful not to overplay naval power as a power political tool. In the American War of Independence (1776–83) France had allies, Britain did not. Paris secured the strategic initiative and along with Spain took revenge for previous humiliations by aiding the American rebels. Once again both Bourbon powers were bankrupted by the effort, and France soon had her own revolution. In America British naval power possessed limited utility against a largely hostile population able to exist without commerce, supported by a naval coalition with more ships of the line than the Royal Navy. When the British wrote off the American colonies the tide began to turn. Naval dominance was restored at the Battle of the Saintes in 1782, but this victory could not re-impose imperial authority in America. The French fleet lived to fight another day, forcing the British to keep their fleet concentrated, rather than supporting offensive operations. Naval power appeared incapable of applying a killing stroke in war. All this would change at the end of the sailing ship era.

nelson and the reformulation of naval power

The Wars of the French Revolution and Empire (1792–1815) posed a new challenge for navies, ships and naval strategy. In the eighteenth century large warships spent much of their time at anchor, many being decommissioned in winter, but the political impulse of the Revolutionary Wars caused a fundamental shift in strategy. Total war required the British fleet to be at sea in all weathers, because the cost of failure was no longer the loss of overseas possessions, but the complete destruction of the nation's political, economic and religious systems. France employed new, terrifying methods of war: ideologically motivated mass conscript armies, supported by revolutionary fifth columns, annihilated entire nations. To counter the invasion threat

British fleets remained on station in all weathers and all seasons from 1799 to the end of the war. This strategy crippled the French navy, imprisoning fleets and cutting supply lines.[15] It also wore out the British fleet at an unprecedented rate, forcing major changes in methods of construction and funding.

Nelson solved the strategic problems by transforming the art of war at sea to a new level. Having mastered the complex business of sailing and fighting early in his career Nelson refined his understanding of how to use naval power in war. As a naval commander he has no equal, his mastery of the art enabled him to render the complex business of naval battle simple for his followers. Nelson's concerns were the strategic and political aims of his country; battle was merely a means of advancing national aims, not an end in itself. Consequently he used different tactics in each battle, because each served a different purpose, in different circumstances. At the Nile in August 1798 he annihilated the French fleet, marooned Bonaparte's army in Egypt, reversed the balance of power in the Mediterranean, and inspired a fresh European alliance against France. The capture or destruction of 11 French battleships from a force of 13 was unprecedented, as was his decision to divide his fleet and turn command of the sea to strategic account.

At Copenhagen in April 1801 Nelson wanted to remove Denmark from the Armed Neutrality quickly, without leaving any lasting animosity, so his Fleet could attack the real enemy, Russia. He micro-managed the battle, and ensured his offer of an armistice reached the Danish Crown Prince at the precise moment the last Danish ship surrendered. Russia gave way without a fight. Nelson also exposed the make-believe invasion threat Napoleon was relying on to bounce Britain into a harsh peace. Instead the 1802 Peace of Amiens became an armed truce between the land and sea powers. When war broke out again in 1803 Nelson needed to secure British sea control. At Trafalgar in 1805 he used high risk tactics to annihilate Villenueve's fleet before a storm broke. He died in the hour of victory, but he had won the last major sea battle for a century.

Nelson's strategic genius and sound management transformed the impact of naval power, to counter the rampant, dynamic armies of Revolutionary and Napoleonic France. Without this enhanced naval power Britain would not have survived war with France. Invasion was the least of her worries, the real threat was the destruction of her commercial system, leading to economic ruin and pathetic capitulation.[16] Unable to contest command of the sea the French fell back on commerce destroying – which the British rendered impotent with convoys, insurance and the capture of outlying bases.[17]

After Trafalgar the Royal Navy was reconfigured for power projection, the natural role of a navy. The British destroyed the French and Dutch overseas empires, and imposed a savage blockade that led to war with the United States. In a total war for national survival the British were not overly concerned by legal niceties: they needed sea power, in its most extreme form, to fight Napoleon. The blockade ruined the French economy, and so distressed Russia that by 1812 she was obliged to leave Napoleon's Continental System. British maritime total war combined rigorous economic blockade with coastal and amphibious operations from Copenhagen and Cape Town to Buenos Aires and Baltimore.[18]

development after 1815

Between 1793 and 1815, Britain provided a master-class in sea power. The Royal Navy began its post-war service subduing the powerful coastal fortress of Algiers by naval bombardment, considered impossible or insane only a generation before. Weapons and tactics developed for war with France forced Algiers to renounce slavery. Mortars, rockets and long-range artillery would be improved over the succeeding decades, for increasingly effective sea-based attacks. Steam propulsion and armour plate shifted the balance further to favour sea power, expanding the British Empire and imposing European control over the rest of the world. Now naval power was effective in coastal waters and rivers, areas where sailing ships had been reluctant to operate. With a dominant battlefleet and a powerful coastal assault force Britain sustained a unique global empire. The threat of an endless economic war, punctuated by overwhelming naval assaults on key positions, was more than enough to deter any aggressive thoughts in St Petersburg, Paris or Washington. The steady increase in global maritime activity provided transport and logistics for large scale expeditionary warfare. Nations with effective sea control could send steam-powered amphibious forces to distant locations and support them on foreign territory for prolonged periods. Those without such assets could only wait to be attacked.

The increased strategic weight of naval power was demonstrated in the Crimean War (1853–56). Anglo-French maritime strategy combined speed of movement and reliable logistics to enable numerically inferior allied armies to invade Russia and destroy the naval base at Sevastopol. A clear British threat to destroy St Petersburg ended the war. At no stage were allied troops, up to 200,000 strong in the Crimea, ever more than one day's march from the sea, the real basis of their strategy.[19] Steam power significantly enhanced the strategy and tactics of amphibious operations. This conflict introduced several new weapons, underwater mines, submarines, rifled artillery, rifled small arms and ironclads. Iron steamships provided reliable logistics support, while industrial production created a major coast assault flotilla in a year. Steam ships so improved the blockade that Britain agreed to respect private property at sea in return for the abolition of privateering.

The lessons of the Crimea were largely repeated in the American Civil War (1861–65). The Union used superior industrial and manpower resources to impose a harsh blockade, before exploiting navigable rivers to penetrate, divide and the crush the Confederacy.[20] The Confederacy employed weapons largely drawn from the Crimean War for coast defence. It also developed a new form of commerce warfare, state funded destruction of hostile merchant shipping, which would feature in the world wars of the twentieth century. These conflicts were won by sea power and a superior industrial base, like every major war since 1793.

Industrial technology enhanced the impact of sea power, forcing coastal nations to invest in costly new defence systems. Steam warships were countered by moored mines, ironclads with locomotive torpedoes. Coast assault strategies prompted naval powers to hide key arsenals far inland, at Rochefort, Nicolaiev and Chatham, while protecting the remainder with ever more costly and complex fortress systems. United States defence spending between 1800 and 1900 was dominated by coastal fortification.[21] By dominating the ocean the British could deter their enemies, and force them to conform to British strategy, by putting most of their money into fortresses. The result was a century of cheap security, imperial expansion and trade dominance. When France, the second naval power throughout the nineteenth century, tried to do the same her fleet proved useless. In the Franco-Prussian war of 1870–71 the French fleet was not ready to attack the German coast before the Prussians had invested Paris.[22] Sea power was not a universal panacea. Consequently Britain's rivals were unable to sustain an effective challenge to her predominance because other security tasks took precedence, and their economies were far less dependent upon overseas trade and investment.[23]

Britain's great power rivals sought strategic and tactical counters to this ubiquitous, overwhelming power. The French invested in the locomotive (or Whitehead) torpedo and the torpedo boat, both British inventions. These could be used for local defence and commerce destroying, which the 1880s *Jeune Ecole* strategy expected would terrorize the British marine insurance market into surrender. Attempting to strike at the City of London, the heart of British power, rather than the Royal Navy was clever. However, the City funded additional ships to sustain British dominance, and enhance the blockade.

While the railway offered continental powers the opportunity to move troops to counter amphibious operations, this option was only available in regions where the rail network was particularly dense, in essence north-west Europe. Furthermore railways, as the American strategist Captain Alfred Thayer Mahan observed in his pioneering geo-strategic study *The Problem of Asia*, compete in vain with the sea and rivers for sustained logistics.[24] In this respect, it was highly significant that the first modern military literature to achieve a global perspective was American. Mahan's book opened the debate about the relative weight of sea and land power in the international balance. He argued that by engaging Russia on the Asian coast the Western powers could exploit their advantages, while Halford Mackinder's famous essay of 1904 'The Geographical Pivot of History' was a suggestive party polemic, not a doom-laden prognosis.[25]

intellect and experience

The British operated an effective global strategy without significant public discussion until the late nineteenth century. When that discussion began naval history was developed to educate the public, and the next generation of naval officers.[26] Before the 1850s the experience of war before 1815, transmitted by senior officers, ensured new technology was integrated into clearly thought out strategies and tactics. After the Crimean and American wars coastal power projection and the likelihood of an asymmetric war ensured most analysts focused on the role of navies in war, not on naval war.

The second half of the nineteenth century saw navies struggle to master new ships and weapons. Yet, amidst the endless discussions of boilers and breech loaders the underlying strategic concepts were constant. Between 1865 and 1889, half of all British capital ships were designed to attack coastal fortresses and fleets in harbour.[27] Only when rival fleets capable of engaging in serious sea battles emerged, in the mid 1880s, did the British re-examine fleet action. Before that, the only subjects to cause any concern were the possibility of invasion or of economic dislocation caused by commerce warfare.

Because the major navies experienced little or no fleet action between Trafalgar and Tsushima in 1905, they were forced to rely on historically based theories provided by Mahan, Corbett and others to think about a future in which ships and weapons had been transformed. Andrew Gordon has demonstrated that rather than understanding how fleets were controlled in the eighteenth century the officers of the late nineteenth century concentrated on improved communication systems, removing the need for individual initiative. As a result, the first modern fleet battle, at Jutland in 1916, was fought under a system that constrained all officers to follow the decisions of a commander in chief who could not see either end of his fleet.[28]

In 1900 any nation with pretensions to international significance was buying into the 'Sea Power' concept so cogently argued in Mahan's *The Influence of Sea Power Upon History, 1660–1783*, published in 1890. Mahan used history to show how the acquisition, maintenance and exploitation of battlefleet based naval mastery led to the growth and triumph of empires, exemplified by British global dominance. The failure of Britain's rivals, notably France, was attributed to feeble governments whose under-funded navies were diverted to secondary strategies of commerce raiding, rather than seeking sea control in battle. Although aimed at American statesmen and naval officers the book had a global impact; by 1900 it was a universal text for the Imperial age.

Yet Mahan's audience expected the next conflict would see purely naval warfare, settled by a single decisive battle, acting as the dominant factor in great power relations. This would not involve merchant shipping, civilians, or collateral damage.[29] Sadly this was an illusion, based on wishful thinking and wilful ignorance. War at sea turned out to be a grim attritional struggle, and while the results were decisive they were so lacking in glamour that after

1918 naval power was not simply removed from the exaggerated position it had occupied before 1914, but was demoted to a significance below its true worth in the minds of inter-war statesmen obsessed with the human cost of the Western Front.

roles

By the 1890s navies had become the defining symbols of imperial rivalry, more useful for prestige than war. For commercial and industrial concerns, navies were the key to colonial imperialism. To avoid the fate of other non-European nations Japan became a Western-style imperial power, with her own British built battlefleet. Imperial states used colonies to secure markets, raw materials and decant surplus population. Unfortunately, the rhetoric of empire was more effective than the reality: few states profited from their new lands, and fewer still could consider their empire secure. Mahan's Sea Power was not open to all: it was a very singular form of power. This power belonged to the British, who possessed the largest fleet and a unique chain of bases, Portsmouth, Plymouth, Gibraltar, Malta, Alexandria, Aden, Bombay, Trincomalee, Singapore, Hong Kong, Sydney, the Falkland Islands, Vancouver, Bermuda and Halifax, from which it could operate. These bases were connected by submarine telegraph cables, and contained unrivalled supplies of best Welsh steam coal. Furthermore, the Royal Navy was effectively as strong as the next two or even three navies. In 1898 the Anglo-French clash over the headwaters of the Nile, at Fashoda, was resolved without war because France understood that any war would destroy her overseas empire. As the Kaiser observed, 'the poor French, they have not read their Mahan!'[30]

technology

After decades of technological and doctrinal uncertainty the instruments of war at sea reached a development plateau with the 'pre-Dreadnought' ships of the 1890s: steel armour, triple expansion steam engines, breech loading guns and torpedoes. The two wars of the decade, the Sino-Japanese of 1894–95 and the Spanish-American of 1898 witnessed 'decisive' fleet actions where better-equipped Japanese and American forces annihilated weak enemies, and territory was captured by expeditionary armies. Sea power had produced rapid and decisive results.

However, such lessons were misleading. Total wars between major modern powers had never been settled by a single battle. It took Britain and France 22 years to resolve their differences over Europe between 1793 and 1815. Even Trafalgar, the most 'decisive' victory at sea, had not been enough. Napoleon was finally worn down by economic attrition, as Mahan had argued in his second *Sea Power* volume of 1892, but these conclusions were largely ignored. In part, this reflected the intellectual failings of contemporary navies. While armies adopted the Prussian/German staff system and planned for war, navies focused on technical issues. The Royal Navy was content to apply the strategies that had worked in previous wars, without a staff, or the educational system to equip officers for such work in wartime. Other navies were little better prepared.

There were alternatives to Mahanian sea control. Smaller nations used miniature battleships, torpedo boats, mines and shore batteries to protect coastal cities and colonies. Commerce destroying, using fast cruisers to attack merchant shipping, still had devotees, although only in France. The universal acceptance of 'Sea Power' led Brazil, Chile and Argentina to build dreadnought battleships against one another between 1906 and 1914. Not one of these ships ever fired a shot in war, although the Brazilian and Chilean ships fired on their own people.

After 1900, the final wave of Imperialism saw the imperialists fighting among themselves. The British defeated the South African republics in the Second South African (Boer) War (1899–1902) because they had undisputed command of the sea, both to move troops and supplies to the theatre, and to deter foreign intervention. In 1904–05, Russia and Japan fought over Korea and Manchuria, pitting Russia's enormous military resources, deployed down the Trans-Siberian railway, against Japan's smaller sea-based army. Japan began with a pre-emptive strike, crippling the Russian fleet at Port Arthur, to cover troop landings in Korea. Russian military reinforcements could not keep pace with the Japanese, because Russia could not contest command of the sea, losing two fleets in the process. The catastrophic Russian defeat at Tsushima settled the war and joined Trafalgar as the pinnacle of modern naval achievement.

In 1906, naval weaponry made another quantum leap with HMS *Dreadnought*, the first all big gun battleship. However, this was more significant as a British attempt to deter further naval challenges. Only America and Germany responded. These costly ships were powerful propaganda tools, linked to the fate of empires. They were to be prized, not used. Nowhere was this more apparent than in the German navy, revitalized and reoriented by Navy Secretary Admiral Alfred Tirpitz in 1898 as a world power political lever to secure concessions from Britain. This policy called into question Britain's fundamental interests: peace and European stability as the ideal conditions for trade. British strategy relied on the deterrent threat of overwhelming naval force, and long wars of economic attrition. If British naval mastery were challenged the British deterrent became less credible. Admiral Lord Fisher deployed the deterrent to uphold British interests, while forcing the Germans into an all-out arms race. He knew Germany could not sustain a massive army and compete with Britain at sea. The naval race ended in 1912, but the outbreak of the First World War was determined by the strategic Kiel Canal. This was being widened for dreadnoughts, and until it was complete Germany could not go to war. The canal re-opened in July 1914.[31]

In 1904, the Japanese had sacrificed an army to capture Port Arthur, rather than risk their fleet. Between 1914 and 1918, all the major powers would hoard battleships. Instead new weapons were used. Submarines only became effective around 1910 with diesel engines, improved torpedoes and wireless, but they offered a new alternative to command of the sea. The Germans also developed rigid Zeppelin airships for strategic reconnaissance; the British preferred cheaper seaplanes.

the first world war

In August 1914 Britain, France, Russia and Japan went to war with Germany and Austria-Hungary. Despite having superiority in modern capital ships the Entente powers had no idea how to use that advantage to defeat the enemy. Technology had transformed the strategic seascape. Capital ships no longer ventured into enemy coastal waters, fearing mines, submarines and coastal artillery. Fisher had anticipated the North Sea would be left to submarines and destroyers, with the heavy ships held back for more important tasks.[32]

The British sent their dreadnought Grand Fleet to Scapa Flow in the Orkney Islands, where it was well placed to intercept German ships trying to leave the North Sea. Another fleet barred the Straits of Dover and escorted the British army to France. A distant blockade of Germany was established. While Tirpitz still lamely expected the British to come into German coastal waters, his High Seas Fleet had no function in the German Schlieffen Plan.[33] Outside Europe, the cruiser war for oceanic communications was over by Christmas. The British cut German underwater cables and drove German ships from the seas.

In the North Sea the main fleets met but once, late on the afternoon of 31 May 1916. While tactically inconclusive the battle of Jutland was a strategic victory for the British, re-asserting their dominance. Yet, Britain needed to make sea power count as an offensive option. The economic blockade was steadily tightened, but that was a tedious process when millions of men were fighting on the Western Front. The British knew that Swedish iron ore was vital to Germany, and that if the blockade could be tightened Germany should collapse.[34] Fisher was preparing to exploit this weakness when Churchill forced through his own half-baked scheme to attack the Dardanelles and force Turkey out of the war. The Anglo-French fleet attacked on 18 March 1915, losing three battleships on a single, small minefield. The attack failed for want of pre-war preparation for such operations, and ended any prospect of large-scale naval power projection. Within weeks the failure had been reinforced with a major amphibious landing that proved equally flawed. Amphibious power projection was hampered by limited technology and lack of recent experience. There would be no more big naval offensives in this war, wasting the Allies' greatest asset.

Italy did not join her Triple Alliance partners in 1914. With her coast, communications, cities and industry exposed to a superior fleet, Italy could not go to war with Britain. Instead, she joined the Entente in May 1915. With over 1 million men now under arms and nowhere to send them but France Britain became a continental military power by default. The cost was severe: industry and trade were decimated, allowing America and Japan to capture British markets, while Britain liquidated overseas investments to fund the war. Because it was not fought along traditional British lines the war cost Britain her economic pre-eminence. It has been argued that this 'Continental Commitment' was inevitable, but more effective exploitation of sea power might have saved British lives, treasure and power.[35]

The Germans responded to their naval weakness with Zeppelin bombing raids on London, and illegal submarine attacks on merchant shipping. The latter was merely an updated *guerre de course*, the usual strategy of despair for powers unable to contest command of the sea. Tirpitz hoped to cut British food supplies but the sinking of the liner *Lusitania* in 1915 with the loss of 1,201 lives, including 128 Americans, generated diplomatic protests from Washington that stopped the 1915 campaign. Both sides broke pre-war agreements on economic warfare, but in total war legal rights are upheld by armed might, not paperwork.[36]

After Jutland, the German High Command, with the army bled white on the Western Front, agreed to re-launch unrestricted U-boat warfare. They hoped to defeat Britain in six months, by cutting food imports. The Entente would then collapse. They were confident the war would be over before America could act. On 1 February 1917, Germany launched the campaign with 105 U-boats. The United States entered the war on 6 April 1917. By April 1917, shipping losses had reached 860,334 tons per month. However, this success could not be sustained. There were not enough U-boats and the British introduced escorted convoys from April. This removed the key German advantage, the ability to attack merchant shipping without fear of counter-attack. Gradually convoys and increasing use of balloons or aircraft for observation in coastal waters reduced merchant ship losses to manageable proportion, while increasing those of the U-boats. This grim attritional struggle between small craft was vital, for with America in the war victory was inevitable if Britain and France could hold on until the middle of 1918. The movement of American troops and equipment to Europe in 1918 went ahead with very little loss, and once the Ludendorff offensive had failed, victory was assured. Germany had gambled on a knockout blow by U-boat, and the Royal Navy had reduced it to an irritant. Contemporaries who knew their history would have recognized this as yet another indecisive attack on commerce of the type that Mahan had derided. By contrast American belligerence tightened the blockade: food shortages in Germany had a disastrous impact on morale.

British naval offensives operations in 1918 were limited, but portentous. The first aircraft carrier raid destroyed Zeppelins at Tondern. Britain was building a fleet of torpedo bombers to attack the High Seas Fleet at Wilhelmshaven in

1919. Modern coast defences would be out ranged by simply changing the delivery system from gun to aeroplane. The principle of coast attack remained unchanged.

After four years of boredom and poor officer–man relations the German High Seas Fleet mutinied: a futile fleet that had failed in every mission finally imploded. On 15 November 1918 the modern ships were interned at Scapa Flow. The Royal Navy's victory was rendered complete the following year when the Germans scuttled their ships: the British demanded more ships in lieu, leaving Germany with no warships from the Dreadnought era. The Treaty of Versailles in June 1919 deprived Germany of battleships and submarines. Germany was no longer a naval power. After four years of unremitting effort by the Royal Navy, the enemy was condemned to utter defeat. What the victory lacked in drama and immediacy was more than compensated for in effect. Without command of the sea the Entente powers would have been defeated, for it was the power to bring men, materials and supplies from all corners of the globe that enabled them to defeat Germany. Those who try to apportion relative values to the British war effort on land and sea miss that cardinal point. The Entente *might* have won without British armies, they *would* have lost without the British Fleet. After the war, British naval squadrons supported anti-communist groups in Russia, helping secure the independence of the Baltic States with a motor torpedo boat raid on the Russian naval arsenal at Kronstadt. However naval power could not compensate for the failure of the White Russian land forces.

During the war, the United States began major battleship programmes in 1916 and 1918. The first sought to influence British policy by making the United States navy equal to the Royal Navy. The 1918 programme reminded Britain not to underestimate American ambition at the peace conference. It was soon cancelled, but not before Japan responded, presaging another naval arms race. America had the economic power to contest command of the sea, the question was did she have the will?

Britain ended the First World War with a commanding lead in numbers of warships, and in experience of modern naval warfare from fleet action to anti-submarine escort. Her chain of global bases had been extended, her Middle Eastern fuel oil supplies were secure and her empire had demonstrated an impressive depth of commitment. However, the price had been high, in men, money and materiel. Naval power had been the backbone of Allied victory, the blockade steadily wearing down the German war effort. But the only major naval offensive, at the Dardanelles, suggested naval power had been reduced to a defensive asset. The new striking power would come from the air, and Britain had been the first to create an independent air force, which adopted strategic bombing as a *raison d'être*, threatening the primacy of the Royal Navy in British strategy. By contrast Japan and the USA retained separate army and navy air forces.[37]

the era of naval limitation

Despite the lack of dramatic operations in the First World War, naval power remained a major political tool. However, the escalating cost of new warships, which were now three times bigger than the original 1906 *Dreadnought*, saw the post-war build up brought to rapid conclusion in the Washington Treaty process of 1922. In America Congress refused to fund President Wilson's 1918 programme, which would have given the United States dominance in battleships. Instead the Americans offered to sacrifice the projected 1918 ships if the other major powers took similar action. The Washington Conference of 1922 restricted the size of future warships, the numbers each power could own, and their replacement ages. Several half-finished American and Japanese battleships were scrapped, along with an armada of older battleships, including the *Dreadnought*. Britain and the USA had a ratio of five ships to three for Japan and 1.75 each for Italy and France. No-one else mattered. Submarine campaigns against merchant shipping were declared illegal, but few can have been under any illusion about the value of such a stipulation. The Washington Treaty headed off a naval race, which suited disinterested Americans and bankrupt Europeans, but it was also a massive blow to the role of naval power in contemporary strategy. When deepened and extended in the London conference of 1930 the results were nothing short of disastrous for Britain.[38] Not only did they devastate the naval infrastructure needed to build the fleet,[39] but they left Britain without the naval assets to defend a global empire.

Naval arms limitation was abandoned in 1936 but only after it had seriously degraded naval power as a strategic factor: armies and air forces had remained unlimited in size and power. This severely disadvantaged the British, who depended on the fleet to secure their global communications, trade and possession, and as their deterrent. Only when Britain was too weak to uphold her vital interests between 1939 and 1941 was the real value of naval power appreciated. As Admiral Sir Herbert Richmond had observed in the 1930s a major naval base at Singapore was useless if the Royal Navy could not detach a force to the area capable of dealing with Japan.[40] The problem was exacerbated when Germany, Italy and Japan rebuilt their navies, as symbols of aggressive intent, with the Stalinist Soviet Union about to follow suit by 1939.[41] As war approached Britain and France drew closer, and sought a strategic edge at sea, both Churchill and the French Admiral Darlan saw knocking out Italy as the best way to make sea power count, while relying on the Maginot Line and economic warfare to defeat Nazi Germany. They could only hope that success in Europe would deter Japan.[42] The United States had begun a major naval reconstruction programme as part of Roosevelt's New Deal, to drag the country out of recession, but Britain and France doubted America would enter the war. They knew that in the long run sea power would win, but had good reason to fear the initial impulse of German aggression.

During the 1930s the aeroplane developed from a 100 mph stick and string biplane with a tiny weapon load into a 300 mph all metal monoplane flying long distances with heavy weapons. Air power proponents argued that they could replace navies in the oceanic security role – the USAAF developed the four-engined B-17 Flying Fortress for the role. Mines and submarines had limited the offensive use of naval forces in 1914–18: with aircraft added to the defensive assets it seemed the sea power no longer had an offensive role. However, every new development prompted a response. The experience of 1914–18 had thrown up new ideas and weapons, purpose built landing craft, aircraft carriers for inland strike missions, and improved gunnery systems and projectiles for shore bombardment. While these developments were important, their impact on the strategic balance between land and seas was limited before the war by the Washington process, which restricted the size and number of platforms. By contrast naval forces acquired new sensors. British sonar (ASDIC) to detect submarines was in operational service by 1939, and the second electronic breakthrough, radar, was in development. Both would be critical.

the second world war

The Second World War witnessed the ultimate expression of naval power in global strategy. Allied sea control, contested but never broken, allowed them to concentrate their resources and overwhelm the essentially isolated Axis powers. In 1939, Germany had few naval assets. With Italy remaining neutral until June 1940, German naval efforts were restricted to diversionary attacks on oceanic trade. Then Germany overwhelmed Denmark and southern Norway with a high-risk, high-tempo operation using land based air power to protect the troops ashore against the Anglo-French response. Crippled by the lack of suitable carrier based fighters the British lost the Norwegian campaign although they destroyed much of the German navy. This first major contest between sea and air power had been won by the air. The fall of France and the evacuation from Dunkirk were followed by the threat of a German invasion. However, the Germans lacked the warships and invasion shipping to cross the Channel in the presence of the world's greatest navy, even with air superiority. With invasion impossible the Luftwaffe changed from targeting RAF bases to bombing London, seeking a psychological knockout. Sea power had won.[43]

The Germans used French Atlantic ports to open the Battle of the Atlantic, the longest-running campaign of the war, and perhaps the most important. With occasional surface and air support U-boats attempted to interdict British supply lines, but losses were kept to manageable levels by the convoy system, intelligence breakthroughs, and improved weapons, sensors and training regimes. Furthermore, Britain had acquired a great mass of shipping from occupied Europe which, along with increasingly effective American shipbuilding effort, ensured the Germans could not win.[44]

When Italy entered the war and France surrendered Britain was outnumbered at sea. Prime Minister Churchill ensured the powerful French Fleet was either sunk or demilitarized. Admiral Cunningham then used an aircraft carrier to cripple the Italian battlefleet based at the port of Taranto, acquiring an enduring moral ascendancy over the Italian fleet. Sea control enabled British ground forces to seize Italian possessions in Ethiopia and Libya before a diversion to Greece and the arrival of German land and air units turned the strategic balance. Luftwaffe bombers sank or damaged Royal Navy warships, hammered the key base at Malta and supported Rommel's offensive in North Africa. Operation Barbarossa allowed a British army with secure maritime supply lines to overwhelm Rommel at El Alamein. At the end of 1942, the Americans landed in Morocco and Algeria to link up with the British. Their army had crossed the Atlantic direct to the beach, the most impressive strategic movement of the war for scale, speed, and success. Further landings in Sicily and Italy were conducted with air cover from carriers, and beach head bombardment by battleships. These landings defeated Fascist Italy.

For much of the war Britain and her allies were content simply to keep the Atlantic sea lanes open. However, in early 1943 the American army was ready to move to Europe. Roosevelt was unwilling to risk his men and material, so it was time to annihilate the U-boats. Allied naval, air and intelligence assets, with improved training, tore the heart out of the U-boat arm in April and May, sinking over 50 boats. Arctic convoys to Russia kept Stalin onside, and later in the war drew German naval and air assets into one-sided attritional battles.[45]

The last maritime strategic task in Europe, the invasion of France on 6 June 1944, deployed Atlantic crossing American and Canadian armies in an amphibious warfare master class. The Allies demonstrated the offensive character of sea power against well prepared defences, with strong ground reserves. Gallipoli had been avenged.

The Pacific War opened with a stunning strategic surprise attack carried out by a carrier task force, in a manner the Japanese had employed in previous wars, at Pearl Harbor on 7 December 1941. The Japanese then swept across Southeast Asia and the South Pacific, seizing the Philippines, Indonesia, Malaya and Burma. The carrier task force overwhelmed weak land based air defences. Off the Malayan coast, land-based Japanese bombers sank the British capital ships *Prince of Wales* and *Repulse*. Air power was dominant: it seemed the battleship could not survive.

However, while the Japanese aircraft carrier was a powerful strike weapon, it was very vulnerable. In the 1930s, both America and Japan had expected their carriers to be annihilated in an exchange of air attacks before the main fleet battle. At Midway in June 1942, the Americans profited from good intelligence, and slack Japanese procedures to ambush an over-confident enemy, sinking the Japanese carriers before they could launch their own strike. It was a stunning, one-sided victory.[46] After Midway the Americans steadily and irresistibly built up their naval and amphibious power, using overwhelming mobile logistics and armadas of carriers to cut off and capture key islands until they were within heavy bomber range of the Japanese home islands. Then the USAAF began a massive bombing offensive, culminating in firestorm raids and atomic bombs. The US submarine fleet had annihilated largely unconvoyed Japanese merchant shipping. This *guerre de course* only worked because the Americans were dominant at sea and in the air, and also had access to Japanese signal codes.[47] It was not the strategy of a power without surface and air power in the theatre, like Germany. By 1945, sea power had annihilated the Japanese Empire, and prepared for the amphibious conquest of Japan. Atomic bombs averted the need, but this option had been secured by sea power. Naval power had won a total war against a powerful opponent. The sheer scale of the Pacific war forced the Americans to create new ways of using naval power, notably afloat support forces to extend the operational range of fleets, refuelling and replenishing at sea.

naval power during the cold war

After 1945, the atom bomb and the creation of a bipolar world order with the flashpoint in central Germany reduced interest in naval power. With the USA and Britain allied together, and the Soviet fleet a chaotic shambles until the late 1950s, sea control was not in question. The Americans developed carrier 'Attack at Source' and submarine offensive strategies that reflected Pacific war experience, laying the intellectual foundations for key developments in the land/sea balance in the 1980s.[48] The creation of NATO focused attention on the North Atlantic link, yet despite a sustained Soviet build-up from the later 1950s to the mid 1980s their fleet never challenged the strategic power of the Western alliance. Consequently the West could use naval power to control many of the local conflicts that punctuated the Cold War, and the interconnected Wars of Decolonization. The Korean War (1950–53) demonstrated that not all conflicts would be nuclear, and consequently carrier aviation, amphibious forces and naval logistics would give the West a critical advantage. Naval successes in this war also defeated attempts by the US Air Force and Army to emasculate the US navy, by stripping it of air and marine assets. The reign of USAF Strategic Air Command as the pre-eminent weapons delivery system on the planet – satirized in the 1961 film 'Dr Strangelove' – was brief. In the late 1950s, the need for a secure second strike nuclear capability led to the Polaris submarine-launched ballistic missile. When these weapons were mounted in nuclear powered submarines, another 1950s development, navies wrested nuclear dominance from air forces. Modern ballistic missiles can be fired from their home ports to most targets. Aggressive anti-submarine warfare against these strategic assets led the Soviets to keep their missile submarines in defended 'bastion areas' off Murmansk and Vladivostock. The USA and the USSR built large numbers of these boats; Britain and France relied on four each to sustain permanent seats on the United Nations Security Council. In Britain, the RAF no longer has a strategic role, or any nuclear weapons capability. Other powers will move in the same direction. To complement the ballistic missile America perfected submarine-launched cruise missiles, with small, nuclear capable warheads for precision strikes. These, like their ballistic cousins, relied on extensive space based targeting systems. Space sensors, targeting and communications systems give information dominant navies, such as the US navy, a massive advantage over potential rivals.[49]

However, the exponential rise in the cost of nuclear age naval power left only one nation capable of building the new capital ship, the super carrier. The United States developed the 65,000 ton 90 plane *Forrestal* into the 90,000 ton nuclear powered *Nimitz*, which has remained in production since the 1960s. These strategic power projection centres carry a massive weapon load, using air tanking and cruise missiles to strike targets as far inland as Kabul. In 1967, the Royal Navy was denied new carriers, focusing on anti-submarine warfare in the North Atlantic to secure the NATO supply line. However, it still produced a balanced fleet with air and amphibious assets for the Falklands Campaign of 1982.

The Falklands War highlighted the key problem for post-1945 surface operations, the inability of anti-aircraft and anti-missile defences to keep up with the progress of offensive systems. German and Japanese guided weapons had inflicted severe losses on surface ships in 1943–45, and although anti-aircraft missile systems entered service in the 1950s radar systems and control technology could not cope with mass attacks. Micro-processors transformed the situation in the late 1970s. The American *Aegis* system allows one ship to engage over 20 targets at once. With *Aegis* American surface forces could take on the powerful Soviet naval air fleets. It emerged just as Reagan's mid 1980s 'Second Cold War' peaked with a '600 ship' US navy. This build-up was justified by publicly promulgating an updated version of the 1940s 'Attack at Source' called 'The New Maritime Naval Strategy' in 1986. Led by Second World War-era battleships, armed with cruise missiles, and supported by air, submarine and space assets, the US navy would threaten Soviet ballistic missile bastion areas in the Arctic.[50] This major increase in the strategic use of naval assets in global strategy played a significant part in the ultimate collapse of the Soviet Union, which could not afford the electronic power and production line facilities that produced the key American weapons. The collapse of the Soviet Union was followed almost immediately by the implosion of the Soviet fleet, which was revealed to have been a force without secure foundations in the security or commercial needs of the state. The tragic loss of the nuclear powered cruise missile submarine *Kursk* in 1999 restated a simple truth: navies without sustained political support and long-term funding are doomed. The rising navies of the twenty-first century are linked to burgeoning maritime economies in Britain, Japan, China and India.[51]

post cold war

Navies, still reconfiguring for a new era of asymmetric warfare, are acquiring power projection assets and amphibious craft. Britain has ordered two very large carriers for global joint service deployment. Naval warfare as a contest between navies for sea control has not been a realistic prospect since 1945. Instead, the ability of naval force to support and sustain strategic operations with air and land forces will dominate the next decades. This has been the reality of naval power for most of history. It is a simple truism to observe that all the major wars of the modern age have been won by the dominant naval power or coalition. It would appear that sea power is critical. Whether that reflects strategic necessity, or the superior industrial, economic and financial power of the open, democratic societies that wield it is a question that has begun to exercise historians.[52]

further reading

Any brief attempt to direct further reading in this vast field would be unwise, but the following texts repay study, and provide a sense of direction in history and historiography: J. A. Beeler, *British Naval Policy in the Gladstone–Disraeli Era, 1866–1890* (Stanford, 1997); J. S. Corbett, *Some Principles of Maritime Strategy* (London, 1911); H. Eccles, *Logistics in the National Defense* (Harrisburg, 1959); J. Ehrman, *The Navy in the War of King William III, 1689–1697: Its State and Direction* (Cambridge 1953); D. C. Evans and M. R. Peattie, *Kaigun: Strategy, Tactics and Technology in the Imperial Japanese Navy, 1887–1941* (Annapolis MD, 1997); A. G. Gordon, *The Rules of the Game: Jutland and British Naval Command* (London, 1996); E. J. Grove, *Vanguard to Trident: British Naval Policy Since World War II* (Annapolis MD, 1987); J. F. Guilmartin, *Gunpowder and Galleys: Changing Technology and Mediterranean Warfare at Sea in the Sixteenth Century* (Cambridge, 1974); K. Hagan (ed.), *In Peace and War: Interpretations of American Naval History, 1775–1984* (Westport CT, 1984); C. I. Hamilton, *The Anglo-French Naval Rivalry, 1840–1870* (Oxford, 1993); R. Harding, *Amphibious Warfare in the Eighteenth Century: The British Expedition to the West Indies, 1740–1742* (Woodbridge, 1991); R. Harding (ed.), *Naval Warfare 1680–1850* (Aldershot, 2006); P. M. Kennedy, *The Rise and Fall of British Naval Mastery* (London, 1976); A. D. Lambert, *The Crimean War: British Grand Strategy Against Russia, 1853–1856* (Manchester, 1990); N. Lambert, *Sir John Fisher's Naval Revolution* (Columbia SC, 1999); A. T. Mahan, *The Influence of Sea Power Upon History, 1660–1783* (Boston, 1890); A. T. Mahan, *The Influence of Sea Power upon the Wars of the French Revolution and Empire, 1793–1812* (Boston, 1892); J. Maiolo, *The Royal Navy and Nazi Germany, 1933–39* (London, 1998); M. Milner, *Battle of the Atlantic* (London, 2003); A. Offer, *The First World War: An Agrarian Interpretation* (Oxford, 1989); N. A. M. Rodger, *The Safeguard of the Sea: A Naval History of Britain* (London, 1996); N. A. M. Rodger, *The Command of the Ocean: A Naval History of Britain* (London, 2004); L. Sondhaus, *The Habsburgs and the Seas: Austrian Naval Policy, 1797–1866* (Purdue IN, 1989); L. Sondhaus, *Preparing for Weltpolitik: German Sea Power before the Tirpitz Era* (Annapolis MD, 1997); J. T. Sumida, *In Defence of Naval Supremacy: Finance, Technology and British Naval Policy, 1889–1914* (London, 1989); G. Symcox, *The Crisis of French Sea Power, 1688–1697: From the Guerre d'Escadre to the Guerre de Course* (The Hague, 1974); D. Syrett, *The Defeat of the U-boats: The Battle of the Atlantic* (Columbia SC, 1994); and J. Y. Wong, *Deadly Dreams: Opium and the Arrow War (1856–1860) in China* (Cambridge, 1998).

For the first serious attempt at naval historiography see: J. B. Hattendorf (ed.), *Ubi Sumus? The State of Naval and Maritime History* (Newport RI, 1994); J. B. Hattendorf (ed.), *Doing Naval History: Essays towards Improvement* (Newport RI, 1995); A. D. Lambert, *The Foundations of Naval History: John Knox Laughton, the Royal Navy and the Historical Profession* (London, 1998); J. K. Laughton, 'Historians and Naval History' in J. S. Corbett (ed.), *Naval and Military Essays* (Cambridge, 1913); D. M. Schurman, *The Education of a Navy: The Development of British Naval Strategic Thought, 1867–1914* (London, 1967); D. M. Schurman, *Julian S. Corbett, 1854–1922: Historian of British Maritime Policy from Drake to Jellicoe* (London, 1981); and J. T. Sumida, *Inventing Grand Strategy and Teaching Command: The Classic Works of Alfred Thayer Mahan Reconsidered* (Washington, 1997). For a study of the economic dimension, see: P. J. Cain and A. G. Hopkins, *British Imperialism: Innovation and Expansion, 1688–1914* (London, 1993). For future trends in naval developments, see: J. Hattendorf, 'The Uses of Maritime History in and for the Navy' in Hattendorf, *Naval History and Maritime Strategy* (Malabar FL, 2000).

notes

1. A. D. Lambert, *The Foundations of Naval History: John Knox Laughton, the Royal Navy and the Historical Profession* (London, 1998).
2. J. S. Corbett, *Some Principles of Maritime Strategy* (London, 1911), p. 14.
3. C. Grey's *The Leverage of Sea Power: The Strategic Advantage of Navies in War* (New York, 1992) is a classic statement by a prominent strategic analyst.
4. J. T. Sumida, *Inventing Grand Strategy and Teaching Command: The Classic Works of Alfred Thayer Mahan Reconsidered* (Washington DC, 1997).
5. The contrast between Admiral Rodgers's Mahanian study of early modern galley warfare, produced at the United States Naval War College in the 1920s, and the modern treatment by Professor Guilmartin in the 1980s, is fundamental, although both addressed military audiences. See W. L. Rodgers, *Naval Warfare under Oars, 4th to 16th Centuries: A Study of Strategy, Tactics and Ship Design* (Annapolis MD, 1940) and J. F. Guilmartin, *Gunpowder and Galleys: Changing Technology and Mediterranean Warfare at Sea in the Sixteenth Century* (Cambridge, 1974).
6. See Lambert, *Laughton*.
7. P. P. O'Brien, *British and American Naval Power: Politics and Policy, 1900–1936* (London, 1998).
8. N. A. M. Rodger's *The Safeguard of the Sea: A Naval History of Britain, 660–1649* (London, 1997) is the most comprehensive guide to these developments.
9. The best sudy available is W. H. Sherman's *John Dee: The Politics of Reading and Writing* (Amherst MA, 1995).
10. J. Brewer, *The Sinews of Power: War, Money and the English State, 1688–1783* (London, 1989).
11. G. Symcox, *The Crisis of French Sea Power, 1688–1697: From the Guerre d'Escadre to the Guerre de Course* (The Hague, 1974).
12. D. Syrett, *Neutral Rights and the War in the Narrow Seas, 1778–1782* (Fort Leavenworth KS, 1985); H. J. Bourguignon, *Sir William Scott, Lord Stowell: Judge of the High Court of the Admiralty, 1798–1828* (Cambridge, 1987); and R. Pares, *Colonial Blockade and Neutral Rights, 1739–1763* (Oxford, 1938). R. Hill's *The Prizes of War* (Gloucester, 1998) contains a very thorough discussion of the British prize system between 1793 and 1815.
13. R. Harding, *Amphibious Warfare in the Eighteenth Century: The British Expedition to the West Indies, 1740–1742* (Woodbridge, 1991).

14. D. Syrett, *Shipping and the American War, 1775–1783* (London, 1970).
15. C. B. Arthur, *The Remaking of the English Navy by Admiral St. Vincent. Key to the Victory over Napoleon. The Great Unclaimed Naval Revolution (1795–1805)* (Boston, 1986); R. Morriss (ed.), *The Channel Fleet and the Blockade of Brest, 1793–1801* (Aldershot, 2001).
16. A. D. Lambert, *Nelson: Britannia's God of War* (London, 2004).
17. P. Crowhurst, *The French War on Trade: Privateering 1793 to 1815* (Folkestone, 1977).
18. See Wade Dudley's *Splintering the Wooden Wall* (Annapolis MD, 2003) for an interesting comparative analysis of the impact of British Blockades on France and America. However, F. Crouzet's *L'economie britannique et le blocus continentale (1806–1813)* (Paris, 1958) remains the standard work.
19. A. D. Lambert, *The Crimean War: British Grand Strategy Against Russia, 1853–1856* (Manchester, 1990).
20. R. Reed, *Combined Operations in the Civil War* (Annapolis MD, 1978).
21. E. R. Lewis, *Sea Coast Fortifications of the United States* (Annapolis MD, 1970).
22. P. Colomb, *Naval Warfare* (London 1891).
23. P. J. Cain and A. G. Hopkins, *British Imperialism: Innovation and Expansion, 1688–1914* (London, 1993).
24. A. T. Mahan, *The Problem of Asia* (Boston, 1900).
25. H. J. Mackinder, 'The Geographical Pivot of History', *The Geographical Journal* 23 (1904): 421–37.
26. D. M. Schurman, *The Education of a Navy: The Development of British Naval Strategic Thought 1867–1914* (London, 1967) reviews the key theorists. His *Julian S. Corbett, 1854–1922: Historian of British Maritime Policy from Drake to Jellicoe* (London 1981) and Lambert, *Laughton* examine two of the key figures in greater detail.
27. J. F. Beeler, *British Naval Policy in the Gladstone–Disraeli Era, 1866–1880* (Stanford CA, 1997); J. F. Beeler, *The Birth of the Battleship: British Capital Ship Design, 1870–1881* (London, 2001).
28. A. G. Gordon, *The Rules of the Game: Jutland and British Naval Command* (London, 1996).
29. Mahan knew better, as his work on international law and blockade made clear. See A. T. Mahan, *Some Neglected Aspects of War* (Boston, 1907).
30. P. M. Kennedy, *The Rise and Fall of British Naval Mastery* (London, 1976), p. 206.
31. A. Mombauer, *Helmuth von Moltke and the Origins of the First World War* (Cambridge, 2003); F. Fischer, *War of Illusions: German Policies from 1911 to 1914* (London, 1975), p. 163; and I. N. Lambi, *The Navy and German Power Politics, 1862–1914* (London, 1984), p. 383.
32. N. Lambert, *Sir John Fisher's Naval Revolution* (Columbia SC, 1999).
33. See Mombauer, *Moltke*.
34. A. Offer, *The First World War: An Agrarian Interpretation* (Oxford, 1989); T. Munch-Petersen, *The Strategy of Phoney War* (Stockholm, 1981).
35. The key texts in this debate are: B. H. Liddell Hart, 'Economic Pressure or Continental Victories', *Journal of the Royal United Services Institute* 76 (1931): 486–510; M. Howard, *The Continental Commitment: The Dilemma of British Defence Policy in the Era of Two World Wars* (London, 1972); D. French, *The British Way in Warfare, 1688–2000* (London, 1990); and D. A. Baugh, 'Great Britain's "Blue-Water" Policy, 1689–1815', *International History Review* 10 (1988): 33–58.
36. J. W. Coogan, *The End of Neutrality: The United States, Britain and Maritime Rights, 1899–1915* (Ithaca NY, 1981); J. Grainger (ed.), *The Maritime Blockade of Germany in the Great War* (Aldershot, 2003).

37. W. H. Trimble, *Admiral William A. Moffett: Architect of Naval Aviation* (Washington, 1993); M. Peattie, *Sunburst: The Rise of Japanese Naval Airpower* (Annapolis MD, 2002).
38. J. Ferris, *The Evolution of British Strategic Policy, 1919–1926* (London, 1989).
39. G. A. H. Gordon, *British Seapower and Procurement between the Wars: A Reappraisal of Rearmament* (London, 1988).
40. C. Bell, '"How are we going to make War?" Admiral Sir Herbert Richmond and British Far Eastern War Plans', *Journal of Strategic Studies* 20/3 (1997): 123–41.
41. J. Rohwer and M. S. Monakov, *Stalin's Ocean-Going Fleet, Soviet Naval Strategy and Shipbuilding Programmes, 1935–1953* (London, 2001); R. Mallet, *The Italian Navy and Fascist Expansionism, 1935–1940* (London, 1998); and J. A. Maiolo, *The Royal Navy and Nazi Germany, 1933–39* (London, 1998).
42. G. E. Melton, *Darlan: Admiral and Statesman of France, 1881–1942* (Westport CT, 1998); A. D. Lambert, 'Sea Power 1939–40: Churchill and the Strategic Origins of the Battle of the Atlantic', *Journal of Strategic Studies* 17/1 (1994): 86–108.
43. D. Grinnell-Milne, *The Silent Victory: September 1940* (London, 1958).
44. C. B. A. Behrens, *Merchant Shipping and the Demands of War* (London, 1955); M. Doughty, *Merchant Shipping and War: A Study of Defence Planning in Twentieth Century Britain* (London, 1982); K. Smith, *Conflict over Convoys* (Cambridge, 2002); and M. Milner, 'The Battle of the Atlantic', *Journal of Strategic Studies* 13/1 (March 1990): 45–66.
45. A. D. Lambert, 'Seizing the Initiative: The Arctic Convoys, 1944–45' in N. Rodger (ed.), *Naval Power in the Twentieth Century* (London, 1996).
46. J. Lundstrom, *The First Team: Pacific Naval Air Combat from Pearl Harbor to Midway* (Annapolis MD, 1984).
47. C. Blair, *Silent Victory, the US Submarine War Against Japan* (Hagerstown MA, 1975).
48. M. A. Palmer, *Origins of the Maritime Strategy: American Naval Strategy in the First Postwar Decade* (Washington DC, 1988); M. Isenberg, *Shield of the Republic: The US Navy in an Era of Cold War and Violent Peace, 1945–1962* (New York, 1993); and E. J. Grove, *Vanguard to Trident: British Naval Policy since 1945* (Annapolis MD, 1987).
49. N. Friedman, *Sea Power and Space from the Dawn of the Missile Age to Net-Centric Warfare* (Chatham, 2000).
50. N. Friedman, *The US Maritime Strategy* (Annapolis MD, 1988).
51. In his 1976 study *The Rise and Fall of British Naval Mastery* Paul Kennedy made the connection very clear, but his economic indicator – industrial output – would not be used today.
52. P. Padfield's *Maritime Supremacy and the Opening of the Western Mind* (London, 1999) and his *Maritime Power and the Struggle for Freedom* (London, 2003) address this issue, as does the unsatisfactory A. Herman, *To Rule the Waves: How the British Navy Shaped the Modern World* (London, 2005).

10
war in the non-european world

bruce vandervort

It all began with Cortés. The victory of Hernán Cortés and his handful of Spanish conquistadors over the glittering empire of the Aztecs in Mexico in 1521, followed a little more than a decade later by the overthrow at the hands of an even smaller band of Spanish adventurers of the equally dazzling empire of the Incas in Peru, gave rise to one of history's most enduring legends: the legend of the world-beating character of the 'Western way of war'. It was, or so the legend has it, the superior technology, disciplined professionalism and assertive quest for decisive battle of Western armies like that of early modern Spain that secured victory – for Cortés and Pizarro *and* for the centuries-long parade of imperial soldiers who followed in their footsteps and succeeded in bringing most of the rest of the world under European (and European American) domination.[1]

The verdict of Tenochtitlán appeared to have been sealed for all time by the nineteenth-century onslaught of Western armies that brought almost all of Africa, large chunks of Asia, all of the Pacific islands and the 'Indian country' of Argentina, Canada, Chile and the USA under white rule. 'The West had now indeed arisen', wrote Geoffrey Parker at the conclusion of his immensely influential *The Military Revolution: Military Innovation and the Rise of the West, 1500–1800*. 'Thanks above all to their military superiority, founded upon the military revolution of the sixteenth and seventeenth centuries, the Western nations had managed to create the first global hegemony in History.'[2] By this time, or so mainstream military history contended, the technological and organizational superiority of Western armies had become so crushing that the campaigns they were called upon to wage outside Europe had been reduced for the most part to 'wars against nature', in the well-known phrase of the dean of Victorian theorists of colonial warfare, Colonel Charles Callwell. These 'small wars' were fought only secondarily against human foes, the real enemies being climate, disease, distance, lack of food and water, and inhospitable terrain. The great challenge in wars of this type, then, was to get troops in and out of the theatre of conflict as quickly as possible and, while there, to keep them healthy and well supplied.[3] The 'savage' or 'fanatical' enemies European and European American soldiers faced, while greatly varied in their ways of war, were nonetheless doomed to defeat by their lack of the 'higher mental faculties' that provided Europeans with seemingly unique powers to 'co-ordinate, to think strategically, and to innovate tactically and technically'.[4] Thus, US military historian John Gates could argue that while North American Indians were 'widely known for their stealth and ferocity', they possessed only a rudimentary knowledge of strategy and tactics. 'They fought as they did because it was the only way they knew how to fight, and their success in keeping the field as long as they did resulted as much from the [US] Army's meager size as from the Indians' prowess as warriors.'[5] The superiority of Western soldiery was so overwhelming, the generals and their civilian masters believed, that it was unnecessary to formulate a doctrine for waging 'small wars'. Any specific knowledge that was required could be picked up through on-the-job experience or from listening to the old hands. Besides, to focus on these campaigns against irregulars was to distract the attention of the military professionals from their primary task: preparing for war against their peers, other European powers. 'Orthodox war was European war.'[6]

other paradigms

If, then, the ways of war of non-European peoples were, by definition, unorthodox, they were also considered irrelevant, and not only by the soldiers and statesmen of Europe's imperial age. Little more than a decade ago, popular military historian Gérard Chaliand could still write that 'Our Western-centeredness, in the military domain, leads us to treat the contributions of other societies as of no consequence.' This, Chaliand suggested, could be attributed to the lack of interest in military matters on the part of most experts on non-Western societies. But, equally important in his view, was the fact that because many of these societies had been defeated or gone into decline in the era of Western imperial expansion, they were looked down upon in the West.[7] If there were exceptions to this pattern, they were those peoples who had made a valiant – but necessarily futile – effort to adopt the Western military model or, on the contrary, those who, like the Mamluks or Zulus, had dismissed gunpowder weapons as dishonourable instruments of war and had gone down to barbarous but glorious defeat, sword or spear in hand, against the disciplined volley fire of squares of European infantry.

Most remarkably, even China, with its long history as the dominant power in Asia and its manifold contributions to military science and technology, not the least of which was gunpowder, received little attention from Western military historians until quite recently. China's long and glorious military past was obscured in Western eyes by the Qing dynasty's economic and political collapse in the nineteenth century and the country's seeming inability to find itself under the Republic from 1911 to 1945. Over this same period, 'the West is associated with modernity, virility, progress, honesty, efficiency, rationality, and a preference for manly combat' while China, 'cast as a declining Oriental civilization, is associated with their opposites', according to the Cambridge historian of China's military, Hans van de Ven.[8] 'It took the unexpected victory of Mao Zedong' in the 1946–49 Chinese Civil War, adds Gérard Chaliand, to bring about a rediscovery of Sunzi, the soldier and martial philosopher of ancient China, whose *Art of War* is now recognized as one of the classic primers on military strategy,[9] and whose maxims were for a time embraced by the more aggressive, upwardly mobile denizens of the City and Wall Street. Sunzi (also transliterated as Sun Zi or Sun Tzu) had furnished, as it turned out, much of the strategic guidance for Mao and his communist armies.[10]

Communist victory in the Chinese civil war and the subsequent re-emergence of China as a military power in Asia have given rise to a renaissance of sorts in Chinese military studies. Perhaps the most important outcome of this renewed interest in Chinese military history has been the progressive abandonment of the long-held perception of Chinese civilization, conditioned by its Confucian system of ethics to distrust military men and the use of force, as essentially passive in relations with its neighbours. This view had held that through most of their history the Chinese relied upon a system of static defence, as symbolized in the famous Great Wall, bribes and cultural seduction to wear down and eventually overcome their enemies, principally the formidable nomadic peoples who encroached upon their northern and western borders.[11] More recent scholarship holds that this passive approach to international relations coexisted with – or, perhaps better, overlaid – a more or less continuous strategic culture which emphasized the use of offensive warfare to secure and ultimately expand China's frontiers. The authoritative statement of this new view came in political scientist Alastair Iain Johnston's 1995 study, *Strategic Culture and Grand Strategy in Chinese History*. Johnston argued that the function of the passive approach derived from Confucian ethics was not to inform decision-making with respect to war, but to 'justify behavior in culturally acceptable terms'. The notion that China has been basically defensive, non-expansionist and complacently superior is, he contends, a twentieth-century inheritance, reflecting a time when the country was weak and under attack. In reality, 'Chinese history is full of examples of ruthless, offensive use of military force against weaker enemies for territorial expansion'.[12]

The revision of Chinese international relations theory to reflect a more predatory approach has been accompanied by new studies of the wars and military campaigns of the past, particularly those of the more expansionist dynasties, the Han, Tang, Ming and Qing. What these studies demonstrate is a long-term Chinese preoccupation with overcoming the advantages in war enjoyed by the nomadic peoples along its frontiers, particularly their superior mobility, and with mastering the formidable problems with terrain and supply that hampered operations in the homelands of these pastoral enemies. In short, agrarian China had to raise large contingents of mounted men to supplement their traditional infantry armies and find the means to keep them in the field across mountains and deserts deep into the grasslands, deserts and mountains of Central Asia and Mongolia. That the Chinese ultimately were able to field numerous and effective mounted forces, acquired by dividing and conquering and then recruiting among their nomadic foes as well as by developing home-grown cavalry, was a considerable feat. Equally impressive was the administrative and fiscal apparatus which made possible expeditions of huge armies deep into enemy territory. In the mid 1700s, Qing China was perhaps the world's greatest military power, doubling the size of its empire by conquering most of Central Asia and occupying Tibet. 'In the eighteenth century', writes Hans van de Ven,

> the Qing was an expansionist empire able to sustain large-scale campaigns over enormous distances in inhospitable territory. Napoleon's inability to supply his troops in Russia provides a good foil for understanding China's logistical capacity at the time.[13]

China's way of war, then, followed a trajectory at considerable odds with that pursued by its European contemporaries, the infantry-heavy trend rooted in Europe's 'military revolution' of the sixteenth and seventeenth centuries. And, while the armies of imperial China possessed many of the technological accoutrements sported by European counterparts – gunpowder weapons, for example, not just handguns but light and heavy artillery as well – these weapons were most often indigenous products. One of the great wars of the early modern era, of the period of the European 'military revolution' in fact, was the Japanese invasion of Korea (1592–98), which drew the armies of Ming China into the fray. It was the cavalry and artillery of the Chinese, plus the famous armoured warships ('turtle boats') of the Koreans, which drove off the Japanese. This was a much larger conflict than anything that would take place in Europe until the Napoleonic era, with around half a million soldiers engaged on the two sides.[14]

The trajectory followed by China's armies took its inspiration throughout its history from a candid appreciation of the military environment in which China had to operate, one which was quite different from that facing the Europeans. The Chinese military experience brings into relief the problems that inevitably beset any attempt to prescribe a universal paradigm of military capability, much less excellence.

There are important lessons to be learned from the Japanese military experience as well. If China provides us with an example of the primacy of the strategic environment in the shaping of a military paradigm, Japan offers some of the most impressive evidence available of the paramount importance of socio-cultural and political factors in that same process. It is clear that, in the forging of both of these national paradigms, technology was very much a *dependent variable*, though the Japanese example is by far the most dramatic in this regard, as will be shown below.

Early Japanese combat, largely an affair of clashes between shield-bearing spearmen supported by archers, underwent a profound change after *c.* AD 400, when the Japanese encountered horses in the course of one of many invasions of Korea. 'Soon fighters combined archery with horse riding, and the resulting fighting technology dominated war in Japan until 1300.'[15] Here, as elsewhere in the world, this kind of warfare was necessarily the province of the aristocracy, who were the only people who could afford to breed and keep horses and to equip and keep the men who rode them. The original *samurai* ('those who serve') thus were mounted retainers of the great Japanese lords, wielders of bow and sword in the incessant battles for regional, and sometimes national, supremacy that, aside from periodic incursions into Korea, dominated warfare down into the 1600s. Although the regional potentates were capable of fielding large armies, mass warfare often was eschewed in favour of individual combats between samurai warriors.[16]

This way of war would receive a rude shock in the course of the Mongol amphibious assaults on Japan in 1274 and 1281. Although these invasions were, of course, ultimately thwarted by typhoons – the famous 'divine winds' or kamikaze – enough Mongol warriors managed to get ashore before the winds started to blow to give their Japanese hosts a considerable fright. The Mongols brought along primitive gunpowder weapons, a jolting novelty to the Japanese, but, more importantly, they fielded large bodies of infantry supported by cavalry, a style of mass warfare they had borrowed from the Chinese. The lesson the Japanese took away from these encounters was not so much that firearms were the wave of the future, though there would be attempts now to obtain guns from the Chinese and, later, European traders, but that in encounters between horsemen, however fearless, and massed infantry, it was the latter that, if kept well in hand by their commanders, usually won. Infantry now became the mainstay of the Japanese military.

Having given itself a mass army based on foot soldiers, Japan promptly took up a position at the forefront of the gunpowder revolution. On the basis of samples of modern muskets bought from Portuguese traders in the mid 1500s, the Japanese within a generation had set up a metallurgical industry to manufacture and repair guns. In 1575, at the battle of Nagashino, a force of some 3,000 musketeers in the army of the great lord (*daimyō*) Oda Nobunaga used volley fire to smash charges of cavalry of the rival Takeda clan and give Nobunaga control of most of the country. Such tactics were unknown in Europe or the rest of Asia at the time.[17] The heyday of the gunpowder revolution in Japan came in the closing years of the sixteenth century, in the invasion of Korea by Nobunaga's great general (and successor as Japanese strongman), Toyotomi Hideyoshi. The 1592–98 war against the Koreans and their Chinese allies, already alluded to above, ended in defeat for the Japanese in spite of an advantage in shoulder arms. The Ming Chinese monopoly on artillery and the use by the Koreans of their armoured ships to seize control of the intervening seas proved to be the decisive factors.[18]

Japan's attempt to conquer Korea with the aid of gunpowder weapons ran parallel, oddly, some might think, to an effort by the great Hideyoshi to severely restrict access by the populace to guns. A policy known as *katanagari* (or, literally, 'sword collection') was begun prior to the general's death in 1598 and continued with even greater rigour by the Tokugawa shogunate[19] which took power two years later. Fearful of the socio-political consequences of putting gunpowder weapons and knowledge of their use in the hands of the lower classes, with the attendant effect of eroding the warrior ethos and thus the overawing power of the aristocracy, the shogunate forbade the ownership or use of firearms in the kingdom. Reversion to a culture of war built around the code of the samurai swordsman would be an integral part of the Tokugawa policy of *sakoku* or closing off the country from the rest of the world. For the next 250 years, while the Western world and its emulators elsewhere were undergoing two 'military revolutions' centred around the employment of firearms, the bow, spear and sword remained the standard weapons in the Japanese arsenal.[20]

a verdict overturned

Though it still boasts adherents, the metanarrative of the evolution of Western military superiority sketched out at the beginning of this chapter has lost much of its explanatory value over the last two decades, and not just because of the existence of multiple military paradigms in this as in any given age. To begin with, the 'verdict of Tenochtitlán' that seemed to have launched the Western 'military revolution' paradigm on its course to world dominance, has long since been overturned.[21] While Cortés was surely content to have it thought that victory over the Aztecs came as a result of Spanish military prowess and acumen (and his own genius, of course), his correspondence from Mexico told a different story. The empire of the Aztecs, he had learned relatively early on in his *entrada* into Mexico, was seething with the discontent of recently subdued peoples. Through a combination of bribes and threats, Cortés was able to obtain the services as guides, porters and warriors of up to 150,000 of these malcontents in the run-up to the final assault on the Aztec capital.[22] Thus, like so many other European conquering armies in the centuries to come, by securing local support the Spanish invaders of Mexico 'acquired men with knowledge of the local terrain; had their numerical inferiority redressed; and obtained advice and information from their allies'.[23] Not to mention the cannon fodder needed to overcome the Aztecs' tenacious defence of Tenochtitlán. A defence rendered all the more remarkable by the appalling inroads made into the Aztec population by smallpox and other epidemic diseases introduced into Mexico by the Europeans and to which the Indian population could offer no natural resistance. It is thought that some 50 per cent of the inhabitants of Tenochtitlán perished of disease in 1520–21, on the eve of the Spanish conquest.[24] Even mainstream encyclopedias nowadays stress the crucial role of epidemic disease in Cortés's victory over the Aztecs. The *Grolier Encyclopedia of Knowledge*, on sale in supermarkets across the USA, for example, tells readers that Tenochtitlán fell, after a three-month siege, '*only* because an epidemic killed many defenders'.[25]

More important, the Spanish successes in Mexico and Peru have been shown to be the exception rather than the rule in the extra-European wars of the early modern period. Despite the 'military revolution' in Western Europe alluded to above, which put gunpowder weapons on distant battlefields and cannon-bearing, ocean-ranging war ships on distant seas, Europeans proved able to do little more than carve out trading enclaves in most parts of the non-European world until the eighteenth century. Economic historian David S. Landes is simply wrong to assert that 'in the four, five hundred years following the millennium' European military technology had 'created a decisive disparity of power at any point of conflict to which Europeans could deliver arms and men'.[26] To begin with, from a global perspective the 'great powers' of the early modern era were not Britain, France, Portugal or even Spain, but Ming China and the expansionist Muslim empires of Asia, the Ottoman Turks, the Safavids of Persia and the Mughals of India. The 'decisive disparity of power' Landes refers to would begin to take shape only in the 1700s, when these empires had entered into decline, due as much to internal stresses as to demonstrations of European military superiority. 'Even as late as 1750, the eventual triumph of western arms in India was not taken for granted.'[27] And, in some regions of the non-European world, the hegemony of the West was even slower in coming.

As late as 1854, the *khalifa* of the Tukolor *jihadi* empire in West Africa, al-Hajj 'Umar, could still say of the French, two centuries after their arrival on the coast of Senegal:

The whites are only traders. As long as they bring me merchandise in their ships, as long as they pay me a good tribute ..., I will live at peace with them. But they are not to build any more forts or to send war ships up the [Senegal] river.[28]

A scant two decades later, however, al-Hajj 'Umar would be dead and the empire he had built would be reeling under pressure from the French that ultimately would carry them to the bend of the Niger River and fabled Timbuktu. Whereas in 1876 less than 10 per cent of Africa was ruled by Europeans, by 1914 only Ethiopia and Liberia had managed to elude the imperial grasp. East of Suez, Britain had contrived to bring all of India under her rule, weather a bid for independence in the Great Mutiny of 1857 in India, and add Burma to her South Asian holdings; France had conquered Indochina; by subduing the Sumatran kingdom of Aceh, the Dutch had finally succeeded in imposing their will upon the sprawling Indonesian archipelago; Filipino rebels had succeeded in escaping from Spanish misrule only to find themselves in the grip of a new entrant in the Asian imperial contest, the USA; and once-powerful China had been forced to grant humiliating territorial concessions to a series of European powers (and the USA) and even to regional upstart Japan.

moral force

At the time these events occurred and for some time afterwards, they would be widely interpreted in the West not so much as the result of superior military technology, but, rather, as proof of 'the superior moral force of the European invaders', wrote the British historian of East Africa, Terence Ranger.[29] For a number of prominent architects of nineteenth-century imperialism, this 'moral force' sprang from white racial and/or European cultural superiority. Britain's greatest Victorian colonial soldier, Sir Garnet Wolseley, made this abundantly clear in an exhortation to his troops on the eve of the Ashanti War of 1873–74: 'It must never be forgotten by our soldiers that Providence has implanted in the heart of every native of Africa a superstitious awe and dread of the white man that prevents the negro from daring to meet us face to face in combat.'[30] It was no different with Asians, in the view of Colonel Callwell, the small wars theorist. '[T]he way to deal with Asiatics', he famously wrote, 'is to go for them and cow them by sheer force of will.'[31]

While this sort of explanation for European success in empire-building may have satisfied Victorian and Edwardian public opinion and informed subsequent historical commentary, it increasingly wore thin as the twentieth century wore on. By the post-1945 era, as colonized peoples in Africa and Asia began agitating for and winning independence, the 'moral force' perspective had become something of an embarrassment and had largely given way, wrote Terence Ranger, once again, to 'assumptions concerning the overpowering military superiority of the Europeans' and, on the part of non-Western peoples, a corresponding 'inability ... to determine their own fates'.[32]

technological determinism

Historians might be excused for leaping to the conclusion that rapid and sweeping developments in military technology were determinant in the equally rapid and sweeping conquest of most of the non-Western world by European and European American armies in the nineteenth century. For this rapid European expansion coincided with a revolution in military technology of even more imposing proportions than its sixteenth-century predecessor.

Until the mid 1800s, European and European American armies enjoyed only a slight technological edge over those of their colonial adversaries. Military weaponry seemed stuck on the plateau reached during the Napoleonic Wars: the smoothbore muzzle-loader remained the standard shoulder weapon in all armies using gunpowder arms; although field artillery had been made lighter during the previous century, it was still too cumbersome for effective use in the mountains and jungles of the colonial world. Nor had European navies progressed much since the days of Nelson. Though steamships had become familiar sights on the rivers and in the coastal waters of most Western countries, they were mostly civilian craft until well into the nineteenth century. The wooden sailing ship still predominated in most Western navies at mid-century.[33]

But the rough technological parity that existed between European and European American armed forces and those of their adversaries began to undergo a profound shift in the 1850s and '60s. For perhaps the first time, technological innovations appeared that raised little or no echo in the non-Western world. These included, among others, the submarine telegraph, steam-powered iron warships, breech-loading, rapid firing shoulder arms, handguns and artillery, and, ultimately, the machine gun.

Navies led the way in implementing this revolution. Steam-driven iron ships slowly began replacing wooden sailing craft in Western navies in the 1840s and by the 1850s were starting to assist imperial expansion on the seas and up the rivers of the non-Western world. Steam-powered fighting ships contributed to British triumph in the 1850s Opium War with China; it was a French naval landing team, coming off gunboats in the Niger River, that first entered the storied city of Timbuktu, on the edge of the Sahara desert, in 1893, much to the disgust of an approaching army of French marines and allied African infantry.[34] Although naval historians later would complain that the sailors got little credit for it at the time, it is clear that the ability of European navies to control the sea lanes and to move men and supplies quickly from place to place was one of the imperial powers' greatest assets.[35]

There were some very effective demonstrations of Western armed might on battlefields in the non-European world as well. In West Africa, although the *jihadis* of al-Hajj 'Umar charged French lines 'as if they are seeking martyrdom; it is clear that they want to die', it was the French squares 'with their measured fire control' that carried the day and consigned the *khalifa*'s Tukolor empire to the refuse heap of history by the 1880s.[36] In East Africa, meanwhile, an army of some 1,000 Portuguese and allied African soldiers, formed up in square and armed with magazine rifles and machine guns, routed a Gaza Nguni impi ten times its size, at the battle of Coolela Lake in Mozambique in November 1895. The Portuguese commander, Colonel Rodrigues Galhardo, likened the encounter to a 'cotillion'.[37] But, it was in the Anglo-Saxon world that the cult of what became known (to its detractors) as 'technological determinism' would sink the deepest roots.

The widespread enthusiasm that soon greeted the 'technological determinist' explanation for European success in the nineteenth-century colonial wars no doubt owed something to the Cold War, with its obsession with the comparative megatonnage of nuclear bombs and the 'throw-weight' of ballistic missile warheads. The more substantial origins of its popular appeal lie, however, in its suitability as a consensus view, acceptable to contemporary Western and non-Western historians alike. We have seen how the Military Revolution thesis used to explain the rise to power of certain European states in the sixteenth century became, in the hands of Geoffrey Parker, an explanatory vehicle for the eventual triumph of the West over the Rest, or at least those of the Rest who could not or would not emulate Western military science and employ Western military hardware. This perspective now was embraced by historians in the emerging ex-colonial states as well, since it could be employed to absolve their peoples from shortcomings of their own that might have led to defeat at the hands of Western armies. 'Above all', wrote the Ghanaian historian A. Adu Boahen, 'technologically and logistically, African armies were at a great disadvantage in comparison with their invaders .... What chance would such an army have against a well-trained, professional one armed with cannons and repeater rifles [and] maxim guns and enjoying naval and logistic support?'[38] Thus, if the subjugation of African and Asian peoples could be ascribed to the technological edge enjoyed by Western armies, a discreet veil could be cast over the part played in European victory by the failure of non-European peoples to present a united front to invasion or by the outright and often massive collaboration of African and Asian peoples in the campaigns of imperial conquest. Such discretion was understandable – finger-pointing of this sort threatened to further weaken the already fragile unity of many newly-independent nations – but it nonetheless represented a serious distortion of the historical record.

The 1980s and early 1990s were the heyday of the 'technological determinist' rationale for the rapid imperial conquests of the nineteenth century. The seminal statement of this position came at the very beginning of the period, in Daniel R. Headrick's often-cited (if less often read) *Tools of Empire: Technology and European Imperialism in the Nineteenth Century* (1981). Headrick, however, had set his sights on technological developments during the era of imperial conquest itself and devoted less attention to the historical links between these nineteenth-century innovations and the Military Revolution of the 1500s and 1600s or to the emulation of Western military organization and technology in the non-European world.[39] These oversights were addressed, of course, in Geoffrey Parker's 1988 study. The period of what we can call the hegemony of the 'technological determinists' reached its apogee two years later, with the publication of David B. Ralston's *Importing the European Army:*

The Introduction of European Military Techniques into the Extra-European World,
1600–1914 (1990).

By the time Ralston's book appeared, however, a reaction had set in. Indeed, in retrospect, it can be seen that a potentially deadly pre-emptive strike had been launched against 'technological determinism' as early as the 1960s, with the publication of Ronald Robinson and John Gallagher's *Africa and the Victorians: The Official Mind of Imperialism.*[40]

Although Robinson and Gallagher's book was a work of diplomatic and political, not military, history, it contained insights that would go to the heart of the debate over the factors behind the rapid spread of European imperialism in the nineteenth century. A major contribution was the authors' success in shifting the locus of initiative in the scramble for empire from metropolitan capitals to the global periphery, thus not only portraying the European imperial powers as *reactive* as opposed to *proactive* with respect to imperial ventures, but making the extra-European world an indispensable participant in the process. Robinson spelled out the salient implications of this position in a later essay that deserves more attention than it has received from the military historians of empire. 'The expansive forces generated in industrial Europe', he wrote,

> had to combine with elements within the agrarian societies of the outer world to make empires at all practicable.... It ought to be commonplace therefore that from beginning to end imperialism was a product of interaction between European and extra-European polities. *European economic and strategic expansion took imperial form when these two components operated at cross-purposes with a third and non-European component – that of indigenous collaboration and resistance.*[41]

This 'third element', Robinson continued, had the potential to serve as the 'missing key' to a more historical theory of imperialism and, we might add, of the military conquest of the non-European world in the nineteenth century. Europeans, he wrote, had to obtain the backing of indigenous elites in the non-European world if they wanted to establish a foothold there.

> Without the voluntary or enforced cooperation of their governing elites, economic resources could not be transferred, strategic interests protected or xenophobic reaction and traditional resistance to change contained. *Nor without indigenous collaboration, when the time came for it, could Europeans have conquered and ruled their non-European empires.*[42]

Leaving aside his characterization of indigenous resistance as 'xenophobic' and 'traditional' – like many Western historians of his day Robinson assumed that African and Asian resistance to empire had emanated from the most backward elements of the indigenous population and thus was doomed to defeat – his essay points the way forward to a more satisfying, reliable and, yes, historical explanation of European success in the colonial wars than the thesis of triumphant technology: the ability of Europeans to recruit and deploy large armies of indigenous soldiers.

In this regard, remarkably little had changed since the early modern era. Just as Portugal and the Netherlands, with populations of some 2 million each, had been forced to rely on indigenous troops in order to hang on to their empires in the 1600s, so nineteenth-century European armies, faced with major commitments elsewhere and still wary of exposing their white soldiers to tropical diseases, bad water and sunstroke, turned to mass recruitment of 'native' troops to wage war on their behalf in Africa and Asia. These troops generally were of two types: irregulars, who functioned as specialized auxiliaries attached to the regular colonial armies, but not integrated into them; and indigenous levies, equipped and trained along professional lines and formed into 'native' units within the colonial armies, under European officers and, usually, non-coms as well.

Most European regular armies on colonial service employed large numbers of irregulars, considered indispensable for purposes of scouting, protecting the flanks of armies on the move, and sowing terror among the enemy populace with their rapacity and ruthlessness. John Keegan has left a colourful sketch of the relationship between these irregulars and the professional soldiers alongside whom they served in the armies of the nineteenth century.

> From the unlawful and uncivilised means by which these irregular warriors rewarded themselves on campaign and from their barbaric methods of fighting, the officers of the civilised states averted their gaze; yet without the services they offered, the over-drilled armies in which Clausewitz and his kin had been raised would scarcely have been able to keep the field.[43]

In Asia, while most of the attention of military historians has focused on indigenous units within the European colonial armies, such as the sepoys who made up such a large part of Britain's Indian army, irregulars also featured prominently in Asian colonial campaigns. Dutch 'pacification' of vast, populous Indonesia would have been impossible without the aid of large numbers of Moluccan and Ambonese auxiliaries.[44] The Russian army, to take but one more example, made great use of irregulars in its conquest of the Caucasus and Central Asian regions in the mid 1800s. Though Russian army commanders employed Christian and dissident Muslim mercenaries to good effect in their colonial wars, their most sought after allies were those notorious 'freemen' of the steppe, the Cossack cavalry who scouted and raided for them and sometimes set themselves up as permanent garrisons in conquered territory by displacing the enemy population.[45]

In Africa, meanwhile, colonial armies also availed themselves of support from auxiliaries, although greater efforts seem to have been made to recruit

Africans for service as 'native' regulars. The French managed to incorporate many of the Arab and Berber irregular cavalry units that had fought alongside them in the conquest of Algeria in the 1840s into Spahi regiments of the *Armée d'Afrique* permanently stationed in North Africa. By contrast, the *goumiers*, fierce hill tribesmen from Morocco, continued to serve the French as auxiliary cavalry and infantry down through the Second World War.[46] Although irregulars were employed in sub-Saharan Africa, the more common practice was to enrol Africans in regiments or battalions that served within – indeed often made up the bulk of – European colonial armies in the region. Thus, while the Italian colonial army took along a contingent of Tigrean irregulars on its disastrous invasion of Ethiopia in 1896, the great majority of its African troops were Eritrean *ascaris*, long-service infantry led by Italian officers.[47] Great Britain, meanwhile, formed the Royal West African Frontier Force (1897) and the King's African Rifles (1902) to facilitate the conquest of West and East and Central Africa, respectively.[48] Indeed, in 1902, the 11,500 soldiers following the British flag in Black Africa included only some 300 white officers and NCOs.[49]

It was, however, France which recruited the most Black regular troops for service in its colonial armies in Africa. Its famous *Tirailleurs sénégalais* (Senegalese light infantry) regiments, first formed in the 1850s for service alongside troops of the French Marine Corps, soon were bearing the burden of French colonial warfare in the Western Sudan and Equatorial Africa. 'The Senegalese light infantry are the real soldiers of the Sudan', wrote Lieutenant-Colonel Joseph Gallieni, who commanded them in the 1880s. 'By turns engineers, gunners, couriers, porters, always ready, always loyal, it is because of them that we hold the vast territory from [the Senegal River] to the Niger River.'[50] On the eve of the First World War, the defence of France's empire in sub-Saharan Africa was assured almost entirely by troops from Senegalese light infantry units.[51]

The recruitment of great numbers of indigenous troops for service in European colonial armies inevitably had a considerable impact on how those armies were organized and how they fought. In both Africa and Asia, European commanders were forced to accept that, for their 'native' troops, war was a family affair. Often accompanied by their children, the wives of African soldiers followed their husbands into the field, pitching tents, cooking for them and carrying their gear. When French officers of the *Tirailleurs sénégalais*, worried that too much 'domestication' might blunt the fighting edge of their troops, tried to send the soldiers' families home, they were threatened with mutiny and obliged to desist.[52]

Just as the general shortage of European troops, increasingly in demand back home as international relations worsened, had combined with the ecology and epidemiology of the extra-European world to dictate a heavy reliance upon 'native' soldiers to wage the imperial wars of the great powers, so did this emerging pattern play a considerable role in shaping the colonial 'way of war'. In much of Africa and Asia, the climate and terrain precluded employment of the mass armies and the industrial style of warfare that characterized contemporary European military conflict. When the German army exported its 'way of war', the late nineteenth century's military paradigm be it remembered, to South West Africa to put down the Herero Revolt of 1904–05, it ran into great – and apparently unanticipated – difficulties.

[D]ependence on the railroad seriously compromised the mobility of the forces in the field. Artillery, machine guns, and rapid-fire rifles gave the Germans overwhelming superiority in firepower, but it was purchased at a high cost, for it tied the German soldier to a bulky, slow-moving, and highly vulnerable supply train, without which their weapons were useless.[53]

Light infantry, usually indigenous, thus became the Queen of Battles in the colonial world. Lightly-equipped, able to live off the land if necessary, supported by clouds of irregulars who scouted the terrain ahead and cowed the population along the route of march, armies like the *Tirailleurs sénégalais* or the Royal West African Frontier Force fought the wars and won the battles that gave the European powers control over most of the non-Western world by 1914.

conclusion

A recent analysis of the triumph of the East India Company in its long struggle for control of India in the eighteenth and early nineteenth centuries sheds much light on the overall approach which won Europe her empires and enables us to give final point to the thesis of this chapter. Indian scholar Kaushik Roy observes that John Company 'emerged supreme because the British were able to strike a balance between the European elements of war and certain indigenous military techniques and utilize the natural, human and animal resources of India in warfare'. Roy styles this 'a Balanced Military Synthesis'. At the same time, he maintains, those Indian peoples which were most successful in holding off the British-led armies were those which, like the Marathas and Sikhs, had recognized that 'the imported European way of war was inadequate to meet the varied demands of warfare and ecology in South Asia' and so had effected a melange between elements of the imported Western art of war and traditional Indian methods. Those Indian states that failed to make the necessary adjustments, whether because of the opposition of feudal nobles, cultural resistance to innovation or, most often, lack of the means to finance a more modern military, could only manage a 'Defective Military Synthesis', in Roy's terms, and quickly succumbed.[54]

Thus, it was not European expeditionary forces, in quest of decisive battle and equipped with the weaponry and techniques of Europe's successive 'Military Revolutions', that carved out the great European empires of the late nineteenth century. Surely there were enough appearances of the 'thin red line' and its equivalents from other imperial powers to give an aura of verisimilitude to the legend of the all-conquering Western 'way of war'. In the end, however, victory in the scramble for empire ultimately required the formation of armies of indigenous regulars, equipped for the most part with the cast-off weapons of their European employers but subjected to discipline imposed by their white officers. What David Killingray has written of the way victory came in Africa should stand as true for the gamut of European conquests.

European empires in Africa were gained principally by African mercenary armies, occasionally supported by white or other colonial troops. In what Kipling described as 'savage wars of peace' the bulk of the fighting was done by black soldiers whose disciplined firepower invariably defeated numerically superior armies.[55]

Killingray's verdict, now nearly two decades old, may represent a new consensus among historians of imperial warfare, in replacement of the older 'verdict of Tenochtitlán', but it would appear that it has yet to penetrate the consciousness of the larger academic community. This is the way one of the most widely used world history textbooks in the USA explains the imperial conquests of the nineteenth century to today's undergraduates.

During the nineteenth century industrialists devised effective technologies of transportation, communication, and war that enabled European imperialists to have their way in the larger world.... [Advances in weaponry] provided European armies with an arsenal vastly stronger than any other in the world [thus] enabling European armies to impose colonial rule almost at will.[56]

further reading

The following books are all recommended: D. Ayalon, *Gunpowder and Firearms in the Mamluk Kingdom: A Challenge to a Mediaeval Society* (London, 1978); J. Belich, *The Victorian Interpretation of Racial Conflict: The Maori, the British and the New Zealand Wars* (Montreal and Kingston, 1989); J. Black (ed.), *War in the Early Modern World* (Boulder CO, 1999); J. Black (ed.), *War in the Modern World since 1815* (London, 2003); C. Callwell, *Small Wars: Their Principles and Practice* [1896] (Lincoln NE, 1996); W. W. Farriss, *Heavenly Warriors: The Evolution of Japan's Military, 500–1300* (Cambridge MA, 1992); D. Headrick, *Tools of Empire: Technology and European Imperialism in the Nineteenth Century* (New York, 1981); G. Parker, *The Military Revolution: Military Innovation and the Rise of the West, 1500–1800* (Cambridge, 1988); D. M. Peers (ed.), *Warfare and Empires: Contact and Conflict between European and non-European Military and Maritime Forces and Cultures* (Brookfield VT, 1997); N. Perrin, *Giving Up the Gun: Japan's Reversion to the Sword, 1543–1879* (Boston, 1979); D. B. Ralston, *Importing the European Army: The Introduction of European Military Techniques into the Extra-European World* (Chicago, 1990); M. Restall, *Seven Myths of the Spanish Conquest* (Oxford, 2003); R. Robinson and J. Gallagher (with A. Denny) *Africa and the Victorians: The Official Mind of Imperialism* (London, 1961); J. K.

Thornton, *Africa and Africans in the Making of the Atlantic World, 1400–1800* (Cambridge, 1998); S. Turnbull, *Samurai: The Warrior Class of Japan* (New York, 1977); H. van de Ven (ed.), *Warfare in Chinese History* (Leiden, 2000); and B. Vandervort, *Wars of Imperial Conquest in Africa, 1830–1914* (London and Bloomington IN, 1998).

notes

1. 'Hernán Cortés and the Creation of the Model Conqueror' in B. Pastor Bodmer, *The Armature of Conquest: Spanish Accounts of the Discovery of America, 1492–1589* (Stanford CA, 1992).
2. Geoffrey Parker, *The Military Revolution: Military Innovation and the Rise of the West, 1500–1800* (Cambridge, 1988), p. 154.
3. C. Callwell, *Small Wars: Their Principles and Practice* [1896] (Lincoln NE, 1996), pp. 21, 25, 57.
4. J. Belich, *The Victorian Interpretation of Racial Conflict: The Maori, the British and the New Zealand Wars* (Montreal and Kingston, 1989), p. 316.
5. J. Gates, 'Indians and Insurrectos: The US Army's Experience with Insurgency', *Parameters*, 13 (1983): 59–68. Quote is at 62. 'Insurrectos' was the name given to Filipinos who offered armed resistance to US occupation of their homeland after the Spanish-American War of 1898.
6. H. Strachan, *European Armies and the Conduct of War* (London, 1983), p. 76.
7. Gérard Chaliand, *The Art of War in World History: From Antiquity to the Nuclear Age* (Berkeley CA, 1994), pp. 15–17.
8. H. van de Ven, 'Military Mobilisation in China, 1840–1949' in J. Black (ed.), *War in the Modern World since 1815* (London, 2003), p. 21.
9. Chaliand, *Art of War in World History*, p. 15. The classic rendition of Sunzi's *Art of War* in English is Samuel B. Griffith's translation, published by Oxford University Press in 1971.
10. G. Bjorge, *Moving the Enemy: Operational Art in the Chinese PLA's Huai Huai Campaign*, Leavenworth Paper No. 22 (Fort Leavenworth KS, 2004), pp. 2, 5–6. Bjorge sees Sunzi as the originator of the now much ballyhooed concept of 'operational art', defined as 'the employment of military forces to attain strategic goals in a theater of war or theater of operations through the design, organization, and conduct of campaigns and major operations'. Ibid., p. 2.
11. This view is most conveniently summarized in J. K. Fairbank (ed.), *The Chinese World Order: Traditional China's Foreign Relations* (Cambridge MA, 1968).
12. Johnston's arguments are nicely laid out in P. C. Perdue, 'Culture, History, and Imperial Chinese Strategy: Legacies of the Qing Conquests' in H. van de Ven (ed.), *Warfare in Chinese History* (Leiden, 2000), pp. 252–5. Quotes are at pp. 254, 255. Johnston is at pains to distinguish his notion of a 'ruthless, offensive' long-term Chinese 'strategic culture' from the strikingly similar view of Soviet global strategy held by Western experts during the Cold War – that it was based on a long-standing Russian tradition 'which believed in the virtues of expansion through pre-emptive, offensive war'. Nonetheless, it would seem obvious that his analysis is bound to resonate with Western policy-makers eager to paint populous, rapidly-developing China as a would-be hegemon. Ibid., p. 254.
13. Van de Ven, 'Military Mobilisation in China', p. 20.
14. K. W. Swope, 'Crouching Tigers, Secret Weapons: Military Technology Employed during the Sino-Japanese-Korean War, 1592–1598', *Journal of Military History* 69/1 (2005): 11–41.

15. W. W. Farris, 'Japan to 1300' in K. Raaflaub and N. Rosenstein (eds), *War and Society in the Ancient and Medieval Worlds: Asia, the Mediterranean, Europe and Mesoamerica* (Cambridge MA, 1999), p. 50.
16. For this period of Japanese military history, see W. W. Farriss, *Heavenly Warriors: The Evolution of Japan's Military, 500–1300* (Cambridge MA, 1992).
17. J. Black, *War and the World: Military Power and the Fate of Continents, 1450–2000* (New Haven CT, 1998), pp. 50–1.
18. Swope, 'Crouching Tigers, Secret Weapons', 38–9.
19. The shogun was, in the beginning in the late 1100s, the military adjunct of the Japanese Emperor in Kyoto. By the 1300s, shoguns had become the real power in the country, to the extent that they were able to enforce their will upon leaders of rival clans, all of whom employed private armies of samurai. The Tokugawa were simply the most successful clan in this regard, dominating Japanese government from 1600 until the Meiji Restoration of 1868.
20. The standard source for the abandonment of gunpowder weapons in Japan is N. Perrin, *Giving Up the Gun: Japan's Reversion to the Sword, 1543–1879* (Boston, 1979). As is well known, Japan never became completely isolated from the rest of the world. The port of Nagasaki was kept open to limited foreign trade. The Chinese were permitted access to the port under close supervision and the Dutch were allowed to maintain a trading post on a small island in Nagasaki harbour, which the Japanese government used as a kind of window on developments in the West. There were also contacts with Korea. E. O. Reischauer, *Japan, the Story of a Nation* (New York, 1976), p. 95.
21. The most authoritative statement of the revisionist position can be found in M. Restall, *Seven Myths of the Spanish Conquest* (Oxford, 2003), chs 1, 3.
22. Hernán Cortés, *Letters from Mexico* (trans. A. Pagden) (New York, 1971), pp. 70, 62, 262.
23. G. V. Scammell, 'Indigenous Assistance in the Establishment of Portuguese Power in Asia in the Sixteenth Century', *Modern Asian Studies* 14/1 (1980): 1–11, 7.
24. J. A. Sokolow, *The Great Encounter: Native Peoples and European Settlers in the Americas, 1492–1800* (Armonk NY, 2003), p. 99.
25. 'Cortés, Hernán' entry in *Grolier Encyclopedia of Knowledge* (Danbury CT, 1991), v, p. 271. Emphasis added.
26. D. S. Landes, 'The Foundations of European Expansion and Dominion: An Equilibrium Model', *Itinerario* 5/1 (1981): 44–61, 50.
27. D. M. Peers (ed.), *Warfare and Empires: Contact and Conflict between European and non-European Military and Maritime Forces and Cultures* (Brookfield VT, 1997), p. xix.
28. L. L. C. Faidherbe, *Le Sénégal. La France dans l'Afrique Occidentale* (Paris, 1889), p. 140.
29. T. Ranger, 'African Reaction to the Imposition of Colonial Rule in East and Central Africa' in L. H. Gann and P. Duignan (eds), *The History and Politics of Colonialism in Africa* (Cambridge, 1969), i, p. 293.
30. Wolseley, 'Memorandum on Bush Fighting', 20 December 1873. Quoted in A. Lloyd, *Drums of Kumasi: The Story of the Ashanti Wars* (Harlow, 1964), p. 85.
31. Callwell, *Small Wars*, p. 72.
32. Ranger, 'African Reaction', p. 293.
33. '[T]he wooden ship of the line remained the heart of the European battle fleet through the 1850s, its life extended by the screw propeller'. L. Sondhaus, 'Naval Power and Warfare' in J. Black (ed.), *European Warfare, 1815–2000* (London, 2002), p. 172.

34. This remarkable episode is recounted in great detail in D. Grévoz, *Les cannonières de Tombouctu: les Français a la conquête de la cité mythique (1870–1894)* (Paris, 1992), pp. 128–66.
35. See, for example, W. L. Clowes's lament about the lack of recognition of the Royal Navy's contribution to victory in the Second South African (Boer) War in *The Royal Navy: A History from the Earliest Times to the Death of Queen Victoria* (London, 1903), vii, p. 463.
36. M. Hiskett, 'The Nineteenth-Century Jihads in West Africa' in *The Cambridge History of Africa* (London, 1976), v, p. 159.
37. D. Wheeler, 'Gungunhana' in N. R. Bennett (ed.), *Leadership in Eastern Africa: Six Political Biographies* (Boston, 1968), pp. 207–8. The Gaza Nguni were cousins to the Zulus of South Africa and used the same 'cow's horn' formation in attacking. Gungunhana was their king at the time of the 1895 war against the Portuguese.
38. Boahen, *African Perspectives on Colonialism* (Baltimore MD, 1985), pp. 56–7.
39. Headrick went some way toward compensating for his earlier neglect of the spread of European military technology to the non-European world in his *Tentacles of Progress: Technology Transfer in the Age of Imperialism* (New York, 1988).
40. Written with Alice Denny (London, 1961).
41. R. Robinson, 'Non-European Foundations of European Imperialism: Sketch for a Theory of Collaboration' in R. Owen and B. Sutcliffe (eds), *Studies in the Theory of Imperialism* (London, 1975), p. 118. Emphasis added.
42. Ibid., p. 119. Again, emphasis added.
43. Keegan, *A History of Warfare* (New York, 1994), p. 5.
44. G. Teitler, 'Manpower Problems and Manpower Policy of the Dutch Colonial Army, 1860–1920', *Acta Politica* 37/1 (2001): 24–37.
45. W. E. D. Allen and P. Muratoff, *Caucasian Battlefields: A History of the Wars on the Turco-Caucasian Border, 1828–1921* (Cambridge, 1953), is good on Russia's wars against the Chechens and other peoples of the Caucasus regions. For the role of the Cossacks as auxiliaries with the Russian army, see R. H. McNeal, *Tsar and Cossack, 1855–1914* (New York, 1987).
46. The best general source on France's colonial armies in Africa is A. Clayton, *France, Soldiers and Africa* (London, 1988).
47. B. Vandervort, *Wars of Imperial Conquest in Africa, 1830–1914* (London and Bloomington IN, 1998), p. 160.
48. A. Haywood and F. A. S. Clarke, *The History of the Royal West African Frontier Force* (Aldershot, 1969); H. Moyse-Bartlett, *The King's African Rifles, a Study in the Military History of East and Central Africa* (Aldershot, 1956).
49. L. H. Gann and P. Duignan, *The Rulers of British Africa, 1870–1914* (Stanford CA, 1978), p. 84.
50. Quoted in M. Michel, *Gallieni* (Paris, 1989), p. 119.
51. C. Mangin, *La force noire* (Paris, 1910), pp. 175–6. While France may have enrolled more African soldiers in its colonial army than any other European power, it was the German *Schutztruppe* in Africa which employed the largest percentage of black troops. Outside of German South West Africa, where the occupation forces were composed entirely of white mounted infantry, German troops in Africa included 226 whites, of whom 108 were officers and physicians, and 2,664 Africans. Gann and Duignan, *The Rulers of German Africa, 1884–1914* (Stanford CA, 1978), p. 118.
52. C. J. Balesi, *From Adversaries to Comrades-in-Arms: West Africans and the French Military, 1885–1918* (Waltham MA, 1979), pp. 43–5.

53. J. Bridgman, *The Revolt of the Hereros* (Berkeley CA, 1981), p. 169.
54. K. Roy, 'Military Synthesis in South Asia: Armies, Warfare and Indian Society, c. 1740–1849', *Journal of Military History* 69/3 (July 2005): 651–90, 655–7.
55. D. Killingray, 'Colonial Warfare in West Africa, 1870–1914' in J. A. De Moor and H. L Wesseling (eds), *Imperialism and War* (Leiden, 1989), p. 146.
56. J. H. Bentley and H. F. Ziegler, *Traditions & Encounters: A Global Perspective on the Past* (New York, 2006), pp. 914–15.

11
imperial military history

peter stanley

Australian, New Zealand and Indian historians writing about war in the past century have made a crucial nexus between imperial relations and national consciousness. Constitutionally, their history has been literally post-colonial: since 1901 in the case of Australia, 1910 for New Zealand and 1947 for India. Their awareness as nations in historical writing, however, has been and largely remains figuratively post-colonial. All three nations have used their military history as a way of disengaging from the imperial past, a point established as a generalization in relation to New Zealand and especially India and tested in this chapter with detailed reference to Australia.

The twentieth century is often depicted as the period when the British Empire went from a brief apogee via its transformation into a Commonwealth before the Second World War to its gradual atrophy thereafter. Viewed from the perspective of the constituent parts of the former empire the great project of the twentieth century is the gradual confirmation of an independent constitutional, political and social national identity. Just as wars, and especially the world wars, proved to be critical points of stress in the relationships between Britain and its dominions, so the scholarly and popular writing about those wars has been a further battleground in which interpretations have been contested and revised in a series of decisive stages. While Australia, India and New Zealand began the century as components of the empire, they ended it as independent nations. Their military historiography reflects that transformation, though with individual inflections, suggesting how 'imperial military history' might be regarded as a useful way to counter the tendency towards an unproductive national particularism.

214

Australia, India and New Zealand represent different models by which military history has become associated with national identity. Each manifests traditions of scholarship, though at very different intensities and in different ways. A brief survey of India and New Zealand suggests questions which can be pursued through a detailed discussion of the Australian literature.

Indian military history, within living memory the subject of a British romantic or nostalgic interest, has become a route to the confirmation and validation of a national consciousness.[1] As a national institution, the armed forces have become a symbol for both unification within a disparate nation and a bulwark against neighbours – especially Pakistan – with whom independent India has fought a series of wars since 1947.[2] Pakistan, which inherited a proportion of the pre-independence army, has experienced a similar process.[3]

Both Indian and international scholars have studied India's military past. Academic and international scholars tend to concentrate on the period before independence, but see it as part of a vigorous tradition of imperial history: works by international scholars of the armies of the Raj constitute a substantial portion of the current scholarship.[4] Post-independence studies tend more to military sociology, often asking the question, 'why has India's large military not intervened in politics?' The resultant literature is vast, but is notable overall for its disinterest. Scholars of Indian military history tend not to engage at an emotive level with their subject. This approach is exemplified in Stephen Cohen's *The Indian Army* or Apurba Kundu's *Militarism in India*.[5]

Paradoxically, perhaps, Indian scholarship has also manifested a strong post-colonial flavour, a determination to view the British period from an Indian perspective rather than continue to be complicit in an imperial viewpoint. There have been some inflections to this general equilibrium, such as the tendency to valorize the Indian National Army of 1942–45 and to accord a disproportionate attention to it compared to the vast army that fought for rather than against the British.[6] The overall result has been to transmute a potentially distorting nationalism into more detached scholarship.

By contrast, in New Zealand, a nation with a strong historical culture, military history has traditionally been a minor and weak part. While individual scholarship is often superb (such as several classic studies of the Anglo-Maori wars or modern works by Ian McGibbon and Christopher Pugsley) military history has been either marginal to the field as a whole or less distinct from it. Even in relation to the wars following European settlement (variously described as the Maori, Anglo-Maori, Land or New Zealand wars, according to ideological persuasion) they have been much more closely integrated into mainstream imperial and national historiography than has the more contentious Australian frontier conflict. Traditional military history, now practised by a small but active coterie, was denied the stimulus of a large and significant military (as in India) or an active founding myth and myth-maker (as in Australia, see below). Accordingly, it has been much less significant even in proportion to the relatively minor part military endeavour has played in national history.[7]

New Zealand's historians have always taken a strong interest in their country's colonial wars, the critical process by which Aotearoa became New Zealand. While the political and social history of Maori-Pakeha contact and conflict (and their consequences) have been extensively studied, the military aspects of the wars have generally been left to military historians, often amateurs and at the local level. Only with the appearance of James Belich's *The New Zealand Wars and the Victorian Interpretation of Racial Conflict* was the military narrative of the wars linked to profound themes in British imperial conception of the world.[8]

New Zealand's part in the Great War was marked by a few short official histories written hastily in the immediate aftermath of the war, with a long gap until the renaissance of the late twentieth century, when a new generation of New Zealand historians, led by Christopher Pugsley and Ian McGibbon, began its modern re-interpretation. Pugsley's *Gallipoli: The New Zealand Story* inspired a new wave of scholarship; though it also may have unwittingly fostered an Australia-style parochialism.[9] McGibbon's *The Path to Gallipoli* remains a unique study connecting colonial and dominion military policy and showing why defence policies led to the commitment to empire in 1914.[10]

The Second World War, though chronicled by an outstanding official history series, was also left fallow for decades. John Crawford's *Kia Kaha* demonstrates the potential of a unified approach to the operational, diplomatic and social understanding of the war and its impact.[11] New Zealand's part in the post-1945 conflicts has been interpreted through Ian McGibbon's *New Zealand and the Korean War*.[12] Unlike Australia, New Zealand has produced historians who seek to resist periodization; Ian McGibbon is the outstanding example, whose *Blue-Water Rationale* explains the naval defence of New Zealand across periods, though John Crawford's study of New Zealand's contribution to peacekeeping operations necessarily follows a unified rather than fragmentary approach.[13]

For Australia, however, the twentieth century has both been largely dominated by an engagement with the idea of nationhood and has made military history a key aspect of that national consciousness. It opened with the proclamation of the federation of the Australian colonies to form a nation. In the ensuing century, the idea of nationhood has been explored, asserted and celebrated through the creation of a body of military historical literature. Military history has not only traced the development of a national identity: it has itself shaped and embodied ideas of what the nation was and what it continues to mean. In effect, military history, ostensibly the most conservative and often least challenging intellectual segment of the discipline, has in Australia been a focus for the development of a continuing post-colonial critique of Australia's relationship with its imperial and de facto imperial powers and allies. That paradigm has been challenged, it is true, but national perspective seems inevitably to shape Australia's military history, at least for the twentieth century.

The six Australian colonies all raised defence forces of varying characters and strengths. They presented bewildering combinations of volunteer, 'partially-paid' and 'permanent' units, and eclectic combinations of warships. While detailed histories of the defence forces of some colonies exist, no one has definitively traced their history, but Craig Wilcox's *For Hearths and Homes* offers a strong analysis of the 'citizen-soldier' tradition which until the mid twentieth century dominated military endeavour in Australia.[14] The best survey of colonial naval forces is Colin Jones's *Australian Colonial Navies*.[15]

In the 40 years before Federation in 1901 Australian forces – that is, units raised by the Australian colonies – served in several imperial campaigns. The New Zealand colonial government raised volunteers from the eastern colonies and South Australia to form regiments of the Waikato Militia during the land wars in the 1860s, though these were in effect mercenaries. The first official Australian involvement in an overseas war came in 1860 when the Victorian sloop HMCS *Victoria* was sent to assist imperial and New Zealand troops against the Maori of the Taranaki. Its role has been treated mainly by antiquarian writers: indeed, the besetting fault of the colonial period as a whole is that it has been barely incorporated into a coherent narrative.

Likewise the colonial contributions to British campaigns in the Sudan (in 1885) and in China (1900–01) have been mainly documented by amateurs. The War Office's acceptance of New South Wales's offer of what would later be called a 770-strong 'battalion group' suggested how troops from European colonies represented an imperial military resource. The involvement of small naval brigades from New South Wales and Victoria, and the cruiser *Protector* (South Australia's entire navy) in the suppression of the 'Boxer rebellion' in China reinforced the idea. The former is significant in that it represented the first use of Australian troops (as opposed to sailors) in an imperial war: presaging a pattern of Australian reaction which became (and arguably remains) the dominant Australian relationship to imperial powers. Ken Inglis's *The Rehearsal* stands out in placing what might be seen as a curious anomaly in the context of colonial–imperial relations and a developing Australian consciousness.[16]

Conceptions of nationalism – the prevailing and now orthodox mindset of most Australians writing about war in the past 40 years – dominate the literature about the Australian part in the South African (or 'Boer') War of 1899–1902. This was the first major conflict of the national century. For Australia, which sent about 16,000 volunteers to South Africa, the Boer War was its third most costly conflict, subordinate only to the world wars. Volunteers enlisted in colonial contingents and served in small groups incorporated into larger British forces, and were commemorated on local or state war memorials. (Only late in the war did Australian volunteers serving in the Australian Commonwealth Horse see minor action, the first troops raised for war by a federal Australian government.)

The Australian treatment of these troops in historical writing reflects the influence of national identity dominant in Australian historiography. The war was documented in Australia initially by journalists – including A. B. 'Banjo' Paterson, a hugely popular bush balladeer, who served as a correspondent with New South Wales contingents in 1899–1900. While Paterson's despatches were soon forgotten, his Boer War verse both celebrated a distinctive Australian 'bushman' archetype and reflected disillusionment with imperial commanders, neither of which seriously undermined imperial attachment. Overshadowed by the Great War, very little was published in Australia on the Boer War until Laurie Field's *The Forgotten War*, a study largely directed at the raising of the contingents as a manifestation of colonial nationalism rather than at the course and effects of the war.[17] Meanwhile, Peter Weir's 1981 film, *Breaker Morant*, created a popular view of Morant – an Australian serving in an imperial unit who was executed for killing Boer civilians – as a victim of British conspiracy and hypocrisy. This view reflected the turn in late twentieth-century Australia that asserted an Australian national identity by denigrating the British connection and relationship. In 2002 the reception of Nick Bleszynski's *Shoot Straight You Bastards!* (supposedly Morant's defiant last words) confirmed the popularity of this view.[18]

Craig Wilcox's *Australia's Boer War*, the only Australian study based on archival sources in Britain, South Africa and the dispersed colonial records in Australian state archives, was commissioned by the Australian War Memorial as a simulacrum of an official history, intended to 'fill the gap' in official histories before 1914.[19] While implicitly contesting the nationalist interpretation of the Morant case it also demonstrated that the Australian part in the war needed to be understood from more than an Australian perspective. Wilcox's strength was to place the Australian dimension within an imperial context, an unfashionable but justifiable stance. Thus the Boer War is remembered largely only because of Morant's execution and vague notions of British complicity in his death. Despite Wilcox's subtle, informed and authoritative exposition of the case, Australian historical and popular interpretation of the war tends to hinge on the nationalist–imperial allegiances represented by the case.

While the literature on the Boer War and Australia has been a century in the making, it delineates what became the essential paradigm of Australian military history: the elaboration of a distinctive Australian identity as revealed through Australian experience of war and Australians' encounters not so much with enemies as with allies, and especially Britain. The origins of this inescapable frame of reference is the official history of Australia's part in the Great War, Charles Bean's official history, beginning with *The Story of Anzac*.[20]

'Anzac' is the crucial idea running through Australian military history from the moment on 25 April 1915 that Australian (and later New Zealand) troops landed under fire on the Gallipoli peninsula and – as importantly – Charles Bean witnessed and recorded their actions for posterity. The reports of war correspondents such as Bean (and perhaps initially even more the British

Ellis Ashmead-Bartlett) celebrated the invasion of Ottoman Turkey. Though a failure operationally, reports of the invasion created and valorized Australian and New Zealand heroism and endurance that soon crystallized around the idea of the 'Anzac legend' (or 'Anzac myth' to later sceptics and detractors). Bean edited the official history of Australia in the Great War, a 12-volume work of immense detail built around the belief that the war represented the greatest trial and the finest achievement of the young Australian nation. It was said – and was widely believed – that Australian nationhood was born on the cliffs of Anzac Cove, and Australian military historians continue to either play out that idea or to struggle against it. So complete was Bean's vision, however, that little was written on the Great War for a further 50 years, except for a plethora of unit histories which detailed the legend he had either recorded, created or fabricated (depending on the critics' taste). Anzac Day, 25 April, became an annual reaffirmation of the heroic qualities and noble sacrifice of Australians in the Great War, a rhetoric permeating and stultifying Australian military history. Not until the 1960s, with the fiftieth anniversary of the Great War, did the Anzac legend become the subject of challenge and exploration. The re-awakening occurred against the awakening national imagination and a critique of Australia's relationship with Britain.

Work by Ken Inglis and Lloyd Robson in the late 1960s is regarded as the genesis of the 'modern' interest in Australia's Great War.[21] Their articles and books sparked a resurgence of interest in the experience and impact of it which remains an engine of both scholarly research and popular publishing in Australia. In 1974 Bill Gammage's *The Broken Years* appeared, the single most influential text since Bean's official history.[22] Gammage, conscious that a profound experience of the Great War had barely been recognized by academic historians – despite the growth in Australian history from the late 1940s – devoted his doctoral thesis to examining the writings of Australian soldiers. He was able to do this because the Australian War Memorial held a large collection of soldiers' letters and diaries which had been almost unused since their donation. The Memorial, created by Charles Bean during the Great War, comprised a museum and archive within a commemorative edifice, a unified, national expression of grief at the loss of the 60,000 Australian dead of the war. Moribund for decades, it was about to become a key element in the reinvigoration of interest in military history.

While *The Broken Years* could not be described as crudely nationalist, it did exemplify several approaches to the study of the nature and impact of war. It explicitly looked at the Australian experience, in contrast to other nations'. This was of course partly a function of the relative difficulty of mounting a trans-national study at that time. (It is interesting that with international research easier 30 years on, because of, say, cheaper travel and better finding and copying aids, cross-national research is becoming both more feasible and usual.) It also explicitly contrasted Australian attitudes with British, and celebrated and mourned both Australian achievement and Australian casualties. Gammage's work has never been equalled in its powerful evocation of a generation whose lives were shaped and often ended by war, but it did inspire many studies of the Great War from an Australian perspective.

These included many that, while sometimes sceptical of the veneration at the heart of Bean's work, nevertheless followed his parochial agenda and the all-too-easy assumption that Australia's contribution was different or its performance superior. They included Eric Andrews's *The Anzac Illusion* or John Robertson's under-rated *Anzac and Empire*.[23] Andrews espoused a sceptical attitude of British motives, Robertson a more moderate attitude.

While the Great War remains a strong focus in Australian military historical writing books have tended to concentrate on some aspects and hardly at all on others. Military biography has been a strong strand, deriving from the existence of a group of mainly Canberra-based writers such as Alec Hill, Chris Clark and David Horner, who have written and fostered a school of such studies, often with a strong leaning towards times as well as life.[24]

While most Australians died on the Western Front (about 45,000 out of 60,000) the battles on the Western Front have been surprisingly poorly served by Australianist historians. While Australian achievement has been asserted, it has hardly been tested through detailed operational studies. Major actions – Fromelles, the Somme in 1916, the two battles of Bullecourt, Messines, the Australian part in the German and Allied offensives of 1918, all battles with major Australian involvement – have largely been accorded not much more attention than Bean's volumes, all published before 1942. With few notable exceptions (such as Peter Pedersen, whose *Monash as Military Commander* examined Monash in the light of the problems of command on the Western Front), most work on this theatre has taken as its subject individuals or units.[25] The major qualification to this must be that of Robin Prior and Trevor Wilson, two historians in Australia who are explicitly not Australian military historians, who have written several influential revisionist studies of the Western Front, notably *The Somme*, which address the war on the Western Front as a whole and not from a parochial stance.[26]

The question might be asked: what have Australian historians of the Great War been investigating if not the Western Front? The answer in one word is: Gallipoli. The centrality of Gallipoli to Australia's conception of its national identity is reinforced each 25 April with Anzac Day. Gallipoli and all it connotes for national identity has fuelled a succession of studies, a trend that has intensified in recent years, many of which have exacerbated the connection between the campaign and an often crude nationalism. As with Breaker Morant and the Boer War, popular understanding of Gallipoli was shaped by a film, Peter Weir's *Gallipoli* (1981). Several, mainly popular, works have fostered a relentlessly parochial view of the campaign. This is exemplified by Les Carlyon's *Gallipoli*, whose turgid lyricism portrays Australians as the victims of callous British 'high command', fostering the view that the real enemies were British rather than Turkish.[27] By contrast, serious studies have taken a broader approach, notably Chris Pugsley (a New Zealander with Australian connections), who has put the Australian part into both an imperial and trans-Tasman context in his *The Anzac Experience*; likewise Peter Stanley in *Quinn's Post*, which represents the holding of this critical part of the Anzac line as part of a related Australian–New Zealand–British campaign.[28]

Otherwise, the Great War has been treated patchily. The Light Horse's long campaign in Sinai-Palestine has not been addressed since Alec Hill's biography of its commander, Chauvel, though the Royal Australian Navy's involvement in an imperial naval war has been addressed, albeit through a series of articles or chapters.[29] Both it and the Australian Flying Corps still await revisionist historians, though both have been the subject of promising graduate work and (as with most aspects of Australian military history) many amateur articles. While medical history generally has been relatively poorly addressed, the exception is the experience of army nurses, notably in Jan Bassett's *Guns and Brooches*.[30]

The Great War's profound impact on Australian society has been extensively addressed by historians who would not all identify as 'military'. Lloyd Robson's *The First AIF*, combining analysis of a statistical sample with conventional documentary research, showed the potential of seeing the Australian Imperial Force as an expression of Australian society.[31] A later, definitive analysis by historians at the Australian Defence Force Academy of the entire 324,000 men and women who served overseas is awaited. Michael McKernan's *The Australian People and the Great War* identified issues in social and class responses to the war in ways that advanced understanding beyond Ernest Scott's official history *Australia During the War*.[32] Local or regional studies, such as Marilyn Lake's *A Divided Society* (dealing with Tasmania), or John McQuilton's *Rural Australia and the Great War*, tested generalizations against one state's experience.[33] In *Sacred Places*, Ken Inglis explored the importance of the local war memorial as a complex communal expression of enduring grief. Michael McKernan's *Here is their Spirit*, a history of the Australian War Memorial, explored the development of the war's most influential institutional expression for Australia.[34] Graham Seal has traced the various manifestations of the Anzac legend in *Inventing Anzac*, while Alistair Thomson's *Anzac Memories* traced the complex evolution of popular conceptions of the Great War.[35]

Following the lead of the official histories, which are such a strong part of the tradition of Australian military historical writing, studies tend to coalesce closely around wars and around particular services. The inter-war period is therefore barely addressed beyond some graduate theses and as sections of biographies, though Chris Clark's study of the inter-war Royal Australian Air Force (RAAF) is notable.[36]

The Second World War was until the 1990s poorly developed historically relative to the Great War. The impetus of anniversaries such as the 1995 'Australia Remembers' year and the opening of archives and access to veterans, encouraged interest in the war. Several general works have stimulated interest, especially John Robertson's argumentative *Australia at War 1939–1945* and Joan Beaumont's incisive synoptic survey, *Australia's War, 1939–1945*.[37] The historiography reflects some of the characteristics of writing on the earlier war: a parochialism shading off into nationalist rhetoric and a reluctance to connect the Australian experience productively to the broader Allied war effort. However, the scale of work on the war offers worthy exceptions to these easy generalizations.

Australia's war entailed a large commitment to the Mediterranean until 1942, when Australian divisions were withdrawn to the South-West Pacific, leaving airmen to fight against Germany, and from 1942 a concentration on the war against Japan. The 22-volume series of the official history (published between the early 1950s and the late 1970s) documents both military operations and the impact of the war on politics and government and the economy.[38] Unlike Britain or the United States, the Australian official historians did not produce a volume on strategy or the higher direction of the war. This crucial deficiency was redressed by the publication of David Horner's *High Command* in 1982.[39] Followed by a study of the workings of the War Cabinet and by a biography of Sir Thomas Blamey, commander of Australia's military forces for the entire war, Horner has given a decisive impetus to the full understanding of the direction of Australia's war.[40]

The war in the Mediterranean has been surprisingly poorly treated. With the exception of biographies of commanders (such as Lavarack and Morshead) major commitments such as to the defence of Tobruk and the Greek campaign have not been re-interpreted, despite the release of records since the publication of the official histories.[41] The only exception is Alamein, which has been addressed, explicitly as an Australian contribution to a Commonwealth force.[42] All works dealing with this theatre, however, cannot but address the relationship between British and Australian (indeed, dominion) commanders. The assumptions of British generals clashed with the aspirations and expectations of their Commonwealth counterparts. Commanders such as Blamey and Morshead both owed allegiance to their national governments and sought to be treated as equals with British officers. The resultant tensions have become a staple of Australian historiography, usually considered from a national stance.

Australian military history is dominated by the history of the Second Australian Imperial Force – almost to the exclusion of the Militia, the conscript home defence force that served in Australian New Guinea. While no studies of Tobruk, Greece or Syria-Lebanon campaigns have superseded the official histories, studies of significant formations by Mark Johnston and of Alamein show what needs to be tackled.[43] *Alamein: The Australian Story* attempted to place the distinctive Australian contribution to the desert war in 1942 without falling for the strident nationalism so often seen in Australian military history.[44]

The most striking instance of the tense relationship between the two arises from the Malaya-Singapore campaign. The historiography generally splits on national lines, continuing allegations and counter-claims first aired among squabbling officers in captivity.[45] British authors such as Peter Elphick raised allegations of Australian culpability for the Japanese lodgement on Singapore in February 1942; Australian writers, especially popular authors such as Cameron Forbes, counter with allegations of British ineptitude.[46] While scholarly authors generally avoid invective, popular understanding is indelibly coloured by assertions of national identity.

Fiftieth anniversary observations ended the general neglect of the Pacific campaigns. Pre-eminent is Kokoda, when Militia and AIF troops halted a Japanese advance on Port Moresby. Kokoda (either as 'track' or 'trail') has entered into the nationalist pantheon second only to Gallipoli, and a string of books has celebrated this new legend. Peter Brune has published a set of books on phases of the campaign, beginning with *Those Ragged Bloody Heroes* and culminating with *A Bastard of a Place*.[47] Paul Ham's *Kokoda* is the most thorough of the many books written by journalists. The over-looked Huon Peninsula and Markham-Ramu Valley campaigns of 1943–44 have been described in detail by John Coates and Phillip Bradley, more interested in operational detail than in ideological alignment.[48] A counter to the classic nationalist view of the controversial 'final campaigns' in Borneo – a view popularized by Peter Charlton's *The Unnecessary War* – is offered by Peter Stanley's *Tarakan*.[49]

The fall of Singapore had significant consequences for the Australian nation and for its historians, including the capture or internment of 22,000 Australian men and some hundreds of women, the collapse of British power in Southeast Asia and the exposure of Australia to Japanese attack or even invasion. While historians have largely overlooked the fate of Australian prisoners of the Germans and Italians, the ordeal of the 22,000 Australians captured by the Japanese has been addressed by a wealth of studies since about 1980. Hank Nelson's *POW: Australians under Nippon*, a book based on an extensive oral history project, rightly re-awakened interest in what had been regarded as an embarrassing episode. Studies of particular episodes, such as Joan Beaumont's unflinching study of captivity on the island of Ambon, stand beside many published diaries and memoirs.[50]

The profound changes that war brought to Australian economy, society and politics have been unevenly traced. Studies of wartime politics in Australia have been marked by a tendency to overlook the government of Robert Menzies (the United Australia Party Prime Minister 1938–41) in favour of the Labour Party leader John Curtin who, becoming prime minister weeks before Japan's entry into the Pacific war, faced an arguable threat to national survival. Allan Martin's scholarly two-volume biography of Menzies has not been reflected in the popular works, which continue to boost a Curtin legend.[51] This strongly nationalist, though not necessarily left-wing, strain is expressed in a series of books by David Day, such as *Menzies and Churchill at War*, *The Great Betrayal*, and his biography of Curtin. Day argues that 1942 represented a decisive break between Britain and Australia, in which Churchill betrayed Australian interests.[52] This view, reflecting a fusion of nationalist and republican sentiment and revisionist historiography, has become orthodoxy in Australia. Though it has been challenged – by, for example, John Edwards – it now reflects the views of many conservatives who portray the war in the South-West Pacific not as the secure base for a counter-offensive, but as a three-year 'Battle for Australia', a phrase drawn from Curtin's rhetoric following the fall of Singapore.[53] Michael McKernan's *All-in!* offers a stimulating overview, while Kate Darian-Smith's *On the Home Front* represents works detailing an argument about the social and moral transformations of war.[54] Military-historical works such as John Barrett's *We Were There* – based on questionnaires completed by hundreds of veterans – and Mark Johnston's studies of attitudes and character in his two books, *At the Front Line* and *Fighting the Enemy*, add greatly to our knowledge of the personal make-up of these veterans.[55]

Because they served generally in isolation from the army, the Royal Australian Navy (RAN) and the Royal Australian Air Force's part in the war has been interpreted independently. Naval history has recently emerged from the shadows of antiquarianism, and apart from the official histories, the best introduction to the RAN's service is David Stevens's survey.[56] The air force in the Pacific is still best chronicled by official and squadron histories, but the European war, at least the Australian involvement in Bomber Command, has fared better. John McCarthy's *Last Call of Empire* portrayed the 'surrender' of Australian aircrew to an imperial war effort in accordance with the mainstream nationalism. Hank Nelson's *Chased by the Sun* took a less strident view while expressing a distinctive Australian sensibility.[57]

After 1945, Australia's foreign policy shifted as the country's orientation went from Britain to the USA. At the same time, Australia was drawn into a series of military commitments in the adjoining but distinct Southeast Asia region (what is sometimes referred to as the 'Asia-Pacific' region). Securely a part of the Western alliance, especially after the election of the conservative Menzies Liberal-Country Party government in 1949, Australia became a dependable ally for both Britain and the United States during the Cold War. Menzies anticipated that Australia would again send expeditionary forces to serve alongside Western allies in the Middle East – as it had in 1914 and 1939 – and Australian fighters were stationed in Malta during the 1950s.[58] Australia committed its forces to meeting communist or nationalist insurgency or aggression in a succession of conflicts during the Cold War. Australian forces served in Korea from the start of the war, throughout the Malayan emergency, in the Commonwealth's resistance to Indonesia's confrontation in Borneo and in support of the USA during the Vietnam War.

Robert O'Neill's official history of Australia's part in the Korean War remains the most comprehensive study; Jeffrey Grey and Peter Dennis's *Emergency and Confrontation* provides similarly comprehensive coverage of Australia's involvement in the Malayan emergency and confrontation.[59] The Vietnam War's social impact and its consequences for Australia's relations with the region and with the United States has always been more significant than the relatively minor combat operations involved. The social impact is examined in the official history, edited and written by Peter Edwards, particularly the volumes entitled *Crises and Commitments* and *A Nation at War*.[60] The impact of the Vietnam War on Australian society has become a strong theme in Australian studies of the war.[61] The memory of the war, a phenomenon complicated by the influence of American culture, is discussed in Jeffrey Grey and Jeff Doyle's *Vietnam: War, Myth and Memory* and Peter Cook and Corinne Manning's *Australia's Vietnam War*.[62]

Australia's turn to America, anticipated by John Curtin's premature appeal in December 1941, finally occurred in the 1960s. The protracted British withdrawal from east of Suez obliged Australia to engage more closely with regional neighbours and left it more securely within the ANZUS alliance. Jeffrey Grey has traced the impact of this gradual and in some ways reluctant shift in his official history of the Royal Australian Navy during the long engagement with Southeast Asia, *Up Top*.[63] Chris Clark's companion volume, *The RAAF in Vietnam*, describes the RAAF's parallel re-orientation towards the United States.[64] As with earlier periods, Australian historians have used biography as a route to understanding broader periods. Jeff Grey's *Australian Brass* and David Horner's *Strategic Command* span the changes which occurred across the post-1945 period.[65]

In the same period, Australia has been involved in peacekeeping operations, mainly under the auspices of the United Nations. An official history of Australian peacekeeping operations – and post-Cold War conflicts – under the direction of David Horner, is now in preparation. The first general survey of the subject, however, is Peter Londey's *Other People's Wars*.[66] Londey espouses a conscious internationalism in contrast to the perennial Australian preoccupation with national identity. Post-Cold War conflicts have been less thoroughly addressed, partly because of the dearth of accessible sources. David Horner's *The Gulf Commitment* gives a useful introduction to Australia's part in the first Gulf War, pending the publication of Prof. Horner's forthcoming official history.[67]

Australian military history, having enjoyed a boom in popular and scholarly interest over the past 25 years, stands at something of a crossroads. Academic interest remains high and is beginning to connect with trends in international military history. Simultaneously, the popular nationalism which has been such a strong element in military history in Australia shows no sign of moderating. The tension between the internationalist academic and the nationalist popular strains will surely make for a more fecund field.

Australia, India and New Zealand regard their military history as important for different reasons, but with differing degrees of commitment. India's military history seems relevant to a tiny fraction of academic or service readers, attracting few general readers. New Zealand's share of the Anzac 'legend' seems much more modest than Australia's – indeed, the word occurs relatively rarely in its literature. Australia's military history, on the other hand, has been harnessed to, or arguably hi-jacked by, the nationalist conception of Anzac. In each case, though, military history is viewed through the lens of the idea of nation. It is worth reflecting on whether our understanding of the military history of Australia has been as well served as has India's by having been written by Australians. India's military history, though sometimes the victim of parochial tendencies, has always been and probably always will be of interest to scholars internationally. That imparts a breadth of vision and a resistance to special pleading largely absent among its Australian counterparts. Perhaps imperial military history in a post-colonial era demands an imperial, or at least a supra-national, vision if it is to do justice to its subject matter.

further reading

The excellent Oxford Companion to New Zealand Military History and its Australian counterpart are indispensable guides: Ian McGibbon (ed.), *The Oxford Companion to New Zealand Military History* (Auckland, 2000) and Peter Dennis et al., *The Oxford Companion to Australian Military History* (Melbourne, 1995). Sadly, no Oxford Companion to Indian Military History yet exists. Several useful surveys of Australian military history exist, such as Chris Clark's *The Encyclopaedia of Australia's Battles* (Sydney, 2001) and John Coates' *Atlas of Australia's Wars* (Melbourne, 2002). Individual volumes of the *Oxford Centenary History of Australian Defence*, and especially Joan Beaumont's *Australian Defence: Sources and Statistics*, provide an authoritative point of departure to the literature: Joan Beaumont (ed.), *Australian Defence: Sources and Statistics* (Melbourne, 2001).

notes

1. The romantic strand in Indian military history is exemplified by Philip Mason's *A Matter of Honour: An Account of the Indian Army, its Officers and Men* (London, 1974) or Byron Farwell's *Armies of the Raj: From the Mutiny to Independence, 1858–1947* (New York, 1989).
2. The 'Indianization' of Indian military history is exemplified by, say, B. Singh and S. Mishra (eds), *Where Gallantry is Tradition* (New Delhi, 1987); K. C. Praval, *Indian Army after Independence* (New Delhi, 1987); and Gautam Sharma, *Nationalisation of the Indian Army, 1885–1947* (New Delhi, 1996).
3. Fazal Muqueem Khan, *The Story of the Pakistan Army* (Karachi, 1963).
4. David Omissi, *The Sepoy and the Raj: The Indian Army, 1860–1914* (London, 1995); Tan Tai Yong, *The Garrison State: The Military, Government and Society in Colonial Punjab, 1849–1947* (New Delhi, 2005).
5. Stephen Cohen, *The Indian Army: Its Contribution to the Development of a Nation* (New Delhi, 1990); Apurba Kundu, *Militarism in India: The Army and Civil Society in Consensus* (London, 1998).
6. See Mohan Singh, *Soldiers' Contribution to Indian Independence: The Epic of the Indian National Army* (New Delhi, 1974); K. K. Ghosh, *The Indian National Army: Second*

Front of the Indian Independence Movement (Meerut, 1969); and Hugh Toye, *Subhas Chandra Bose: The Springing Tiger* (Bombay, 1991).

7. For a useful summary of New Zealand history and historians, see Jeffery Grey's entry ('Military history and historians') in Ian McGibbon (ed.), *The Oxford Companion to New Zealand Military History* (Auckland, 2000), pp. 321–3.

8. James Belich, *The New Zealand Wars and the Victorian Interpretation of Racial Conflict* (Auckland, 1989).

9. Christopher Pugsley, *Gallipoli: The New Zealand Story* (Wellington, 1984).

10. Ian McGibbon, *The Path to Gallipoli: Defending New Zealand, 1840–1915* (Auckland, 1991).

11. John Crawford, *Kia Kaha: New Zealand in the Second World War* (Auckland, 2000).

12. Ian McGibbon, *New Zealand and the Korean War. Volume 1. Politics and Diplomacy* (Auckland, 1991) and McGibbon, *New Zealand and the Korean War. Volume 2. Combat Operations* (Auckland, 1996).

13. Ian McGibbon, *Blue-Water Rationale: The Naval Defence of New Zealand, 1914–1942* (Wellington, 1981); John Crawford, *In the Field for Peace: New Zealand's Contribution to International Peace-Support Operations, 1950–1995* (Wellington, 1996).

14. Craig Wilcox, *For Hearths and Homes: Citizen Soldiering in Australia, 1854–1945* (Sydney, 1998).

15. Colin Jones, *Australian Colonial Navies* (Canberra, 1986).

16. K. S. Inglis, *The Rehearsal: Australians in the Sudan, 1885* (Adelaide, 1985).

17. L. M. Field, *The Forgotten War: Australian Involvement in the South African Conflict of 1899–1902* (Melbourne, 1979).

18. Nick Bleszynski, *Shoot Straight You Bastards! The Truth behind the Killing of Breaker Morant* (Sydney, 2002). Morant was executed with his friend and fellow officer Peter Handcock for the murder of up to twelve Boer civilians. Morant has always captured the popular imagination because he was a colourful bush-balladeer. Ironically, for a nationalist hero, he was a British migrant.

19. Craig Wilcox, *Australia's Boer War* (Melbourne, 2002).

20. C. E. W. Bean, *The Story of Anzac* (Sydney, 1922). The two-volume *Story of Anzac* (which dealt with the Gallipoli campaign) was followed by four volumes on the Australian Imperial Force on the Western Front, and volumes on the campaign in Sinai-Palestine, Royal Australian Navy, the Australian Flying Corps, the war at home and the occupation of German New Guinea. There is also a photographic volume and three volumes of medical history. The volumes appeared at intervals until 1942, and were reprinted in the 1980s. Detailed and remarkably useful still, they continue to form the foundation of scholarship on the Great War in Australia, having been published on the web by the Australian War Memorial at <http://awm-public/histories/ww1/intro.asp>.

21. K. S. Inglis, 'The Anzac Tradition', *Meanjin Quarterly* 24/1 (1965): 25–44; K. S. Inglis, 'The Australians at Gallipoli', *Australian Historical Studies* Parts 1 and 2, 14/54 and 14/55 (1970): 219–30, 361–75; and L. L. Robson, *Australia and the Great War, 1914–1918* (Melbourne, 1969).

22. Bill Gammage, *The Broken Years: Australian Soldiers in the Great War* (Canberra, 1974).

23. Eric Andrews, *The Anzac Illusion: Anglo-Australian Relations during World War 1* (Melbourne, 1993); John Robertson, *Anzac and Empire: The Tragedy and Glory of Gallipoli* (Richmond, 1990).

24. Alec Hill, *Chauvel of the Light Horse* (Melbourne, 1978); C. D. Coulthard-Clark, *A Heritage of Spirit: A Biography of Major-General Sir William Throsby Bridges KCB,*

CMG (Melbourne, 1979); David Horner (ed.), *The Commanders: Australian Military Leadership in the Twentieth Century* (Sydney, 1984). The tradition continues with biographies such as Ross McMullin's *Pompey Elliott* (Melbourne, 2003) and Peter Sadler's *The Paladin: A life of Major-General Sir John Gellibrand* (Sydney, 2000). Clark's *No Australian Need Apply: The Troubled Career of Lieutenant-General Gordon Legge* (Sydney, 1988) connects Legge's life with nationalist aspiration.

25. Peter Pedersen, *Monash as Military Commander* (Melbourne, 1985).
26. Robin Prior and Trevor Wilson, *Command on the Western Front: The Military Career of Sir Henry Rawlinson, 1914–18* (Cambridge MA, 1992); *The Somme* (Sydney, 2005).
27. Les Carlyon, *Gallipoli* (Melbourne, 2001).
28. Christopher Pugsley, *The Anzac Experience: New Zealand, Australia and Empire in the First World War* (Auckland, 2004); Peter Stanley, *Quinn's Post, Anzac, Gallipoli* (Sydney, 2005).
29. The best introduction to Australian naval historiography is David Stevens's volume in the *Oxford Centenary of Australian Defence* series: *The Royal Australian Navy* (Melbourne, 2002).
30. Jan Bassett, *Guns and Brooches: Australian Army Nursing from the Boer War to the Gulf War* (Melbourne, 1992).
31. Lloyd Robson, *The First AIF: A Study of its Recruitment* (Melbourne, 1970).
32. Michael McKernan, *The Australian People and the Great War* (Sydney, 1984).
33. Marilyn Lake, *A Divided Society: Tasmania during World War I* (Melbourne, 1975); John McQuilton, *Rural Australia and the Great War: From Tarrawingee to Tangambalanga* (Melbourne, 2001).
34. Michael McKernan, *Here is their Spirit: A History of the Australian War Memorial, 1917–1990* (St Lucia, 1991).
35. Graham Seal, *Inventing Anzac: The Digger and National Mythology* (St Lucia, 2004); Alistair Thomson, *Anzac Memories: Living with the Legend* (Melbourne, 1994).
36. Chris Coulthard-Clark, *The Third Brother: The Royal Australian Air Force, 1921–39* (Sydney, 1991).
37. John Robertson, *Australia at War 1939–1945* (Melbourne, 1981); Joan Beaumont (ed.), *Australia's War, 1939–1945* (Sydney, 1996).
38. Gavin Long (ed.), *Australia in the War of 1939–1945* (22 vols) (Canberra, 1953–77). The full text of the series can be obtained on the Australian War Memorial's website at <http://awm-public/histories/volume.asp?conflict=2>.
39. David Horner, *High Command: Australia and Allied Strategy, 1939–1945* (Sydney, 1982).
40. David Horner, *Inside the War Cabinet: Directing Australia's War Effort, 1939–1945* (Sydney, 1996); *Blamey: The Commander-in-Chief* (Sydney, 1998).
41. Brett Lodge, *Lavarack: Rival General* (Sydney, 1998); David Coombes, *Morshead: Hero of Tobruk and El Alamein* (Melbourne, 2001).
42. Mark Johnston and Peter Stanley, *Alamein: The Australian Story* (Melbourne, 2002).
43. Mark Johnston, *That Magnificent 9th: An Illustrated History of the 9th Australian Infantry Division, 1940–46* (Sydney, 2002); Mark Johnston, *The Silent 7th: An Illustrated History of the 7th Australian Division, 1940–46* (Sydney, 2005).
44. Mark Johnston and Peter Stanley, *Alamein: The Australian Story* (Melbourne, 2002).
45. Peter Stanley, '"The Men who did the Fighting are now all Busy Writing": Australian Post-Mortems on Defeat in Malaya and Singapore, 1942–45' in Brian Farrell and Sandy Hunter (eds), *Sixty Years On: The Fall of Singapore Revisited* (Singapore, 2003).

46. Peter Elphick, *Singapore: The Pregnable Fortress: a Study in Deception, Discord and Desertion* (London, 1995); Cameron Forbes, *Hellfire: The story of Australia, Japan and the Prisoners of War* (Sydney, 2005).

47. Peter Brune, *Those Ragged Bloody Heroes: From the Kokoda Trail to Gona Beach, 1942* (Sydney, 1991); Peter Brune, *A Bastard of a Place: The Australians in Papua: Kokoda, Milne Bay, Gona, Buna, Sanananda* (Sydney, 2004).

48. John Coates, *Bravery Above Blunder: The 9th Australian Division at Finschhafen, Sattelberg and Sio* (Melbourne, 1998); Phillip Bradley, *On Shaggy Ridge: The Australian Seventh Division in the Ramu Valley from Kaiapit to the Finisterres* (Melbourne, 2004).

49. Peter Charlton, *The Unnecessary War: Island Campaigns of the South-West Pacific, 1944–45* (Melbourne, 1983); Peter Stanley, *Tarakan: An Australian Tragedy* (Sydney, 1997).

50. Joan Beaumont, *Gull Force, Survival and Leadership in Captivity, 1941–1945* (Sydney, 1988).

51. A. W. Martin, *Robert Menzies: A Life. Volume 1: 1894–1943* (Melbourne, 1993); Martin, *Robert Menzies: A Life. Volume 2: 1944–1978* (Melbourne, 1999).

52. David Day, *Menzies and Churchill at War: A Controversial New Account of the 1941 Struggle for Power* (Sydney, 1986); Day, *The Great Betrayal: Britain, Australia and the Onset of the Pacific War, 1939–42* (Sydney, 1988); and Day, *John Curtin, a Life* (Sydney, 1999); *Reluctant Nation: The Politics of War* (Sydney, 2003).

53. The 'Battle for Australia' interpretation has been disseminated not so much by books as by websites offering a highly partial interpretation, and one based on an exaggerated view of the imminence of the Japanese threat. John Edwards, *Curtin's Gift: Reinterpreting Australia's Greatest Prime Minister* (Sydney, 2005).

54. Michael McKernan, *All-in! Australia in the Second World War* (Sydney, 1983); Kate Darian-Smith, *On the Home Front: Melbourne in Wartime, 1939–1945* (Melbourne, 1990).

55. John Barrett, *We Were There: Australian Soldiers of World War II* (Melbourne, 1987); Mark Johnston, *At the Front Line: Experiences of Australian Soldiers in World War II* (Melbourne, 1996); and Johnston, *Fighting the Enemy: Australian Soldiers and their Adversaries in World War II* (Melbourne, 2000).

56. David Stevens (ed.), *The Royal Australian Navy in World War II* (Sydney, 1996).

57. John McCarthy, *A Last Call of Empire: Australian Aircrew, Britain and the Empire Air Training Scheme* (Canberra, 1988); Hank Nelson, *Chased by the Sun: Courageous Australians in Bomber Command in World War II* (Sydney, 2002).

58. David Lowe, *Menzies and the 'Great World Struggle': Australia's Cold War, 1948–1954* (Sydney, 1999).

59. Robert O'Neill, *Australia in the Korean War, 1950–53. Volume 1. Strategy and Diplomacy* (Canberra, 1981); O'Neill, *Australia in the Korean War 1950–53. Volume 2. Combat Operations* (Canberra, 1985); and Jeffrey Grey and Peter Dennis, *Emergency and Confrontation: Australian Military Operations in Malaya and Borneo, 1950–66* (Sydney, 1996).

60. Peter Edwards, *Crises and Commitments: The Politics and Diplomacy of Australia's Involvement in Southeast Asian Conflicts, 1948–1965* (Sydney, 1992); Peter Edwards, *A Nation at War: Australian Politics, Society and Diplomacy during the Vietnam War, 1965–1975* (Sydney, 1997).

61. See, for example, Greg Pemberton, *Vietnam Remembered* (Sydney, 1990); Jeff Doyle and Jeff Grey, *Vietnam Days: Australia and the Impact of Vietnam* (Melbourne, 1991); and John Murphy, *Harvest of Fear: A History of Australia's Vietnam War* (Sydney, 1993).

62. Jeff Grey and Jeff Doyle, *Vietnam: War, Myth and Memory. Comparative Perspectives on Australia's War in Vietnam* (Sydney, 1992); Peter Cook and Corinne Manning (eds), *Australia's Vietnam War in History and Memory* (Melbourne, 2002).
63. Jeffrey Grey, *Up Top: The Royal Australian Navy and Southeast Asian Conflicts, 1955–1972* (Sydney, 1998).
64. Chris Coulthard-Clark, *The RAAF in Vietnam: Australian Air Involvement in the Vietnam War, 1962–1975* (Sydney, 1995).
65. Jeff Grey, *Australian Brass: The Career of Lieutenant General Sir Horace Robertson* (Melbourne, 1992); David Horner, *Strategic Command: General Sir John Wilton and Australia's Asian Wars* (Melbourne, 2005).
66. Peter Londey, *Other People's Wars: A History of Australian Peacekeeping* (Sydney, 2003).
67. David Horner, *The Gulf Commitment: The Australian Defence Force's First War* (Melbourne, 1991).

12
technology, science and war

matthew hughes

Alongside his works of art, Leonardo da Vinci (1452–1519) produced sketches for tanks, breech-loading guns, rifled firearms, wheel-locked pistols, rapid-fire catapults, steam cannons, parachutes, submarines, balloons and flying machines. His tank, operated by crank handles, held eight men, had holes for the guns and an opening in the top for ventilation.[1] The problem for da Vinci – probably the greatest mechanical engineer and military scientist of his day – was the mismatch between his creative genius and the productive capabilities of the workshops of Renaissance Europe. This highlights one of the key debates in this chapter: the interaction between the ideas and theories (or science) and the means of production (or technologies, defined as the systematic study of techniques for designing and making things) available to transform the drawings of those such as da Vinci into practicable weapons. It was not until the nineteenth and twentieth centuries that advances in engineering technology facilitated the practical realization of scientific ideas on weapons development to produce, among other things, breech-loading guns, recoil systems, poison gas, the tank, the warplane, the battleship, the submarine, the digital battlefield and, above all, the atom bomb. As the two merged, it made it difficult to distinguish between scientific enquiry and technological activity. By the mid twentieth century, soldiers were being pushed aside as warfare became a duel between highly qualified scientists who, with the advent of nuclear weapons, wielded destructive power on an almost inconceivable scale.[2]

Another issue to consider is that of technological determinism in warfare. In *Technology and War: From 2000 B.C. to the Present* (1991), Martin van Creveld declares that his book 'rests on one very simple premise which serves as

231

its starting point, argument, *raison d'être* rolled into one. It is that war is completely permeated by technology and governed by it.'[3] While it is true that better weapons may win battles, one should be careful to place them in the wider context of a given war, particularly the quality of the men who control and wield them. After all, Dr Richard Gatling thought that his newly-invented machine gun would not only defeat the Confederacy and end slavery, but it would also help stop wars; the British military thinker J. F. C. Fuller believed that tanks were war winners; in 1942, the British airman Arthur 'Bomber' Harris promised that his heavy bombers could force a German surrender.[4] None proved to be right and, while new technologies have played a vital part in military history, readers should be sceptical of technological determinism: a state of affairs whereby new, apparently lethal, weapons are the determining factor for victory or defeat in war. In certain situations, such as colonial warfare, new weapons have been decisive but even here, as Bruce Vandervort argues in his chapter in this volume, victory is invariably a product of a number of factors, of which technology is just one component. The introduction of an apparently unstoppable weapon forces modern armies on both sides to produce effective counter-measures: depth charges to destroy submarines, or dispersed infantry tactics and portable firepower to cope with machine guns. This creates a cycle of technological development in which warring groups quickly copy, counter and check new technologies introduced by opponents. This militates against new technologies having a decisive impact on warfare.

Instead of examining these issues, much (perhaps too much) of the literature on technology and war focuses on military hardware and assessments of theoretical capabilities – 'killing power' – rather than an analysis of technology, science and war within a wider historical narrative, taking into account political, economic and social factors. The best studies analyse the interaction between military technology/science and national history, thus providing a counter-weight to those who see the subject only in terms of an unhealthy interest in guns and their technical specifications.[5]

The literature on war and technology is also Eurocentric. While there is a range of books that examines African, South Asian, Native American and Islamic/Middle Eastern military technology, the focus in mainstream military history is typically on changes in war and technology in Europe; ones that then had profound effects as Europe expanded overseas after 1500. Europe was one of a number of distinct military eco-spheres: Mesoamerica, African, Middle Eastern, Japan, India–South-east Asia, China and Europe, of which the Chinese and European were the most advanced technologically and had the most enduring influence. Of the others, while some had developed military technologies that were well adapted to local conditions, they were not 'particularly advanced', at least not when compared to what the Europeans were using.[6] The impact of Europe (and, later, America) on the world was so great in this period that it overshadows developments in war and technology elsewhere. The extensive entry on 'War, technology of' in the *Encyclopaedia Britannica* makes this point explicitly: 'Because European methods of warfare ultimately dominated the world, and because the technology of war, with few exceptions, advanced first and fastest in Europe, this article devotes most of its attention to the European military ecosphere.'[7]

David Parrott picks up on the imbalance in the scholarship in his review of Geoffrey Parker's *Cambridge Illustrated History of Warfare: Triumph of the West* (1995) and Jeremy Black's *Cambridge Atlas of Warfare: Renaissance to Revolution, 1492–1792* (1996), pointing out:

'Thus the warrior-dominated civilisations of Mesoamerica are accorded considerable attention at the moment of confrontation with the Spanish conquistadores.... But the global triumph of the West remains, historically, a relatively recent phenomenon, and societies which never came into contact with Western arms and armies, or did so relatively late in the day, receive little attention.'[8]

While Parker, who discusses non-European technology in volumes such as his *The Military Revolution: Military Innovation and the Rise of the West, 1500–1800* (1988), rightly emphasizes the dominance of the 'western way of warfare', it is true that, where non-European military technology is examined, it tends to be in the context of an encounter with Western military forces. Readers interested in this subject are directed to Chapter 10 of this volume and to the further reading section at the end of this chapter.

Finally, while this chapter examines war and technology after 1500, readers should consider the fact that weapons development was not confined to the Western-dominated modern age. In the pre-classical, classical and medieval periods, military technology went through momentous changes as man invented, and used in battle, wheeled chariots, stirrups, catapults, trebuchets, compound crossbows and metal (bronze and iron) edged weapons, all of which had an immense impact on the ways that wars were fought. In the Mediterranean, in the seventh century AD, combatants deployed 'Greek fire', a mysterious admixture of chemical combustibles that was squirted from a tube and ignited upon contact with the water. Even earlier, in 424 BC, at the siege of Delium, the Greeks used sulphur fumes against the enemy, an example of a gas attack long before its more notorious use in the First World War.

So why is the period after 1500 special? Firstly, the span of time from 500 BC to AD 1500 was marked less by the introduction of new weapons as by 'endless alterations and combinations of existing ones'.[9] As a result, while fortifications improved in this period, tactics changed very little, as is illustrated by the fact that, throughout the medieval period, military commanders still used Roman military textbooks for instruction. Secondly, while there were undoubtedly great changes in military technology before 1500, there was a revolutionary development in weapons technology about this date associated with the use of gunpowder – which went hand-in-hand with wider changes in Europe as it entered the early modern period – that, fitfully, unevenly but inexorably, transformed the face of battle. Robert L. O'Connell sees it as change from mechanical weapons before 1500 to an era of chemical weapons, starting with guns and gunpowder and ending with nuclear bombs.[10] Van Creveld's periodization is more complex: firstly, an age of tools, 2000 BC–AD 1500; secondly, an age of machines driven by gunpowder, wind and water, 1500–1830; thirdly, an age of integrated machines when technology was properly organized, 1830–1945; finally, an age of automated war, 1945–present, when war was 'waged with the aid of machines that are not only linked to each other in systems, but are capable within limits, of themselves detecting changes in their environment and of reacting to these changes'.[11]

the gunpowder revolution

The Europeans obtained gunpowder, the combustion material for the gun, from the Chinese (possibly brought to Europe by the Mongols) who, from the twelfth century, were using it in simple bamboo guns, grenades and rockets. Although cannons were appearing on European battlefields by the fourteenth century and hand-held firearms in the fifteenth century, the rise of gunpowder weapons was a gradual, stuttering process over the next two centuries. In the nascent armaments industry emerging in northern Italy and the Low Countries in this period, artisans had to overcome significant technological problems before guns could come to dominate the battlefield. These included eradicating impurities from the metal used for gun barrels and achieving greater precision in their manufacture; there were also problems with the ammunition used (for instance, early shells were simply stone balls). At the same time, discovering the best technique for maximizing the explosive quality of the gunpowder required much trial and error. In the early days, premature explosions or burst barrels often killed or maimed gunners and infantrymen. There was also the difficulty of transporting guns over Europe's poor road system. Consequently, catapults, crossbows and longbows continued in use for hundreds of years after the arrival of gunpowder, not finally dying out until the seventeenth century or later. Van Creveld dates the dominance of the firearm to the War of the Austrian Succession (1740–48) that finally relegated all older weapons technology 'to the scrapheap'.[12]

Having said this, siege guns quickly proved their value, especially against the thin, high-walled fortifications of the time, designed only to withstand scaling ladders. Mechanical artillery such as catapults, however well developed, never acquired the power to bring down entire fortress walls in the manner made possible by gunpowder and cannon. In 1453, at the siege of Constantinople, the Ottoman besiegers employed a Hungarian gunner, Orban, who deployed in front of the city walls a number of muzzle-loading guns including one huge cannon that fired a stone ball weighing a ton. While the effect of this gun was perhaps as much psychological as physical, Roger Crowley in his *Constantinople: The Last Great Siege, 1453* (2005) sees its use as decisive and he is right to devote a whole chapter to the technological leap it represented.

Even with their imperfections, siege guns were capable of packing much greater power and hurling much heavier projectiles with much greater force than the largest catapults and trebuchets. In consequence, from the sixteenth century, the fortresses of Europe had to be redesigned, walls lowered, steeply sloped, buttressed and thickened, and defensive glacis pushed out to threaten attackers and keep them from closing in with artillery and infantry. This led to what became known as the *trace italienne* style of fortress, epitomized in the massive fortress building programme of the French military engineer, Sébastien Le Prestre de Vauban (1633–1707).

The impact and relationship of the new fortifications to European society is tied in with a wider debate generated by Michael Roberts in the 1950s in which he argued that significant changes in European government and society could be traced back to new battlefield tactics instituted by Maurice of Nassau and Gustavus Adolphus in the late-sixteenth and seventeenth centuries. These changes involved the introduction of more linear military formations to maximize the potential of the new musket-armed infantry alongside aggressive cavalry charges.[13] Roberts' argument pulled battlefield tactics and technology out of an academic ghetto, arguing that these military changes (his so-called 'military revolution' – still hotly debated amongst historians) were the motor for wider societal, political and economic change (and not the other way round). In the 1970s and 1980s, as part of a critique of Roberts, Geoffrey Parker turned to the *trace italienne* fortification system, arguing that these formidable fortresses built in response to the growing power of the siege guns tipped the balance back in favour of the defence.[14] Battles thus became less common as war became a matter of sieges – sometimes very prolonged – that in turn demanded money and manpower on an unprecedented scale. Simultaneously, the growth of the population and wealth of Europe made it possible to meet this demand: 'By emphasizing the *trace italienne*, Parker added a key new ingredient to the military revolution debate: military technology as a causative factor.'[15] This is significant inasmuch as military historians usually show how revolutions in military technology (and tactics) can transform the art of war, as opposed to showing how these can alter entire societies.[16] Laurent Henninger and Alan James discuss these issues in more depth in their chapters in this volume.

In 1525, at the battle of Pavia, the troops of the Habsburg Emperor, Charles V, routed those of Francis I of France. In the battle, a decisive moment came when the Emperor's Spanish musketeers – or arquebusiers – threw the French cavalry into utter confusion.[17] While the battle of Pavia symbolizes the impact of the gunpowder revolution, it is easy to forget how slowly the revolution took place. Infantry edged weapons and armour held on tenaciously and by the sixteenth century field armies were fighting with a fantastic variety of weapons: muskets, pikes, swords, lances and artillery of every shape and size. Finding an efficient firing mechanism for early muskets was always a problem, reflected in the evolution from touchholes to matchlocks to wheellocks to flintlocks to percussion caps. There was always the risk of a premature musket pan flash that could horribly burn one side of a soldier's face as he leant down to aim and fire the weapon (and blind him). Moreover, until the advent of breech-loading mechanisms in the nineteenth century, the loading of these muskets (and field guns) from the front was a fussy, time-consuming business, requiring the soldier to stand upright on the battlefield and go through the slow procedure of forcing powder, wadding and a ball down the barrel preparatory to firing. One estimate is that early matchlock muskets required 96 separate motions by the soldier for each round of firing.[18] As they slowly loaded and fired, perhaps managing at most two rounds per minute, the soldiers with muskets needed to be protected against enemy cavalry and infantry charges. This required the deployment of soldiers with traditional weapons – usually pikemen – interspersed among their vulnerable comrades who were busy loading and reloading their muskets. The relatively simple technology of the bayonet, first used at the end of the seventeenth century, changed all of this. The French invention of the socket bayonet, which fixed over the end of a musket while still allowing firing, meant that the infantryman could stand alone. The bayonet spelt the end of the pikeman and marked the final fusion of the two major infantry arms – projectile and edged weapons – into one.[19]

Field guns and firearms transformed the battlefield in other ways. To get the most from firearms it came to be recognized that precision drill, which had made the Swiss pike squares so effective in the fifteenth century, would have to be extended to the new fire-powered infantry. This was because gunpowder firearms remained very inaccurate and often misfired. Thus, soldiers with firearms could only deliver effective fire through salvos on command, which also required the men in the fire team all to go through the complicated re-loading process at the same time, and to remain as a coherent group on the battlefield. This necessitated an increase in the ratio of commissioned and non-commissioned officers to the other ranks and a great deal of unit training – or drill – before a campaign. The first great drill master of modern times was Maurice of Nassau, and the first drill books were published in the Netherlands early in the seventeenth century. Van Creveld puts it bluntly: 'it is hardly surprising that the best armies of the period were those which were most successful in turning their men into soulless robots goose-stepping forward at exactly 90 paces [to] the minute'.[20] Killing was also no longer directly related to soldiers' physical prowess and steely courage in the face of hand-to-hand combat. Instead, it became a matter of trained, professional skill that, with greater weapon range, distanced the soldier from death. New technology meant drill and the professionalization of soldiering, both of which would shape combat over the coming centuries. In the eighteenth century, one could expect a third of an advancing army to be cavalry; by the nineteenth century, this was reduced to between a quarter and a sixth. Inexorably, the musket-equipped soldier supported by field artillery replaced the mounted knight and cavalry of the Middle Ages. Vestiges of the old world remained: thus, at Waterloo in 1815, the French mounted cuirassier's mirror-shining helmet and breastplate were left on the field of battle, relics from an earlier age (they even made a brief re-appearance in 1914 when the French army again went to war). As van Creveld concludes: 'Overall, the period between 1500 and 1830 was characterised by continuous and fairly steady technological progress. In contrast to the previous age, this meant that there could be no periodic return to old weapons.'[21] While true, it is worth noting that weapons could come and go, and then re-appear. Thus, the British army in 1799, building on fourteenth-century ideas about using gunpowder in rockets, introduced the Congreve military rocket, only to phase it out in 1885. Later, in the 1940s, German rocket technology would transform warfare and lay the foundation for the Cold War era of nuclear tipped inter-continental ballistic missiles and the current fashion for super-accurate cruise missiles.

non-military technologies

War and technology in the early modern period should not be viewed solely through the prism of weapons development. Other technological developments changed warfare; most of these developments had little or nothing to do with warfare, at least not at first. Thus, the spread of writing, printing and paper had a huge impact on armies. Large, modern armies cannot function without effective written orders and signals communicated from one literate signaller to another. Along with the development of metalled roads, canals and, later, railways, modern signals and communications meant that a commander no longer had to stay close to his army in the field. The railway was of particular importance to modern warfare, as Dennis Showlater shows in his *Railroads and Rifles: Soldiers, Technology and the Unification of Germany* (1975). Printing presses and paper came into use at about the same time as gunpowder. Along with this, there was the invention of double-entry book-keeping – vital for managing the finances of large standing armies – and the use of Arabic numerals. The latter led to the discovery of the decimal system by Simon Stevin (1548–1620), one of the outstanding military engineers of his age. Dependable maps were also vital for the movement of armies and ships, and soldiers and sailors were at the forefront of early mapmaking.

Preserving food was another pressing issue for quartermasters and commanders. Without modern refrigeration and canning/packaging techniques, armies took food on the hoof or soldiers lived off the land, with all the negative implications that this had for the local civilian population forced to feed large armies. With this in mind, in 1795 the French revolutionary government offered a 12,000-franc prize for the discovery of a practical method of food preservation. In 1809, Nicolas Appert, a Parisian confectioner, won the prize with his system for preserving certain foods in specially made glass bottles by prolonged immersion in boiling water. Appert was the father of the modern canning industry and his discovery led, in 1839, to the first tin-coated metal cans in the USA.[22] Watches (or chronometers) were another civilian invention with significant implications for armed forces. Before proper timekeeping instruments were available, generals could never be sure that subordinate commanders would arrive on the battlefield at the right time; meanwhile, sailors were unable accurately to determine longitude without a marine chronometer, not invented until John Harrison (1693–1776) painstakingly built a set of instruments that, eventually, won British Admiralty approval for use on Royal Navy ships. (Harrison's amazingly intricate and beautiful time-keeping devices, designed to stay true despite the sway of the ship, are on display in London's Greenwich Observatory.)

Finally, one should not ignore the effect that aesthetics and morality had on the appearance of weapons. Anthropological, psychological and cultural factors have influenced the evolution of weapons throughout the ages. Weapons have been embellished and engraved as ornaments or to make them look elegant; fortifications put up with imposing beauty rather than military purpose in mind; ships built with bas relief and gilding or impressively large even though this reduces their ability to fight effectively. The Lateran Council in 1139 tried to ban all bows (including crossbows) as being unfair, although it allowed their use against non-Christians. More recently, international conventions have outlawed 'dum-dum' expanding bullets as being unusually cruel. Whether it is crossbows, gas or weapons of mass destruction, morality, war and technology is an interesting theme examined by, among others, Michael Howard and Geoffrey Best.[23]

These essentially non-military technologies and concerns – whether it is maps, canning, printing or the need to make something pleasing to the eye – probably did as much to shape warfare, and particularly its strategic dimensions, as did technologies designed solely for military use. Moreover, many purely military technologies (such as the email system originally designed for the US military in 1968), with some adjustments, found a place in non-military technologies designed for everyday civilian use. Military needs also hastened new technologies. Thus, the intervention of the US military brought forward the invention of the ordinary computer by 12–15 years. Michael White's interesting if sometimes tenuous study, *The Fruits of War: How Military Conflict Accelerates Technology* (2005), makes this point, highlighting the symbiotic relationship between war and technology, and arguing that many of the day-to-day technologies that we take for granted – such as transport, communications, consumer electronics and medicine – are the result of military technological developments made during the Second World War.

technology and the war at sea

As Andrew Lambert shows in his chapter in this volume, naval warfare has been heavily dependent on new technologies. Before the Renaissance, ships had limited seaworthiness. *Pace* the voyages of the Vikings and the Pacific islanders, before *c*.1500, because of poor technology, ships were unable to make long journeys on a sustained and regular basis. Sailing close to the wind and with imprecise navigation methods, ships (oared or sailed) hugged the coast on even short journeys, heaving to at night to anchor or dock by land. Thus, ships were unable to command the high seas in the 'Mahanian' way that they have done in more recent times (although air power has recently come to challenge this dominance).

This all changed after 1500 as sailing skills improved and new building techniques transformed the galleys and coastal trading vessels of the era into ocean-going vessels capable of circumnavigating the globe. Much of this change was technical in nature. Shipbuilders attached another sail, the spritsail, to a mast jutting forward from the bows of sailing ships. This sail provided leverage against the rudder – which by now had become standard on all ships and was built into the sternpost. The spritsail enabled vessels to sail as close as 80 degrees to the wind and to pull away from a lee shore. This meant that ships could sail out to sea, tack against an adverse wind, and thus make their way across the high seas. At the same time, rigging on ships underwent further improvements.[24] This led to the development along Europe's Atlantic littoral of new fully-rigged ships called carracks and caravels. These ships were sturdy and seaworthy, had better navigation tools, required fewer crewmen and, with increased energy per crewman, had almost unlimited endurance. The Europeans also mounted guns into these ships, turning them into men-of-war. These new ships had a profound effect on European and world history. In Europe, they heralded an era lasting until the mid nineteenth century of naval warfare between fully-rigged, wooden-built men-of-war divided in classes based on the number of guns mounted on board. Outside of Europe, they laid the foundation for Europe's expansion overseas. Between 1519 and 1522, Ferdinand Magellan, sailing under a Spanish flag, circumnavigated the globe for the first time. Thereafter, equipped with fully-rigged ships and 'reliable instruments of navigation, European sailors, merchantmen, and soldiers were able to embark on an adventure of epic proportions, one which transformed Western Europe from a small peninsula of Asia into the mistress of the world'.[25]

In terms of firepower, as early as the sea battle of La Rochelle in 1372, handguns were being used, helping the French and Spanish secure a victory over a smaller English squadron.[26] The important change came when bigger guns, capable of doing damage to an enemy ship's hull, were placed below deck with holes cut in the ship's side enabling gunners to lay their guns in time of battle. These advances spelt the end of the oared galley with its ram and boarding tactics as a war-fighting vessel, although their presence lingered on in the calmer waters of the Mediterranean until the battle of Lepanto in 1571 (in fact, galleys carried on being used on a diminishing scale for inshore work in the Mediterranean and Baltic seas after this date). Non-Europeans had no effective military response to these new gun-equipped vessels and quickly felt their effect. In 1509, at Diu off the coast of India, the Portuguese used their longer range naval guns (up to 200 yards) to defeat a more numerous Muslim fleet accustomed to close with the enemy, board and fight it out hand-to-hand.[27] Instead, the Portuguese stood off from the enemy and used their guns to blow the enemy out of the water. It was not long before non-European shipping in the Indian Ocean had to carry passes from the Portuguese to secure their passage across waters now controlled by Europeans.[28]

In just a few decades in the early sixteenth century, the new man-of-war allowed the Europeans to establish their absolute predominance over the oceans:

> Religion supplied the pretext and gold the motive. The technological progress accomplished by Atlantic Europe during the fourteenth and fifteenth centuries provided the means.... The gunned ships developed by Atlantic Europe in the course of the fourteenth and fifteenth centuries was the contrivance that made possible the European saga.... When the sailing vessels of Atlantic Europe arrived, hardly anything could resist them.[29]

While the Europeans now controlled the high sea, on land, outside Europe itself, they remained highly vulnerable, not least from diseases such as malaria that made any attempt to establish coastal forts, let alone move inland, highly problematic. And in the East, they faced powers in India and China that could field far larger armies than they could. Indeed, greater numbers could still neutralize better Western military technology and methods until at least the late eighteenth century.

In terms of ships, the next big round of changes to naval technology came in the nineteenth century. From the 1840s, engineers started to develop coal-fired, steam-driven ships, obviating the need for sails altogether, that were, at first, metal-clad and then all-steel vessels. Warships got steadily bigger, and more heavily armed, culminating in Britain's launch of the all-big-gun 18,000-ton, steam-turbine driven *Dreadnought*-class of battleship in 1906 that marked a new era in sea fighting, making all previous battleships obsolescent. At the same time as the shift from sail to steel in ship design, there was the development of the torpedo. The torpedo threatened to sink the big warship, especially when mounted in an underwater delivery system such as the submarine. Prototype submarines were made in the 1770s and tried out in the American and French Revolutionary wars – Napoleon was little interested – but not until the development of petrol and, more especially, diesel engines in the 1890s were submarines practical as a means of threatening enemy shipping.

The damage caused by the submarine in both world wars is testament to the impact of this new technology; one that forced the major naval powers such as Britain and America to develop anti-submarine technologies such as Asdic/Sonar. After the Second World War, the major powers developed nuclear-driven submarines capable of staying under the water for months at a time and armed with nuclear missiles. If the submarine's threat to battleships could be contained that of the aircraft carrier at the end of the First World War could not and eventually resulted in the phasing out of battleships after the Second World War. Over this period, propulsion systems also changed from sail to coal to oil to nuclear power. Sea power is now expressed in nuclear-driven carrier battle groups equipped with jet warplanes, cruise missile technology and advanced electronic warfare capability.

the industrial revolution

In terms of advances in military technology and science, the French Revolutionary and Napoleonic Wars (1792–1815) were unremarkable. There were some new inventions but the commanders were not much interested in them. Napoleon closed down his army's 'aeronautical' department; Congreve's rockets frightened the Duke of Wellington more than the enemy; Lord Cochrane's interest in chemical warfare won him more enemies than friends; the possible naval use of steam power was wholly ignored; and when the American engineer Robert Fulton produced his idea of using his pioneer submarine to attack the Royal Navy ships blockading the port of Brest the French were horrified, arguing that this was a 'disgraceful way of making war.... those engaged in it deserved to be hanged'.[30] Industrial technology at this stage of history was adding to the size of the combatants' armouries rather than to the quality of their weaponry. With the exception of better maps and roads, and the Chappé telegraph, technological innovation does little to explain Napoleon's victories and ultimate defeat.[31]

However, from about 1830, the Industrial Revolution resulted in myriad changes to weapons technology and more general technology that had military uses (such as railways and the telegraph).[32] As van Creveld notes, the Industrial Revolution also combined weapons: 'Until about 1830, warfare was very largely an affair of using individual tools and machines. Some of these tools and machines were steam-operated... however, they were not integrated into complexes or systems'.[33] The science and technology that were integral to industrialization produced the new technologies – some purely military, some not – associated with war in the modern era: railways, breech-loading rifles and guns, quick-firing artillery (such as the French '75'), recoil systems on which modern guns relied, the telegraph, wireless, aeroplanes, explosives such as TNT and dynamite, the internal combustion engine, steam-powered ships and torpedoes. Above all there was the machine gun, an exemplar of modern, industrialized warfare, and the subject of John Ellis's *The Social*

History of the Machine Gun (1975). Later on, there were cheap, mass-produced automatic assault rifles, epitomized by the Soviet-built AK-47, whose story is told in Mikhaïl Kalchnikov's *Ma Vie en Rafales* (2003).[34] There is even a growing literature devoted to barbed wire, invented to fence off the prairies of America but soon put to good defensive use by armies, and then electrified by the combatants in the Russo-Japanese War of 1904–05.[35] At the same time, populations became more literate and sophisticated and so able to use the new technologies. By the South African War (1899–1902), soldiers were in khaki – drab was now the order of the day for soldiers who fought lying down with personal weapons that could kill opponents up to 2,000 yards away on a dispersed (or 'empty') battlefield stretching for many miles.

Even before the American Civil War (1861–65) and Wars of German unification (1864–71), European armies were practising the large-scale movement of troops by railway; after 1871, every general staff had a railway department.[36] The mass technologies of the Industrial Revolution threatened soldiers' individual heroism and skill in the 'art of war'; armies were becoming mass killing machines.[37] War became a business of huge, conscript armies moved by railways, equipped with a formidable array of weaponry and fed by home-front industrial bases. Jan Bloch's six volume *The War of the Future in its Technical, Economic and Political Aspects* (1898–1900, the last volume appeared in English as *Is War Impossible?*) is remarkable not only for its predictions of the application of new technology to warfare that presaged the total wars of the twentieth century, but also for the fact that its author was not a military man but a Polish Jewish banker, a fact that allowed the military experts to ignore his predictions.

technology and the war in the air

New technology also meant that warfare in this period became three-dimensional, an issue discussed in full in John Buckley's chapter in this volume. In 1783, the Montgolfier brothers built a hot-air balloon capable of carrying up to two persons. The first military use of the balloon during the Napoleonic Wars was not auspicious. The balloon rose to 3,000 feet and sailed for 15 miles before landing near a peasant village whereupon 'the superstitious villagers filled it full of bullet holes, tore it to pieces with their scythes, and tied it to the tail of a horse'.[38] Balloons were also used in the American Civil War and in 1870 during the Franco-Prussian War. Then, in 1903, the Wright brothers in the USA made the first powered flight of a fixed-wing aircraft at Kitty Hawk, North Carolina. It was a revolutionary new development that quickly had an impact on war and strategy. In 1909, Louis Bleriot flew across the English Channel in 31 minutes. Bleriot's flight marked the end of the long period of British invulnerability to attacks from abroad. The first military use of aeroplanes was in 1911–12 in Italy's war in Libya, when bombs were first dropped on the enemy.

government and technology

The full mobilization required by the world wars coupled to the importance of new weapons technologies – especially in the Second World War – meant that government policy and technology merged. Government ministries took over technology and integrated research, science, technology and production.[39] The most successful warring states created 'command technologies' where government tasked industry to satisfy the specific strategic and tactical needs of the armed services, rather than going about its usual business of fulfilling market demand. As industry was not always able or willing to fulfil this role, the state often financed private companies to conduct ambitious defence research. The sums involved were huge. In the USA, military research budgets went up from $13 million in 1939 to $1.5 billion in 1944.[40] In all of this, the Allies in both world wars were more successful than their enemies.

Tim Travers' *How the War was Won: Command and Technology in the British Army on the Western Front, 1917–1918* (1992) examines the issue of how decisive the new technologies produced by these centrally-mobilized industries were on the battlefields of the Great War. Travers poses the valid question – did new weapons and technology shift the balance, particularly tanks and aeroplanes? – answering with a qualified yes.[41] The protagonists used many other new weapons technologies for the first time, gas and flamethrowers being obvious examples. Moreover, weapons that had been partially deployed in the nineteenth century were now mass-produced and used in great quantities: mines, machine guns, barbed wire, high explosives, breech-loading rifles, recoilless artillery pieces and the advanced artillery percussion contact fuses (known to the British as the 106 fuse). At the same time, pre-existing civilian technologies such as the wireless, petrol-driven vehicles and railways were co-opted for the war effort. The successful use of these technologies did not win the First World War on its own, but it played a vital part in the combination of factors that secured Allied victory in 1918. As William Philpott argues in his chapter in this volume, the First World War was the arena in which, for the first time, a new style of technologically-driven three-dimensional 'deep battle' emerges. While science, as Guy Hartcup shows, also played its part in the Great War, it is in the Second World War that we see the full application of scientific endeavour for the war effort.[42]

science and the world wars

Science had always been important in warfare. Hellenistic geometry and the work of scholars in Alexandria made possible Roman siege weapons and fortifications. Much later, Galileo's experimental work on ballistics in the sixteenth and seventeenth centuries (1564–1642) is just one example of theories being worked on in the early modern period that had significant military resonance. Increasingly, the job of gunners required them to work with mathematics, a subject formally taught in the artillery schools established in France and Spain in the sixteenth and seventeenth centuries.[43] More generally, scientific enquiry was being institutionalized; in 1663, the Royal Society for the Promotion of Natural Knowledge was founded in London and three years later the French established the *Académie Royale des Sciences*.

In the twentieth century, scientists assumed a critical role in warfare unseen in previous eras, working on theories and production methods that were of paramount military significance. The First World War was a period of transition as scientists began to intrude into the workings of the military machine.[44] The apogee for science came with the Second World War. Michael Howard is right to emphasize how decisive technology now was:

> Nevertheless technology had introduced a factor which had not been present in the Napoleonic era, and which rendered all comparisons with the past of very doubtful value. A little more concentration by the Germans on the development of jet aircraft might have changed the course of the air war. Had they devoted more resources to missile technology they might have produced rocket weapons which would have laid central London waste and made the Allied landings in Normandy impossible. And if their nuclear research had taken a rather different turn and received greater political backing, they might have developed nuclear weapons.[45]

Many of the discoveries made after 1939 were completely new, while others were improvements on existing ideas and technologies that were now operationalized and mass-produced. In the Second World War, 'the scientists in the laboratory touched almost every aspect of the war operations and profoundly influenced tactics and strategy'.[46] Looking at both Axis and Allied science, Guy Hartcup highlights six important developments or devices that arose from the war: atomic energy, radar, rocket propulsion, jet propulsion, automation and operational research.[47] As never before, contemporary armed forces came to rely on science to provide combat capability.[48]

In 1940, the British and Americans established a joint scientific mission:

> These moves marked the beginning of what was to grow into a gigantic co-ordinated effort, in which hundreds of academic scientists, all the leading British, American and Canadian universities, and an immense number of industries, as well as the research departments of all the armed services in all the Allied countries, worked at top speed to perfect old weapons, to invent new ones, and to invent countermeasures which could lessen the deadliness of enemy weapons.[49]

The results were impressive and far-ranging: radar, proximity fuses, electronic fire control equipment, anti-submarine weapons such as Hedgehog and Squid, incendiaries, rockets, frangible bullets, flail tanks, bailey bridges, Mulberry harbours, DUKW floating vehicles, landing craft, the 'colossal' computer and 'asdic' (later developed by the Harvard Underwater *Sound* Laboratory into 'sonar'). Not all of these were the result of scientists working in laboratories. The flail tank was the brainchild of a South African officer, A. S. J. Du Toit, who, before the war, had driven from Johannesburg to London in 13 days. After attending a lecture on mines in North Africa, Du Toit came up with the idea for the flail tank. His commanding officer sent him to Cairo to develop the idea. By the Christmas of 1941, the flail tank was ready for use.[50]

Some of these inventions were so good that the Allies were loath to use them lest they fall into enemy hands and be cloned and turned against Allied troops. This was the case with the proximity fuse, sometimes called the variable time fuse, a remarkable invention whereby scientists built a small radar set – power plant, transmitter and receiver – into an explosive shell enabling it to explode right next to a target rather than on contact.[51] The Americans first tested the proximity fuse in 1942 but only allowed its use over sea where the enemy could not recover lost, unexploded fuses. Used in conjunction with radar guided fire control systems the effect was devastating: 'The men at the guns merely loaded and reloaded, confident that the aiming and firing were being accurately handled elsewhere.... the electronic computers used in the director systems were the forerunners of the great wartime and postwar electronic computers'.[52] The Allies finally released the proximity fuse for use in Europe in 1944 to combat the V1 flying bomb threat. The results were amazing: in the first week of their use, they destroyed 24 per cent of V1s launched against Britain; 46 per cent in week two; 67 per cent in week three; 79 per cent in week four. In one final attack launched from Holland, proximity fuse shells from anti-aircraft guns brought down all 24 V1s launched before they even reached the British coast.[53] When the Allies knew that the war was almost over, they used proximity fuses on land against German troops in battles around the Rhine in 1945. Able to burst above enemy troops, proximity fuse shells inflicted terrible casualties and aided the Allied advance into Germany.[54]

There were failures, one extraordinary example being Project Habakkuk. This was a project to build floating platforms made of a new material called pykrete, a mixture of wood, pulp and water which when frozen became as hard as concrete. The aim was to create huge, floating pykrete aircraft carriers stationed in the mid-Atlantic for use in the battle of the Atlantic. The British developed a 1,000-ton prototype in Canada with an on-board refrigerating plant. The plan was then to make a 2,000-feet 2.2 million ton pykrete ship to take 200 fighters and 100 Mosquitoes. The cost would have been £17 million. The British eventually scrapped Project Habakkuk as it was impractical. In a less dramatic fashion, scientific projects that did not have good government backing often foundered. Thus, while Britain was successful with its development of radar, directed by the government from the 1930s, it was less successful with jet propulsion, in part because it failed to support Frank Whittle, Britain's leading jet scientist.[55]

The contrast with the Axis powers' use of science and technology is striking. The Germans made tremendous advances in certain areas of science and technology, notably in ordnance, aero-dynamics and rocketry.[56] The Allies had no countermeasures against the V2 rocket, except to destroy its launching sites, and there was little that they could do when faced with German jet fighters such as the Me-262. The Germans also invented special devices such as the *schnorkel* that allowed submarines to run underwater while charging their batteries. However, the Nazis were generally hostile to science and many of Germany's best scientists – certainly the Jewish ones – left if they could in the 1930s. Assuming that the war would be a short one, the Nazis failed to organize scientists for war or to initiate long-range projects until they made belated efforts after 1942, when it was too late.[57] The Germans thought that they could win the war with the weapons they had developed in peacetime.[58] They were wrong. Writing just after the war, James Phinney Baxter put it nicely, arguing that the Germans produced 'almost' weapons that provided the basis for post-war military technology but did little to help Germany during the war.[59]

While Italy and Japan led the field in certain areas such as aeroplane and torpedo technology, they were, generally speaking, in an even worse state than Germany. Not until late 1944 did the Japanese army and navy combine to set up a joint technical committee. As with Germany, by then it was too little, too late. Moreover, in Japan the military distrusted scientists, especially if they had been trained, as many of them had been, in the West.[60] The results were, at times, farcical as, for instance, when the Japanese navy and army developed separate systems for radar identification of planes. As a result, neither could identify the other's planes from those of the Americans.[61]

the atom bomb

The Manhattan Project, the Allies' development of the atom bomb, brought together scientists and engineers in one huge endeavour: 'Besides being the most revolutionary military development of modern times, if not of all time, it was the first time in which the very boundaries of scientific knowledge were pushed outward on a grand scale in the pursuit of a weapon.'[62] The Manhattan Project utilized the work of European, often Jewish émigré, scientists such as Albert Einstein, Max Born, James Franck, John von Neumann, Edward Teller, Leo Szilard, Enrico Fermi and Niels Bohr. Einstein arranged for some of these fugitive scientists to meet US government officials – a decision that the pacifist Einstein later regretted. In October 1942, the US President gave the go-ahead to build the bomb: 'From this time onward the scientists became in a very real sense captives of the enterprise, or simply "scientific personnel", obliged to submit to military forms of control.'[63] No longer was weapons technology just tapping into existing scientific knowledge. Instead, the desire for new weapons was driving science.[64] The dropping of the atom bombs on Hiroshima and Nagasaki in 1945 ushered in an age of mutually assured destruction that did away with 'total' war. The thermo-nuclear age after 1945 seemed to have no need for soldiers. Had a new technology transformed war in the West?[65] The answer is that while nuclear weapons made another world war highly unlikely, they did not prevent a series of wars and insurgencies outside of Europe in which Western powers were often involved.

the nuclear age and beyond

After 1945, NATO and the USA often looked for technological solutions to their security problems. Technology provided a less costly way of deterring aggression and acted as a force multiplier.[66] This meant a big growth in research and development (R&D). Before 1940, total R&D in the USA was about $1 billion; by the mid 1980s, this figure had increased to $100 billion. Just after 1945, the USA committed 5 per cent of its defence procurement budget to military R&D; by the mid 1970s, the ratio was 50:50. Defence research became the vanguard of scientific advances: 'From the 1940s until the 1970s, military research and development led rather than followed the ideas of industry in a number of critical product sectors, such as electronics and aerospace.'[67] The result was an unprecedented growth in military and non-military technology after 1945, coterminous with an era of nuclear deterrence theory in which the military's task was not to win wars but to avert them.[68] How effective all of this technology would have been had there been a superpower war is unclear. When NATO war-gamed potential wars with the Soviet Union the results showed that, even with all the new conventional weaponry, it still lost, forcing it in the final instance to use nuclear weapons.[69]

America's involvement in the Vietnam War (1960–75) gave it the opportunity to try out its new technologies to secure a quick victory at little loss in American lives. Early computers manned by Harvard Business School graduates processed information on everything from Vietnamese rice production to the battles being fought: 'They then spewed forth a mighty stream of tables and graphs which purported to measure "progress".... So long as the tables looked neat, few people bothered to question the accuracy, let alone the relevance, of the data.'[70] It was expected that America's vast technological superiority would deliver a quick victory over North Vietnam. Its use of precision-guided munitions (PGMs) in 1972 to bring down the Paul Doumer and Thanh Hoa bridges in North Vietnam is one example of major new US-developed weapons systems successfully tested out in Vietnam.[71] Others include the helicopter and air mobility, firepower (B-52s, C-130s and smart weapons) and electronic sensors to detect the enemy. This was a technical, capital-intensive war.

Instead, America lost the war, a defeat that seriously undermined the self-confidence of the US military, prompting soul-searching of why its far greater technology had not been enough.[72] The answer, of course, is that technology, in Vietnam as in earlier periods, is but one factor in explaining victory and defeat in war, and the Americans were misguided in thinking that weapons, computers and management systems could, alone, win the war. The Americans lost no major battlefield encounters and their technologies usually worked very well in exclusively military terms. The problem obviously lay elsewhere: in deficiencies in soldiers' morale, government policy, military strategy, political will and home-front support.[73] In comparison to the resilience of the Vietnamese people and government and their readiness to expend whatever it took in lives and time to win, advanced US technology counted for little. The war in Vietnam prompted a wider debate on America's over-reliance on technology, one that has rumbled on into the twenty-first century and the wars in Afghanistan and Iraq.

After Vietnam, the USA developed new theories of war such as active defence and then, in 1982, the air-land battle, all of which attempted to incorporate new technologies at the tactical and operational level more effectively to produce quick victories with low casualties. These new approaches to warfare were highly dependent on information technology (IT), so much so that some authors see this as another revolution in military affairs (RMA).[74] US-led Coalition forces tested out the IT-led air-land battle in the Gulf War of 1990–91, where it achieved phenomenal success, vindicating, it seemed, a style of warfare that relied heavily on advanced technology and 'digital soldiers'. The Gulf War was characterized by electronic fire operations, electronic surveillance, electronic warfare, stealth fighters, cruise missiles and smart bombs: 'Something extraordinary happened during Operation Desert Storm. The sheer one-sidedness of the victory...points to a qualitative shift in military power... the Iraqi Army, a reasonable force for the post-war world, had met an enemy from the post-Cold War world. A generational shift had taken place.'[75] Yet, as Michael Handel observes, this triumph of military technologies that smashed the Iraqi army, re-taking Kuwait and inflicting huge casualties for very few Coalition losses, masks the political planning and preparation that were so vital to success in 1991 – precisely the political planning that was absent in America's involvement in Vietnam three decades earlier.[76] There remains the fact that vastly superior military technology, while winning on the battlefield, will not necessarily win the war, as the recent (2003) invasion of Iraq demonstrates.

The new technologies of war also meant the end of mass production of weapons and a return to low-productivity, highly-skilled cottage industry-style production methods. One example of this is the guidance system for the American MX missile of the 1980s that, while being the size of a basketball, contained 19,000 parts.[77] It remains to be seen how successful the new technologies will be in the long run. As the events of 9/11 and after show, simple means of attack by determined terrorists, or the use of crude but potentially deadly nuclear, chemical or biological weapons, can dramatically undercut the sophisticated new weapons technologies of the West. Mark Bowden illustrates the predicament for the users of high-tech weaponry in his book *Black Hawk Down*[78] (2000) that describes the defeat suffered by the Americans in Somalia in 1993 at the hands of crudely armed militia opposition fighting in a built-up area (who brought down advanced US helicopters with simple, hand-held weapons). More recently, Sean Naylor, who spent time with the 101st Airborne Division on operations in Afghanistan in 2002, does the same in his *Not a Good Day to Die: The Untold Story of Operation Anaconda* (2005). Naylor's description of the serious problems that the US paratroopers – reliant on IT systems and satellite imagery – faced when fighting Taliban fighters is a cautionary tale for those who think that advanced weapons technologies can transform the US military into a lighter, smaller force using air support and futuristic communications equipment in place of soldiers and artillery on the ground.[79]

medicine and war

Until the mid to late nineteenth century, medical advances lagged behind military technology. One might even argue, as Piers D. Mitchell does in *Medicine in the Crusades: Warfare, Wounds and the Medieval Surgeon* (2005), that medicine in the medieval period was superior to what followed. Reading the literature on military medicine from 1500 up to the nineteenth century, one is shocked at the appalling treatment of wounded and sick soldiers and sailors, and left with a sense of wonder at how any survived the surgeon's knife. As the ability to kill and maim improved, doctors' skills diminished. The standard text on this period and subject – Richard Gabriel and Karen Metz's *A History of Military Medicine: From the Renaissance through Modern Times: Volume II* (1992) – recounts this in grisly detail. Believing that pus and suppuration aided healing, surgeons introduced dirty material into wounds. This made as much sense as Kenelm Digby's (1603–45) sympathetic powder, in which physicians of the age placed great faith. The powder was made from moss scraped from a dead man's skull mixed with powdered mummy's flesh. No less a figure than Francis Bacon included sympathetic powder in his scientific collection of drugs. Then there was the transplantation cure in which a piece of wood was dipped in the blood or pus of the wound and then wedged in a tree. If the sliver of wood took root and grew, the patient recovered. Perhaps most amazing was the weapon salve cure in which an ointment was applied not to the wound but to the wounded man's weapon.

Too often, surgeons favoured amputation for wounded limbs. While some advances were made in developing ligatures for arteries – the usual means of stemming blood after a limb had been lopped off was cauterization with boiling oil – and devices that cut off blood flow allowing upper leg amputations, infection was always a problem, not least as there were no effective antiseptics available. A Bavarian army medical chest for a campaign against the Turks in 1688 contained the following 'medicines': powdered sandalwood, rhubarb, palm oil, spermaceti, mummy dust, scorpion oil, rainworm oil, oil of vipers, angle worms, earwigs, zinc oxide, Vigo's plaster of frog spawn, mercury, human and dog fat, aloes, tartar emetic, sugar of lead, alum, sassafras and opium. Most of this was worse than useless and compared poorly to what a Roman military surgeon took when he went on campaign. The cities of Europe teemed with crippled and maimed veterans, most of whom had no other option than to beg for their livelihoods. Poor military hygiene, the cause of so much infection and disease, changed little after 1500 as nobody was able to develop a cogent theory of disease transmission.

In the eighteenth century, there were improvements. John Hunter, a surgeon, wrote a *Treatise of the Blood, Inflammation and Gun Shot Wounds* (1794) which dealt sensibly with wound management. At the same time, physicians made links between cleanliness and infection, but it was not until Joseph Lister (1827–1912) that the medical world discovered antiseptic treatment. Consequently, disease and infections rather than battle were the main cause of deaths among soldiers until the First World War. In the American Revolutionary War, 90 per cent of all deaths were from disease. As the French physician Hugues Ravaton noted, the death rate from disease increased massively the longer the army was in the field. In 1718, the British army's medical staff for an army of 18,000 about to go on campaign was 173.

In the course of the nineteenth and twentieth centuries this changed. The medical discoveries made in these centuries – building on more general advances in science – were immensely significant and vastly improved military medicine. These discoveries not only recognized diseases and their causes but also came up with remedies: Ether, Chloroform, Plaster of Paris, Bacteria, Carbolic Acid, Tetanus, X-rays, blood groups, sulphonamides, blood transfusions, penicillin and DDT. Surgeons could now operate on soldiers under anaesthetic in a clean environment with the aim of saving rather than removing limbs, using for post-operative care the new anti-bacterial drugs. Among unwounded soldiers, immunization and anti-disease treatment programmes – such as against the mosquito that causes malaria – meant resistance and/or eradication of many diseases.

By the First World War, for the first time, more soldiers were dying in battle than of disease and post-wound infection. In a perverse way, this was an advance, certainly for the generals who could now field and sustain larger, healthier armies in which wounded or sick men were now more likely to recover and be available, once again, for service. The 1930s and 1940s saw huge advances in blood transfusions – whole blood and plasma – that kept wounded men alive and increased their chances of recovery.[80] Perhaps the biggest breakthrough came with the antibiotic (anti-infection) drug penicillin, discovered in the 1920s, but not mass-produced until, under the pressures of war, the USA took on production from 1943. Penicillin worked wonders against infections and by 1944 was widely available to Allied troops – the Axis powers had to rely on sulphonamide drugs, when they were available. The United States turned out over 21 billion units of penicillin in 1943, 1,633 billion units in 1944 and 7,052 billion units in 1945.[81] One of its first uses was on the vast number of Allied soldiers with sexually-transmitted diseases (STDs), *hors de combat* for relatively long periods while they were treated with the old drugs. For syphilis, the old treatment with arsenical drugs and bisimuth took 40–50 days; penicillin did the job in eight days and it would clear up gonorrhoea in 1–2 days (especially important as 60 per cent of gonorrhoea cases were sulphonamide drug resistant).

Mark Harrison's *Medicine and Victory: British Military Medicine in the Second World War* (2004) breaks new ground in analysing medicine and war, using the British army in the Second World War as a case study. Harrison shows how forward thinking the British were with military medicine after 1939, creating a medical service the likes of which Britain had never seen before. Having learnt its lessons in North Africa, Italy and Burma, the British army medical services reached its apogee in Normandy in 1944: 'Never before in history has a British Expeditionary Force left the country so well equipped medically', claimed one senior British medical officer quoted by Harrison.[82] This is contrasted with Orde Wingate's Chindit operations behind Japanese lines in Burma where poor medical provision severely hampered operations. Similarly, as a result of inadequate German medical provision, Erwin Rommel's *Afrika Korps* suffered badly, reducing its combat effectiveness. For Harrison, it was the creation of 'medical consciousness' among British commanders that gave their army a crucial edge in key theatres of war – notably North Africa and Burma.[83]

Field Marshal B. L. Montgomery declared that the contribution of the military medical services to Allied victory had been 'beyond all calculations'. Harrison concludes: 'In an age of total war, with manpower at a premium, all resources had to be used to their fullest extent and good medical services were essential if the maximum benefit was to be derived from Britain's forces.'[84] Too little has been written on military medicine and it is to be hoped that Harrison's volume – which won the Society for Army Historical Research's prestigious Templer Medal prize in 2004 – will encourage further scholarship.

The behaviour of US General George Patton in the Second World War illustrates some of the tensions for the medical services. A doctor recalled a harangue from Patton in which the latter said: 'If you have two wounded soldiers, one with an arm or leg blown off, you save the sonofabitch with the lung wound and let the goddam sonofabitch with an amputated arm or leg go to hell. He is no goddam use to us anymore.' The doctor felt uneasy with this, concluding, 'perhaps it takes this hard-boiled attitude to win battles but...'.[85] Racism also played its part: the US military medical service refused to accept blood donations from black troops, fearful of the effect this would have on white troops, even though it knew full well that there was no scientific reason to refuse blood from black donors.[86]

The USA began widespread helicopter evacuation of the wounded in the Korean War (1950–53), after which they went to 'MASH' hospitals close to the front, a procedure that vastly improved chances of recovery. By the time of the Vietnam War, the average flying time for a wounded US soldier going to a forward hospital was 35 minutes. The idea that the world wars created the conditions for medical advances has not gone unchallenged, as is shown by Roger Cooter, Mark Harrison and Steve Sturdy's edited volume *War, Medicine and Modernity* (1998), a book that also tackles the question of the place of military medicine within more general ideas of 'modernity'.

Alongside medicine, military psychiatry, which developed after the American Civil War, dealt with the combat-related psychiatric problems among soldiers. This led to ideas of shell shock and, more recently, post-traumatic stress disorder. These topics are dealt with in Hans Binneveld's *From Shellshock to Combat Stress: A Comparative History of Military Psychiatry* (1997), Ben Shephard's *A War of Nerves: Soldiers and Psychiatrists, 1914–1994* (2002), Edgar Jones and Simon Wessely's *Shell Shock to PTSD: Military Psychiatry from 1900 to the Gulf War* (2005) and some doctoral theses.[87] The literature examines the two approaches taken to military psychiatry: the 'tough' and 'tender' approaches; between those interested in finding out more about the medically fascinating disorders of mentally-unbalanced soldiers, and those wishing to make them better so that they could go back to being soldiers.[88]

conclusion

An obsession with military technology and science in isolation can distort the general picture of war whose character in any given case is the product of many factors – political, social, economic as well as technological. In the current age of advanced technology, there is a natural proclivity to overestimate the role of weapons and underestimate the more general environment in which technology operates. Technology has been an important driver in success and defeat in war, especially against non-Western societies, but the West's belief that superior technology in war will always prevail over 'primitive' societies has been shown to be spectacularly wrong in a number of cases since 1945 – Vietnam and Afghanistan being obvious recent examples. Thus, readers should approach ideas of technological determinism in warfare with caution. The best histories take the technical knowledge of the military purists on war, science and technology and intertwine it with wider societal, economic and political developments after 1500. In doing so, they advance our knowledge not just of war but also its place in history.

further reading

For general texts on technology and war, readers should look at the following, all of which are well-written and informative, and provide comprehensive coverage of the subject: Bernard and Fawn Brodie, *From Crossbow to H-Bomb* [1962] (London and Bloomington IN, 1973); Martin van Creveld, *Technology and War: from 2000 B.C. to the*

Present (London, 1991); J. F. C. Fuller, *Armament and History: A Study of the Influence of Armament on History from the Dawn of Classical Warfare to the Second World War* (London, 1946); William McNeill, *The Pursuit of Power: Technology, Armed Force and Society since A.D. 1000* (Oxford, 1983); Robert L. O'Connell, *Of Arms and Men: A History of War, Weapons and Aggression* (New York, 1989); and Maurice Pearton, *The Knowledgeable State: Diplomacy, War and Technology since 1830* (London, 1982). There are also two relevant journal articles, of which the first is especially useful: George Raudzens, 'War-Winning Weapons: The Measurement of Technological Determinism in Military History', *The Journal of Military History* 54/4 (1990): 403–33; and Alex Roland, 'Technology and War: The Historiographical Revolution', *Technology and Culture* 34/1 (1993): 117–34. More generally, the journal *Technology and Culture* is useful for this topic.

For naval developments in the early modern period, Carlo M. Cipolla's *Guns and Sails in the Early Phase of European Expansion, 1400–1700* (London, 1965) is the basic text. On war and technology in the computer age, James Dunnigan's *Digital Soldiers: The Evolution of High-Tech Weaponry and Tomorrow's Brave New Battlefield* (New York, 1996) is very useful.

Readers interested in weaponry should consult the following texts: Kenneth Chase, *Firearms: A Global History to 1700* (Cambridge, 2003); *Engels as Military Critic* (Manchester, 1959); Ian Hogg, *The Weapons that Changed the World* (London, 1986); A. J. Smithers, *A New Excalibur: The Development of the Tank, 1909–1939* (London, 1986); John Terraine, *White Heat: The New Warfare, 1914–18* (London, 1982); and Tom Wintringham and John Blashford-Snell, *Weapons and Tactics* (London, 1973).

Warfare and technology in the non-Western world is well served by a set of specific key volumes that covers Africa, Asia and the Americas: J. F. Ade Ajayi and R. Smith, *Yoruba Warfare in the Nineteenth Century* (Cambridge, 1964); David Ayalon, *Gunpowder and Firearms in the Mamluk Kingdom* (London, 1956); Simon Digby, *War-horse and Elephant in the Delhi Sultanate* (Oxford, 1971); Robert Elgood, *Firearms of the Islamic World* (London, 1995); Jos Gommans and Dirk Kolff (eds), *Warfare and Weaponry in South Asia* (New Delhi, 2001); Robert Smith, *Warfare and Diplomacy in Pre-Colonial Africa* (London, 1976); Patrick Malone, *The Skulking Way of War: Technology and Tactics Among the New England Indians* (Lanham MD, 1991); Joseph Needham, *Science and Civilisation in China* (Cambridge, 1954–, multi-volumed); V. J. Parry and M. E. Yapp (eds), *War, Technology and Society in the Middle East* (London, 1975); and John Thornton, *Warfare in Atlantic Africa, 1500–1800* (London, 1999).

There are also more general texts that cover war and technology in the non-European world that readers may wish to examine. These include: Jeremy Black, *War in the Early Modern World* (London, 1998); Black, *War in the Modern World* (London, 2003); Brenda Buchanan (ed.), *Gunpowder: The History of an International Technology* (Bath, 1996); Daniel Headrick, *The Tools of Empire: Technology and European Imperialism in the Nineteenth Century* (Oxford, 1981); and John Keegan, *A History of Warfare* (London, 1993).

On the role of science in war, readers should consult the following: James Phinney Baxter, *Scientists Against Time* [1946] (Cambridge MA, 1968); David Egerton, 'British Scientific Intellectuals' in Paul Forman and José M. Sánchez-Ron (eds), *National Military Establishments and the Advancement of Science and Technology* (London, 1996); Guy Hartcup, *The Challenge of War: Scientific and Engineering Contributions to World War Two* (Newton Abbot, 1970); G. I. Pokrovsky, *Science and Technology in Contemporary War* (London, 1959); Tom Shachtman, *Terrors and Marvels: How Science and Technology Changed the Character and Outcome of World War II* (New York, 2002); and Solly Zuckerman, *Scientists and War: The Impact of Science on Military and Civil Affairs* (London, 1966).

For medicine and war, the following texts cover both general medicine and military psychiatry: Anthony Babington, *Shell-Shock: A History of the Changing Attitudes to War Neurosis* (London, 1997); Hans Binneveld, *From Shellshock to Combat Stress: A Comparative History of Military Psychiatry* (Amsterdam, 1997); Roger Cooter, Mark Harrison and Steve Sturdy (eds), *War, Medicine and Modernity* (Stroud, 1998); Roger Cooter, Mark Harrison and Stephen Sturdy (eds), *Medicine and Modern Warfare* (Amsterdam and Atlanta, 1999); Albert Cowdrey, *Fighting for Life: American Military Medicine in World War II* (New York, 1994); Richard Gabriel and Karen Metz, *A History of Military Medicine: From the Renaissance through Modern Times: Volume II* (New York, 1992); Mark Harrison, *Medicine and Victory: British Military Medicine in the Second World War* (Oxford, 2004); Edgar Jones and Simon Wessely, *Shell Shock to PTSD: Military Psychiatry from 1900 to the Gulf War* (Hove, 2005) and Ben Shephard, *A War of Nerves: Soldiers and Psychiatrists, 1914–1994* (London, 2002).

notes

1. Bernard Brodie, *Strategy in the Missile Age* (Princeton NJ, 1965), p. 71.
2. Michael Howard, *War in European History* (Oxford, 1976), p. 120. See also Martin van Creveld, *Technology and War: From 2000 B.C. to the Present* (London, 1991), p. 85.
3. Creveld, *Technology and War*, p. 1.
4. Examples from George Raudzens, 'War-Winning Weapons: The Measurement of Technological Determinism in Military History', *Journal of Military History* 54/4 (October 1990): 403–33, 403.
5. David Egerton's provocatively titled book *Warfare State: Britain, 1920–1970* (Cambridge, 2005), which makes the case that military technology and the military-industrial complex have been written out of contemporary British history, is not as ground-breaking as some reviewers might think. Authors such as John Lynn, Richard Overy and Hew Strachan have argued the same point in studies that pre-date Egerton. See Huw Richards, 'The Might of the Military Tendency', *Times Higher Education Supplement* (25 November 2005): 18.
6. *Encyclopaedia Britannica* (15th edn) (London, 2002), xxix, p. 530.
7. Ibid.
8. Review by David Parrott of G. Parker, *Cambridge Illustrated History of Warfare: Triumph of the West* (Cambridge, 1995) and J. Black, *Cambridge Atlas of Warfare: Renaissance to Revolution, 1492–1792* (Cambridge, 1996) in *War in History* 4/4 (1997): 477–93.
9. Creveld, *Technology and War*, p. 21; Bernard and Fawn Brodie, *From Crossbow to H-Bomb* [1962] (London and Bloomington IN, 1973), p. 34.
10. Robert L. O'Connell, *Of Arms and Men: A History of War, Weapons and Aggression* (New York, 1989), p. 12.
11. Creveld, *Technology and War*, pp. 2–3.
12. Ibid., pp. 21–2.
13. Michael Roberts, *The Military Revolution, 1560–1660* (Belfast, 1956); Clifford J. Rogers (ed.), *The Military Revolution Debate: Readings on the Transformation of Early Modern Europe* (Boulder CO, 1995), pp. 2, 14. See also J. Black, *A Military Revolution? Military Change and European Society, 1550–1800* (Basingstoke, 1991) and David Parrott, 'Strategy and Tactics in the Thirty Years' War: The "Military Revolution"', *Militärgeschichtliche Mitteilungen* 38 (1985): 7–25, reprinted in Rogers (ed.), *The Military Revolution Debate*.

14. Geoffrey Parker, *The Military Revolution: Military Innovation and the Rise of the West, 1500–1800* (Cambridge, 1996). See also Geoffrey Parker, *The Army of Flanders and the Spanish Road, 1567–1659: The Logistics of Spanish Victory and Defeat in the Low Countries' Wars* (Cambridge, 1972).
15. Rogers (ed.), *The Military Revolution Debate*, p. 4.
16. Rogers in Rogers (ed.), *The Military Revolution*, pp. 1–2.
17. Creveld, *Technology and War*, pp. 90–1.
18. Brodie, *From Crossbow to H-Bomb*, p. 55.
19. Ibid., p. 83.
20. Creveld, *Technology and War*, p. 94.
21. Ibid., p. 96.
22. Brodie, *From Crossbow to H-Bomb*, p. 107.
23. For more information on this, see Michael Howard et al. (eds), *The Laws of War: Constraints on Warfare in the Western World* (New Haven CT, 1994); Howard, *War and the Liberal Conscience* (London, 1978); and Geoffrey Best, *Humanity in Warfare* (New York, 1980).
24. Creveld, *Technology and War*, p. 126. See also J. H. Parry, *The Age of Reconnaissance* (London, 1963); C. R. Boxer, *The Portuguese Seaborne Empire, 1415–1825* (London, 1969); and C. R. Boxer, *The Dutch Seaborne Empire, 1600–1800* (London, 1973).
25. Creveld, *Technology and War*, p. 129.
26. Brodie, *From Crossbow to H-Bomb*, p. 64.
27. William McNeill, *The Pursuit of Power: Technology, Armed Force and Society since A.D. 1000* (Oxford, 1983), p. 101.
28. Carlo M. Cipolla, *Guns and Sails in the Early Phase of European Expansion, 1400–1700* (London, 1965), p. 143.
29. Ibid., pp. 136–7, 140.
30. Examples and quote from Geoffrey Best, *War and Society in Revolutionary Europe, 1770–1870* (London, 1982), p. 143.
31. Creveld, *Technology and War*, p. 167.
32. Geoffrey Best dates the change to the mid nineteenth century. Best, *War and Society*, p. 300.
33. Creveld, *Technology and War*, p. 153.
34. An English translation of Kalchnikov's biography by Polity Press is forthcoming. See also E. C. Ezell, *The AK47 Story: Evolution of the Kalashnikov Weapons* (Harrisburg PA, 1986). There is also a biography of Hiram Maxim and numerous specialist books available on the technical side of weaponry.
35. Henry and Norman McCallum, *The Wire that Fenced the West* (Norman OK, 1965); Alan Krell, *The Devil's Rope: A Cultural History of Barbed Wire* (London, 2002); Oliver Razac, *Barbed Wire: A History* (London, 2002); and Reviel Netz, *Barbed Wire: An Ecology of Modernity* (Middletown CT, 2005).
36. Creveld, *Technology and War*, p. 159.
37. G. Jensen, 'Introduction' in Jensen and A. Weist (eds), *War in the Age of Technology* (London and New York, 2001), p. 2.
38. Brodie, *From Crossbow to H-Bomb*, p. 109.
39. Maurice Pearton, *The Knowledgeable State: Diplomacy, War and Technology since 1830* (London, 1982), p. 254.
40. Warren Chin, 'Technology, Industry and War, 1945–1991' in Jensen and Weist (eds), *War in the Age of Technology*, pp. 44–5.
41. Tim Travers, *How the War was Won: Command and Technology in the British Army on the Western Front, 1917–1918* (London, 1992), pp. 1–2.

42. Guy Hartcup, *The War of Invention: Scientific Developments, 1914–1918* (London, 1988).
43. Brodie, *From Crossbow to H-Bomb*, p. 88.
44. Solly Zuckerman, *Scientists and War: The Impact of Science on Military and Civil Affairs* (London, 1966), p. 13.
45. Howard, *War in European History*, p. 135.
46. Brodie, *From Crossbow to H-Bomb*, p. 200.
47. Guy Hartcup, *The Challenge of War: Scientific and Engineering Contributions to World War Two* (Newton Abbot, 1970), p. 17.
48. G. I. Pokrovsky, *Science and Technology in Contemporary War* (London, 1959), pp. 12–13.
49. Brodie, *From Crossbow to H-Bomb*, p. 202.
50. Hartcup, *The Challenge of War*, p. 196.
51. Brodie, *From Crossbow to H-Bomb*, p. 213.
52. Ibid., p. 213.
53. Hartcup, *The Challenge of War*, p. 179.
54. James Phinney Baxter, *Scientists Against Time* [1946] (Cambridge MA, 1968), ch. 15.
55. Eric Bobo, 'Scientists at War' in Jensen and Weist (eds), *War in the Age of Technology*, p. 258.
56. Brodie, *From Crossbow to H-Bomb*, p. 201.
57. Hartcup, *The Challenge of War*, p. 29; Baxter, *Scientists Against Time*, p. 9.
58. Baxter, *Scientists Against Time*, p. 7.
59. Ibid., p. 51.
60. Hartcup, *The Challenge of War*, p. 30.
61. Baxter, *Scientists Against Time*, pp. 9–10.
62. Brodie, *From Crossbow to H-Bomb*, p. 233.
63. Ibid., p. 252.
64. Chin, 'Technology, Industry and War, 1945–1991', p. 6.
65. Howard, *War in European History*, p. 135.
66. Chin, 'Technology, Industry and War, 1945–1991', pp. 46, 48.
67. Ibid., p. 47.
68. O'Connell, *Of Arms and Men*, p. 296.
69. Chin, 'Technology, Industry and War, 1945–1991', p. 54.
70. Creveld, *Technology and War*, p. 247.
71. George and Meredith Friedman, *The Future of War: Power, Technology and American World Dominance in the 21st Century* (New York: Crown, 1996), pp. x–xi.
72. Michael Handel, *Masters of War: Classical Strategic Thought* (London, 2001), pp. 9–10.
73. Ibid., p. 9.
74. Chin, 'Technology, Industry and War, 1945–1991', pp. 54–7.
75. Friedmans, *The Future of War*, p. x.
76. Handel, *Masters of War*, p. 12.
77. Chin, 'Technology, Industry and War, 1945–1991', p. 60.
78. Made into a film of the same name in 2001 (directed by Ridley Scott).
79. See Peter Siegel, 'A Military Lesson America Must Grasp', *Financial Times*, 12 September 2005.
80. Albert Cowdrey, *Fighting for Life: American Military Medicine in World War II* (New York, 1994), p. 167.
81. Ibid., p. 187.

82. Mark Harrison, *Medicine and Victory: British Military Medicine in the Second World War* (Oxford, 2004), p. 237.
83. Ibid., p. 283.
84. Ibid., p. 1.
85. Quoted in Cowdrey, *Fighting for Life*, p. 118.
86. Ibid., pp. 170–1.
87. Such as Nafsika Thalassis, 'Treating and Preventing Trauma: Military Psychiatry during the Second World War' (PhD thesis, University of Salford, 2004).
88. Ben Shephard, *A War of Nerves: Soldiers and Psychiatrists, 1914–1994* (London, 2002), p. xxii.

13
new military history
joanna bourke

The term 'new military history' is a misnomer. Judged by its chronological birth during the social, political and intellectual upheavals of the 1960s, it is distinctly middle-aged. Nevertheless, new military history remains dynamic and innovative, inciting youthful exuberance amongst its proponents. Indeed, new military history is arguably the most popular brand of military history in the academy today. However, new military history also arouses keen irritation amongst opponents, provoked (perhaps) by the implicit assumption that they are writing 'old' military history. Despite these tensions between different schools of war writing, all share a dedication to accurately describing and convincingly explaining historical problems arising out of armed conflicts in the past.

Designating a piece of historical research 'new military history' is often simply a convenient sobriquet. Innumerable historians have attempted to define it. As the historian Peter Karsten put it, 'old' military history concerned itself with 'campaigns, leaders, strategy, tactics, weapons, and logistics'. In contrast, the 'new' military history represented

> a full-fledged concern with the *rest* of military history – that is, fascination with the recruitment, training, and socialization of personnel, combat motivation, the effect of service and war on the individual soldier, the veteran, the internal dynamics of military institutions, inter- and intra-service tensions, civil–military relations, and the relationship between military systems and the greater society.[1]

In such a formulation, new military history becomes an unwieldy hotchpotch of diverse topics, thrown together for reasons difficult to fathom. Furthermore, many self-designated new military historians work on topics not mentioned by Karsten.

What is generally agreed upon is that the definition of new military history has conventionally been highly politicized. Both proponents and opponents use the term lazily, as a shorthand way of registering approval or disapproval. As a result, the relationship between new military historians and their more traditional colleagues is sometimes tense. New military historians, for instance, have concluded that some traditional military history is objectionable. In particular, its attitude to women has excited much fury. It is relatively easy to find examples of what new military historians deplore. For instance, the prolific military historian John Laffin did not endear himself to many of his readers when he wrote in *Women in Battle* (1967) that a 'woman's place should be in the bed and not the battlefield, in crinoline or terylene rather than in battledress, wheeling a pram rather than driving a tank'.[2] More recently, Martin van Creveld's polemic against women in the armed forces has been received by new military historians with dismay.[3]

But new military historians' critique of the ways military history has conventionally been written is much broader than this implies. They suggest that the traditionally narrow focus on battlefields, commanders and issues of strategy seriously distorts 'what really mattered'. The fact that much traditional military history takes place within military academies or with the financial help of the defence industry is seen as evidence of collusion with warmongers. New military historians reject the suggestion that they should provide (in the words of Benjamin Franklin Cooling) 'better and more *useful* national security history' because military historians have a duty both 'to interpret the past' and 'to lead policymakers in the study of war in all its ramifications'.[4] It is precisely any institutional bond between military historians and the military establishment that alarms many (although by no means all)[5] new military historians. If military history is sponsored by the same institution it is studying (and one which happens to be among the most powerful institutions in society), won't its independence be curtailed? At the very least, many of the topics that new military historians regard as important might be inhibited by institutional ties with the armed forces.

Benjamin Cooling admitted that the older type of military history 'connotes traditional drum and trumpet operational history with heroic, often panegyric coverage of the past'. In contrast, new military history 'may represent the liberal wing, while the drum and trumpet school upholds the conservative right of the line'.[6] Traditional military historians responded to such characterizations defensively. In the words of the distinguished historian John A. Lynn, writing in *The Journal of Military History* in 1997, traditional military history has always been 'something of a pariah' in universities. 'We used to be condemned because we were believed to be politically right-wing,

morally corrupt, or just plain dumb', he complained, but 'from bad we have
gone to worse, much worse'. One of his colleagues had sniped that 'Military
history is to history as military music is to music'. Lynn, however, went on
to observe that:

> Military history has always been regarded as politically and morally
> questionable, but now military history also suffers because it represents the
> opposite of the dominant, and increasingly intolerant, trends in historical
> studies.... Military history is a remarkably male field, both in that we study
> institutions that have been overwhelmingly male and in that women are
> underrepresented among military historians as a group.... And, of course,
> military history is not tied to any high-minded political or social cause,
> such as the plight of minorities or the drive for equality for women. We
> might try to defend ourselves as somehow concerned with ending wars, but
> that is a stretch. Military history is not the continuation of peace studies
> by other means. Too bad, but it seems to embody everything they disdain.
> They have met the enemy, and it is us.[7]

He was exaggerating the crisis, but his defensive mood was widely shared. Among
the general reading public, there was an enormous market for traditionally-
inspired military histories, but in the academy, these same scholars found
themselves marginalized. At a time when conferences addressing traditional
military concerns were dwindling and their cohort aging, the vibrancy of
academic conferences addressing new military topics and approaches was
discomforting. Even worse, traditional military historians found themselves
caricatured as compulsive war-gamers, elaborately setting up battle mock-
ups on ping-pong tables where they obsessively second-guessed Confederate
General Robert E. Lee and Union General George Meade at Gettysburg.

As in all conflicts, however, the military history wars have not been one-
sided. More traditional military historians accuse their 'new' colleagues of
ignorance about basic details of battle. By rashly dismissing the significance
of logistics, strategy, weapons development and intelligence (to name just a
few), new military historians simply misread the historical record. The fact
that most new military historians had never been remotely 'in the thick of
things' is sometimes proffered as evidence that new military historians were
especially out of touch. (Of course, most traditional military historians had no
military experience either, but since they tended to be men at least they could
claim gender solidarity.) The wariness of many new military historians towards
histories of 'dead white men' could blind them to crucial historical actors.
Indeed, as some more traditional military historians suggest, new military
history sometimes threatens to reduce the complexity of armed conflict to
mere crises of masculinity or tropes in the literary imagination. What use
were post-structuralist theories, such as Lyotard's postmodernism, Roland
Barthes' and Jean Baudrillard's criticism, the psychoanalytic theories of Jacques

Lacan and Julia Kristeva, Michel Foucault's philosophical historicism, and the deconstructionist philosophy of Jacques Derrida, in understanding the cut and thrust of actual battle?[8] Might these theories even eclipse historical evidence and argumentation? As Lynn quipped, deconstruction 'means one thing to our "cutting edge" colleagues; to us it just means something like carpet bombing'.[9]

It is important to observe that these history wars are relatively new and they arose within a specific historical context. Military history – in whatever guise – does not exist in a vacuum but is fundamentally positioned within a diverse and shifting range of social and political relations. New military historians, for instance, situate themselves within a number of spheres of influence, including the fields of traditional military history, the historical profession more generally, and the wider non-historical academic community. They both echo and contribute to the themes and approaches preoccupying these diverse groups.

It is no coincidence that new military history arose in a period of sweeping social change from the 1960s. Protests against the war in Vietnam, a rejection of authoritarianism, and fury about gender and racial oppression fuelled its development. At a time when the social esteem of the armed forces was plummeting, many young scholars were attracted by approaches that assumed that war was irrational as opposed to instrumental. Departments where war was studied, along with academic books and articles on military matters, began to be scrutinized for signs of a nationalist agenda. Was jingoism being propagated in the guise of academic respectability? Richard Buel Jr observed that

> Those dissatisfied with histories that focused on the deeds of white males, dead or alive, had two additional reasons to view [traditional] military history with suspicion. Not only had warmaking through the ages been a special masculine province, but western warmaking had established the global hegemony of European males and given their imperialism a decidedly racist caste.[10]

From its conception, new military history was invested with a powerful critique of power structures in contemporary society.

In order to infuse the way military history was written with this more radical ethos, while still retaining its commitment to historical veracity, new ways of thinking about war and conflict were required. To a large degree, many of the pioneers who turned to look afresh at war were not military historians at all. The largest group of revisionists included people like Arthur Marwick, Angus Calder and Paul Addison, who wrote pioneering books on 'the people' at war. They remained primarily social historians who happened to write about events occurring in wartime.[11] For such scholars, it was obvious that a history of war must be a history of *all* participants, and not simply of elites and leaders. Rather than battle-plans and bazookas, interactions between the home front and the battlefield became important. Instead of generals, new military historians shifted their attention to so-called ordinary people (who inevitably turned out to be quite extraordinary). Previously neglected groups were examined: nurses, farm labourers and munitions workers. The ethnicity of the participants broadened.[12] Privates replaced officers; minority groups edged out majorities; conscientious objectors began appearing alongside heroes. The result can only be described as a blitzkrieg upon popular histories of war.

Even more striking than this infusion of social historians into military history was the entry of scholars whose approach was primarily cultural. We shall be discussing these historians in more detail later but a significant number of them were interested with issues of gender relations in wartime. They would be astonished to have the label 'military historian' appended to their names. Instead, they identified themselves as cultural historians or historians of gender. Ironically, some of the most quoted writers in new military history would not identify themselves as military historians of either the traditionalist or new bent.

Freed of the need to call themselves 'military historians', with all the intellectual and methodological baggage associated with that designation, new military historians greedily incorporated methodologies from other disciplines. Indeed, it may even be argued that much of what was identified as new military history was being written outside of the historical discipline altogether. These historians drew upon approaches, ideas and methodologies from an eclectic mix of disciplines: sociology, anthropology, economics, psychology and literature, to name just a few.

Anthropological insights have had a lasting impact upon the work of many new military historians. Cultural and symbolic anthropology, as espoused by scholars such as Clifford Geertz, Mary Douglas and Victor Turner, have been influential. Geertz's *The Interpretation of Cultures* (1973) encouraged a shift of interest away from personality and internalized values and toward collective symbols and the creation of meaning within society. In Geertz's words, 'culture is not a power, something to which social events, behaviours, institutions, or processes can be causally attributed; it is a context, something within which they can be intelligibly... described'. Geertz's concept of culture was

> essentially a semiotic one. Believing with Max Weber that man is an animal suspended in webs of significance he himself has spun, I take cultures to be those webs, and the analysis of it to be therefore not an experimental science in search of laws but an interpretive one in search of meaning.

Like ethnographers, new military historians sought to come 'into touch with the lives of strangers' by developing a 'thick description' of their symbolic and social worlds.[13] Historians, like anthropologists, were concerned with 'searching out and analyzing the symbolic forms – words, images, institutions, behaviours – in terms of which, in each place, people actually represented themselves to themselves and to one another'.[14]

The fundamental insistence of all these approaches was that of meaning. In the words of Eric Leed, author of the dazzling book *No Man's Land: Combat and Identity in World War I* (1979), the war experience was 'an ultimate conformation of the power of men to ascribe meaning and pattern to a world, even when that world seemed to resist all patterning'. He argued that the 'myths and fantasies of war' were

> firmly anchored in the realities of war, however much they might mobilize traditional themes, images, and formulas. One must see illusion in general, and the myths and fantasies of war in particular, as an attempt to dissolve and resolve the constraints upon vision and action that define the reality of war.[15]

The historian George Mosse concurred, noting that the myth of war was the way 'the reality of war was masked and made bearable'.[16]

In other words, rites and rituals that seemed incomprehensible to many civilians in today's society made sense when placed within the symbolic worlds of individuals in the past. For instance, many people have commented on the almost ubiquitous taking of often gruesome souvenirs by combatants. In my book *An Intimate History of Killing: Face-to-Face Killing in Twentieth Century Warfare* (1999), I discuss the taking of souvenirs by British and American servicemen during the two world wars, observing that, although the extent of such gruesome trophy-hunting varied according to the racial nature of the enemy ('Japs' and 'Gooks' more frequently than 'Huns'), opportunity (small patrols during the Second World War in the Pacific theatre and in Vietnam more than in the mass entrenched armies of the First World War), and national narrative traditions (American troops placed more emphasis on scalping their enemies 'like the Indians'), it was a frequent practice. Buttons, epaulettes, piccolos, medals, helmets and tassels from the enemies' bayonets were common trophies. Even the young poet, Wilfred Owen, sent his brother a blood-spattered handkerchief which he had taken from the pocket of a dead German pilot.[17] But more gruesome souvenirs – ears, fingers, skulls and so on – were also taken. At a political level, these rituals of collecting and remembering performed a crucial function in enabling men to cope with the problem of the transition from an identity based upon the Commandment 'thou shalt not kill' to one in which killing was the measure of identity and self-worth. Carnivalesque rites of killing could be enjoyable: they helped create individual identity as a 'warrior' engaged in a life-and-death struggle, and they helped cement group bonds – comradeship between men, all of whom were 'set apart' from both their pre-war personas *and* civilian society back home, by acts of violence. This was why, in combat, cruel and often carnivalesque rites constituted what Mikhail Bakhtin called 'authorized transgression':[18]

military authorities officially disapproved of gruesome photographs and 'fooling around' with enemy corpses, but 'turned a blind eye' to such antics, accepting them as necessary for effective combat performance.[19]

While military history influenced by anthropological insights tended to focus on the interpretation of meaning through signs and the ephemeral debris of individual lives, there was a contrasting approach that took much of its stimulus from sociology and worked with the hard data of economic calculation and demographic trends. This represented a return to the scientific values of predictability, verifiability and model-generating. Once again, the pioneers in this field were less 'military historians' and more 'economic historians'. One of the most eminent – Avner Offer – wrote a book on property and politics in late nineteenth- and early twentieth-century Britain before turning his attention to the First World War, and he went on to write about the economics of well-being. In his book, *The First World War: An Agrarian Interpretation* (1989), however, Offer trained his meticulously analytical eye to explaining why Germany lost the First World War. Although not a reductive economic analysis (indeed, the cultural psychology of the consumption of food was at the heart of his analysis), Offer was able to elaborate a theory about the significance of nutritional habits in sustaining quality of life. He showed why the naval blockade, which resulted in severe food shortages in Germany, played a significant role in Germany's defeat. On the home front, malnutrition and low morale magnified the effects of military defeats, forcing the Germans into signing the Versailles Treaty. Of course, Offer admitted that the battlefield offensive was important, but once the quality of life had declined to a certain level, the will to fight faded away. His was a sophisticated and multi-layered analysis. As Offer put it:

Economic factors are important. Land, productive equipment, population, finance, the detail and sum of productive resources, define the possibilities and the opportunities of individuals and statesmen alike. But economic factors require human agency.... Economic history is inseparable from social history, and from history in general.[20]

Quantitative analysis was equally influential when social historians began investigating the impact of war. This is best illustrated in the work of Jay Winter, whose classic, *The Great War and the British People* (1985) explained the great paradox of the 1914–18 war: why, at a time of immense carnage, did the lives of British civilians (especially those at the poorest end of the social scale) undergo immense improvement? Winter was able to show that full employment, rationing and rent control, as well as improved social provision more generally, were responsible for these improvements. Like Offer, Winter did not rely solely on economic arguments to make his point (he made good use of literary approaches), but the book was a brilliant illustration of the value of the methodologies of social and economic history. As Winter argued, quantitative methods permit

> us to enter into one of the most difficult, and yet most important, areas which confront the historian of war. Such methods provide a strict framework for asking counter-factual questions about what would have happened had there been no war. The use of counter-factual arguments in history is highly controversial. However, population historians who approach such counter-factual questions do not suffer from the maddening difficulties facing economic historians who engage in such exercises as constructing a counter-factual railway-free economy in order to estimate the contribution of railways to national income. Fortunately demographic historians can construct realistic counter-factual models without entering such realms of historical fantasy, and they are therefore able to distinguish between the effects of war and the passage of time, a problem bedevilling all historians concerned with armed conflict in the past.[21]

It was an ambitious project.

However great the disciplinary influences of anthropology, economics and demography on the development of new military history, they pale next to the significance of psychology and literature. Indeed, one of the founding texts in new military history – John Keegan's *The Face of Battle* (1976) – reveals a fascination with psychological concepts (such as crowd behaviour) and the emotional life of combatants. Keegan used psychological insights to analyse the three battles of Agincourt in 1415, Waterloo in 1815 and the Somme in 1916. Although he rightly insisted that the story of battle was 'not a study only for the sociologist or the psychologist, and indeed ought not perhaps be properly a study for either', his employment of sociological and psychological insights enabled him to avoid the 'laboratory approach' of many social scientists, in order to focus on 'the human group in battle, and the quality and source of the stress it undergoes'. As Keegan put it,

> What battles have in common is human: the behaviour of men struggling to reconcile their instinct for self-preservation, their sense of honour and the achievement of some aim over which other men are ready to kill them. The study of battle is therefore always a study of fear and usually of courage; always of leadership, usually of obedience; always of compulsion, sometimes of insubordination; always of anxiety, sometimes of elation or catharsis; always of uncertainty and doubt, misinformation and misapprehension, usually also of faith and sometimes of vision; always of violence, sometimes also of cruelty, self-sacrifice, compassion; above all, it is always a study of solidarity and usually also of disintegration – for it is towards the disintegration of human groups that battle is directed.

The result was breathtaking, featuring pain, fear, torrents of blood and epidemics of diarrhoea. Readers can almost hear the screams of men and horses. The effect was to emphasize chaos, confusion and the irrationality of war, as opposed to the more glamorous clash of swords and heroics. The 'fog of battle' was transformed into a storm of emotion. The humanity of the individual soldier was laid bare. Despite being written 30 years ago, *The Face of Battle* still merits study.[22]

The inner world of combatants remains at the heart of new military history, spawning a vast amount of research.[23] There was a shift in emphasis from passive suffering to active killing. Humanity's extraordinary gift for slaying each other was veiled in much traditional military history. As I wrote in *An Intimate History of Killing*,

> The characteristic act distinctive of men at war is not dying, it is killing. For politicians, military strategists, and many historians, war may be about the conquest of territory or the struggle to recover a sense of national honour but, for the man on active service, warfare is concerned with the lawful killing of other people. Its peculiar importance derives from the fact that it is not murder, but sanctioned blood-letting, legislated for and policed by the highest civil authorities and obtaining the consent of the vast majority of the population.[24]

The ways in which men (and occasionally women) experienced the violence of combat, and the ways they even derived excitement from the bloodletting, remains a highly sensitive topic of discussion. Nevertheless, the morale of front-line soldiers, including their ability to control states of fear and retain a belief in the military enterprise, came to be seen as crucial to the outcome of battle. Instead of discipline and courage, individual self-respect and small-unit cohesion were shown to be the major ways combatants were able to cope with the urgency of war.

Although there was courage, this school of historians also pointed out that most front-line soldiers struggled to keep the emotions of fear and disgust under control. The balance between coercion and comradeship in helping to retain control was always delicate. People trapped within such a landscape of terror may be forgiven for attempting to escape. They could desert (a highly risky venture: a deserter could be condemned to death if caught).[25] Shirking or malingering was a less risky way to gain release from the unbearable tension. In wartime, attitudes to such men tended to be harsh. As one officer insisted during the First World War, 'if a man lets his comrades down, he ought to be shot. If he's a looney, so much the better!'[26] All signs of fear carried with them the stigma of cowardice. After all, in wartime, the nation had a right to demand that servicemen gave their 'nerves' for their country, as much as their limbs, eyes, or lives. In other words, instead of the traditional emphasis on domination, new military historians were more likely to emphasize the often creative ways individuals and groups responded to oppressive power structures. Traditional approaches to military medicine (which tended to focus on institutions such as the Royal Army Medical Corps and to tell a rather 'improvement tale') gave way to a bottom-up history in which shell-shock and dismemberment took centre-stage.[27] When the official medical corps appeared, they tended to be assigned harsh disciplinary roles.[28] This was history that sidelined the heroes, in order to look at the damaged men.

The military establishment had to make sure that the 'virus' of cowardice did not spread. Terror of the enemy had to be matched with fear of the consequences of malingering or running away. What kept most men in the front line was not a sense of the rightness of the cause, nor the fear of being executed, but that sense of loyalty to their comrades combined with a powerful resolution to ignore the threatening environment. Fate was deemed responsible for everything: 'if the bullet has my name on it, there is nothing I can do'. For men who could not maintain such a pose of stoic passivity, the war might never end.[29]

In such studies of emotional reactions, many new military historians adopted implicit psychological models. Others, however, were more bold. Psychoanalytical theories, for instance, were employed in the work of Graham Dawson. He used the Kleinian tradition of psychoanalysis to look at masculinity and fantasy in the First World War, showing how a 'cultural imaginary' produced meaning through connections between fantasies and culture.[30] As already implied, Eric Leed's *No Man's Land* also grappled with psychoanalytical approaches. He merged anthropological and psychoanalytical theory, particularly the insights of Claude Levi-Strauss, Bronislaw Malinowski, Sigmund Freud and Sandor Ferenczi, to explain how soldiers coped with becoming 'anonymous functionaries of impersonal mechanisms of destruction'. Concepts like regression, ego, the unconscious and drives are scattered throughout his text. By employing the term liminality (Latin for threshold), Leed was able to describe how a civilian's identity was fundamentally altered in moving through stages that turned him into a soldier. Soldiers were stranded between front and home: they had a psychic need 'to close the gap between the surprising realities of life and initial expectations'.[31] They did this with remarkable creativity.

Finally, the other most important interdisciplinary approach influencing new military historians was that of literary scholarship. Although controversial, these scholars reminded historians that history was a 'dialogical exchange' between the past and the present. Texts were not 'simple sources of information on the level of content analysis', as Dominick LaCapra put it. Rather, texts were 'important events in their own right'. They posed 'complex problems of interpretation' and had 'intricate relations to other events and to various pertinent contexts'.[32] Rhetorical strategy was an integral part of historical interpretation.[33] Whether they admit it or not, all historians have a philosophy of history, and new military historians were at the forefront of reminding their more traditional colleagues that history involved more than simply 'finding out what happened'.

As with the other branches of new military history, the incursion of non-historians into the killing fields was crucial in this revolution as well. Literary scholars such as Paul Fussell, Elaine Showalter, Samuel Hynes and Dominic Hibberd turned their formidable intellects onto war.[34] The result was dramatic, encouraging new military historians to be interested not only in 'what happened', but in how 'what happened' was imagined.

Fussell's book, entitled *The Great War and Modern Memory* (1975), was one of the most influential texts of the new wave. This American literary scholar, much influenced by the theories of Northrop Frye, was concerned with the reciprocal relationship between life and literature. He showed 'the way the dynamics and iconography of the Great War... proved crucial political, rhetorical, and artistic determinants on subsequent life. At the same time the war was relying on inherited myth, it was generating a new myth, and that myth is part of the fiber of our own lives.' The writers most influential in forging that myth were Siegfried Sassoon, Edmund Blunden, Robert Graves, Wilfred Owen, Isaac Rosenberg and David Jones. Participants in war used pastoral and archaic languages in their attempt to make sense of what seemed like chaotic violence all around them. The result was an essentially ironic[35] understanding of the modern world.[36]

Samuel Hynes took Fussell's argument in a different direction. He also argued that the First World War did not only alter the way people thought about military events, but about a universe of topics. In particular, the sense of disjuncture took the form of the myth of war. According to this myth:

> A generation of innocent young men, their heads full of high abstractions like Honour, Glory, and England, went off to war to make the world safe for democracy. They were slaughtered in stupid battles planned by stupid generals. Those who survived were shocked, disillusioned, and embittered by their war experiences and saw that their real enemies were not the Germans, but the old men at home who had lied to them. They rejected the values of the society that had sent them to war, and in doing so separated their own generation from the past and from their cultural inheritance.

This myth took shape in the 1920s and was firmly fixed by the 1930s. As a result, the war inspired modernism, or a sense of history as 'discontinuous, the past remote and unavailable, or available only as the ruins of itself, and the present a formless space emptied of values'.[37]

Although both Fussell's and Hynes' books have been immensely influential, Fussell's continues to excite the most heated debates. It has been over 30 years since *The Great War and Modern Memory* was published and, in that time, Fussell has been attacked on a number of grounds. Robin Prior and Trevor Wilson launched a furious attack on Fussell for misunderstanding the more military aspects of war. According to them, Fussell presented an extraordinarily narrow view of war. His analysis was ahistorical. They suggested that 'if diplomatic and battle narratives will not explicate all facets of modern war', neither would 'imaginative writings and personal accounts'.[38] Equally trenchantly, other historians have observed that the canon Fussell focused upon was a peculiarly narrow one, involving 'the cultural elite of the men who fight our wars (i.e., white British or American soldiers well-versed in the canon of English literature)'.[39] In the canon of war-writers identified by Fussell, Lynne Handley was struck by

> the utter absence of women. Women are nowhere to be seen. They are not at the front, they are not at the rear, they are not tending the home fires, they are not writing their memoirs.... The myth Fussell means to instill of World War 1, the memory he wants to create of soldiers as the tragic victims of war, can survive only if we imagine war as impinging on no one but soldiers.[40]

Fussell had ignored the huge amount of war literature written by women.[41]

Another type of criticism came in an article by Ted Bogacz entitled '"A Tyranny of Words": Language, Poetry, and Antimodernism in England in the First World War'. In this article, Bogacz noted that once the gaze turned away from the elites, 'high diction' was actually extremely prevalent, contrary to Fussell's argument. By high diction, Bogacz was referring to the elevated rhetoric of words like sacrifice, transfigured, chivalry and honour. Rather than Wilfred Owen, Bogacz insisted that historians read the popular poetry and prose being published in the press of the times. There, euphemistic language and religious imagery flourished. The point was not that these writers (and their readers) were ignorant of the 'true facts' of war, but that this elevated language was a way of spiritualizing barbaric reality. High diction (not irony and disillusionment) was a response to the horrors of modern, industrial war.[42]

Even more crucially, however, the sense of rupture in both Fussell's and Hynes' work was directly challenged by Jay M. Winter. In *Sites of Memory, Sites of Mourning: The Great War in European Cultural History* (1995), Winter argued that the rupture caused by the First World War had been exaggerated by historians. The emphasis of many literary scholars on the 'modernism moment' forged out of the war blinded them to older traditions – religious, romantic and classical – that survived and even thrived after the war. In their grief and bewilderment, survivors turned to traditional forms of culture in order to understand what had happened. Through traditional languages, the bereaved learnt to cope with their pain. They 'walked backwards into the future'.[43]

Whatever the interdisciplinary approach, the main function it performed was to extend dramatically the focus of military scholarship. Aside from the ways already mentioned, there was one other major way new military historians approached the study of war: they introduced the concept of gender. Warfare is a highly gendered exercise of violence. It is collective cultural practice, a multifaceted phenomenon requiring complex levels of analysis. To reduce it to biology (masculinity run riot), or, indeed, to a single cultural phenomenon such as patriarchy, is not only reductionist, but perverse. Rather than biological divisions, gender concerns itself with knowledge about sexual difference. It is a social category and, as such, changes over time. For a huge range of writers, war culture was fundamentally gendered, both in the senses that war was constructed through gender and that war contributed towards the construction of gender.

Although most scholars conceive of gender as a relationship (not a taxonomy), the employment of the concept of gender in war studies started with a feminist concern to make women visible. A lively debate was started about whether war affected women's lives in substantive ways. Immediately after the First World War, for instance, many people believed that the war had helped advance women politically and economically. Thus, Mrs Millicent Fawcett, leading feminist, founder of Newnham College Cambridge and President of the National Union of Women's Suffrage Societies from 1897 to 1918, said in 1918: 'The war revolutionized the industrial position of women – it found them serfs and left them free.' The early writings on women and war in Britain agreed with this verdict.[44] More recently, however, this view has come under fire from a more pessimistic group of historians who conceded that war might have improved the living standards of women but argued that most of the gains were short term.[45] At the end of each conflict, men and women wanted to re-establish gender patterns that had been skewered (or crushed) in the context of conflict. By promoting a militaristic masculinity, wars might even have blocked female progress.

Another area of debate concerned bellicosity. Some historians began focusing on women in peace movements, fuelling the myth that women were the peace-loving sex.[46] More recently, scholars have written about martial motherhood, in which female bellicosity was located within traditional female roles. After all, women were often an integral part of the killing process, even if their bellicosity did not translate into the large-scale presence of armed women in the front lines. On the American frontier, for instance, hand-to-hand combat with Native Americans was considered to be behaviour wholly *appropriate* to the good American wife and mother. The American War of Independence saw many female combatants. There is also a formidable history of individual female combatants. 'Molly Pitcher' (1778), Lucy Brewer (War of 1812), Sarah Borginis (Mexican War), Sarah Edwards (American Civil War), and great icons such as the Amazons, Bodicea, Joan of Arc and Mata Hari.[47]

But even more 'ordinary' women were much more than Handmaidens, Madonnas and Patriotic Mothers. Women did not thrust bayonets into living flesh, but they imagined doing so. In the context of British women during the two world wars, when they were refused arms, they fought back: demanding combat training and taking it upon themselves to learn how to fire weapons. Most importantly, they did this in the name of womanhood. Women could frequently be heard wishing that they could be allowed to kill the enemy with their own hands. Men in the trenches were much more liable to feel pity for their opponents: after all, front-line servicemen knew that the men in the opposing trenches were suffering in similar ways to themselves. Womenfolk back home – scared witless about the safety of their lovers, husbands and brothers, yet unable to externalize their terror through aggressive 'hitting back' at the enemy – responded with profound verbal hatred and aggressiveness against the foe.[48] And, of course, women were crucial in persuading men that dishonour was worse than death, and then buckling on men's psychological (if not military) armour. As Virginia Woolf put it in *A Room of One's Own* (1929), women served as magnifying mirrors 'reflecting the figure of man at twice its natural size. Without that power... the glories of all our wars would be unknown.' Such mirrors, she continued, 'are essential to all violent and heroic action'.[49]

Nevertheless, militarism has traditionally been associated with manliness.[50] It is the specifically masculine nature of war that has interested new military historians the most. Exhortations to 'be a man' have been 'all pervasive in Western culture', as Mosse observed in the first sentence of his *The Image of Man* (1996). Never was this so powerful as in the context of war, when the male body and the masculine ideal become society's central symbol of personal and national regeneration. According to Mosse there was a general feeling in western Europe during the First World War that a 'new type of man had emerged from the trenches'. According to him, these new men were defined largely in terms of an alteration in outward appearance: new men had 'supple, lean, muscular bodies'.[51] These men were supposed to be expected to be able to cope with battle: if they 'broke' under the strain, their lack of will power and self-control dealt a fatal blow to their manliness, and (more importantly) to the myths of 'civilized society'. After all, as Mosse continually emphasized,

> Although the warrior image of masculinity had existed ever since the French revolution and the Napoleonic wars. The Great War further accentuated certain aspects of masculinity that of themselves did not have to be warlike but – like willpower, hardness, or perseverance – were qualities that peacetime society prized as well.[52]

In other words,

> the fears engendered by a presumed attack on the fundamental pillars of society – strong nerves, will-power and a clear separation of sexes – all relevant to the comprehension of shell-shock, were increased by the threat

of degeneration which had haunted society and culture ever since the turn of the century.[53]

In other words, men who failed to find a way – whether through language or through visual representation – to make sense of what was often senseless violence in combat were 'incomplete men' whom, by their very existence, weakened the social fabric. Whether shell-shock was seen as a form of psychological emasculation or a protest against the inhumanity of modern war, it was fundamentally about embodied trauma as well as about masculinity and its discontents.

All of these shifts mentioned so far distinguished new military historians from their colleagues. They also led to two changes. The first was a modification in the new military historian's relationship to his or her historical subjects. A greater reflectivity was introduced. As objectivity in history-writing came to be questioned, it was noted that discourses – all discourses – are exercises in power. They are never 'pure' or 'innocent'. As Alon Confino dryly observed: 'The often-made contention that the past is constructed not as fact but as myth to serve the interest of a particular community may still sound radical to some, but it cannot (and should not) stupefy most historians.'[54] The role of the historian as memory-maker was crucial. New military historians followed the lead of cultural history in seeking to situate themselves as well as their historical subjects in an historical context. Political engagement was not a dirty secret but was seen as necessary both in unmasking the false assumption of objectivity implicit in traditional military history and in situating the writing of history within a political project. This willingness – indeed, requirement – to engage was shared by a large proportion of new military historians.[55]

The second change concerned the nature of the sources used to make historical arguments. No longer would historians take the word of the autobiographies of the officer class or the official histories. Instead, they sought non-official documents. In addition, memoirs, novels and poems, postcards, photographs and comic strips, graffiti, diaries and letters entered the historical archive to be read in much the same way as literature was read.[56] Some historians even turned to material culture, or the ways in which meaning becomes associated with objects, to understand war. Artefacts such as toy soldiers and ash-trays could provide insights into a society's values and assumptions in wartime.[57] More traditionally-inspired military historians had also used these sources, but in a way that tended to be more haphazard. Diary accounts, for instance, were used for 'local colour', before attention returned to 'real stuff' of history (that is, the official accounts or battle plans). After all, given the questions asked by more traditional military historians, the individual in battle had no idea of what the real strategic point was of his sacrifice. In contrast, for new military historians, it was precisely the subjective nature of these sources that made them valuable.

Clearly, these new sources required different forms of interpretation. It also became even more necessary to discuss the instability of memory: it could be false, recovered, or implanted. In the crimson heat of battle, historians recognized that experiences were often confused, indeterminate, and incapable of articulation. As a soldier in a Manchester Regiment described his recent experience in battle:

> 'Ay! but that was a fight. If only somebody could describe it. But, there, they can't, for it was dark, with very little room, and nobody could exactly say what he saw.'[58]

Equally honest was the diary entry which began: 'one thing that I can remember seeing quite distinctly (although I know I never did, but dreamt it in the hospital – it was a true story nonetheless)'.[59] Historians even questioned the statements of men recorded under the influence of so-called truth drugs. When hysterical servicemen were given barbiturates to enable them to recover from amnesia they would recite emotional accounts of their combat experiences, enacting scenes of attack and lunging at psychiatrists, believing them to be the enemy. Psychiatrists initially interpreted such behaviour as part of the process of recovering forgotten memories. However, further investigation found that most of the events they recollected were fictional or highly distorted versions of what had occurred.[60]

But for many new military historians, bewilderment, hope and fantasy were the very stuff of human experience. Of course, in historical time, many things actually did (or did not) 'happen', but the very act of narrating changed and formulated the 'experience'. From the moment of action, the event entered into imagination and language, to be interpreted, elaborated, re-structured. As the Vietnam story-teller, Tim O'Brien, wrote in *The Things They Carried* (1990):

> it's difficult to separate what happened to what seemed to happen. What seems to happen becomes its own happening and has to be told that way. The angles of vision are skewed.... And then afterwards, when you go to tell about it, there's always that surreal seemingness, which makes the story seem untrue, but which in fact represents the hard and exact truth as it seemed.[61]

The act of narration is never more dependent upon the ordering mechanisms of grammar, plot and genre than when attempting to 'speak' when in the midst of the ultimate terror of combat.

New military historians were at the forefront of developments in the history of 'memory' and commemoration. War did not begin with the declaration of hostilities, nor did it end with the signing of treaties. Maurice Halbwachs in *Collective Memory* (1980) and Frances Amelia Yates in *The Art of*

Memory (1966) reminded historians to examine the ways in which war was remembered by groups, even nations.[62] As Jay Winter and Emmanuel Sivan insisted, memory was the 'socially-framed property of individuals (or groups of individuals) coming together to share memories of particular events, of time past', while collective memory is 'the process by which individuals interact socially to articulate their memories'.[63] This strand of new military history was fundamentally moulded by the holocaust. The near annihilation of European Jewry was the near annihilation of Jewish memory. There was 'no choice but to remember'. The question was: how?

Historians who work on collective memory represent a diverse range of scholars, with some examining the ways in which people who lived through historical events recalled these events in later years, and others focusing on representations of the past more generally.[64] It is not surprising that the best work on memorialization focuses on the First World War. After all, memorial-building was extensive after that conflict. And, whatever country you look at, it was a popular movement. Of course, there were significant differences between different cultures. Thus, in Britain the war memorials were of the ordinary Tommy, in contrast to the heroic figures in Germany and the 'stylized *poilus*' in France.[65] However, in all cases, these historians were engaged with the question of how personal grief was transformed into public expression of bereavement.

Finally, new military history does not – and never did – stand alone. It is impossible to regard traditional military history as separate from new military history. All the best traditionally-inspired histories integrate the best of the new approaches. Trevor Wilson's *The Myriad Faces of War: Britain and the Great War, 1914–1918* (1986) is a particularly sophisticated example of this combination of traditional and new military history, partly due to his commitment to interdisciplinary ways of thinking, but also due to his insistence that 'if the Great War seems to reduce humanity to ciphers, [my] book does not doubt that its proper subject is man – or rather, men and women, in high estate and low, in handfuls and large masses, in political and social and military groupings'.[66] Memory, in particular, is being successfully integrated into studies that are otherwise more traditional in approach.[67]

Nevertheless, although new military history is one of the most exciting and innovative forms of history currently being written, inevitably, there are areas of weakness. Many new military historians have been less than clear about their theoretical underpinnings. The best military history proves the aphorism that historians are better than their theories. In other words, good military history (in whatever guise) does not simply apply some preconceived theoretical stance, with tasty morsels picked from the archives, but is firmly and exhaustedly based on research and the exploration of varying hypotheses. Some cultural approaches to war can fall into a kind of cultural reductionism, with everything that cannot be explained being set aside as 'cultural'. The emphasis on cultural constructionism has meant that issues of agency and political economy can sometimes be forgotten. As the eminent historian Peter Burke wisely argued in his critique of cultural history more generally, it is crucial to ask 'who is doing the construction? under what constraints? out of what?'[68]

Conceptually, some of the work on memory suffers from a lack of focus, and slips from personal remembering and collective remembrance. As Alon Confino correctly observed:

> There is too often a facile mode of doing cultural history, whereby one picks an historical event or a vehicle of memory, analyzes its representation or how people received it over time, and draws conclusions about 'memory' (or 'collective memory')…. As a field of study, memory has a label more than a content; that is, though the label is an attractive one, in itself memory does not offer any true additional explanatory power. Only when it is linked to historical questions and problems, via methods and theories, can memory become illuminating.[69]

Too often, memory is portrayed as simply an elite production, imposing a dominant view on the populace. While not disputing the fact that the state is certainly at the heart of memory-making, it remains important to identify what and which part of the state is imposing their script on which others. Equally, the concept of gender is often not sufficiently conceptualized and, in its worse form, becomes simply a description of what women (or men) 'do'.

Furthermore, there remain a number of areas of analysis that are ripe for more historical work. Comparative history is one such area. The paucity of comparative work – and, therefore, a tendency to assume a kind of cultural homogeneity – continues to plague much historical writing.[70] The stranglehold of the nation state is partly a result of the linguistic limitations of many academics (and, as such, may be getting worse). Other topics have only recently been given due attention. Peace, for example, is still (relatively speaking) ignored, as is the peacetime military.[71] Emotions have been examined in the context of war, but hypotheses for change over time in the emotional expressions of fear, hatred, joy and love have still not been adequately tested.[72]

To conclude, military history was once the Cinderella of the historical profession, working in one of the least glamorous sectors of human history. New military history has been one factor in changing its status. Most important, new military history has opened the door for a wider dialogue with mainstream history. Ironically, its very success means that it lacks a firm identity: new military history is simply those forms of military history which embrace new ideas within the profession more broadly. In the past three decades, this has meant an adoption of the approaches and methodologies first of social history and then of cultural history. The vibrancy of new military history resides precisely in the energizing uncertainty about where it may go next.

further reading

It is impossible to do justice to the full range of new military history. Much new military history is concerned with the experience of combat. Some of this work can be seen in: Tony Ashworth, *Trench Warfare, 1914–1918: The Live and Let Live System* (London, 1980); Joanna Bourke, *An Intimate History of Killing: Face-to-face Killing in Twentieth Century History* (London, 1999); John Keegan, *The Face of Battle: A Study of Agincourt, Waterloo and the Somme* (Harmondsworth, 1978); and Eric J. Leed, *No Man's Land: Combat and Identity in World War I* (Cambridge, 1979). An excellent critical analysis can be found in Gail Braybon (ed.), *Evidence, History, and the Great War: Historians and the Impact of 1914–18* (Oxford, 2004). For a taste of the strong demographic and economic themes running through much new military history, see Jay Winter, *The Great War and the British People* (Basingstoke, 1985). It is impossible to summarize the histories of women and war, but good starting points would be Gail Braybon and Penny Summerfield (eds), *Out of the Cage: Women's Experience in Two World Wars* (London, 1987); Susan R. Grayzel, *Women's Identities at War: Gender, Motherhood, and Politics in Britain and France During the First World War* (Chapel Hill NC, 1999); and Penny Summerfield, *Women Workers in the Second World War: Production and Patriarchy in Conflict* (London, 1989). In recent years, the history of masculinity has come to the fore. Examples include Joanna Bourke, *Dismembering the Male: Men's Bodies, Britain and the Great War* (London, 1996); Leo Braudy's *From Chivalry to Terrorism: War and the Changing Nature of Masculinity* (New York, 2003); Graham Dawson, *Soldier Heroes: British Adventure, Empire, and the Imagining of Masculinities* (London, 1994); and George L. Mosse, *The Image of Man: The Creation of Modern Masculinity* (New York, 1996). For books that examine specific technologies, two excellent examples are Alan Krell, *The Devil's Rope: A Cultural History of Barbed Wire* (London, 2002) and Patrick Wright, *Tank: The Progress of a Monstrous War Machine* (London, 2000). There is a huge and rich literature on war medicine, war neuroses, and psychiatry, including Roger Cooter, Steve Sturdy and Mark Harrison (eds), *War, Medicine, and Modernity* (Stroud, 1999); Mark Harrison, *Medicine and Victory: British Military Medicine in the Second World War* (Oxford, 2004); Paul Lerner, *Hysterical Men: War, Psychiatry, and the Politics of Trauma in Germany, 1890–1930* (Ithaca NY, 2003); and Jeffrey S. Reznick, *Healing the Nation: Soldiers and the Culture of Caregiving in Britain During the Great War* (Manchester, 2004). Finally, collective memory and remembrance is a strong area of research. Some excellent examples include Paul Fussell, *The Great War and Modern Memory* (London, 1975); Samuel Hynes, *A War Imagined: The First World War and English Culture* (London, 1990); George Mosse, *Fallen Soldiers: Reshaping the Memory of the World Wars* (Oxford, 1990); Jay Winter, *Sites of Memory, Sites of Mourning: The Great War in European Cultural History* (Cambridge, 1995); and Jay Winter and Emmanuel Sivan (eds), *War and Remembrance in the Twentieth Century* (Cambridge, 1999).

notes

1. Peter Karsten, 'The "New" American Military History: A Map of the Territory, Explored and Unexplored', *American Quarterly* 36/3 (1984): 389–418, 389.
2. John Laffin, *Women in Battle* (London, 1967), p. 185.
3. Martin van Creveld, *Men, Women and War: Do Women Belong in the Front Lines?* (London, 2001).
4. Benjamin Franklin Cooling, 'Towards a More Usable Past; A Modest Plea for a Newer Typology of Military History', *Military Affairs* 52/1 (1988): 29–31.

5. John Keegan, for example, taught at the UK's Royal Military Academy, Sandhurst.
6. Cooling, 'Towards a More Usable Past', 29–31.
7. John A. Lynn, 'The Embattled Future of Academic Military History', *Journal of Military History* 61/4 (1997): 777–89, 782.
8. For wider discussion of these theories, see the journal *History and Theory*.
9. Lynn, 'The Embattled Future', 778, 782.
10. Review by Richard Buel of J. Keegan's *History of Warfare* in *History and Theory* 34/1 (1995): 90–106, 90.
11. Paul Addison, *Now the War is Over: A Social History of Britain, 1945–1951* (London, 1985); Angus Calder, *The People's War: Britain, 1939–1945* (New York, 1969); Arthur Marwick, *Britain in the Century of Total War* (London, 1968); Arthur Marwick, *The Deluge: British Society and the First World War* (Harmondsworth, 1967). See also Bernard Waites, *A Class Society at War, England, 1914–18* (Leamington Spa, 1987).
12. John H. Morrow, *The Great War: An Imperial History* (London, 2004); Richard Smith, *Jamaican Volunteers in the First World War: Race, Masculinity and the Development of National Consciousness* (Manchester, 2004); and Heather Streets, *Martial Races: The Military, Race and Masculinity in British Imperial Culture, 1857–1914* (Manchester, 2004).
13. Clifford Geertz, *The Interpretation of Cultures* (London, 1973), pp. 5, 14.
14. Clifford Geertz, *Local Knowledge: Further Essays in Interpretive Anthropology* (New York, 1983), p. 58.
15. Eric J. Leed, *No Man's Land: Combat and Identity in World War I* (Cambridge, 1979), pp. x, 116.
16. George L. Mosse, 'The Knights of the Sky and the Myth of War Experience' in Robert A. Hinde and Helen E. Watson (eds), *War: A Cruel Necessity? The Bases of Institutional Violence* (London, 1995), p. 132.
17. Letter, Wilfred Owen to Colin Owen, 9 April 1917 in Harold Owen and John Bell (eds), *Wilfred Owen: Collected Letters* (London, 1961), p. 451. He asked that the handkerchief be kept for him.
18. Mikhail Bakhtin, *Rabelais and His World* (trans. H. Iswolsky) (Bloomington IN, 1985).
19. For a discussion of this, see Joanna Bourke, *An Intimate History of Killing: Face-to-Face Killing in Twentieth Century History* (London, 1999).
20. Avner Offer, *The First World War: An Agrarian Interpretation* (Oxford, 1989), p. 20.
21. Jay M. Winter, *The Great War and the British People* (Basingstoke, 1985), p. 2. See also Richard Wall and Jay Winter (eds), *The Upheaval of War: Family, Work and Welfare in Europe, 1914–1918* (Cambridge, 1988).
22. John Keegan, *The Face of Battle: A Study of Agincourt, Waterloo and the Somme* (Harmondsworth, 1978), p. 303.
23. For instance, see Tony Ashworth, *Trench Warfare, 1914–1918: The Live and Let Live System* (London, 1980); Bourke, *An Intimate History of Killing*; George Mosse, *Fallen Soldiers: Reshaping the Memory of the World Wars* (Oxford, 1990); and Frederic Rousseau, *La guerre censurée: Une historie des combatants européens de 14–18* (Paris, 1999).
24. Bourke, *An Intimate History of Killing*, p. 1.
25. Gerald Christopher Oram, *Military Executions During World War 1* (Basingstoke, 2003).
26. Dr H. W. Wills, 'Footnote to Medical History', no date, in Liddle Collection, Leeds (UK), General Aspects: Shell Shock, item 1, p. 2.

27. Peter Barham, *Forgotten Lunatics of the Great War* (New Haven CT, 2004); Deborah Cohen, *The War Come Home: Disabled Veterans in Britain and Germany, 1914–1939* (Berkeley CA, 2001); Peter Leese, *Shell Shock: Traumatic Neurosis and the British Soldiers of the First World War* (Basingstoke, 2003); Paul Lerner, *Hysterical Men: War, Psychiatry, and the Politics of Trauma in Germany, 1890–1930* (Ithaca NY, 2003); and Antoine Prost, *In the Wake of War: Les Anciens Combattants and French Society 1914–1930* (Oxford, 1992).
28. For instance, see Roger Cooter, Steve Sturdy and Mark Harrison (eds), *War, Medicine and Modernity* (Stroud, 1999).
29. For a discussion, see Joanna Bourke, *Dismembering the Male: Men's Bodies, Britain, and the Great War* (London, 1996).
30. Graham Dawson, *Soldier Heroes: British Adventure, Empire and the Imagining of Masculinities* (London, 1994).
31. Leed, *No Man's Land*, pp. 116, 200. See also the remarkable Modris Eksteins, *Rites of War: The Great War and the Birth of the Modern Age* (London, 1989).
32. Dominick LaCapra, *History and Criticism* (Ithaca NY, 1985), pp. 9, 38.
33. Hayden White, *Metahistory: The Historical Imagination in Nineteenth Century Europe* (Baltimore MD, 1974).
34. Dominic Hibberd, *The First World War* (Basingstoke, 1986); Elaine Showalter, *The Female Malady: Women, Madness, and Culture in England, 1830–1980* (New York, 1986).
35. That is, contrasts between expectation and reality, intention and outcome, and illusion and reality.
36. Paul Fussell, *The Great War and Modern Memory* (London, 1975), pp. ix, 35. See also Paul Fussell, *Wartime: Understanding and Behavior in the Second World War* (New York, 1989).
37. Samuel Hynes, *A War Imagined: The First World War and English Culture* (London, 1990), pp. x, 433.
38. Robin Prior and Trevor Wilson, 'Paul Fussell at War', *War in History* 1/1 (1994): 63–80, 63.
39. Lynne Hanley, *Writing War: Fiction, Gender and Memory* (Amherst MA, 1991), pp. 27–8.
40. Ibid., p. 31.
41. This is a huge literature, but includes Nicola Beauman, *A Very Great Profession: The Woman's Novel, 1914–39* (London, 1983); Sandra M. Gilbert and Susan Gubar (eds), *The Female Imagination and the Modernist Aesthetic* (London, 1986); Sandra Gilbert and Susan Gubar, *No Man's Land: The Place of the Woman Writer in the Twentieth Century* (London, 1988); Lynne Hanley, *Writing War*; and Suzanne Raitt and Trudi Tate, *Women's Fiction and the Great War* (Oxford, 1997).
42. Ted Bogacz, '"A Tyranny of Words": Language, Poetry and Antimodernism in England in the First World War', *Journal of Modern History* 58/3 (1986): 643–68.
43. Jay M. Winter, *Sites of Memory, Sites of Mourning: The Great War in European Cultural History* (Cambridge, 1995), p. 221. See also Bourke, *Dismembering the Male*.
44. Marwick, *The Deluge*.
45. Gail Braybon and Penny Summerfield (eds), *Out of the Cage: Women's Experience in Two World Wars* (London, 1987); Susan R. Grayzel, *Women's Identities at War: Gender, Motherhood, and Politics in Britain and France During the First World War* (Chapel Hill NC, 1999); and Penny Summerfield, *Women Workers in the Second World War: Production and Patriarchy in Conflict* (London, 1989).

46. For instance, see Heloise Brown, 'The Truest Form of Patriotism': Pacifist Feminism in Britain, 1870–1902 (Manchester, 2003); Jean E. Kennard, 'Feminism, Pacifism and World War I', Turn-of-the-Century Women 2/2 (1985): 10–21; Claire M. Tylee, The Great War and Women's Consciousness: Images of Militarism and Feminism in Women's Writings, 1914–64 (Basingstoke, 1990); Claire M. Tylee, '"Maleness Run Riot": The Great War and Women's Resistance to Militarism', Women's Studies International Forum 11/3 (1988): 119–210; and Jo Newberry Vellacott, 'Feminist Consciousness and the First World War', History Workshop Journal 23 (1987): 81–101.
47. For instance, see Tammy M. Proctor, Female Intelligence: Women and Espionage in the First World War (New York, 2003) and Julie Wheelwright, Fatal Lovers: Mata Hari and the Myths of Women in Espionage (London, 1992).
48. Bourke, An Intimate History of Killing.
49. Virginia Woolf, A Room of One's Own [1929] (London, 1945), p. 31. See also Angela K. Smith (ed.), Gender and Warfare in the Twentieth Century: Textual Representations (Manchester, 2004).
50. For a brilliant overview, see Leo Braudy's From Chivalry to Terrorism: War and the Changing Nature of Masculinity (New York, 2003).
51. George L. Mosse, The Image of Man: The Creation of Modern Masculinity (New York, 1996), p. 115.
52. Ibid.
53. George L. Mosse, 'Shell-Shock as a Social Disease', Journal of Contemporary History 35/1 (2000): 101–8, 104.
54. Alon Confino, 'Collective Memory and Cultural History: Problems of Method', American Historical Review 102/5 (1997): 1386–403, 1387.
55. For instance, see Chris Hedges, War is a Force That Gives Us Meaning (New York, 2002); Sven Lindqvist, Exterminate All the Brutes (London, 1996); Sven Lindqvist, A History of Bombing (London, 2003); and Wolfgang Sofsky, Violence: Terrorism, Genocide, War (London, 2003).
56. For instance, see Stéphane Audoin-Rouzeau, Men at War 1914–1918: National Sentiment and Trench Journalism in France During the First World War (Oxford, 1992).
57. For instance, see P. H. Liddle and M. Richardson, 'Passchendaele and Material Culture: The Relics of Battle' in Liddle (ed.), Passchendaele in Perspective: The Third Battle of Ypres (London, 1997), pp. 459–66. See also Nicholas J. Saunders, Trench Art (London, 2001).
58. Owen Spencer Watkins, With French in France and Flanders (London, 1915), p. 127.
59. Lt-Col T. S. Wollocombe, 'Diary of the Great War', Imperial War Museum (UK), 98/7/1, p. 34.
60. Edwin Weinstein, 'The Fifth U.S. Army Neuropsychiatric Centre – 601st' in Lt-Gen Hal B. Jennings (ed.), Neuropsychiatry in World War II. Volume II. Overseas Theatres (Washington DC, 1973), p. 137.
61. Tim O'Brien, The Things They Carried (New York, 1990), p. 210.
62. Maurice Halbwachs, Collective Memory (New York, 1980) and Frances Amelia Yates, The Art of Memory (London, 1966).
63. Jay Winter and Emmanuel Sivan, 'Setting the Framework' in Winter and Sivan (eds), War and Remembrance in the Twentieth Century (Cambridge, 1999), pp. 6–40.
64. This is a huge literature, but special mention might be made of Annette Becker, Les Monuments aux Morts: patrimoine et mémoire de la Grand Guerre (Paris, 1988); John Gillis (ed.), Commemorations: The Politics of National Identity (Princeton NJ, 1994);

Adrian Gregory, *The Silence of Memory: Armistice Day 1919–1946* (Cambridge, 1995); Ken Inglis, *Sacred Places: War Memorials and the Australian Landscape* (Melbourne, 1998); Alex King, *Memorials of the Great War in Britain: The Symbolism and Politics of Remembrance* (Oxford, 1998); Alex King, 'Remembering and Forgetting in the Public Memorials of the Great War' in Adrian Forty and Susanne Küchler (eds), *The Art of Forgetting* (Oxford, 1999); George L. Mosse, *Fallen Soldiers: Reshaping the Memory of the World Wars* (Oxford, 1990); and Prost, *In the Wake of War*.

65. Jay M. Winter, 'Catastrophe and Culture: Recent Trends in the Historiography of the First World War', *Journal of Modern History* 64/3 (1992): 525–32.

66. Trevor Wilson, *The Myriad Faces of War: Britain and the Great War, 1914–1918* (Oxford, 1986), p. 3.

67. For instance, see Modris Eksteins, 'Memory and the Great War' in Hew Strachan (ed.), *The Oxford Illustrated History of the First World War* (Oxford, 1998).

68. Peter Burke, *What is Cultural History?* (Cambridge, 2004), p. 98.

69. Confino, 'Collective Memory and Cultural History', 1388.

70. A notable exception is the multi-volume 'capital cities' project of Jay Winter and others. See Jay Winter and Jean-Louis Robert (eds), *Capital Cities at War: London, Paris, Berlin, 1914–1919* (Cambridge, 1997).

71. Exceptions include Paul Laity, *The British Peace Movement, 1870–1914* (Oxford, 2001).

72. Exceptions are Joanna Bourke, *Fear: A Cultural History* (London, 2005) and William Ian Miller, *The Mystery of Courage* (Cambridge, 2000).

index

8